ALLE · ZEIT · WACH · 1842

Human-Computer Interaction: Psychonomic Aspects

Edited by
Gerrit C. van der Veer and Gijsbertus Mulder

With 121 Figures, Some in Color

Springer-Verlag
Berlin Heidelberg New York London Paris Tokyo

Drs. GERRIT C. VAN DER VEER
Free University
P.O. Box 7161
1007 MC Amsterdam, The Netherlands

Professor Dr. GIJSBERTUS MULDER
Institute for Experimental Psychology
University of Groningen
Kerklaan 30
9751 NN Haren, The Netherlands

ISBN-13: 978-3-642-73404-5 e-ISBN-13: 978-3-642-73402-1

DOI: 10.1007/978-3-642-73402-1

Library of Congress Cataloging-in-Publication Data. Human-computer interaction : psychonomic aspects / edited by Gerritt C. van der Veer and Gijsbertus Mulder. p. cm. Based on papers presented at a conference held at the Free University, Amsterdam, organized by the Dutch Human Performance Group, and sponsored by the Dutch Psychonomic Society. Includes bibliographies and index. 1. Human-computer interaction–Congresses. I. Veer, G.C. van der (Gerritt C.) II. Mulder, G. III. Dutch Human Performance Group. IV. Dutch Psychonomic Society. QA76.9.H85H86 1988 004'.01'9–dc 19

Softcover reprint of the hardcover 1st edition 1988

2126/3130-543210 – Printed on acid-free paper

Preface

This book is the final product of a conference organized at the Free University, Amsterdam, by some members of the Dutch Human Performance Group and sponsored by the Dutch Psychonomic Society. We first of all thank the Society for financially supporting this publication, and the Free University for providing technical support. P.J.G. Keuss, A.A.J. Mannaerts, and W. Hulstijn, members of the organizing commitee, and J.A. Michon and W. Molenaar collaborated with the editors in defining the fields dealt with at the conference and in the book and in getting together the team of authors.

All the chapters in this volume have been reviewed by a team of external referees, who generously spent their time to improve the readability, coherence, and scientific standard of the work as a whole: H. Bogers, Institute for Experimental Psychology, University of Groningen, The Netherlands; P. Innocent, Leicester Polytechnic, UK; G.A.M. Kempen, Institute for Cognition Research and Information Technology, Nijmegen, The Netherlands; J. Moraal, Institute for Perception RVO/TNO, Soesterberg, The Netherlands; J.M. van Oorschot, Department of Economics, Free University, Amsterdam, The Netherlands; G.R.E. Ouweneel, Institute for Experimental Psychology, Haren, The Netherlands; J.G.W. Raaymakers, Institute for Perception RVO/TNO, Soesterberg, The Netherlands; G. Rohr, IBM Science Center, Heidelberg, FRG; M.J. Tauber, Department of Computer Science, University of Paderborn, FRG; Y. Waern, Department of Psychology, University of Stockholm, Sweden; G. d'Ydewalle, Department of Psychology, University of Leuven, Belgium.

We would like to mention the staff of Springer-Verlag for their encouraging cooperation during the preparation of the typescript. In particular, we would like to thank Dr. Thiekötter who stimulated this project from the beginning. We are very grateful for his continuing support of this type of project. We also would like to mention Rob Dimbleby for his care in copy-editing all contributions.

Elly Lammers was an indispensable help to the editors during the whole process of the preparation of the book, taking care of the organization and administration, of the layout, and of the preparation of the camera-ready typescript.

Amsterdam/Groningen, April 1988

Gerrit van der Veer,
Gijsbertus Mulder

Contents

Interaction with Information Systems: Input Aspects

Searching for Information in Information Systems

The Use of Natural Language in Interaction with Information Systems

List of Contributors

JOS BEISHUIZEN, Department of Cognitive Psychology, Free University, P.O. Box 7161, 1007 MC Amsterdam, The Netherlands

MARTINUS C. BOSCHMAN, Institute for Perception Research, (IPO), Eindhoven University of Technology, P.O. Box 513, 5600 MB Eindhoven, The Netherlands.

LOUIS G. BOUMA, Computer Science Section, Department of Mathematics and Natural Science, University of Amsterdam, Nieuwe Achtergracht 166, 1018 WV Amsterdam, The Netherlands

BERT BREDEWEG, Department of Social Science Informatics, University of Amsterdam (SWI), Herengracht 196, 1016 BS Amsterdam, The Netherlands

DAVID S. BRÉE, Rotterdam School of Management, Erasmus University, P.O. Box 1738, 3000 DR Rotterdam, The Netherlands

JEROEN BRUIJNING, Section Computer Science, Department of Mathematics and Natural Science, University of Amsterdam, Nieuwe Achtergracht 166, 1018 WV Amsterdam, The Netherlands

HARRY C. BUNT, Computational Linguistics Unit, Tilburg University, P.O. Box 90153, 5000 LE Tilburg, The Netherlands

PETER DESAIN, Experimental Psychology Unit, University of Nijmegen, P.O. Box 9104, 6500 HE Nijmegen, The Netherlands

MICHAEL A.M. FELT, Department of Cognitive Psychology, Free University, P.O. Box 7161, 1007 MC Amsterdam, The Netherlands

ANTHONY JAMESON, Psychological Laboratory, University of Nijmegen, Montessorilaan 3, 6525 HR Nijmegen, The Netherlands

RENÉ JORNA, Faculteit Bedrijfskunde, University of Groningen, P.O. Box 800, 9700 AV Groningen, The Netherlands

PIET A.M. KOMMERS, Department of Education, Division of Educational Instrumentation, Twente University of Technology, P.O. Box 217, 7500 AE Enschede, The Netherlands

MARTIN A.M. LEERMAKERS, Institute for Perception Research (IPO), Eindhoven University of Technology, P.O. Box 513, 5600 MB Eindhoven, The Netherlands

FRANS J. MAARSE, Department of Experimental Psychology, University of Nijmegen, P.O. Box 9104, 6500 HE Nijmegen, The Netherlands

IVO W. MOLENAAR, Informatics of the Social Sciences, Faculty of Social Sciences, University of Groningen, Oude Boteringestraat 23, 9712 GC Groningen, The Netherlands

GIJSBERTUS MULDER, Institute for Experimental Psychology, University of Groningen, Kerklaan 30, 9751 NN Haren, The Netherlands

GERARD L.J. NAS, Faculty of Arts, University of Utrecht, Trans 14, 3512 JK Utrecht, The Netherlands

FLORIS L. van NES, Institute for Perception Research (IPO), Eindhoven University of Technology, P.O. Box 513, 5600 MB Eindhoven, The Netherlands

LEON P.A.S. van NOORDEN, Social Research Department (CASWO), Netherlands Postal and Telecommunications Services (PTT), P.O. Box 30000, 2500 GA The Hague, The Netherlands

LEO G.M. NOORDMAN, Department of Linguistics, Catholic University of Brabant, P.O. Box 90153, 5000 LE Tilburg, The Netherlands

PIETER PADMOS, Nederlandse Organisatie voor Toegepaste Natuurwetenschappelijk Onderzoek (TNO) Institute for Perception, P.O. Box 23, 3769 ZG Soesterberg, The Netherlands

LOUIS C.W. POLS, Institute of Phonetic Sciences, University of Amsterdam, Herengracht 338, 1016 CG Amsterdam, The Netherlands

JACQUES A.J. ROUFS, Institute for Perception Research (IPO), Eindhoven University of Technology, P.O. Box 513, 5600 MB Eindhoven, The Netherlands

PAUL van SCHAIK, Ergonomics Group, Twente University of Technology, P.O. Box 217, 7500 AE Enschede, The Netherlands

LAMBERT R.B. SCHOMAKER, Department of Experimental Psychology, University of Nijmegen, P.O. Box 9104, 6500 HE Nijmegen, The Netherlands

KOENRAAD de SMEDT, Department of Psychology, University of Nijmegen, Montessorilaan 3, 6511 TL Nijmegen, The Netherlands

FRANS N. STOKMAN, Sociological Institute, University of Groningen, Oude Boteringestraat 23, 9712 GC Groningen, The Netherlands

HANS-LEO TEULINGS, Department of Experimental Psychology, University of Nijmegen, P.O. Box 9104, 6500 HE Nijmegen, The Netherlands

ARNOLD J.W.M. THOMASSEN, Department of Experimental Psychology, University of Nijmegen, P.O. Box 9104, 6500 HE Nijmegen, The Netherlands

GERRIT C. van der VEER, Department of Mathematics and Computer Science, Department of Cognitive Psychology, Free University, P.O. Box 7161, 1007 MC Amsterdam, The Netherlands

JOHANNES C. van VLIET, Department of Mathematics and Computer Science, Free University, De Boelelaan 1081 U-420, 1081 HV Amsterdam, The Netherlands

PIETER H. de VRIES, Institute for Experimental Psychology, University of Groningen, Oude Boteringestraat 23, 9712 GC Groningen, The Netherlands

BERNARD A. WEERDMEESTER, Dr. Neher Laboratories, PTT, Leidschendam. Current address: Technical University Twente, CT Kamer 3184, P.O. Box 217, 7500 AE Enschede, The Netherlands

CHARLES M.M. de WEERT, Psychological Laboratory, Faculty of Social Sciences, University of Nijmegen, P.O. Box 9104, 6500 HE Nijmegen, The Netherlands

TED N. WHITE, Ergonomics Group, Twente University of Technology, P.O. Box 217, 7500 AE Enschede, The Netherlands

BOB J. WIELINGA, Department of Social Science Informatics (SWI), University of Amsterdam, Herengracht 196, 1016 BS Amsterdam, The Netherlands

Introduction

Gerrit C. van der Veer and Gijsbertus Mulder

Human-computer interaction is becoming an increasingly important area of research and a field of application of experimental psychology. In 1985 the Dutch Psychonomic Society approached several experminental psychologists whose work was either directly or indirectly relevant to human-computer interaction. These scientists were asked to discuss both the theoretical basis of their work and the practical implications for the interaction between man and machine. The present book is an elaboration of presentations given at the Conference on Human-Computer Interaction in Amsterdam in December 1985, supplemented by some other Dutch contributions in this field.

1. General Structure

The book is structured in such a way as to provide a broad overview of the contribution of experimental research in psychology and related disciplines to the domain of human-computer interaction. The work in this field may be divided into some major topics:

a. *The presentation of visual information*
This part is first of all concerned with the basic aspects of visual information processing. In addition, some relevant applications in the domains of visual presentation of statistical information and of texts are discussed.

b. *The representation of knowledge*
The second major part is concerned with the representation of knowledge. The interaction between man and machine is most effective if both components have an adequate representation of knowledge. Several techniques of representation are shown, and the compatibility between human representation and machine representation is discussed.

c. *Expert systems and artificial intelligence*
The development of expert systems will in many respects change the nature of the interaction between man and machine. In this part are discussed future developments, the current state of expert systems as compared to human experts, and the characteristics of production systems which are so prominent in most expert systems.

d. *The interaction with systems*
In the last part of the book, some interaction features are reviewed. Input aspects mentioned are the ergonomic value of keyboards, and advanced input modes like handwritten text and speech. Procedures for searching information in large databases and for the use of natural language in the interaction between man and machine are increasingly important.

2. Presentation of Visual Information

2.1. Visual Aspects

In Chapter 1 van Nes discusses the legibility of a text, on paper or visual display units (VDTs). Legibility of a text is determined by text properties that influence the visual reading process by influencing the reader's search for certain text parts and their subsequent recognition. Van Nes argues that reading can be divided into two groups of subprocesses: those related to the processing of visual information and those related to modality unspecific cognitive processes, or, rephrased in van Nes' terminology, a look-and-search process and a comprehend-and-absorb process respectively. A distinction should be made between the legibility of a text, determined by such factors as lettercase, contrast, and color, and the readability of a text. The latter property of a text is the result of stylistic factors such as the vocabulary used and the length of sentences (see Chapter 7). Van Nes mainly discusses the factors affecting legibility. An important determinant of legibility is the amount of blank space inserted in the text, a densely packed text being less legible because of the small eye-return angle. Other important factors are the make-up of tables, the number of different colors on a screen, and related general and specific effects like perceptual grouping and use of typographic emphasis.

The issue of color is also discussed by De Weert in Chapter 2. Technical facilities are becoming increasingly available, but advances in the perceptual know-how needed to apply these usefully have not kept pace. Both de Weert and van Nes discuss negative effects of the introduction of color. De Weert first discusses the difference between color and luminance processing. In this case the chromatic and achromatic modulation transfer function is relevant. The visual system is thought of as consisting of optical and neural parts. The modulation transfer function refers to the ratio of the contrast modulation before and after the lens. It is the neural part that causes the difference in chromatic (luminance) and achromatic (color) perception. Detailed information is better processed in the luminance channel than in the chromatic channel. Fundamental processes like accomodation are not or are only minimally subserved by the chromatic system. Isoluminance of figure and background leads to a decrease in perceived depth. Subjective brightness contours, evoked by pure luminance differences, are reduced if color is introduced. In addition, De Weert discusses the effect of color on wanted and unwanted "Gestalts." He emphasizes that a task analysis should precede the discussion of whether or not to use color in the presentation of information. Though our knowledge about the use of color is quite limited, a few guidelines about when *not* to use color are already available.

Visual fatigue is the most frequent health complaint of VDU workers. In Chapter 3 Padmos mentions field studies on office workers, reporting frequencies of complaints from 30% to 90%. Many workers are afraid that their eyes may deteriorate through VDU work. Visual fatigue can be considered as a change in the condition of an organism over time as a consequence of long and/or taxing visual work. This change in condition becomes manifest in the subjective experience of the subject, in the performance of tasks by the subject, and in the physiological state of the subject. Visual fatigue is usually reported by workers in terms of eye complaints such as burning sensations in or behind the eyes. Factors affecting the quality of the visual system such as uncorrected far-sightedness, astigmatism, presbyopia, anisometropia, or problems with binocular balance and fusion may affect visual fatigue. It is, however, quite conceivable that visual fatigue also involves more central brain mechanisms. Important issues are how to measure the contribution of more peripheral and more central effects and how long it takes to recorver from the effects. Subjective measures are suspect for several reasons and therefore more objective measures are preferred. Visual fatigue encompasses different aspects and is certainly not unidimensional. Relevant measures include indices of workload, task performance, psychophysical threshold, eye movements, binocular coordination, accomodation, and pupil diameter. Different aspects of visual tasks can differentially affect these dimensions.

In designing display units visual comfort should be optimized, as Roufs, Boschman, and Leermakers discuss in Chapter 4. They argue that visual fatigue is difficult to measure and as a consequence cannot be used as a design criterion. A more suitable candidate is the comfort with which the subject feels he can read the information on the VDU. To measure visual comfort, we have to acknowledge that subjects can feel comfortable for very different reasons. For example, a system may be rated highly comfortable because it facilitates information intake as indicated by fixation duration and saccade length or the speed of performing a visual search. Roufs et al. show that luminance contrast, physical sharpness, and character font are important parameters determining visual comfort. They emphasize, however, that the visual information processing underlying the observed relation must still be determined.

2.2. Statistical Information

The availability and increased use of computers has caused an information explosion that requires adequate techniques for information reduction. Graphical representation of statistical information in principle has the potential of both reducing the quantity of information, and of presenting it in a useful way. In Chapter 5, however, Molenaar shows that graphs are often misleading, and relates this to mechanisms of human visual information processing. From this analysis are derived some principles of tabular and graphical presentation that are illustrated with examples of statistical data.

Another aspect of visual information is the representation of trends in process control. Trend deviation detection is an important aspect of the diagnosis component of process operators' tasks. White and van Schaik (Chapter 6) report some experimental data about the effect of slope deviation, amplitude, and visibility of deviation. A quantity defined as "rate of perceivability" appears to explain differences in operator performance. Higher perceivability generally leads to fewer missed detections, lower rated difficulty of detecting deviations, higher certainty estimates of correct detection, and shorter observation times. With equal perceivability a large slope of deviation generally favors the same results. This may be useful for designing visual display layouts for industrial applications.

2.3. Linguistic Aspects

In Sect. 2.1. it is argued that it is possible to distinguish different subprocesses in reading: the look-and-search process and the comprehend-and-absorb process. In Chapter 7 Noordman emphasizes the latter. Information perceived during fixation is assumed to be first stored in a buffer. Some models assume that semantic processing of information is delayed until enough information is available, others assume that words are processed semantically as soon as they are fixated. As a consequence fixation duration should correlate with the "semantic difficulty" of the words. Such a relation has been established (see also Chapter 4). In recent models of word recognition it is assumed that there is an interaction between bottom-up and top-down processing at the level of letter features, at the letter level, and at the word level. Such models can explain the well-known word-superiority effect, and factors affecting the speed of word recognition (word length, word frequency). An interesting issue is whether word meaning is indirectly accessed through phonological coding or directly from the visual signs. Evidence suggests that both ways are possible but that for the adult reader phonological coding does not play an important role. At the next level the structure and the meaning of the sentence should be recovered. Does the processing of letter forms, sounds, words, and syntactic and sematic information occur separately or interactively? There are arguments against a modular view of sentence processing. Understanding a text implies relating current information to preceding information. The larger the number of different concepts in a text the less well such a text is recalled. It is important in this respect to distinguish between the sentence grammar and the story grammar. During reading inferences are made. With respect to the reader it is important to consider his knowledge and purpose. The reader's knowledge can be conceived in terms of scripts, i.e., knowledge of more or less stereotypical situations and events. The reader's purpose affects the perspective from which he reads the text. This is believed to be an important determinant of what can be retrieved from memory. The final part of Noordman's chapter is concerned with the implications of basic linguistic research for the presentation of texts on computer displays and discusses issues such as reading from a page versus reading from a display, and the effects of computer presentation on higher-order processes. In this respect Noordman discusses at some length the rapid sequential visual presentation technique (RSVP; see also Hampton, 1987).

What are the effects on reading speed of word divisions at the end of a line? This problem is discussed by Nas in Chapter 8. In four experiments the effects were studied of breaking off words at the end of a line. The first two experiments concerned silent reading, the last two reading aloud. Why should there be any effect? One theoretical view holds that all words, including those consisting of two or more morphemes, are fully represented in the mental lexicon. The other view assumes that words consisting of two or more morphemes are decomposed into their respective morphemic units before the lexicon is consulted. The words that are thus decomposed are then matched with representations in the mental lexicon. It appears that reading a text with word divisions takes longer than reading the same text without any word division. There are, however, negative effects of avoiding word division on indentation and justification: justification sometimes produces gaps which also affect reading rate.

In Chapter 9 Bouma, Bruijning, and van Vliet give an overview of the different systems that have been developed for electronic processing of documents. First the characteristics of word processing systems are discussed. The basic word processing system has a number of relatively simple characteristics. Usually the screen represents a window on a fragment of a document; via a cursor every position in the text can be reached; the system processes plain text and has no knowledge of more complicated documents or of different types or fonts. The system output usually goes to a simple daisywheel or dot-matrix printer. Word processing on personal computers became very popular and WordStar in particular has contributed greatly to this popularity. This program is discussed to some extent. A more advanced stage of text processing is document processing. Four systems are described: Troff under UNIX, T_EX, Scribe, and SGML. The implementations of these systems are batch-oriented.

In contrast, in interactive text processing systems text make-up and graphic design facilities are integrated, and the WYSIWYG principle ("What you see is what you get") is implemented. The desktop metaphor is used as a paradigm for the user interface (see also Chapter 10). Objects in the system are represented on the screen as drawings called icons (see also Chapter 13). The user can manipulate these icons: i.e., he can open, move, send, and store them by moving a small arrow across the screen. "Popup" menus appear if a relevant icon is selected. Two systems, Xerox 8010 and Edimath, are discussed.

3. Representation of Knowledge

The representation of information in human-computer interactions depends on the presentation mode. In Chapter 10 by Jorna the phenomenon of mental representation is considered from the viewpoint of communication between man and computers, and related to presentational and semantic aspects of symbols. Analysis of the representations of novices and expert computer users shows the importance of a distinction between different sense modalities and of a subdivision within modalities. Only an expert is able to abstract information from the mode of presentation used. Current theories of mental representation are reviewed, from which conclusions may be drawn for machine representation of information on behalf of the human user.

Stokman and de Vries (Chapter 11) discuss the application of graphic techniques in relation to knowledge-based systems. Graphs may represent conceptual knowledge, and may be used for structuring, integrating, and comparing knowledge from different sources. Some important methods of knowledge representation and their technical realization in computer programs are illustrated. A procedure is shown for constructing a knowledge graph from text, illustrated with examples of scientific knowledge (texts on medical diagnosis).

The tasks that are being performed with computers are involving increasingly complex knowledge structures. This justifies the distinction of a separate programming level for the representation of the knowledge, requiring special techniques from the field of artificial intelligence. De Smedt (Chapter 12) characterizes styles of symbolic knowledge representation, related to psychological theories in this field, as these are currently applied in artificial intelligence: propositional logic, production rules, procedural representations, semantic networks, and frames. Languages for knowledge representation are briefly discussed in relation to these styles.

Graphical representation may be extremely useful in formal language analysis. In Chapter 13 Desain presents a system for editing graphic structures, and for the manipulation and animation of formal trees. The central idea of the development was to provide a user interface that enabled direct manipulation. The system, called Tree Docter, is of a modular structure, including modules for position specification, tree layout, clustering, parameter adjustment, information supervision, animation, and on-line documentation. The chapter shows some applications from the domain of linguistics.

Another contribution in the field of graphic representation of text is Chapter 14, by Kommers. His system is aimed at the manipulation of conceptual knowledge. The user interface in this case applies the multi-windowing paradigm. The conceptual structure of text is mapped in a graphic environment that may be manipulated by opening a window in order to present a view of a concept that for this purpose is declared "central." Abstraction and relation are the criteria for computation of centrality. Kommers presents some experimental results on learning to design a conceptual network or to elaborate an existing network with the help of the system. The results seem to indicate that there is a change in strategy from a receptive learning mode to a more productive use of information.

Metaphors are often suggested as a way to establish an adequate mental model of a computer system. Van der Veer and Felt (Chapter 15) describe a field study on the development of a conceptual model of an integrated office system from which metaphors are designed for an introductory course. In spite of the methodological difficulties of this type of study, interesting individual variations are found in users' representations of the system, and seem to be related to differences in preference of visualization. The destinction by Moran (1981) of levels of analysis and representation of human-computer interaction could be applied both to the analysis of the system, and to the user's representation.

4. Expert Systems and Artificial Intelligence

Development in computing is very rapid. The potential and variety of both hardware and software are increasing, and there are being developed multimodal terminals and integrated fourth generation toolkits that enable the user to define his own level of interaction with the system. Programming languages are progressing to mathematically oriented representation methods and theorem provers. For the nonspecialist, however, the systems are still far from easy to learn. The manuals provided are often not structured according to the knowledge and language of the intended end-user. Breé's contribution (Chapter 16) shows how artificial intelligence, incorporating notions from cognitive psychology, may provide users with insight into how they can accomplish a certain task. Expert system shells and tutorial systems may even base their cooperation with the user on an internal model of the individual user, including his knowledge and expertise.

Most expert systems do not behave like a human expert. The most striking difference is that the domain of expertise in a system is very strictly defined. Outside the bounderies, the system fails completely, whereas a human expert shows a behavior that can be characterized as "graceful degradation." In fact the system does not know where its domain ends, whereas humans may apply their knowledge in related situations, based on meta-knowledge and analogical reasoning. Wielinga and Bredeweg identify in Chapter 17 the function of different types of knowledge and structural aspects of the expert's knowledge base. They advocate psychonomic research methods to analyze the knowledge of human experts in order to provide basic models for the construction of a second generation of expert systems.

In the near future the applied artificial intelligence systems that users interact with will often be based on some kind of production system formalisms. Chapter 18 shows that production systems are particularly well suited to simulating cognitive processes involved in human-computer interaction. Both applications of the technique require knowledge representation methods that may deviate from basic production system architecture. Jameson offers some background information, starting with a nontechnical introduction to the topic of pattern matching, which is the most difficult problem for implementation. The architectural variants that may be defined are related to efficiency constraints. Two interpretors are mentioned which support experimentation with production systems paradigms.

5. Interaction with Information Systems

5.1 Input Aspects

At present interaction with computers usually occurs via a traditional keyboard. In the course of the time different keyboard layouts have been proposed. New developments in keyboard design are discussed, along with recent research on the use of handwriting for input and user-identification, and the processing of speech as an interaction medium that may be expected to be a useful alternative in the future.

In Chapter 19 van Noorden evaluates a new keyboard, the Velotype. Experimental data show a striking improvement in the speed of text input from an ergonomically designed chord-keyboard, as compared to the traditional "qwerty" device, for comparably skilled users of the two keyboards. However, it is doubtful whether from the user's point of view a keyboard is on all occasions the most efficient way of interacting with a system. Thomassen, Teulings, and Schomaker ask the question of whether handwriting and drawing might not sometimes be a more direct way of interacting with the system (Chapter 20). Taking handwriting seriously as a means of communication not only involves a reappraisal of the skill of handwriting but also demands fundamental insight into its psychomotor and mechanical aspects. The use of handwriting is comparable to the use of natural language as a means to bridge the gap between human communication habits and the requirements for man-computer interaction. Handwriting is especially useful for making notes, for editing comments, and for the composition of nonroutine texts. Typewriters and text editors are difficult devices to use for filling out forms, adressing mail, writing out cheques, etc. The authors discuss a model-based handwriting recognizer. Another interesting aspect of approaching a computer with handwriting is the automatic identification of writers (Chapter 21).

In Chapter 22 Pols gives a review of the problems and the developments with respect to speech input. Recognition of a limited vocabulary from a known speaker in a quiet environment is possible. As yet it is not possible to recognize and correctly interpret an unrestricted text spoken by any speaker. On the other hand, speaker verification based on voice characteristics (compare Chapter 21) is in principle possible.

5.2. Searching for Information

In the future people with different knowledge levels will search in databases for answers to either specific or more general questions. Some ideas on how these systems should be designed can be gained from research on the interaction of users with current systems.

Ideas for facilitating human search of databases may be derived from theories of human memory processes. Information retrieval in human memory as a model for searching external databases is analyzed in Chapter 23 by Beishuizen. Users of a database system are not always aware of the structure, and, moreover, they are forced by the system to work sequentially. This places serious constraints on the analogy to the use of long term memory in human problem solving. Beishuizen reviews experimental results that reveal a prevalence of search strategies based on iteration of retreival cycles, combined with individual differences in preference for a breadth-first or a depth-first approach.

Videotex services like the Dutch system Viditel are examples of large and complex databases that became available for a large user group with no expertise on database retreival methods. At the Dutch PTT an alternative user interface was developed. based on an alphanumeric search system combined with a flexible help facility. Weerdmeester reports experiments showing that the new method was an improvement over existing user interfaces (mostly of the type involving a numerically operated subject index), as indicated by both the number of correct solutions to search problems, and the average time taken to find the answer (Chapter 24).

5.3. Natural Language

Whether we interact with systems by keyboard, by handwriting, or by speech, the processing of natural language would enormously facilitate the interaction from the user's point of view. Problems and possible solutions are discussed by Bunt in the final chapter of the book. Bunt deals especially with dialogues that aim at exchanging factual information, so called "informative dialogues." This type of interaction is the core of many communication transactions, especially when a computer system is involved. Considering the systems that were available until recently, two forms of natural language dialogue paradigms might be considered as state of the art, question answering systems, and interactive dialogue systems that allow a rigid scheme of natural language expressions. Developments in the 1970s were influenced by computational linguistics and involved techniques like augmented transition networks. Semantic theory has led to improvements, and has recently been combined with theoretical developments on mechanisms for natural informative dialogues, including assumptions on the changing state of knowledge of both partners in a dialogue. Bunt illustrates this approach with experimentally simulated terminal dialogues.

6. Conclusions

The research discussed in this book has both fundamental and applied aspects. In the field of man-computer interaction it is quite evident that much research is driven by a certain application which is to be tested or modified. The problem with such an approach is that fundamental questions are not asked. We should develop and use theories about how people communicate with each other and consider their implications for communication between man and machine. We should also investigate whether theories of cognitive skills can be applied to the task of programming, to using a text processor, etc. Most theories in cognitive psychology have been based on quite artificial tasks, and it seems doubtful whether these theories can be easily generalized. It is, however, our belief that knowledge upon which design principles can be based, formulated in production rules, can be derived from basic research principles. Several authors have indicated how the principles they found may be applied. It will be the task of the reader to judge whether the research discussed in this book is really useful for understandig human-computer interaction and to reformulate the principles in such a way that they are also useful for the cognitive engineer.

References

Hampton J.A. (1987). Principles from the psychology of language. In: *Applying Cognitive Psychology to User Interface Design.* M.M. Gardiner and B. Christie (Eds.), John Wiley: New York.

Moran T.P. (1981). The command language grammar: a representation for the user interface of interactive computer systems. *International Journal of Man-Machine Studies*, 15, pp. 3-50.

The Presentation of Visual Information: Visual Aspects

Chapter 1. The Legibility of Visual Display Texts

Floris L. van Nes

1. Introduction

Communicating with computers is becoming increasingly important in our technological environment. Unfortunately the quality of the texts that appear on the display screen is often far from perfect. Numerous complaints - and the occasional alarming press report - testify to this. Is there any possibility of improvement? In most cases visual display texts can indeed be shown in such a way that they can be read perfectly. A lot of improvements can often be made to the layout, the typeform, and use of color. In a number of cases, however, there is still uncertainty about our visual perception capabilities. Further research is thus called for. In what follows, some basic properties of the visual reading process will first be described. Then, the separate effects of the use of layout, color and typography on legibility will be treated explicitly, followed by some illustrations of the combined effect of the three image parameters. These illustrations, as well as all others in this paper, refer to videotex pages as used to be broadcast, regularly or in experiments, by the Dutch Teletext service. Finally, some practical rules are formulated which mostly apply to multicolor text displays in general and, to a certain extent, also to the use of graphics.

2. Visual Processes in Reading

Reading can be divided into two processes: a visual process and a cognitive one, or a look-and-search process and a comprehend-and-absorb process (Bouma, 1980). The searching is linked to the reader's interest: in many cases he or she will wish to actually read only part of the text seen and so will want to find this interesting section as quickly as possible. It will therefore be obvious that the legibility of texts on visual display screens is enhanced by arranging the page on the screen in such a way that the search time is reduced and once the passage has been found it can be read without difficulty.

During the search process the eyes skim over the page, guided by such text attributes as characteristic initials and word lengths and attracted by conspicuous symbols, words, or entire fragments of text. In printed text the headings of paragraphs and suchlike are made to stand out sufficiently by printing them in bold letters or italics. But such subtle possibilities are not yet available on most displays: in this case the text writer is forced to resort to more forceful measures, such as showing the words in question in a different color. Unfortunately those words may then be too striking compared with the rest of the text, so that the reader's attention is involuntarily drawn towards them again and again, even after the search process is completed. As a result the actual reading of the text may be interfered with.

2.1. Distinction Between Legibility and Readability

When we read without interruption our eyes move along the lines of text in a series of rapid movements. Inserted between these are fixation pauses during which the eyes focus on a particular point on the line. The fixations are used for absorbing the information in the text, since this is when words are recognized. Important factors in this recognition process include not only the individual letters but the word contours as well (Bouwhuis, 1979). For example no one would ever identify *h* as *p* or *leg* as *Hottentots*, whereas *h* may be confused with *b* and *leg* with *tap*.

As regards the component letters it should be noted that lower-case letters, with their characteristic ascenders and descenders lend a characteristic contour to a word, far more so than when a word is made up of capitals. In the latter case the only aid to recognition is the length of the word. Apart from letter type, other features of text which affect the visual recognition processes include contrast and color; together these characteristics determine the legibility of a text as defined by, for example, Tinker (1964) and Klare (1969, pp.1-2). This text property is distinct from that which is called readability (Klare, 1969, pp.1-2). This second property, the result of stylistic factors such as the vocabulary used and the length of sentences, determines the intelligibility of the text.

In the reading process the distance between two successive fixations along a line is determined by factors related to recognizability and by text characteristics related to intelligibility, such as redundancy. The eye may move not only from left to right, but also from right to left, the main example of this being from the end of one line to the start of the next. But this reverse movement can also occur within a line. This probably happens when some part of the line already passed has not been correctly recognized or understood.

The movement to the start of the next line may not be directed quite precisely enough if the angle between the required direction of motion and the direction of the lines is small. These small "eye return angles" occur when the lines are long or the distance between lines is small.

3. Legibility and Space

The amount of text which a writer can put onto a visual display screen is usually limited; a "page" of Teletekst or Viditel (the Dutch teletext and videotex systems), or, to use the generic term, a page of videotex contains a maximum of 24 lines containing 40 letters each, i.e., 960 letters or a total of some 150 words (about one-quarter of a page of text in this book). A fragment of text any longer than this must therefore be spread over several of the videotex pages. Due to the operations required, however, it is far more awkward to read a number of videotex pages in succession than a number of pages of a book or magazine, since the latter only have to be turned. Because of these distracting operations it is easy to lose the thread of what several videotex pages are talking about. This makes it tempting for the person writing the pages to cram as many letters as possible onto the lines available. But the distance between these lines is small in relation to their length and this gives rise to the small eye-return angles described earlier. As a result the visual legibility is greatly reduced, so that in actual fact the writer has defeated the object.

Figure 1. A visual display text spread over two columns. As a result of this layout the lines have become half as long as with a single-column layout, so that the text is easier to read. The letters here are from a 6 × 10 dot matrix.

One way of overcoming this is to divide the visual display text into columns (normally two), as is done in newspapers. Figure 1 show this kind of text lay-out in columns, and also shows the problem that may now arise: because of the limited number of letter positions, 40 in the case of videotex, only 18 or 19 letters and spaces can fit on each column line, compared with 32 - 34 in a normal newspaper column. This low number makes satisfactory line filling difficult.

3.1. Texts on Paper and on Visual Display Screens

Tests have shown that for texts printed on paper, a page with a great deal of blank space amongst the text is regarded as easier to read and more interesting than pages entirely filled with text (Smith & McCombs, 1971). Such a view constitutes the subjective interpretation of the objective reduction in visual legibility caused, among other things, by the small eye-return angles in densely packed text. With display screens whose legibility is often rather limited (owing to the blurred letters, which in some cases vibrate a little, etc.) the inclusion of blank spaces on a page is probably even more important than

Figure 2. The division of this text into three paragraphs separated by blank lines and the open spaces in the second and third paragraphs enhance legibility. The letters here are formed from a 12 × 10 dot matrix.

on paper for getting people to actually read the page; the blank lines (3 and 10) in Figure 2 and the only partly filled lines (2, 7, 9, and 15) thus have a favorable effect.

3.2. Layout Aspects

Figure 3 (see color plate at the end of the book) shows a so-called index page, the Teletekst *General Index* from the end of 1981; it illustrates two layout aspects. First, the use of space; the page contains little open space, which, as explained above, is a pity (though sometimes inevitable on an index page). But in this case the *Teletekst* logo (as it was then) and the unimportant line about the general index in this same test period together take up six of the 24 lines available. That is one-quarter of the entire page, which would seem to be rather wasteful. And the sentence beginning *"De rubrieksoverzichten...."* (the subject indexes), below the middle of the page, which takes up more than three lines, is perhaps not all that informative.

Secondly, I would like to draw attention to the tabulation of the page. It has, apart from the logo, two different systems of two columns plus two fragments of text which run across the entire width; the overall impression is one of confusion. And also on the subject of tables, the order in a table should be according to a system that can be understood, and therefore used, by the reader. This is not the case in Figure 3; the subject indexes and the *"veelgevraagde pagina's"* (popular pages) are neither in alphabetical order nor listed in ascending page numbers.

The latter classification principle *is* used in Figure 4 (see color plate at th end of the book) in the top part of the page. While it is true that such a lis looks neat, this does not help us to find a particular broadcasting compan (left column) or program. This is because with this system they can only b found by reading in full the words or acronyms before the numbers, wherea with an alphabetical list only the initials have to be scanned. Moreover because of the relative distances it is easy to mistakenly read that: "Radi Noord's programs are on page 516." especially since in the page depicted i Figure 3, from the same period as Figure 4, the page numbers are indeed t the left of the corresponding page titles.

4. Legibility and Color

4.1. Color Contrast

The recognition of colored letters against a colored or "black" background depends primarily on the luminance contrast between the letters and the background; color contrast plays a minor role. This is important for the legibility of colored texts, including systems such as videotex, in which no correction is made for the varying sensitivity of our retinas to different colors, which as a result differ in perceived brightness. The seven videotex colors available can be placed in the following descending order of brightness: white - yellow - cyan - green - magenta - red - blue (cyan = green + blue, magenta = red + blue). Against a dark background the first four colors are the most suitable for text reproduction. Red and especially blue are unsuitable since our eyes are relatively insensitive to them. However, against a bright background, i.e., white, yellow, or cyan, it is precisely the other way round; then, the color of the letters must be dark, for example red, blue, or magenta, for there to be sufficient contrast. In Figure 5 (see color plate at the end of the book) the letter and background colors have been selected so that hard-to-read sentences alternate with easy-to-read ones.

About 8% of the male population is to a greater or lesser extent color-blind: for these readers a sufficiently high luminance contrast between letters and background must be provided whenever colors are used which they may have difficulty in distinguishing. Although they perhaps will not see the colors as different, they may still be able to read the text thanks to the difference in luminance between text and background.

4.2. Color and Interpretation

The use of different colors on a visual display screen may have many different effects on the reader, some desirable from the writer's point of view, some undesirable or even unforeseen, but all of them influencing the reading process. Examples are:

1. Connecting fragments of text by means of the same color, known as perceptive grouping
2. Emphasizing parts of a text by making them a different color from that of the surrounding text and thus making them stand out
3. Categorizing parts of the text, for example according to their importance, by colorcoding them
4. Facilitating or impeding the reading process by the number of different colors on a single screen page

We shall now go into these effects in some detail.

1. People have a strong tendency to interpret fragments of a text and/or figure of the same color as belonging together. But this association mechanism, which groups parts of texts and figures without the reader being aware of it, only works as long as there are not more than three or at most four colors on a page (Cahill & Carter, 1976; Reynolds, 1979).

Figure 3 illustrates that the converse can also be true: different colored parts of text are not easily interpreted as belonging together. The titles of the subject indexes, "*Nieuws*" (news), "*Vrije Tijd*" (leisure time), etc., are cyan on the screen (on paper this becomes light blue), while the corresponding page numbers are yellow, as is the introductory line "*PAGINA's met RUBRIEKSOVERZICHTEN zijn:*" (pages showing subject indexes are:) above them. As a result there is at first sight no immediate reason for associating, say, "*Weerberichten*" (weather) with page 305 (here again, incidentally, the impression could be given that the weather is on page 355, since the distance from the word to that number is less than it is to 305).

Since the paragraph below the upper table provides information about the subjects in that table it is rightly the same color as the subject names. But the last sentence in this paragraph is really about something new, namely searching in an alphabetical index, so it could be argued that it should not be in cyan. Anyway, the alternate use of two colors makes it difficult to see that this is a single sentence.

2. As a matter of fact, of course, the designer of the page described did have something in mind when he decided to make "*Alfabetisch zoeken*" (alphabetical index) yellow, which was to make these words stand out. A fragment of a text or figure which is a different color from its environment has an objectively measurable conspicuousness (Engel, 1980), which depends amongst other things on the particular color combination. This means that the eyes are involuntarily attracted to the different colored part as they skim over the page. Color differences can thus be used as efficient aids to searching, for example in a text like that in Figure 6 (see color plate at the end of the book); because the motorway numbers are shown in yellow we can - provided we are familiar with them! - quickly find the traffic news for the road we intend to take and skip the remainder of the text that is of no interest to us.

   Another way to emphasize a text is to put it against a conspicuously colored background. On screens the background is usually black; any bright background then stands out. Returning to Figure 3, it can be seen that the bottom block, showing the popular page numbers, will probably attract a great deal of attention as a result of this. This also used to be true of the page heading: undisturbed searching through the general index was at that time hampered because the eyes were constantly being drawn by the extremely striking nature of the Teletekst logo, partly because of the color and partly because of the unusual letter forms.

3. The color of a text can also be used to code it, i.e., to attach a specific significance to it which is not necessarily conveyed by the content. An example of such coding is the transference of the subjective meaning of a color

Figure 7. This subject index illustrates the difference between the bold numbers and normal letters, allowing a distinction to be made between null and the capital O (bottom line), thanks to the 12 × 10 dot matrix used here.

to the words in that color; words printed with red letters are thus generally assumed to be important. This does not apply, however, to the red letters against a dark background as used in most color displays, as the brightness is then too low in comparison with that of words in other colors. But the last line on Figures 7 and 8 shows that a red background, because of its greater area, may be used to transfer the code of the background color to the text concerned, which in this case is about news flashes. If color coding is applied, the application should be consistent in the sense that the agreed upon connection between color and meaning should remain the same.

4. A comparison of Figure 2 with Figure 3 shows that the number and spatial distribution of colors on a display may create an impression of order or visual chaos, respectively. This could affect the reading process, for instance through causing erroneous eye movements in the chaotic case.

Figure 8. The same page as shown in Figure 7, but now with the current 6 × 10 dot matrix for the letters and numbers.

5. Legibility and Typography

In printed matter typographical methods are used primarily for two purposes, making headings and giving emphasis. The normal technique for headings is to use letters which are larger, sometimes much larger, than those in the text which follows. Emphasis may be used for single words, sentences or entire paragraphs.

Making headings on screens is more difficult because the possibilities for displaying large letters are limited. Videotex systems can reproduce both the normal lower-case letters and capitals at twice the height, as in the heading in Figure 1, but other than this the only solution is to resort to what are known as graphic letters, which can be made up of relatively large blocks as in the headings in Figures 2 - 4, for example.

Even more awkward is the typographical emphasis of fragments of electronically generated text. At the moment the only way to make a distinction between emphasized and nonemphasized text on most screens is to use capitals and lower-case letters. But the use of capitals in straight text is not to be recommended. There are two reasons for this. First, as was said earlier, the contours of words in capitals are less characteristic, at the expense of word recognition - an effect which has even been found to apply to headings (Poulton, 1967). Secondly, the open space between two lines of text in capitals is relatively small, so that the recognition of a word in a line is made even more difficult by the words above and below it exerting a masking effect through being so close (Woodworth & Schlosberg, 1954).

For screens in the lower and medium price ranges there is in fact no typographical method for, say, giving two paragraphs two different characters. Now, however, a 12 × 10 dot matrix has been introduced for videotex, to replace the present 6 × 10 dot matrix (Van Nes, 1986). One of the advantages of this is that, because the new matrix is constructed twice as finely in the horizontal direction, it is in principle possible to make both normal and bold symbol forms. This can come in useful for distinguishing between those capitals and numbers which are easily confused under non-optimal perception conditions, such as the long distances at which Teletekst is read. So as, for instance, to reduce to a minimum the possibility of confusing capitals and numbers, such as *S* and *5* and *B* and *8*, a set of optimally distinguishable alphanumeric symbols was designed and tested at the Institute for Perception Research and the numbers in the set were made bolder in comparison with lower-case letters and capitals. This also solved the notorious problem of not being able to distinguish between the capital letter O and the numeral null, as can be seen in the bottom three lines of Figure 7. This is only true, of course, if the maker of the page has actually typed the numeral null on his keyboard. Figure 4, taken from a Teletekst screen, illustrates that this is not always the case: none of the 0s here is bold and they are thus identical with Os, probably because the maker of this page did not like the present diamond-shaped nought which can be seen in Figure 8.

6. Conclusions

6.1. What Knowledge is Still Lacking?

A great deal of our knowledge of the reading process goes back as far as about the turn of the century. But it is only in recent years that modern research equipment, for example to accurately record eye movements during reading, has become available to obtain objective data regarding the combined effect of layout and color factors on the reading process. Among other things, a quantitative gauge is still needed for the conspicuousness, at first glance or continuously, of different colored text, measurable by means of eye movement registration.

6.2. Golden Rules

Finally, a few golden rules for designing visual display texts:

- A page filled entirely with text is difficult to read. Its legibility can only be increased significantly by inserting blank lines, not by using different-colored text.
- The emptier an index page the easier it is to find an item: therefore such pages should contain only necessary information and be clearly laid out.
- Not more than three or at most four colors should be found on a page of text. Fragments of text in the same color are regarded as belonging together; this effect can be made use of, but may also cause confusion if there is no connection between texts of the same color.
- Part of a text or figure that is a different color from its surrounding stands out and thus attracts attention. This can be used to help readers to scan a text.
- In a particular software environment color should be applied as systematically as possible. For example, in color coding the connection between color and meaning should remain the same.
- Capitals should only be used for the initial letters of sentences and names and for titles and headings, in other words hardly ever for all the letters in a sentence, paragraph, or page.

References

Bouma H. (1980). Visual reading processes and the quality of text displays. In: *Ergonomic aspects of visual display terminals*, E. Grandjean & E. Vigliani (Eds.). Taylor and Francis, London, pp. 101-114.

Bouwhuis D.G. (1979). *Visual recognition of words*. Ph.D. thesis, Catholic University of Nijmegen.

Bruce M. & Foster J.J. (1982). The visibility of colored characters on colored backgrounds in viewdata displays. *Visible Language*, 16, pp. 382-390.

Cahill M.C. & Carter R.C. Jr. (1976). Color code size for searching displays of different density. *Human Factors*, 18, pp. 273-280.

Engel F.L. (1980). Information selection from visual display units. In: *Ergonomic aspects of visual display terminals*, E. Grandjean & E. Vibliani (Eds.). Taylor and Francis, London, pp. 121-125.

Klare G.R. (1969). *The measurement of readability*. The Iowa State University Press, Ames, IA, pp. 1-2.

Nes F.L. van (1984). Limits of visual perception in the technology of visual display terminals. *Behaviour and Information Technology*, 3, pp. 371-377.

Nes F.L. van (1986). A new Teletext character set with enhanced legibility. *IEEE Transactions on Electron Devices*, 33, pp. 1222-1225.

Poulton E.C. (1967). Searching for newspaper headlines, printed in capitals or lower-case letters. *Journal of Applied Psychology*, 51, pp. 417-425.

Reynolds L. (1979). Teletext and viewdata a new challenge for the designer. *Information Design Journal*, 1, pp. 2-14.

Smith S.L. & McCombs M.E. (1971). The graphics of prose. *Journalism Quarterly*, 48, pp. 134-136.

Tinker M.A. (1964). *Legibility of Print.* Iowa State University Press, Ames, IA.

Woodworth R.S. and Schlosberg H. (1954). *Experimental Psychology.* Methuen, London.

Chapter 2. The Use of Color in Visual Displays

Charles M.M. de Weert

1. Introduction

Technical advances have given as enormous increase in the possiblities to use color for the representation of information, and have increased the risk of expectations of color's usefulness being too high. Unfortunately the technical progress has not been accompanied by a proportional increase in knowledge about useful employment of color. In other words, color is in many cases applied in a silly, sometimes even very unprofitable way. In particular, the application of pseudocoloring, i.e., the transformation of unidimensional brightness differences into multidimensional color differences, easily leads to problems if the transformation is not well chosen.

In this contribution attention will first be paid to differences in the processing of luminance differences on the one hand and the processing of color differences on the other. The second part concerns attempts to measure possible equivalences of color and brightness differences. As soon as more forms, colors, and brightnesses occur in a display, we are confronted with the general problem of wanted and unwanted Gestalt formations. Knowledge about the ordering of the "equivalences" of color, and brightness differences and of combinations of these, is just a beginning to the understanding of Gestalt formations in displays. In the following section some attention is paid to the role of color, in comparison with other codes, in the presentation of information. Finally, possible applications of color in displaying complex information are described, starting from the idea that there is more need for guidelines than for rules of thumb for the use of color in displays.

2. Differences in Color and Luminance Processing: Spatial Aspects

2.1. Chromatic and Achromatic Modulation Transfer Functions

In Figure 1 spatial modulation transfer functions for achromatic (luminance) modulation (B) and for chromatic (color) modulation (C) are illustrated. The figure indicates with what attenuation a sinusoidal modulation is transmitted

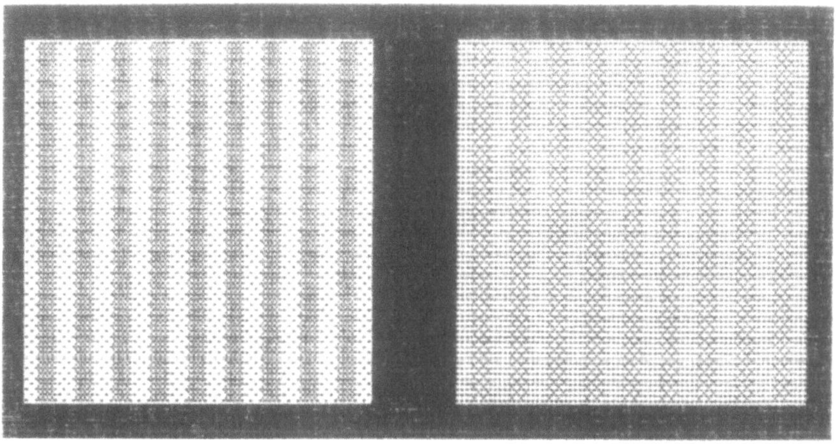

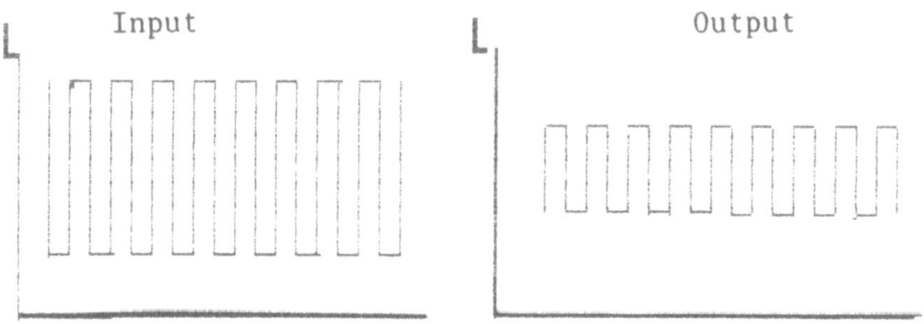

A

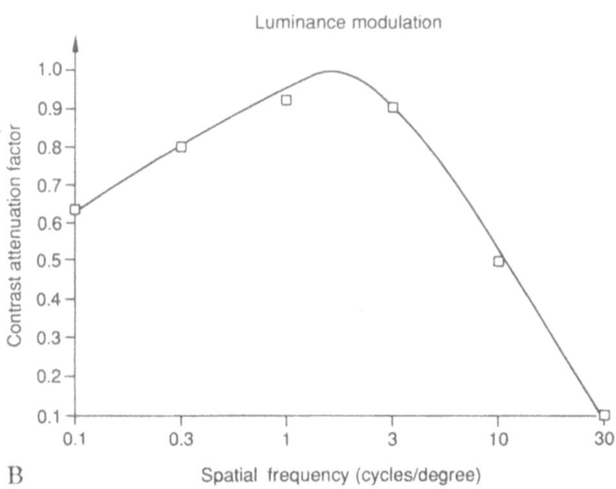

B

Fig. 1. Legend on page 28

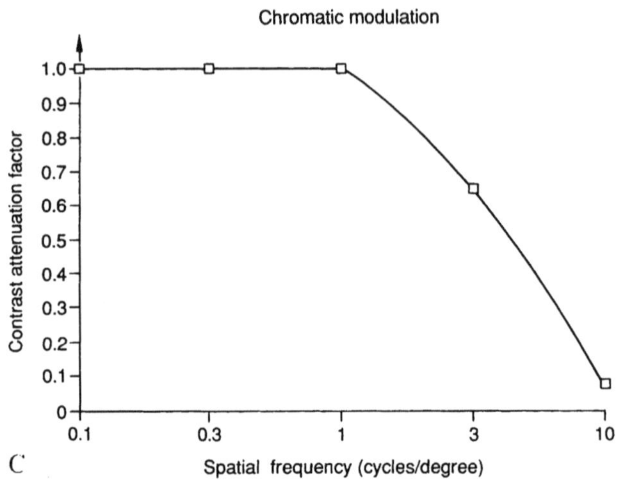

C

Figure 1. Modulation transfer function for an optical system (A). The input wave (left) is attenutated in amplitude by the lens. The ratio of the output amplitude and the input amplitude is a measure of the contrast transfer. B shows schematically the human observer's modulation transfer function for sinusoidal luminance modulations, C for sinusoidal, purely chromatic modulations.

through the visual system. For ease one should first consider the visual system as an optical system only, as in Figure 1A. The ratio of the contrast modulation before and after the lens is called the modulation transfer function. This ratio is dependent upon the spatial frequency of the sinusoidal function at the input side. The visual system is much more complex. It consists of an optical part and a neural part. The neural part is determined by the structure of the receptor layers and the neural connections between them, and by the structure of the further pathways to the cortex. It is the neural part which causes the differences in the two MTFs (Cornsweet, 1970). An important difference between the parts of the figure is concerned with the high-frequency cutoff, which is considerably higher for luminance modulation than for purely chromatic modulation. Detailed information is better processed in the luminance channel than in the chromatic channels. A second difference can be found at the low frequency side of the MTFs. A decrease occurs for the luminance MTF, which is absent in the chromatic MTF. This cannot directly be interpreted as the better functioning of color for low frequency information, but is commonly taken to mean that the bandpass character of the luminance channel represents an ability to contribute to contour formation, whereas the absence of this property in the chromatic channel is interpreted as evidence against involvement in contour processes.

2.2. Accommodation

Some very fundamental processes are not or are hardly subserved by the chromatic channels on their own. Accommodation is an example. Pure color contours do not lead to a stable accommodation response (Wolfe & Owens, 1981). The effect is best illustrated in two-color pictures on a display, when one of the colors is changing gradually around the point of isoluminance. Isoluminance means that the two colors have equal luminance. (Luminance is not identical to brightness. Stimuli of equal luminance may be judged as equally bright but that is not necessarily the case.) It is difficult to illustrate this effect in static color photographs, main reason being the enormous variation in color sensitivity functions even among color-normal observers. The dynamic representation of, for example, a noise pattern consisting of only red and green dots on a TV screen, leads at isoluminance to very unpleasant feelings for many subjects, because not only is the accommodation disabled, but more or less coupled with this, the convergence of the two eyes is also disturbed. For the use of color in displays this particular effect is enough reason to avoid isoluminance in adjacent areas because of variation in V_λ between subjects (V_λ is the spectral sensitivity function).

2.3. The Role of Colors in Some Pattern Recognition Processes

2.3.1. Binocular Stereopsis

The process of depth perception is based upon the detection of small differences in the retinal images in the two eyes (disparity). Here a peculiar effect can occur. For figural stimuli (i.e., the part of the figure to be seen in depth that can be seen in both eyes) isoluminance of figure and background leads to a considerable decrease in perceived depth but does not entirely destroy it; for random dot stereograms, in which the figure to be seen in depth cannot be detected monocularly, depth disappears at isoluminance (Lu & Fender, 1972; Gregory, 1977; De Weert, 1979). Only in very extended series of measurements was some depth found (de Weert & Sadza, 1983). An interesting aspect here was that the luminance difference necessary to obtain a just visible depth sensation, increased with increasing difference in color between the dots and the background (see Figure 2A, derived from de Weert, 1980).

2.3.2. Subjective Brightness Contours

A similar effect has been found in the formation of subjective brightness contours (see Figure 2B). Subjective brightness contours are perceived contours which do not have corresponding physical changes in luminance in the

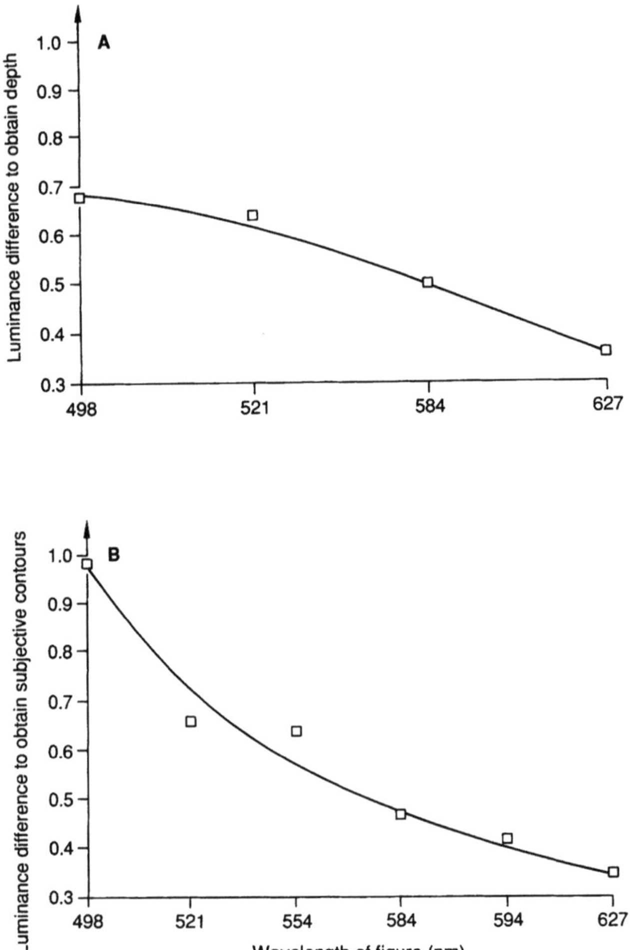

Figure 2. Luminance differences necessary to obtain stereopsis in random dot stereograms (A), and luminance differences necessary to obtain subjective brightness contours (B). Data derived from de Weert (1980). The wavelength of the figure was variable, that of the background was fixed. The luminance of the background was set at unity.

stimuli at the places where the contours are seen. The luminance difference between inducing fields and background, needed to evoke the perception of a subjective contour, is larger when the difference in color between the inducing field and the background is larger (see color example). Note that the contour is seen in the background, where no changes in physically measured intensity occur. The nature of these two visual effects may not be of vital importance to ergonomists. However, the influence of the introduction of color is very instructive: adding color differences apparently leads to a reduction of the effect evoked by pure luminance differences.

There are further effects regarding color differences versus luminance differences. Although these are much better demonstrated in a dynamic display, the principles of some will be illustrated through color plates. There is a striking difference in the perception of Figure 3A and 3B (see color plate at the end of the book). When luminance differences are present (Figure 3A) different depth planes are perceived. This organization in depth planes completely disappears at isoluminance (Figure 3B). As a matter of fact monocular depth information is also quite difficult to grasp in an isoluminant picture (Figure 3D) as compared with a picture with luminance differences (Figure 3C). This is not the place to discuss the possible grounds for the detrimental influence of adding color differences, it suffices here to conclude that it is worth considering the different subprocesses before color is added, because some of them could deteriorate. For a review of psychophysical phenomena occurring in color displays see also Walraven (1985).

3. Gestalt Formation

Of greater importance than the preceding phenomena is the question of what role color plays in the formation of figure-ground relations: which parts connect to which to form a figure? This is the problem of "gestalt" formation. What happens if some visual representation, based on achromatic differences only, is transformed according to some key, into a picture in which both color and brightness differences occur? Achromatic variations are of a one-dimensional nature whereas variations in color are trivariant. There is an increase in possible similarity relations. The problem of this so-called pseudocoloring is to find a key which leads to an improvement of the intended information transfer. In Figure 4 (see color plate at the end of the book) a few relatively simple examples are given. Figure 4A is the original picture in which increasing gray levels correspond to increasing strength of connection between points. In Figure 4B the luminance relations have been retained but color differences added. In Figure 4C the original luminance relations have no longer been retained. One can easily imagine that in this picture a possible loss of corrrect identification of important areas would occur. Here it is harmless, but that is certainly not the case in, say, medical X-ray photographs, or echograms. One should be very careful with the use of pseudocoloring in general; its application requires knowledge about color similarity to start with.

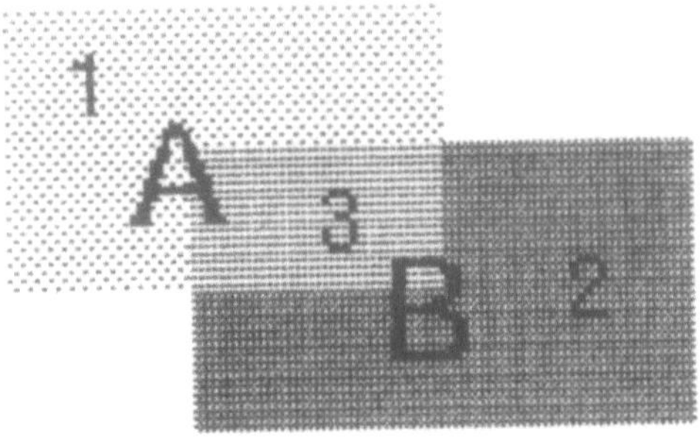

Figure 5. General form of the stimuli used in gestalt measurements. Does area 3 belong to area 1 or to area 2?

3.1. Similarity of Colors and Color Scaling

The similarity problem can easily be demonstrated in the following series of examples, in which for clarity reasons the number of features is extended to three: form, color, and luminance. It should be noted that the pictures to be presented are not meant as stimuli in an experiment. The exaggerated examples only serve demonstration purposes. The stimulus is always built up in the same manner (see Figure 5) and the observer is asked, for every possible configuration, to give in a forced choice procedure a response to indicate whether area 3 belongs to square A or to square B.

In Figure 6A (see color plate at the end of the book) the forms are equal in all three parts, but differ in color and brightness. It is possible that observers use a combination of color and brightness differences, but it is equally possible that an observer "decides" to weight brightness similarity more than hue similarity. This strategy is more clear in the other example in Figure 6, in which in addition an inequality of form is introduced. The question posed to the observer is the same as the one given above. One is inclined of course to say here that observers are able to deal with the clearly different dimensions separately. Although it is easy enough to make examples in which a "strategy" seems evident, one should be careful in concluding that a conscious choice is always possible. In fact it is also very easy to generate pictures in which this choice can hardly be made. This problem is of considerable theoretical interest. Going back to the color domain one may ask to what extent subjects are able to separate dimensions. This question has been dealt with by Raaijmakers and de Weert (1975), Elzinga and de Weert (1978, 1984), and Elzinga (1985). In their experiments so-called cancellation functions were measured, which give measures for the opponent color channel activities. These opponent color channels are supposed to be independent. One can for example quantify the redness of a stimulus by measuring the

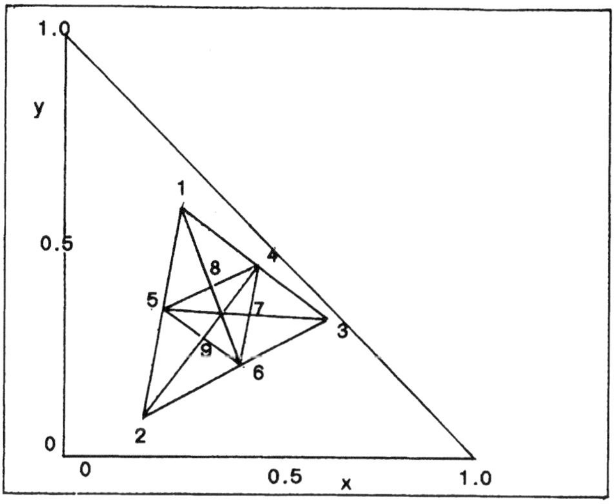

Figure 8. The "isobri" set, consisting of nine colors equated in luminance (15 cd/m^2).

Table 1. The RYG set, consisting of three colors (R, red; Y, yellow; G, green), at three luminance levels (H, high; M, medium; L, low)

Designation	X	Y	Luminance (cd/m^2
HG	0.290	0.580	30
MG	0.290	0.580	15
LG	0.290	0.580	7.5
HY	0.475	0.458	30
MY	0.475	0.458	15
LY	0.475	0.458	7.5
HR	0.634	0.342	30
MR	0.634	0.342	15
LR	0.634	0.342	7.5

amount of a particular green stimulus which must be added in order to cancel this redness. This cancellation function is a psychophysical measure. It turns out that the judgement of redness, however, is not a simple function of the cancellation function alone. It also depends on the activities in the other opponent color channel (yellow/blue) and on the activity in the achromatic channel. This brings us to the question of color scaling. Information is needed about distances in the psychological color-brightness space. In fact there is hardly any knowledge about these distances for large color and brightness differences, and although the data presented here are the result of a pilot study only, they are worth mentioning because of the fundamental problems in scaling large color and brightness differences.

In Figure 7 (see color plate at the end of the book) the stimuli used in this study were illustrated. The subjects are asked to say whether they perceived a triangle pointing to the right or one pointing to the left. The experiments were performed for several sets of colors. In one set three colors each at three luminance levels, were chosen (Table 1) and in another set nine isoluminant colors were selected (Figure 8).

Subjects were first-year students who participated in an experimental practical session. Triadic comparisons were made and the preference data were converted to scales that indicate the order of similarity of each stimulus with respect to all others. These were used as entries in a multidimensional scaling program. In these programs the stimuli are positioned in an euclidic geometrical space in such a way that all ordinal distance relations are optimally retained. The results are depicted in Figure 9, in which the two dimensional solutions are represented. The isoluminant color set (dark background) is remarkably well recognized in the plot (compare Figures 8A and 9A). For the RYG set (three colors, each at three luminance levels) one can see that different clusters occur for different backgrounds. The white background (brighter than the brightest stimulus value, data in Figure 9B) apparently reduces the weight of the luminance dimension and clustering occurs according to similarity in hue, whereas with the dark background (data in Figure 9C) a more even distribution over color and luminance levels seems to occur. Does this really mean that the distance is a combined (euclidian) function of color and luminance differences? This type of data must be analyzed in several "metrics". It remains to be seen whether subjects can freely alter their strategy, and thus change the metric.

4. Task Analysis: Ergonomic Aspects

For the choice of color as a code in a display to carry a certain type of information, careful analysis of the purpose is needed. It is of course impossible to present a scheme of all possible goals and the possible means. It makes much sense, however, to make a division into the types of processes involved, and then look for codes which best serve these processes. In review papers Christ (1975, 1984) presented the relative advantages or disadvantages of color codes, as compared with the use of noncolor codes such as size, brightness, specific form, etc. In brief one can say that color is a superior code for search tasks, because, in contrast to letter forms for example, variations in color can be easily detected in the parafoveal and more peripheral parts of the retina. From fundamental research it has become clear that color discrimination for

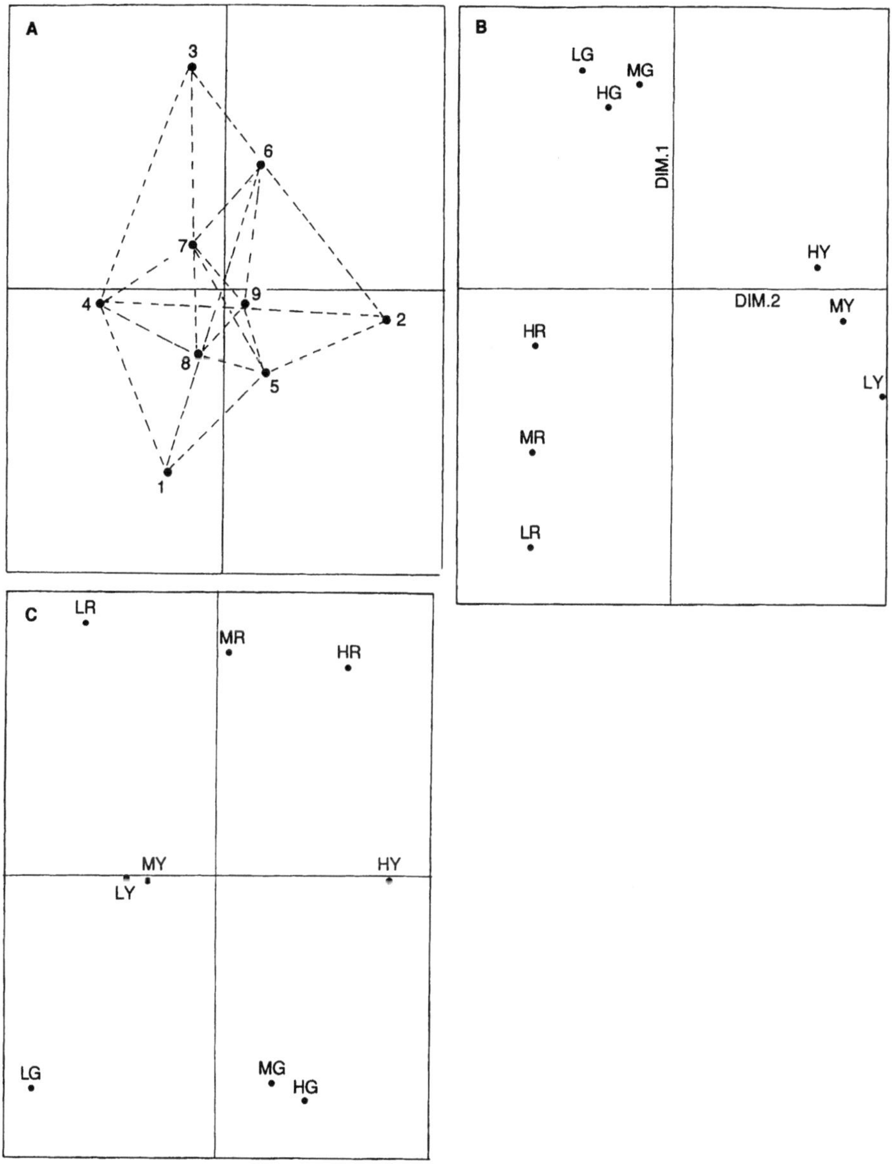

Figure 9. Results for the isobri set (A), for the RYG set (B) presented on a white background which was brighter than the brightest stimulus color, and for the RYG set (C) presented on a dark background.

properly adapted sizes of stimuli remains good even for the far periphery (Van Esch, Koldenhof, Van Doorn, and Koenderink, 1984). Not only does discrimination of color remain at a high level in the periphery, but so too does the capacity to identify color, otherwise a search task would not make sense. For identification tasks letter forms and known geometrical forms seem to do better. This is presumably related to the effort needed to attach names to colors on the one hand and to well known forms on the other. Christ's papers are strongly recommended reading because of the wide review of different practical types of use of color, i.e., as redundant versus nonredundant information, in unidimensional versus multidimensional displays, and for different tasks.

In Treisman's (1982) paper a more fundamental analysis of underlying processes was given. A theoretical framework was presented in which two types of information processes were supposed to coexist: an automatic, preattentive system, working in parallel to form maps of different features, and a serial, attentive system which combined the outcomes of a number of those different feature detection processes. According to Treisman, "figure/ground" separations occur in parallel only within simple feature maps. If form recognition is supposed to occur in the serial process because different features have to be combined, and if color discrimination in Treisman's model is one of the parallel processes, this would explain why color gives quicker results in searching tasks than for example geometric forms. It does not predict differences in identification tasks. Although Treisman's feature integration theory covers a wider field the concepts are quite similar to those of Julesz (1981) in his texture detection theory. The building blocks of the texture elements are processed automatically, preattentively, without "scrutiny", but the distinction of different compositions is an attention controlled process.

Engel's (1971) work can be placed between the pragmatic approach of Christ and the theoretical approach of Treisman. It is concerned with the analysis of visual conspicuity for targets in textured displays. Engel introduced the concepts of attention area, conspicuity area and visibility area. These operationally defined measures might also be useful for the study of color coding. The conspicuity area was defined as that area around the fixation spot in which a target was detected with a certain probability during one short presentation of 75 ms. The visibility area was determined in nearly the same way, with the exception that just before the target presentation the subject was informed about the exact place. The visibility area is larger than the conspicuity area. The third area, called the attention area, is the area with a certain target detection probability around an "attention point," while fixation is kept constant at another point. The three areas are related in a simple geometric way, with the visibility area being composed of attentional areas and with the conspicuity area as the central area around the fixation point.

5. Guidelines Instead of Rules of Thumb: Some Examples

The most important thing to be learned from the literature on the use of color for presentation of information is that there is a need for theoretical concepts, rather than for rules of thumb. Displays are two-dimensional, but objects are three-dimensional. There is a need for presentation of this three-dimensional character in computer assisted design and computer assisted manufacturing (CAD/CAM) for example. If different planes are superimposed as opaque surfaces, the information on the covered parts is visibly lost. Is there a way to present the superimposed information in such a way that the information from the covered planes is still available? Examples of superimposition of different planes are presented in Figure 10A and 10B (see color plate at the end of the book) for equally colored planes.

A similar problem occurs when information must be superimposed because different features belonging to the same location must be displayed (see Figure 10C and D), for example cartographic data. Much simpler examples are found in direction signs in buildings. In all cases one wants the overlapped area to be recognized as belonging to two other areas, and not as a separate object. In de Weert (1984, 1985) an explicit statement was presented about the way in which people can deal with color information. The statement was as follows: observers have implicit knowledge of at least a number of aspects of their physical environment. This body of knowledge also comprises knowledge about physical characteristics of light stimuli. We hypothesized that observers have knowledge of underlying physical rules for transparancy (brightness aspects), and also about additive mixing of lights of a different nature (color aspects).

In a series of experiments the recognizability of two stimuli was measured (de Weert, 1984, 1985). These stimuli were five-letter words (Figure 11, see color plate at the end of the book) with a constant frequency of occurrence. The colors of the words were chosen from sets of nine, either a set of three colors at three luminance values each, or a set of nine isoluminant colors.These sets were the same as those presented in Figure 8. The two words were presented simultaneously and partly overlapping each other. Let the colors of the two words be i and j, and the color of the overlap be k. The background was dark in these experiments. At each presentation two words were chosen from a list of 80, and a new triad of colors (i,j,k) was chosen. The subjects were asked to read the words aloud, and their responses were compared to the input words and registered. This type of stimuli gives rise to several types of data. Simply counting the number of correct words whenever color i is involved results in an ordering of the colors from the set according to their conspicuity. More interesting, however, is to see which color combinations lead to the highest recognition of both word 1 and word 2. The hypothesis was that if the overlap color were the "additive" mixture color of the colors of word 1 and word 2, the subject would recognize this and consequently consider the overlap area as belonging to both word 1 and word 2. If the overlap were not a possible mixture product this would strengthen the interpretation of the overlap as a separate area, and consequently lead to a lower recognition of both word 1 and word 2. Related reasoning can be given for luminance relations. If the luminances of the three areas (and the background) can be interpreted as satisfying the physical relations as they would occur under transparency, i.e., a superposition of translucent layers, a similar statement about the "belongingness" can be made. In brief, we predicted that if the area of the overlap had a luminance higher than the luminance of one of the component luminances, the interpretation of transparency was valid. Indeed, we found a better recognition of both word 1 and word 2 for these particular conditions, just as we found better responses for the conditions satisfying the "additive" color mixture hypothesis. By additive we mean at a place in the chromaticity diagram where the additive mixture of two components is supposed to be, and do not require additivity of luminances. Data can be found in de Weert (1984,1985). The knowledge meant above is implicit knowledge. Subjects do not necessarily have explicit knowledge of physical relations in stimuli. In fact it is very likely that they do not have this knowledge explicitly. In one experiment we tested whether subjects were able to adjust the color of an overlap area of two differently colored areas as if it were the additive mixture product of the two composing colors. The luminance matches were reasonable, but the chromatic matches were deviated strongly from the real additive mixtures, indicating that the active knowledge of the color mixture rules is meager indeed.

6. Concluding Remarks

The state of affairs concerning the use of color in displaying information is not satisfactory: there is a large supply of technical facilities to use color and a lack of knowledge to make proper use of it. One should be careful not to use color for information transfer just because of its fashionable character. From a psychophysical point of view a few hints can be given. Isoluminant or nearly isoluminant colors should not be used in adjacent areas, or for very detailed information, because both the technical properties of the color displays and the psychophysical properties of the observer's visual system are not well suited for processing high spatial frequencies. It should also be noted that some pattern recognition processes do not work for color signals alone, and are poorer for combined color and luminance signals. There are numerous possiblities, however, for useful applications of color coding, as well as the esthetic aspects of its use.

References

Christ R.E. (1975). Review and analysis of color coding research for visual diplays. *Human Factors*, 17, pp. 524-570.

Christ R.E. (1984). Research for evaluating visual display codes: An emphasis on color coding. In: *Information Design*, Easterby & Zwaga (Eds.). John Wiley and Sons, New York, pp. 209-227.

Cornsweet T.N. (1970). *Visual Perception*. Academic Press, New York.

Elzinga C.H.(1985). *On the measurement of color and brightness*. Thesis, Nijmegen.

Elzinga C.H. & De Weert C.M.M. (1978). Hue magnitude estimates as relative judgements. *Perception and Psychophysics*, 23, pp. 372-380.

Elzinga C.H. & De Weert C.M.M. (1984). Nonlinear codes for the yellow-blue mechanism. *Vision Research*, 24, pp. 911-922.

Engel F.L. (1971). Visual conspicuity, directed attention and retinal locus. *Vision Research*, 11, pp. 563-576.

Julesz B. (1981). Textons, the elements of texture perception, and their interactions. *Nature*, 290, pp. 91-97.

Van Esch J.A., Koldenhof E.E., Van Doorn A.J. & Koenderink J.J. (1984). Spectral sensitivity and wavelength discrimination of the human peripheral field. *Journal of the Optical Society of America*, 74, pp. 443-450.

Gregory R.L. (1977). Vision with isoluminant color contrast: 1) A projection technique and observations. *Perception*, 6, pp. 113-119.

Lu C. & Fender D.H. (1972). The interaction of color and luminance in stereoscopic vision. *Investigative Ophthalmology*, 2, pp. 484-489.

Raaijmakers J.G.W. & De Weert C.M.M. (1975). Linear and opponent color coding. *Perception and Psychophysics*, 18, pp. 474-480.

Treisman A. (1982). Perceptual grouping and attention in visual search for features and for objects. *Journal of Experimental Psychology, Human Perception and Performance*, 8, pp. 194-214.

Vicario G. (1978). Chromatic changes due to figural properties. *Italian Journal of Psychology*, 5, pp. 261-264.

De Weert C.M.M. (1979). Colour contours and stereopsis. *Vision Research*, 19, pp. 555-564.

De Weert C.M.M. (1980). Die Bedeutung von Farbkonturen verglichen mit Bedeutung von Helligkeitskonturen. *Farbe und Design*, 15/16, pp. 89-93.

De Weert C.M.M. (1983). The role of colors in the formation of subjective brightness contours. *Psychological Research*, 45, pp. 117-134.

De Weert C.M.M. (1984). Veridical perception: A key to the choice of colors and brightnesses in multicolour displays? In: *Monochrome vs color in electronic displays.* P. Gibson (Ed.). 18, pp. 1-8. RAE, Farnborough.

De Weert C.M.M. (1985). Information in Color. In: *Proceedings of the 5th International Color Association.* Vol. 12, pp. 1-7. Centre Francais de la Couleur, Parijs.

De Weert C.M.M. & Sadza K.J. (1983). New data concerning the role of colors in stereopsis. In: *Colour vision.* J. Mollon & T. Sharpe (Eds.). Cambridge University Press, Cambridge, pp.553-562.

Walraven J. (1985). Perceptual problems in display imagery. *Proceedings of the Society for Information Display*, 16, pp.192-195.

Wolfe J.M. & Owens D.A. (1981). Is accommodation color blind? Focusing chromatic contours. *Perception*, 10, pp. 53-62.

Chapter 3. Visual Fatigue with Work on Visual Display Units: The Current State of Knowledge

Pieter Padmos

1. Introduction

Visual fatigue is the most frequent health complaint of visual display unit (VDU) workers. In field studies on office populations reported frequencies of complaints vary between 30% and 90%. In addition, many workers are afraid that their eyes may deteriorate through VDU work. On the other hand, visual fatigue is also a common health complaint with other types of work. In "classical" office populations the frequency of complaints varies between 20% and 60%.

This paper is primarily devoted to the question of what is known about the possible causes of the increased frequency of visual fatigue with VDU work (see the section on research), but first the symptoms, mechanisms, and methods of measuring visual fatigue will be discussed, and a survey of the visually problematic conditions in VDU work will be presented. Special attention is given to research contributions from The Netherlands. In the final section it is concluded that knowledge in this field is limited and suggestions for future research are presented.

2. What is Visual Fatigue?

Within the scope of this chapter only a cursory description of the complicated subject of visual fatigue can be given. For more details the reader is referred to the reviews of for example Carmichael and Dearborn (1948), Bartley (1976), Östberg (1976) and, probably the most recent and complete, Pluymen (1981).

2.1. Definition and Symptoms

Visual fatigue might be defined in a wide sense as the change in condition of an organism with time, as a consequence of long and/or taxing visual work. The change (deterioration) in condition may be manifested by the subjective experience of the individual, organic changes, or changes in work output or frequency of errors. It should be noted that there is a difference in meaning between visual fatigue and the word "discomfort". The latter is rather an instantaneous phenomenon, although one may say that performing uncomfortable visual work for a longer time may lead to visual fatigue.

The main symptoms of visual fatigue are tears, reddish-looking eyes, an itching or burning sensation in the eyes, a strained, fatigued, or painful sensation in or behind the eyes, and blurred or double vision. Headache or vertigo may sometimes accompany visual fatigue. Most of these symptoms have a subjective character. Several of these or very similar symptoms are generally mentioned in field studies on relations between visual fatigue and VDU work or other types of visually taxing work. This is the reason why we would prefer to define visual fatigue in a narrower sense (following Duke-Elder, 1949) than that stated before, and thus define visual fatigue as being identical to the symptoms just mentioned as far as they are related to performance of a visual task.

The reason for this narrower definition will become apparent in the next section, where so-called objective measures of visual fatigue are discussed; the relation of these measures to subjective symptoms has generally not been established.

There are considerable individual differences in sensitivity to visual fatigue. From clinical experience and rather scarce research the following properties of eyes and spectacles that increase the chance of occurrence of visual fatigue can be mentioned (e.g. Borish,1975): allergies and problems with tear secretion or composition; uncorrected far-sightedness (hyperopia); uncorrected astigmatism; decreased accommodative power (presbyopia); eyes with mutually different refraction (anisometropia); fixation problems; deviations of binocular balance; weakness of binocular fusion mechanisms.

Most complaints seem to be related to problems of the eyes and their direct control by the brain, although the possibility that more central brain functions may also be involved cannot be excluded. For instance, Wilkins (1985) noted that stimuli such as repeated bar patterns or flickering lights which may evoke an epileptic seizure in some persons, can also cause sensations like those of visual fatigue in many other persons.

A common feature of most complaints of visual fatigue is that the effects tend to disappear rather soon after the termination of visual work. Recovery times can be as short as one quarter of an hour. Occasionally, however, symptoms may last for several hours or even days.

2.2. Objective Measures of Visual Fatigue

Since the 1940s research on visual fatigue has been going on. Research has often been directed towards studying the influences on visual fatigue of task conditions like level or sources of lighting, quality of print, microfilm reading and most recently VDU properties. The tasks performed were often reading, searching for errors in texts, or discrimination of details.

Although the symptoms of visual fatigue generally have a subjective character, researchers have often been reluctant to use subjective measures in experimental studies. The main reason is probably the lack of knowledge of or confidence in subjective scaling methods. Of course one apparent disadvantage of subjective methods is their sensitivity to the subject's motivation and bias. Therefore various objective measures have been used to try and quantify visual fatigue. Generally, the change (deterioration) of a specific quantity has been measured as a function of time spent performing a task (Table 1).

Table 1. Objective measures of visual fatigue

Category	Measure
Workload	heart rate, skeletal muscle tension, blinking frequency
Performance	speed of work, errors
Psychophysical threshold	acuity, flicker fusion frequency, contrast threshold
Eye movements	saccade speed, fixation pause, pursuit
Binocular coordination	eye balance, convergence amplitude
Accommodation	speed, range, resting focus, fluctuations
Pupil	diameter change

The interpretation of much of this research is difficult for two reasons. First, an independent estimate of task load (e.g., task visibility) is often lacking. This makes it difficult to compare literature as regards the reported effects of a certain task parameter (e.g., light level, or VDU vs. hard copy) on a proposed measure of visual fatigue. Secondly, and even more important, there is the question of whether the noted change has anything to do with visual fatigue as defined above. Correlation with subjective symptoms of visual fatigue (in the narrower sense) has rarely been studied. This means in general that there may be influences of uncontrolled factors like motivation, learning, or general fatigue. These factors may cause changes of the measured quantity in either direction. Psychophysical or performance measures are particularly sensitive to the spurious influences mentioned.

An example of the importance of relating changes of allegedly objective fatigue measures to changes of subjective visual fatigue sensations was obtained through an (unpublished) experiment conducted by Sadza and myself. The aim of this experiment was to check whether saccade (= fixation jump) speed would be a good indicator of visual fatigue, as the results of Bahill and Stark (1975) and Meyer-Delius and Liebl (1976) suggested. We measured peak saccadic velocities continuously, through on-line computer analysis of the electro-oculogram, and found a very significant reduction (on average 10%) of the speed of the larger (20 °-55 °) saccades during a task that lasted for 2 h. This task consisted of following with the eye a small stimulus spot that changed position once per second to a point, randomly selected from five possible points spaced 12.5 ° apart. Unfortunately, the decrease of saccade speed did not correlate with changes in a subjective measure of visual fatigue that was derived from the responses to various visual fatigue symptom scales, and which subjects filled out each half hour during the task sessions. Rather, saccade speed correlated weakly with the scaled sensations of drowsiness that subjects reported during the tedious sessions. For the visual fatigue symptom scales subjects had to indicate on graded 11-point scales (from 0 "no", via 5 "moderately" to 10 "yes") the answers to nine questions like "Are your eyes feeling fatigued or heavy?" or "Do you have difficulties in focussing sharply?" For the drowsiness scales subjects had to indicate on ten graded scales their sensations between extremes such as awake-sleepy, active-passive, keen-dull.

We concluded that objective measures of visual fatigue, if they have not been calibrated against subjective visual fatigue sensations, are of limited value. On the other hand, the study of changes in functioning that accompany subjective visual fatigue is useful because it may increase knowledge of the physiological mechanisms that underlie visual fatigue. Unfortunately, only in rare instances has research been directed towards the goal of studying the mechanisms of visual fatigue.

Pluymen (1981) concluded on the basis of his extensive literature survey that a correlation with subjective visual fatigue symptoms had not been unequivocally demonstrated for any of the the proposed objective measures. However, considering the clinical and experimental evidence, he thought that the most promising options for objective visual fatigue measures were among the oculomotor functions (eye movements, binocular coordination, accommodation). About 15 studies on visual fatigue and VDU work have been published, the majority of which appeared after Pluymen's review. Among the various fatigue measures used some, at least in some instances, showed an effect of VDU work: decrease of visual acuity (at long distances), error in accommodation (myopization), error in resting focus of accommodation, and delay of fixation movements have been found. However, only one study (Jaschinsky-Kruza, 1984) showed a clear correlation between the objective measure (accommodation error) and subjective visual fatigue. One other study showed a weak indication of correlation of convergence near point with subjective visual fatigue (Gunnarson & Söderberg, 1980).

In The Netherlands several experimental studies on visual fatigue in relation to VDU work have been or are being conducted, until now not with much success. Kalsbeek, Posma, Bosman, and Umbach (1983) from the Technical University at Enschede developed a battery of psychophysical tests that are presented on a VDU and therefore can be administered at regular intervals during normal VDU work. The tests measure the thresholds for contrast, and spatial and temporal resolution, and as such are subject to the spurious influences of motivation, learning, etc., as mentioned before. No correlation with subjective visual fatigue has been established.

Significant threshold increases (the alleged fatigue effect) have been reported for a search task on a VDU lasting 2-3 h, but not for a similar task on hard copy. A typewriting task that involved reading from a handwritten manuscript also showed significant threshold increases. De Groot, from the Occupational Health Service PTT in Groningen, is presently analyzing the results of a field study on visual fatigue in VDU operators, which he conducted recently with the apparatus of Kalsbeek et al. The first results do not indicate correlations between the test results and subjective visual fatigue (personal communication).

At the Netherlands Ophthalmic Research Institute in Amsterdam a series of experiments has been conducted by Ossenblok and van de Berg. Here the fatigue effect of an accommodative load (which lasted 0.5-1 h and subjectively was very fatiguing) was studied by means of the pattern evoked occipital potential. The underlying idea was that more fatigue would lead to less accurate focusing, and that the resulting blurred retinal image would give a smaller pattern evoked potential. However, it appeared that the decrease measured also occurred in a subjectively non fatiguing task.

3. Problematic Visual Conditions with VDU Work

3.1. General Remarks

First of all it should be stated that there is no evidence of any radiation of a level that could possibly be harmful to the eyes (Padmos, Pot, Vos & de Vries-Mol, 1985). Some earlier reports about VDUs causing cataract appear to lack a solid scientific basis. Neither is there any clear evidence for any other kind of deterioration of the eyes as a consequence of the use of VDUs, although it must be said that longitudinal research in this area is scarce. In The Netherlands the two studies that followed eye condition over several years (de Groot & Kamphuis, 1983; Grootendorst, 1983) found no alarming effects.

There are a number of visual conditions that may potentially increase the incidence of visual fatigue. Many have to do with the fact that VDU work is relatively new and rules of (visual) ergonomy are not sufficiently applied, or in some instances not sufficiently well established. In chapter 1 van Nes mentions several potentially problematic visual ergonomic conditions. Others include light flicker on the screen, high contrast between manuscript and screen, and large visual angles between screen, keyboard, and manuscript.

Besides visual ergonomic problems there are also functional problems that may increase the incidence of visual fatigue. VDUs are introduced as part of a process of automation. This may cause the traditional office to change and have a more industrial atmosphere. Possibilities include increased monotony and central monitoring of work output, but we will not discuss this subject further although it is important.

3.2. Guidelines and Recommendations

An increasing number of guidelines and recommendations regarding the use of VDUs are appearing, such as those of Deutsche Industrie-Norm (DIN) (1983), Health and Safety Executive (1983), Commission International de l'Eclairage (1984) and, in The Netherlands, Arbeidsinspectie (1980), den Buurman et al. (1986), and Nederlands Normalisatie Instituut (in preparation). For a detailed comparison of recommendations and guidelines see Padmos et al. (1985).The conclusion of this review is that there is a reasonable correspondence between current recommendations.

3.3. The Visual Ergonomic Situation in Practice

In the literature there are not many concrete data about the degree and extent of violations of ergonomic principles in the practical use of VDUs. The general impression is that, although there have been and still are many unsatisfactory situations, there have been noticeable improvements. To give an impression of items that are often not satisfactory, some preliminary results of a field study conducted by our Institute in cooperation with the Institute for Preventive Health Care TNO will be presented. Further details are given by Padmos and Pot (1986) and Pot, Brouwers and Padmos (1986). In this field study we visited over 200 VDU workers (mostly engaged in data-entry or word processing) at their workplaces. At each workplace we objectively measured or assessed about 160 visual and postural ergonomic items and other physical workplace characteristics. The visual items covered aspects like: VDU legibility, instability, contrast, and reflections, legibility and reflections of manuscript and keyboard, and lighting of the workplace. Each item was rated as "good" or "bad", attached, after comparison with current recommendations or standards. The seven visual items that were most frequently labelled bad (= not meeting standard) are presented in Table 2.

Table 2. Visual ergonomic items that were most frequently labelled bad in a field study

Visual ergonomic item	Percentage bad
Luminance ratio screen-manuscript	74
Handwritten manuscript	72
Manuscript orientation	65
Specular reflection on screen	63
Luminance ratio screen-surround	63
Frequency of fixation changes	59
Space between symbols on screen	57

4. Visual Ergonomic Conditions and Health Complaints

4.1. Introduction

In the last five years there has been an ever-increasing number of publications regarding the health and well-being of VDU workers. Most of the field studies on the complaints of VDU workers have an inventory character, and do not try to relate complaints and possible causes. The laboratory studies mentioned earlier more often attempt to relate complaints to specific changes in conditions. In this section a few aspects and examples will be mentioned, with an emphasis on research carried out in The Netherlands. More extensive information is available in some critical reviews that appeared recently (Dainoff, 1982; National Research Council, 1983; Helander, Billingsley & Schurick, 1984; Padmos et al., 1985).

4.2. VDU Work vs. Non-VDU Work

As indicated before, most field studies that compare VDU work in offices with the more traditional office work find about 1.5 times as many complaints of visual fatigue from VDU workers. There are, however, notable exceptions. For instance, de Groot and Kamphuis (1983) did not find an appreciable difference in frequencies of complaints of visual fatigue in workers in the Dutch telephone inquiry service before and after the introduction of VDUs. In laboratory studies differences in complaints between a VDU task and a "comparable" paper task are sometimes found, but in other instances such differences are not found. The problem with most of these comparative studies is that detailed knowledge about the characteristics of the VDU and the non-VDU tasks is lacking, which makes it impossible to obtain clues about the properties of VDU work that may cause visual fatigue.

4.3. Influence of Task Properties on Visual Fatigue

From the literature it is difficult to draw firm conclusions about which visual task properties cause the increased incidence of visual fatigue (again, we will disregard here the nonvisual task properties). The reason for this difficulty is that in many field studies at most only a few visual items (like flicker or contrast) have been considered in isolation. Eventual effects are then difficult to interpret because of the many other factors that may influence complaints, with many chances for confounding and interaction. These objections are valid to a lesser extent for controlled laboratory experiments but there too the effects found are generally of low significance. If one considers the influences of task properties on both visual fatigue and subjective discomfort then the following items emerge as being the most problematic: high contrast between screen and surround, and between characters and screen; many eye movements required; illegibility of manuscript (rather than illegibility of screen!); and flicker. Opinions differ as regards the beneficial effect of presenting the information on the screen in negative contrast (i.e., black symbols on a white background, sometimes called positive polarity). This subject is dealt with in more detail in chapter 4 on visual comfort by J.A.J. Roufs.

In our field study of over 200 VDU workers, a standardized interview with each worker was also held. In this interview the respondents were asked about their satisfaction with 14 visual ergonomic items. The five items that received most complaints are listed in Table 3.

Table 3. The five visual ergonomic items about which respondents complained most frequently

Visual ergonomic item	Percentage of complaints
Bad manuscript legibility	58
Disturbing screen reflections	49
Much glancing to and fro	41
Glare from lighting or window	41
Workplace often too bright	27

Interestingly, the frequency of complaints about the legibility of the text on the VDU was only 5%. In many instances the frequency of complaints on visual items correlated with our quality assessments based on current recommendations. Among the most striking correlations are the following: complaints about bad manuscript legibility were especially frequent if handwritten manuscripts were dominant; both complaints about disturbing screen reflections and about glare from lighting or window were more abundant at places without, or with ineffective, daylight shielding; "much looking to and fro" correlated with large viewing angles between screen and manuscript or keyboard; "workplace too bright" correlated with dark screens (with respect to the manuscripts) and with low luminance of the screen phosphor.

Relations between the ergonomic quality of the visual workplace factors and eye fatigue were less obvious in our field study. Only for one item (handwritten manuscript) was the labelling as good or bad correlated significantly (single-sided χ^2, $p < .05$) with the frequency of eye fatigue. When we attempted to shift some of the criteria for bad slightly, but without making unreasonable excursions from the a priori criteria, in order to maximize the correlation between complaints of visual fatigue and the good-bad scores, the correlations increased somewhat, as is shown in Table 4.

Table 4. Visual ergonomic items that correlated (after optimizing the criterion for good or bad) significantly (single-sided χ^2, $p < .05$) with complaints of visual fatigue

Visual ergonomic item	Number of workplaces assessed		Complaints about item (%)		P
	Good	Bad	Yes	No	
VDU character sharpness	179	43	32	58	.001
Effectiveness of daylight shielding	135	87	32	45	.04
Handwritten manuscript	65	157	28	41	.05

From our field study it appears that frequencies of complaints of visual fatigue, as well as of other health complaints of VDU workers like musculoskeletal pain, headaches and general fatigue or stress, correlate more strongly, but still weakly, with a combination of the following factors: time spent per day on VDU work, presence of work pressure, and experience in a work atmosphere.

4.4. Influence of Eyes and Spectacles

In some studies the possible influence of characteristics of eyes and spectacles on visual fatigue in VDU workers has been taken into account. A relatively high proportion of these studies were in The Netherlands (de Groot & Kamphuis, 1983; Grootendorst, 1983; Punt, 1983), and the findings can be summarized as follows. People with a relatively low visual acuity tend to have more complaints. Contact lens wearers do not seem to have special problems. Reading glasses that are not matched to the viewing distance (which is generally larger for VDUs than for regular reading) may increase visual fatigue, especially in older workers. Opinions differ about the (dis)advantages of using bifocals. Surprisingly, there is not much evidence of effects of deviating eye balance.

The preliminary results of our own field study which comprised a very detailed optometric measuring program, gave evidence of rather strong influences of several optometric characteristics on complaints. The strongest effects were found for deviations in binocular coordination (weak fusion, unstable balance) and for low visual acuity. Effects of accommodation weakness on complaints of visual fatigue were not very obvious, which is not surprising given the small number of respondents above 40 years of age.

5. Research Needed

There is limited knowledge of the relations between complaints of visual fatigue and the conditions, in a wider sense, under which VDU work is performed. Research must be concentrated on the relative influences of task structure and organizational aspects on the one hand, and on ergonomic and optometric characteristics of the workplace and worker on the other. For this purpose field studies are most appropriate, provided that subjective scales of fatigue are used and a multifactorial design is applied. These studies cannot do more than allow hypotheses to be made about the influence of details of the various conditions. Quantitative knowledge of the properties of VDU workplaces that determine the visual quality is limited. For instance, what are the physical optima for symbol sharpness, luminance ratios, flicker, eye movement pattern? Such questions should be studied, preferably in the laboratory. The most appropriate independent measures are probably subjective comfort or a selected performance measure, rather than fatigue.

Mechanisms of visual fatigue are only partially understood, although the oculomotor systems (eye movements, binocular coordination, accommodation) seem to play an important role. The type of research indicated is a mixture of clinical and laboratory research. Subjective scaling procedures, combined with objective function assessments, should be applied for various types of tasks. Optometric characteristics of subjects should be known and, if possible, studied as an independent factor.

References

Arbeidsinspectie (1980). *Het werken met beeldschermen - Concept voorlichtingsblad* [Working with VDUs - Draft guidance]. Directorate-General of Labour, Voorburg.

Bahill A.T. & Stark L. (1975). Overlapping saccades and glissades are produced by fatigue in the saccadic eye movement system. *Experimental Neurology*, 48, pp. 95-106.

Bartley H. (1976). Visual fatigue. In: *Psychological aspects and physiological correlates of work and fatigue.* E. Simonson & P.C. Weiser, (Eds), pp. 155-175. Thomas, Springfield, IL.

Borish I.M. (1975). *Clinical refraction* (3rd ed.). The professional press, Chicago.

Buurman R. den, Leebeek H.J., Lenior T.M.J., Scholtens S., Verhagen L.H.J.M. & Vrins A.G.M. (1986). *Beeldschermergonomie - beeldschermwerk, ergonomische achtergronden, aanbevelingen* [VDU work, ergonomic backgrounds, recommendations]. Nederlandse Vereniging voor Ergonomie, Amsterdam.

Cakir A., Hart D.J. & Stewart T.F.M. (1980). *Visual display terminals.* Wiley, Chichester.

Carmichael L. & Dearborn W. (1948). *Reading and visual fatigue.* Harrap, London.

CIE. (1984). *Vision and the visual display unit work station* (CIE Publication no. 60). Commission International de l'Eclairage, Paris.

Dainoff M.J. (1982). Occupational stress factors in visual display terminal (VDT) operation; a review of empirical research. *Behavior and Information Technology*, 1, pp. 141-176.

DIN. (1983). *Kennworte für die Anpassung von Bildschirmarbeitsplatzen an den Menschen* [Characteristics of adaptation of VDU workplaces to man]. (DIN standard 66234), Beuth, Berlin.

Duke-Elder W.S. (1949). *Text-book of ophthalmology*, Vol. IV, pp.4466-4498. Kimpton, London.

Groot J.P. de & Kamphuis A. (1983). Eyestrain in VDU users; physical correlates and long-term effects. *Human Factors*, 25, pp. 409-413.

Grootendorst, G. (1983). Oog en beeldscherm [Eye and VDU]. *Tijdschrift voor Ergonomie*, 8, pp. 7-11.

Gunnarson E. & Söderberg I. (1983). Eye strain resulting from VDT work at the Swedish Telecommunications Administration. *Applied Ergonomics*, 14, pp. 61-69.

Health and Safety Executive (1983). *Visual display units.* Her Majesty's Stationery Office, London.

Helander M.G., Billingsley P.A. & Schurick J.M. (1984). An evaluation of human factors research on visual display terminals in the workplace. *Human Factors Review*, 3, pp. 55-129.

Jaschinski-Kruza W. (1984). Transient myopia after visual work. *Ergonomics*, 27, pp. 1181-1189.

Kalsbeek J.W.H., Posma E., Bosman D. & Umbach F.W. (1983). How specific is VDT-induced visual fatigue? *Proceedings of the Society for Information Display*, 24, pp. 63-65.

Meyer-Delius J. & Liebl L. (1976). Evaluation of vigilance related to visual perception. In: *Monitoring behavior and supervisory control.* T. Sheridan & G. Johansson, (Eds), pp. 97-106, Plenum, New York.

National Research Council. (1983). *Video displays, work and vision.* National Academy Press, Washington DC.

Nederlands Normalisatie Instituut. (in preparation). *National specifications for VDU workplaces.* NNI, The Hague.

Östberg O. (1976). *Review of visual strain, with special reference to microimage reading.* Paper read at International Micrographics Congress, Stockholm.

Padmos P. & Pot F. (1986). Determinants of the VDU operator's well-being 1. Visual and postural ergonomics, optometry. *Proceedings Work With Display Units*, pp. 167-170. National Board Occupational Safety and Health, Stockholm.

Padmos P., Pot F.D., Vos J.J. & de Vries-Mol E.C. (1985). *Gezondheid en welbevinden bij het werken met beeldschermen 1. Verslag van een vooronderzoek* [Health and well-being in VDU operators 1. A state of the art report]. Report 8412139, Ministry of Social Affairs, The Hague.

Pluymen J. (1981). *Visuele vermoeidheid* [Visual fatigue]. (Report NI 8101). Doctoral essay, Psychophysiology Department, University of Amsterdam.

Pot F., Brouwers A. & Padmos P. (1986). Determinants of the VDU operators' well-being 2. Work-organization. *Proceedings Work With Display Units*, pp. 322-324. National Board of Occupational Safety and Health, Stockholm.

Punt H. (1983). Ergophthalmologisch onderzoek bij gebruikers van beeldschermen [Ergophthalmological study on users of VDUs]. *Nederlands Militair Geneeskundig Tijdschrift*, 36 (3), pp. 7-14.

Wilkins A.J. (1985). Discomfort and visual displays. *Displays, April 1985*, 101-103.

Chapter 4. Visual Comfort as a Criterion for Designing Display Units

Jacques A.J. Roufs, Martinus C. Boschman
and Martin A.M. Leermakers

1. Introduction

Display units designed for the transfer of alphanumeric information may be found to be quite different in quality. Badly designed units are not read easily and cause visual fatigue when used in long and intensive sessions. This has already received some attention (e.g., Grandjean, 1980; Padmos, this volume; Cakir, Renter, Schmude, & Ambruster, 1978; Cakir, Hart, & Stewart, 1979; Matula, 1981). It became apparent that it was important to match the physical parameters of the displays to the demands of the visual system. However, visual fatigue is known to be very difficult to measure and, consequently, is not an obvious design criterion. Looking for a more adequate measure, therefore, we surveyed other criteria based on two different angles of approach. The most direct candidate is the comfort with which a subject feels he can read the information on the screen. In principle this can be measured at least ordinally by psychometric methods. Another line of approach is the speed at which information is taken in, as reflected by performance measures like reading speed or by eye movement characteristics such as saccadic length and fixation duration.

This paper reports in general terms on part of the results of a research project concerning these problems. More detailed reports will be published elsewhere.

First some background information will be given on the methods we have employed, and this will be followed by the essential details of apparatus and procedures. After that the results of the various methods will be shown and compared. Finally some conclusions will be listed.

2. Background of Methods

To quantify visual comfort in reading alphanumerical text while varying the different physical screen parameters, psychometric scaling is the only direct approach. This kind of complex psychological attribute can, in our experience, be most conveniently scaled at intervals (using either adjectives or numbers). We want to illustrate this important point with an example stemming from an interlaboratory study in which our Institute participated. The study was undertaken within the framework of a European Committee (COST) carrying number 211. In this example, the same moving images displayed by four different image-coding systems had to be assessed by subjects in five different countries by means of the adjectives shown in Table 1. Details are to

Table 1. The adjectives used in the psychometrical experiments for the five European countries which participated in the COST project. Each country used five different adjectives in its native language

France	Great Britain	Italy	Netherlands	Sweden
Excellent	Excellent	Ottimo	Uitstekend	Utmärkt
Bon	Good	Buono	Goed	God
Assez bon	Fair	Discreto	Voldoende	Acceptabel
Médiocre	Poor	Scadente	Onvoldoende	Dälig
Mauvais	Bad	Pessimo	Slecht	Oanvündbar

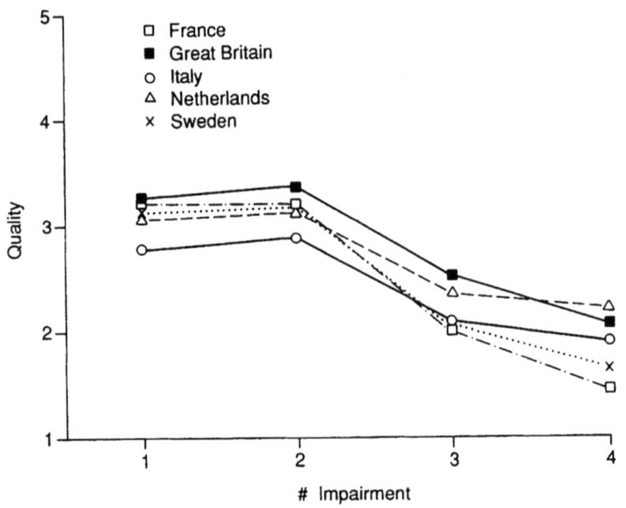

Figure 1. The results from the COST scaling experiment for about 30 subjects per country. Image quality, expressed in numbers, is plotted for four different methods of image coding. Every plot represents the mean results for one country, which used its own native set of adjectives (see Table 1.). The adjective scale running from bad to excellent (in English) has been converted to numbers according to the Thurstone model.

be found in Allnatt, Gleiss, Kretz, Sciarappa, and Van der Zee (1983). The results expressed in numbers, following the usual Thurstone model (e.g., Torgerson, 1958) are shown for four different scenes in Figure 1. Each point is the average of about 30 subjects.

Although the judgements are highly dependent on the kind of scenes that were chosen to expose different image regressions inherent to the coding systems, there is a fair consistency between subjects of different countries. In comparing the scale values one has to keep in mind that the adjectives may carry different emotional values in different languages and moreover that the method allows any linear transformation of the scale values (normalization brings them even closer together).

The results demonstrate that with this type of scaling representative ordering can be obtained. The differences between systems and scenes suggest a reasonable sensitivity. A pertinent advantage of category scaling is that it is fast. For the reasons explained above, category scaling was chosen to measure comfort. Since, however, it is sometimes criticized as being subject to considerable bias (for a review see Roufs & Bouma, 1980), we also looked for objective methods which might provide us with data concerning the ease of information intake. These were found from studies about the reading process.

In reading, the eye does not move continuously over the text but jumps from one fixation point to the other (Figure 2). These saccades and the fixation pauses between them are related to the legibility and to the difficulty of the text among other things (Bouma, 1978; Roufs & Bouma, 1986). During fixations information is taken in. The more difficult the text is, the longer are the fixation pauses and the smaller the saccades (Tinker, 1965). This suggests that fixation duration and saccadic length might be a measure of the ease of information intake. Fixation duration and saccade length are stochastic variables. An example of their distribution for normal reading is given in Figure 3, which is taken from Rayner (1981). The average values of these two eye-movement characteristics are also taken as a measure of the ease with which alphanumeric text can be read from displays. Finally we took the speed of performing a search task, a well-known measure of visual performance, as dependent variable (Blackwell, 1972). It is, of course, closely related to the two preceding characteristics and is relatively simple to measure.

3. Apparatus and Experimental Conditions

Alphanumeric text of different fonts, contrasts, sizes, and sharpnesses were made with the aid of a digital image processing device (Figure 4.). The image to be displayed was stored in a 512 × 512 pixel memory. Different character

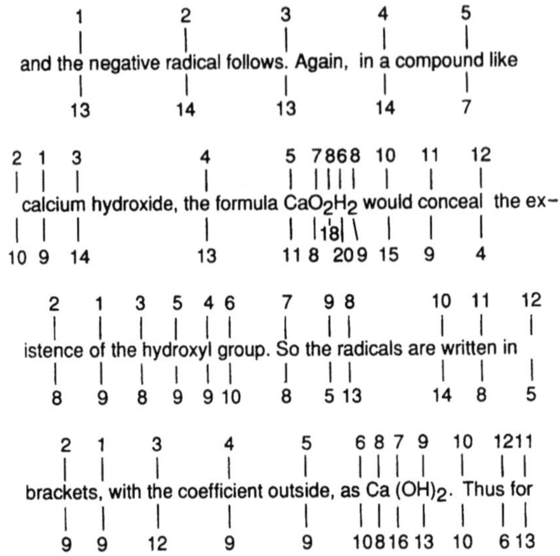

Figure 2. Fixation locations in reading. The vertical lines show the locations of the individual fixations. The numbers at the top show the sequence. Those at the bottom give an indication of the fixation duration; each unit corresponds to 0.02s (from Tinker, 1965).

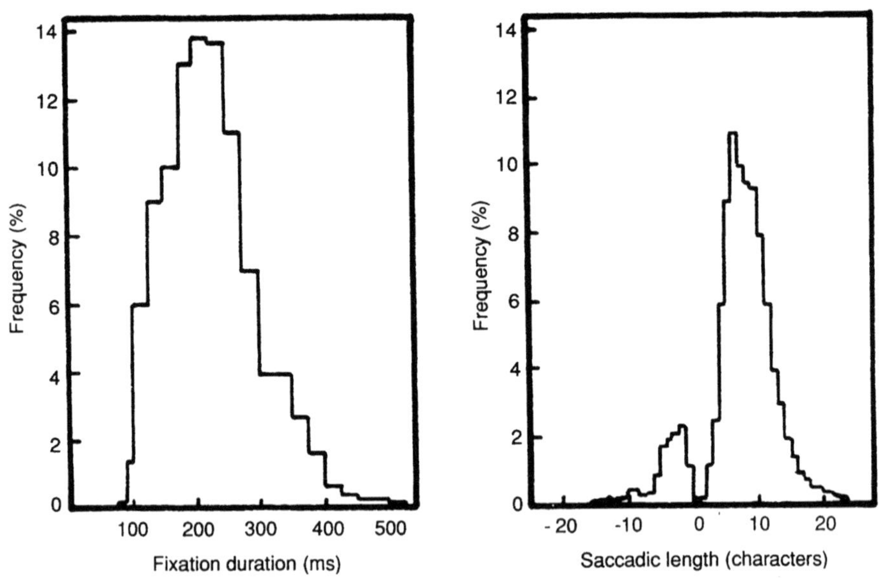

Figure 3. Distributions of the eye movement parameters in reading experiments. The frequency distribution of fixation duration (left) has a median at about 220 ms. In the frequency distribution of the saccadic length (right) regressive saccades have been included. The median length of the forward saccades is about six characters (Adapted from Rayner, 1981).

shapes, stored in disk files, could be transported to the memory and subsequently processed for contrast and sharpness. Sharpness was changed by filters. In this case causal second-order low-pass filters were used, which were characterized by their 6 dB amplitude cut-off frequency. The filtering was effected by convolution in two dimensions, and since in the reported experiments only causal filters were used, convolution took place along the scan-lines of the display unit.

A high quality CRT monitor was used, having a field frequency of 50 Hz and a 1 : 2 interlace. The screen was observed at a distance of 1.0 m. The experiments reported here concerned two character sets, namely Beehive and IPO Normal, examples of which are shown in Figures 5 and 13. The *X* heights for both types are 18 minutes of arc, and their centers are about 14 and 21 minutes apart. Pseudo-alphanumeric text was displayed in 15 and 18 lines of at most 36 and 30 characters respectively, having a vertical distance of 35 minutes of arc. In order to avoid effects of text difficulty and redundancy,

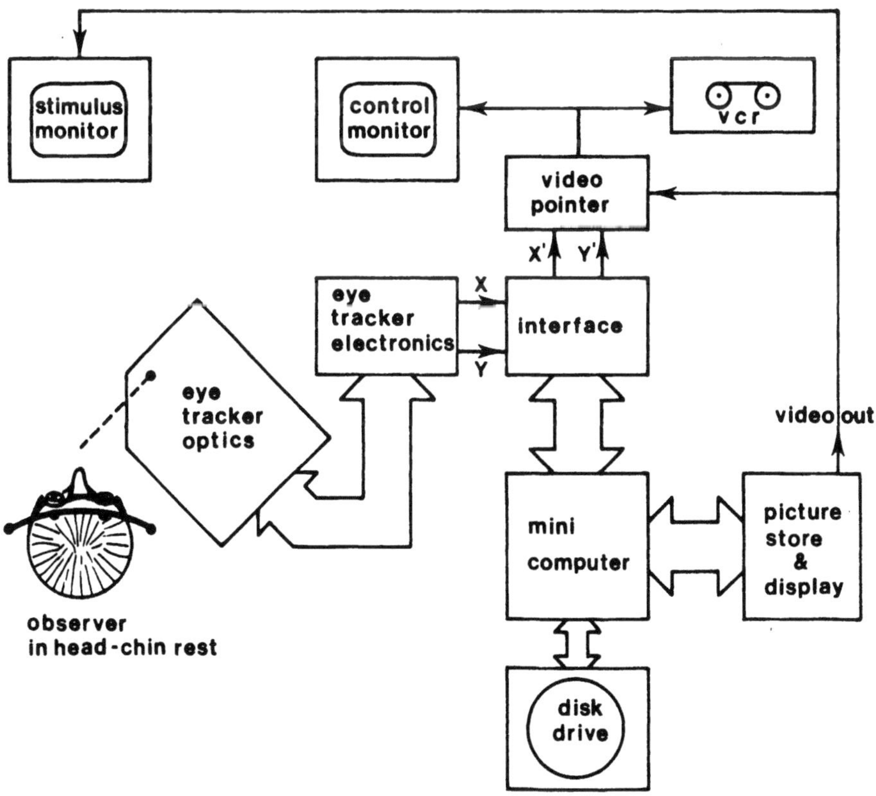

Figure 4. Schematic diagram of the general set-up of the apparatus.

```
6M 4KVGWY09L9VHVI3F TNJY0 7AFS
XDY M8HINOM4EZB6I T08 XAMP 9NF
N7ST6IG4GY YOE6 YA10SQFT BGZIH
LIT CHIL 9LA7ENQ W9HB J1RVHOWG
CSUY1X44C8G EEGITU52L44WJ215N6
I8G ZYH 1SJOQ2 ANQ 8I8X3Y 0LX7
M4 B7HH4FR1H HTU 21EP CC VUOXK
PZRB TS0Q WIWO7 VY4TMH833QI TD
F8H AI4PFYCN7I NH GTY4Q6LV0UHS
W24XD2O TVY 1J AMN2DH9FQE0WGGF
QWGRBA34QL 1R 3789 NNVFX9T5 ZU
1Q5L IY0OV P19V 3R5 IC CF0VR01
MUL VEXS 2XOA4SQL9 NT8G7T 59WI
6T EAX 4MGEZR 5JJHBH DCKY LP3V
```

Figure 5. An example of pseudotext with the Beehive character font, which was used in experiment I. The distribution of the length of the strings resembles the distribution in normal Dutch texts. The target character for the search task was the letter *A*.

meaningless character strings of different length were used, which had a distribution roughly comparable with that of normal text.

Movements of the right eye were recorded with a device based on a dual Purkinje image (SRI) (Figure 8). Before each experiment the subject fixated nine calibration points, which were placed on the monitor in a square matrix enclosing the text field. From these positions a matrix which corrects for the non-linearities in the reading of the X and Y coordinates was derived and used on subsequent readings. In the continuous process of reading, fixation almost never means a complete standstill. Although there is always a drastic decrease in speed of movement, there is hardly ever a complete stop. A special study showed that a good criterion for fixation is a speed below 40 degrees s^{-1}, (see Figure 6), which agrees reasonably with literature data (Reulen, 1984). For high background levels a very dilute mydriatic was used, which kept the right eye pupil open to ensure proper functioning of the eye tracker. It did not affect accommodation.

In the experiments presented here, subjects were asked to search for the letter *A* in the pseudotext on the screen and do this as fast as they felt they could do it reliably. Every time they spotted an *A* they were supposed to push a button. This enabled us to check their performance. Even for very degraded text the subjects rarely made errors, except in extremely poor conditions, which ruled out errors as an adequate measure. After having finished the search the subject pushed a button registering the time needed to accomplish the search

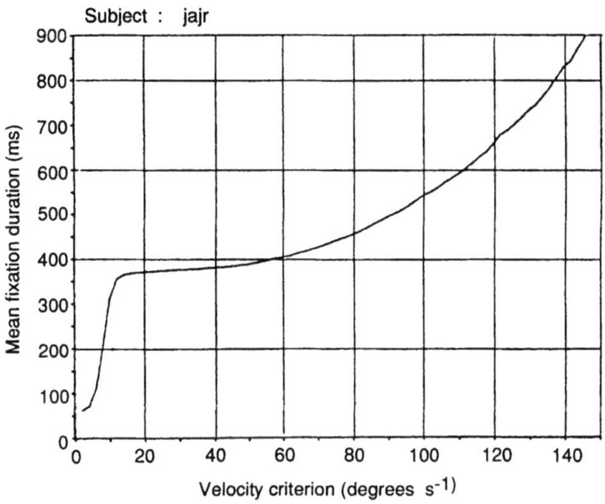

Figure 6. The effect of the speed criterion on the mean fixation duration. The steep increase between 0 and 10 degrees s^{-1} is caused by the fusion of small eye movements with fixations. In the range 20-60 degrees s^{-1} the speed criterion causes only a small increase in fixation duration. Hence, a criterion of 40 degrees s^{-1} was used.

task. The total number of scanned characters divided by this time was taken as a measure of search speed and was used as a global measure of visual performance (local measures will be published elsewere). One sheet of text took 1-2 min. At the end of each sheet a judgement of reading comfort was given on a 10-point scale. Every session started with five sheets of text covering the extremes of the parameters. Every identical condition was repeated twice within each session. A complete session took about 1.5 h. The session was repeated with the same subjects after an interval of a few weeks.

During the search task fixation durations and saccade lengths were measured. Typical distributions of these two variables are shown in Figure 7. There is no reason to assume that these distributions differ essentially from those found with normal reading as shown in Figure 4, although the median values of saccade length are, not surprisingly, somewhat smaller and median fixation durations are longer for the search data.

Character contrast (for definition see next section) was calibrated with a luminance meter having a microscope objective and a circular shaped light stop, providing a measuring field diameter which corresponded to a viewing angle of about 0.25 minute of arc at the viewing distance used. In this report character luminance is for practical reasons defined as the peak luminance of the lower vertical part of the character *F* traced along a scan line, the background

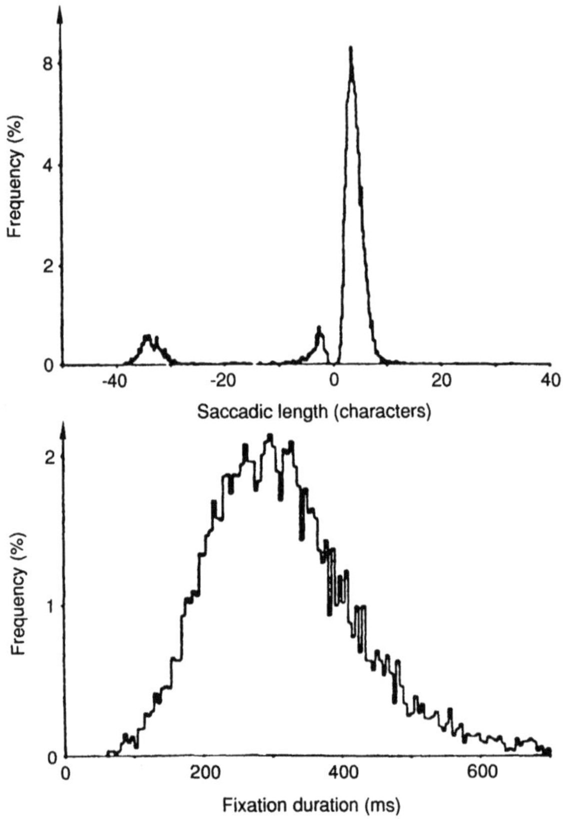

Figure 7. Distributions of the eye-movement parameters for a search task used in the experiments described here. The median fixation duration is about 300 ms, which is significantly longer than the median duration found in reading experiments (Figure 3). The median length of the progressive saccades is about 3.5 characters, which means that searching leads to smaller saccades than during reading.

luminance being the luminance of the undisturbed scan line. Figures 4 and 8 show the general set-up of the apparatus.

4. Results of Experiment I: The Effect of Luminance Contrast

Figure 9A shows the effect of luminance contrast on comfort judgement for the BEEHIVE character set. The averages of three subjects are given. Luminance contrast is defined here as the ratio of character to background lumi-

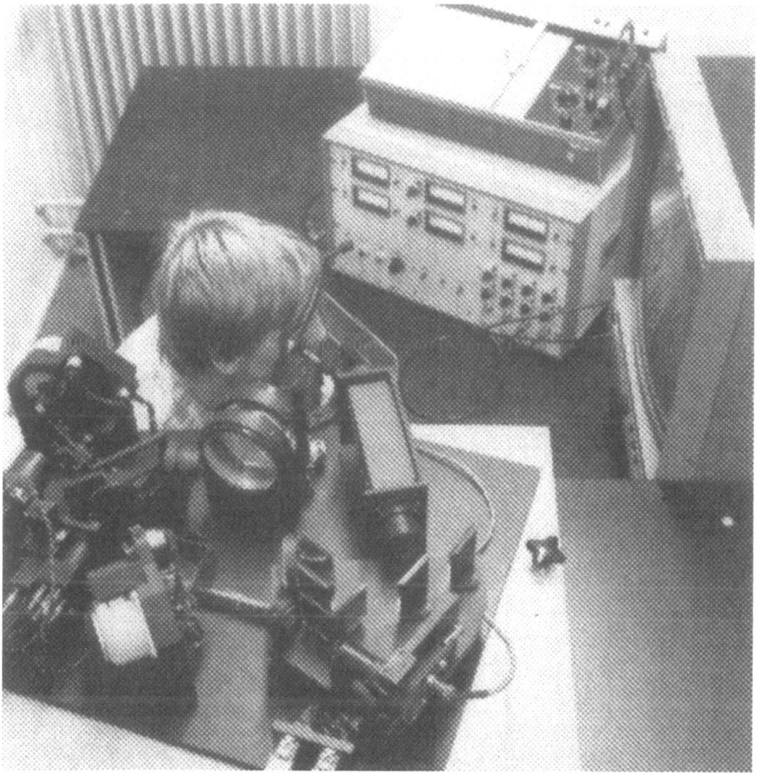

Figure 8. Picture of a subject during recording of the eye movements using the SRI dual Purkinje eye tracker.

nance. In the case of a bright character on a relatively dark background the logarithm of the ratio is positive: in some countries this is called positive contrast, and in others negative contrast. We will avoid this terminology here because of the possible confusion. An important parameter is the adapting luminance, since the contrast transfer properties of the visual system depend closely on this quantity. However, it is not easy to define what the adaptive luminance is, since the relative effects of local and global adaptation cannot be easily estimated. For the experiments described in this chapter the mean luminance in the square enclosing the text was taken as a measure of the adapting luminance. This approximation is more or less justified by the averaging lateral effect of neural activity and stray light of the illuminated retinal elements on their immediate neighborhood and by the averaging effect of movement of the text over the retina during reading.

Since there are reasons to believe that for characters of the correct dimensions black text on a background of relatively high luminance might be better than

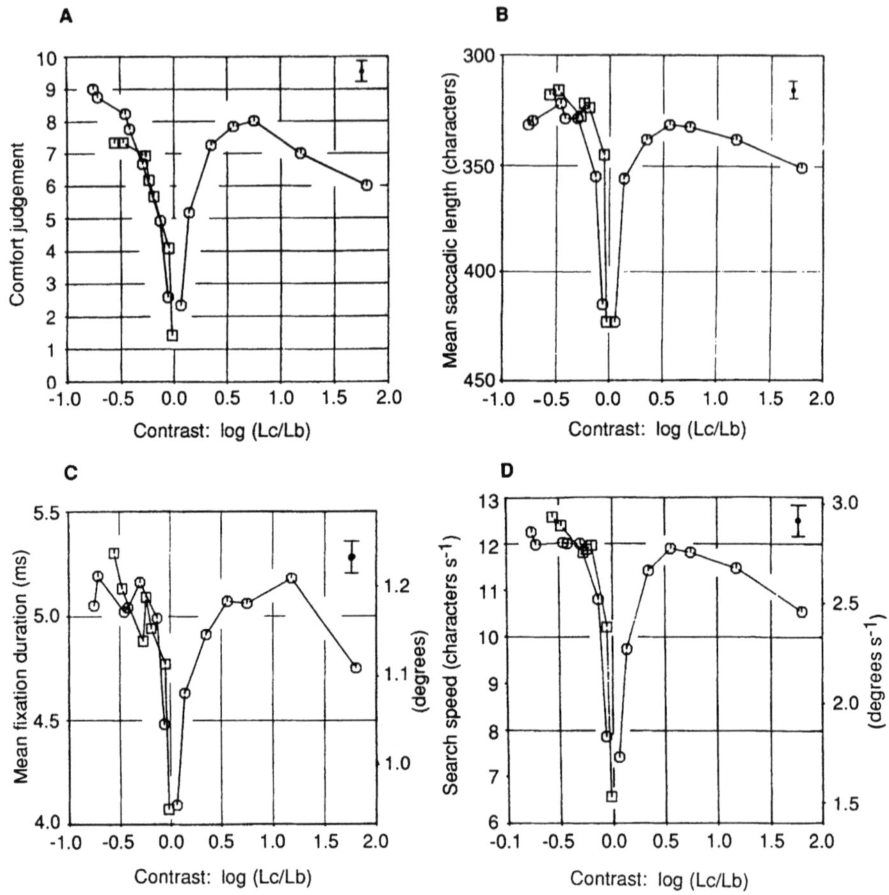

Figure 9A-D. Results of experiment I. Every point represents the average results for three subjects, four presentations per subject (N=12). Two mean luminances were used: L_{mean} = 40 cd/m^2 (O), L_{mean} = 200 cd/m^2 (□). The bars in the top right-hand corners represent twice the average of the standard deviations of the means represented by the drawn symbols. **A** The subjective dependent parameter "judgement of visual comfort" plotted as a function of the logarithm of the luminance contrast ratio (Lc/Lb). **B** The mean fixation duration (ms) plotted with an inverse ordinate as a function of the logarithm of the luminance contrast ratio. **C** The mean length in characters of the progressive saccades as a function of the logarithm of the luminance contrast ratio. **D** Search speed expressed in number of characters scanned per second as a function of the logarithm of the luminance contrast ratio.

the reverse situation, one high level (200 cd/m^2) was also used. Although it would have been interesting to use this high mean luminance level for bright characters on a dark background, technical limitations prevented us from doing so.

The scaled comfort, at the mean luminance level of 40 cd/m^2, increased relatively fast with the logarithme of the contrast ratio for positive and negative values. As Figure 9A shows, this increase is almost symmetrical with respect to the ordinate. In the case of positive log contrast ratios there is a maximum at a ratio of about 5. On the negative side there might also be a maximum at a contrast ratio of about 0.2. Unfortunately the contrast ratio in the latter domain is limited by scatter and bandwidth limitations (this will be analyzed more extensively elsewhere). As a result, the contrast range in this domain is too restricted to show a definite maximum, at least for this character set and monitor. In Figure 9B fixation duration is plotted downwards as a function of the log contrast ratio for the same three subjects. The reason for this reversal in ordinate direction is that the correlation with judgement is better visualized, since faster, and correspondingly easier information intake would mean shorter fixation duration. The correlation with Figure 9A is obvious. The shorter the mean fixation duration found, the better the corresponding comfort judgement. In functional behavior there is one systematic difference. The fixation behavior is less symmetrical in contrast. The initial decrease of the fixation duration is faster for negative log contrast ratios.

In Figure 9C saccadic length is plotted as a function of the log contrast ratio for the same three subjects. Again the correlation is obvious. The better the comfort judgement the larger the saccadic length. The plots of saccadic length and fixation duration almost cover each other if the proper constants and scale factors for the ordinates are used. Figure 9D demonstrates the change of performance speed as a function of the log contrast ratio. A similar correlation is found.

The effect of changing the mean level from 40 up to 200 cd/m^2 for the negative log contrast ratios is small, for the subjective variable as well as for the objective ones, as may be seen from Figures 9A-D. As demonstrated in Figure 7 the relatively large backward saccades to the beginning of the lines and the occasionally occurring regression saccades (backward saccades for a "second view") can easily be identified. The latter appeared to be not very suitable as a global measure of legibility, mostly because of the lack of efficiency.

It is of some importance to have more direct indications of how representative the judgement data are for the average subject. This is relevant not only because of possible large variations in the comfort experienced by different subjects, but also because there might be individual differences of skill in

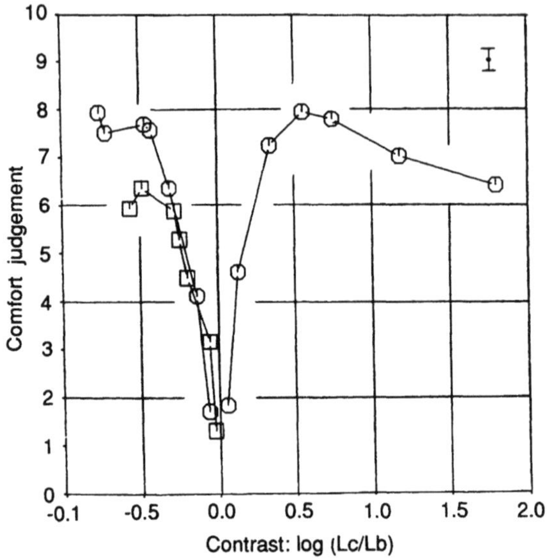

Figure 10. Results of the scaling experiment on 20 inexperienced subjects. As in experiment I, two mean luminances were used: L_{mean} = 40 cd/m^2 (O) and L_{mean} = 200 cd/m^2 (□). Every point is the average of 20 subjects, two presentations per subject (N=40). Again, the subjective comfort parameter is plotted as a function of the logarithm of the luminance contrast ratio.

evaluating them in numbers, since this is not an everyday job for naive subjects. Figure 10 shows the averages of 20 naive subjects. A comparison with Figure 9A indicates that there is no essential difference between trained and untrained subjects. The only difference may be that for large negative values of the log contrast ratio, comfort does not seem to be better than the optimal value for positive values. Nevertheless, ignoring small differences, even naive subjects seem to handle this category scale quite consistently, which is in agreement with the expectations based on results as mentioned in section 2. Moreover, the number of intervals used by the subjects appears to be nicely linear with the psychological scale based on Thurstone's model (see Torgerson, 1958). This can be tested with a scale reconstruction according to Edwards (1957) and is shown in Figure 11 for the pooled data of 20 subjects.

5. Discussion of the Effect of Contrast on Measures of Reading Comfort (in the case of Beehive Character Set)

The four contrast-dependent variables are sufficiently sensitive to be used as criteria for an optimal design. The correlation coefficient between each of the

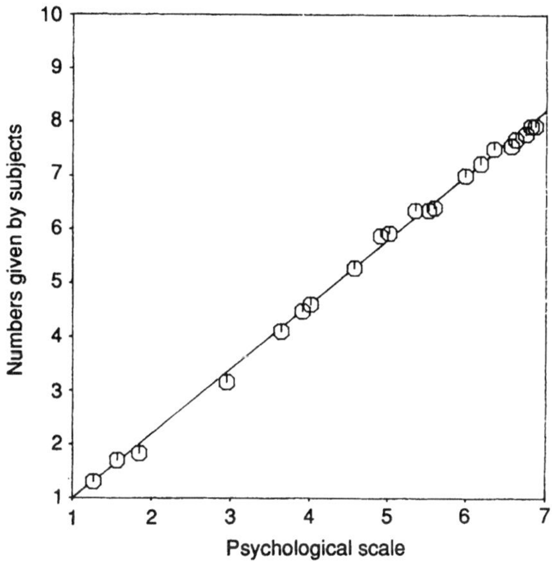

Figure 11. Demonstration of the linearity of the 10-point scale with the psychological scale, based on Thurstone's model and reconstructed using Edwards' (1957) method. Every point in the plot corresponds to the averaged (scale used) or reconstructed (psychological scale) data, concerning one stimulus condition in the scaling experiment with 20 inexperienced subjects, two presentations per subject (see also Figure 10).

Table 2. Matrix of correlation coefficients for the different dependent variables. In all cases $p<.001$ (two-tailed)

	Comfort judgement	Search speed	Fixation duration
Search speed	0.92	-	-
Fixation duration	- 0.86	- 0.98	-
Saccade length	0.85	0.93	- 0.89

variables is given in Table 2. Although a high degree of correlation between the dependent variables does not imply that the connection is understood, it does increase confidence in the validity of the judgement of reading comfort. Comparing the judgements in Figures 9A and 10, it becomes evident that scaling results can be fairly representative. On the other hand, the curves are not exactly identical, which shows that individual differences do occur and have to be taken into account. The currently topical question of whether dark characters on a light background are better than light ones on a dark background cannot yet be answered with certainty. Large variations of all the independent parameters involved must be tested to answer this question with any degree of generality. The same applies for the optimal value of the character contrast ratio. Although an optimal luminance ratio of 5 in the case of positive log contrast seems reasonably well defined. the ratio of 0.2 in the negative domain is not, since scatter of light in the phosphor and in the eye does not allow a sufficiently low contrast ratio in this region with the character set actually used here.

In considering the reasons for the relations between the dependent variables which can be measured objectively, it is relevant to take account of the observable asymmetry around a contrast ratio of 1. An obvious reason for this that should be considered is a possible asymmetry in the subjective brightness contrast. This subjective brightness contrast may be thought of as an effect of the more central processing part of the visual system. Indeed, brightness contrast does seem to increase faster for dark objects on a light background than vice versa (see Figure 12). However, this does not apply to contrast ratios in

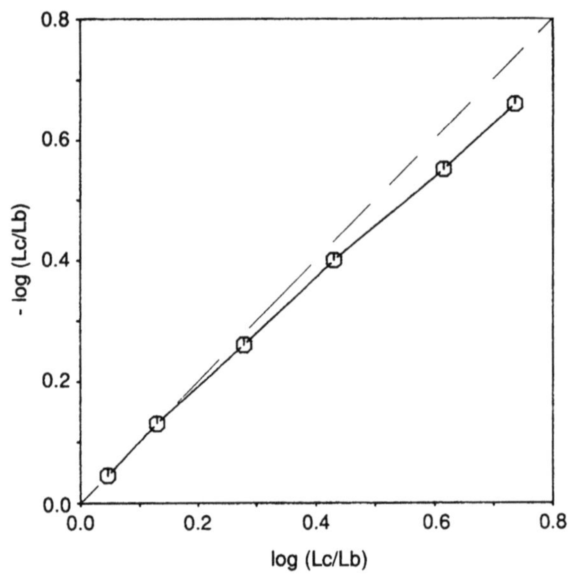

Figure 12. Demonstration of the asymmetry in subjective brightness contrast for dark bars on a light background (negative) and light bars on a dark background (positive). This figure shows the results of one subject in a psychometric experiment using the magnitude scaling method. Every point in the plot represents equal brightness contrast for both negative and positive log luminance contrast conditions (adapted from Burkhardt et al., 1984).

the region of 1 (see also Burckhardt, Gottesman, Kersten, & Legge, 1984). Since at these small values contrasts are almost symmetrical, while fixation duration, saccade length, and search speed show asymmetric behavior, subjective brightness contrast does not seem to be the explanation of the small but significant asymmetry found.

Without considering here the precise nature of the relation between fixation duration and saccadic length, the striking resemblance of the results suggests a common cause. This is an intriguing matter for further study. Search time consists of saccade times and fixation times, and also includes time for movement to a new line, for correction, and for backward regression saccades, and it is clear that search speed is highly correlated with fixation duration, the contribution of which is predominant. By way of example, for one arbitrary sheet fixation pauses account for 92% of a search time of 30 s. The same is true for search speed as shown in Figure 9D. It will not be surprising that the close resemblance of the curves in visual inspection is confirmed by correlation coefficients higher than 0.85 between all measured objective variables and the subjective variable.

The effect of background luminance level is surprisingly small for all four variables studied. However, this may be due to antagonizing effects. For instance, increasing the background luminance level does, up to a certain level, improve the contrast sensitivity for details. This has been demonstrated for example by Blackwell (1946, 1959) for circular objects, and by Van Nes and Bouman (1967) for sinusoidal gratings. One is able to see most sharply at high luminance levels, so to speak. This would increase legibility. On the other hand a higher background level causes an increase in the diameter of the electron beam of the CRT and therefore a loss in physical sharpness. On the basis of evidence not given here we have indications that subjects' judgement is unconciously influenced by flicker. At higher levels flicker sensitivity increases (Kelly, 1961; De Lange, 1954; Roufs, 1972). This is relevant here since a 50 Hz monitor with 25 Hz interlace was used.

6. Results of Experiment II: The Simultaneous Effect of Contrast and Sharpness

In experiment II we changed to a bolder type of character, IPO Normal (see Van Nes, 1985). An example of pseudotext made with this character set is shown in Figure 13. This character shape allowed us to make lower contrast ratios. We also varied the bandwidth, introducing a new independent variable. Since in these experiments we only used low-pass filtering, the effect of the filtering is to blur the image. Four cut-off frequencies of the video signal of

Y3 LMM RZCS RHC4 14V 7L SHH6H6
9LGE TZQ LT2FLA TS09UDJL 9K 10
5ZWQ7940MXH N1 IFVPFUK I8 FHIR
BR58 TUZ JDDDUX PKP BOQN34LR70
2UQ9 ND09Y WF5U RFSAI 6E5 691E
4QI2L5TUJVBK6BW IPN5Z2GN OI LC
TU KBOKA69A7Q QI6U3 KA3WX M6N9
5XXL14 OB9SM1G JW5OA 5NE 6C 4W
988UOJJU IE BRJ5 UXONZIPY 15Q3
1EW Q9RZS ESOK OLGP1 7P23 JFIH
Y4UDG E3S3 KHJ WTG UV OR7U0411
N97 Z2 AJ 3XKJLIJ6JDEDTKJ 9Z9S
PZ4 OGI MN OE AV 9U TI4OXOEH5U
GRA 2L A6R2S V52U 4C 94BOJA KD
8X10 U591K NFQJS99BL BOSMH5NXU
53I 01HO3WO U9 MO6ORUURNGD WGS
ULL 56 8H3OVOGV608R 33 1GXGP93
ZWBX CC7 HCT Q7AOL U2HMVPF4LFE

Figure 13. An example of pseudotext with IPO Normal character set as used in experiment II.

0.5, 1.0, 2.0, and 4.0 MHz were used. This is equivalent to 1.65, 3.3, 6.6 and 13.2 cycles/degree^{-1} of arc.

In the previous section it was shown that comfort judgement does not change very fast with the mean adaptation level. For practical reasons we therefore changed to *background luminance* as a measure of the adaptive state. The background was kept at about 45 cd/m^2 for negative contrast ratios and about 15 cd/m^2 for positive ones, resulting in an average of 40 cd/m^2 throughout this entire experiment.

Figure 14A shows the results of comfort judgement using filtered and unfiltered stimuli. In the case of the filtered stimuli the maximum attainable contrast was used. As a result of blur the effective contrast ratio is diminished. Figures 14B-D show the behavior of the objective dependent variables for the blurred and unblurred images having the same contrast ratio. The results of the filtered images deviate considerably. The unsharpness of the image obviously causes poorer judgement and lower performance. In order to separate the effect of contrast and unsharpness the differences of the measured results were also plotted as a function of the cut-off frequency (Figure 15A-D).

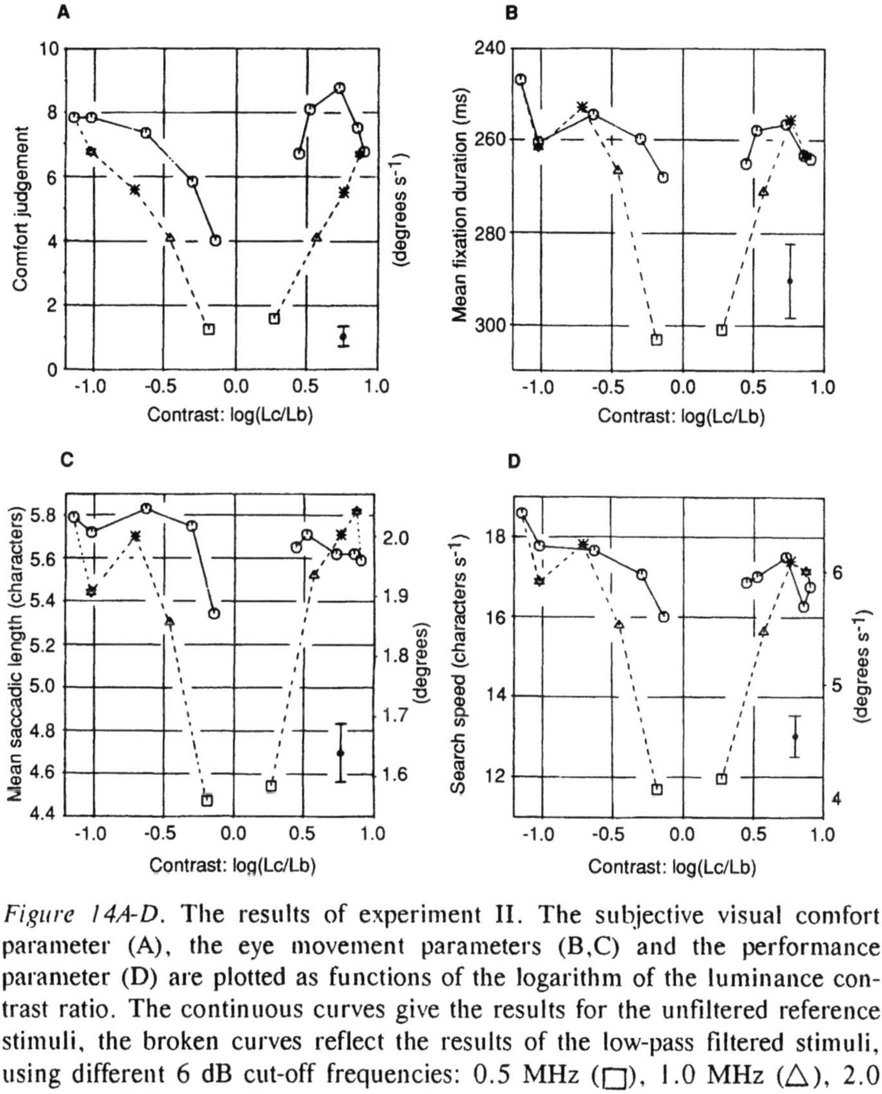

Figure 14A-D. The results of experiment II. The subjective visual comfort parameter (A), the eye movement parameters (B,C) and the performance parameter (D) are plotted as functions of the logarithm of the luminance contrast ratio. The continuous curves give the results for the unfiltered reference stimuli, the broken curves reflect the results of the low-pass filtered stimuli, using different 6 dB cut-off frequencies: 0.5 MHz (□), 1.0 MHz (△), 2.0 MHz (*); 4.0 MHz (✡), and the unfiltered condition (O). Again, an inverse ordinate is used in part B. Every point in the plot represents the results for three subjects, four presentations per subject.

The choice of taking the difference was quite arbitrary and there is no fundamental consideration justifying this choice. The reasoning is that the difference must be caused by the effect of unsharpness. In the case of the objective variables this difference does not increase further beyond 2 MHz. The difference in comfort judgement, on the other hand, does not level off at this fre-

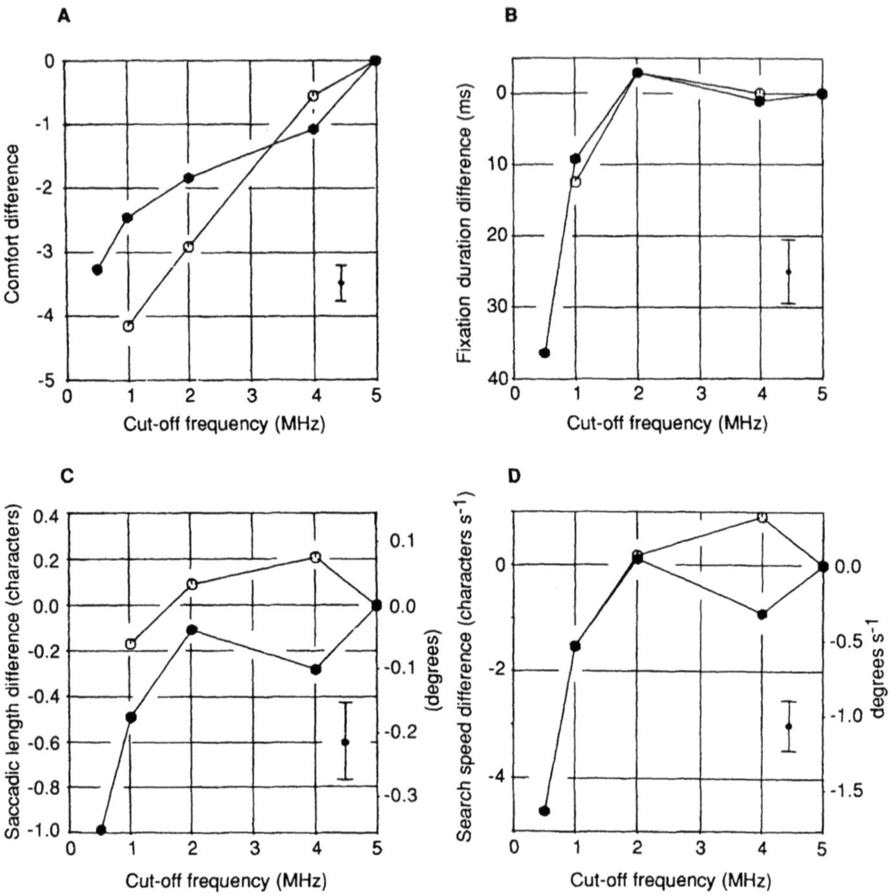

Figure 15A-D Differences between the filtered and the unfiltered conditions in the four dependent variables of experiment II plotted as a function of the 6 dB cut-off frequencies of the digital filters used. These data were obtained by taking for every parameter the interpolated differences between the filtered and the unfiltered situations. The open symbols reflect the results for positive logarithm contrast ratios, and the filled symbols give the results for the negative logarithm contrast ratios.

quency. From the experiments reported here it is the only instance of deviation between the subjective and the objective variables.

7. Discussion of Experiment II

The effect of different character sets becomes obvious if the results of the unfiltered texts of Figure 14 are compared with those of Figure 9. The differences found are most likely due to the effect of character shape. However the general trend of the curves is the same and the same arguments apply as in Sect. 5. Only for the lowest log contrast ratios does one find, at least for the objective variables, a higher outcome than would be expected from the general behavior of the curves. It is not clear at the moment whether this has any significance or whether it is due to an artifact. Sharpness variations, effectuated by changes in the spatial modulation transfer, cause considerable changes in judgement and in the objective variables, as Figure 15 demonstrates. This is in accordance with the widespread notion that sharpness is an important subjective dimension of image quality (Roufs, Soons, & Eising, 1982). More surprising is the tail-off at about 2 MHz, corresponding to 6.6 cycles/degree^{-1} for the objective variables. It seems that the subjective experience of sharpness still increases, while performance and the eye-movement characteristics cannot improve any more. Despite this difference the correlation is still high. The correlation coefficients of the raw data from Figure 14 are presented in Table 3.

Table 3. Matrix of correlation coefficients for the different dependent variables. In all cases $p<.001$ (two-tailed)

	Comfort judgement	Search speed	Fixation duration
Search speed	0.87	-	-
Fixation duration	- 0.84	- 0.99	
Saccade length	0.85	0.96	- 0.94

In order to get the desired insight into the effects of the various parameters the experimental study will have to be extended considerably. The major question raised in the beginning as to whether methods can be found which are a measure of reading comfort and ease of information intake and which are sufficiently sensitive to be used as design criteria seems to be answered in the affirmative. The next step and challenge will be to find out more explicitly what is behind these curves in terms of visual processing and to establish the relation with eye-movement characteristics and visual performance.

8. Conclusions

Scaling of judgement of reading comfort, fixation duration and saccadic length during a search task in pseudotext, and visual performance in terms of search speed have been shown to be highly correlated dependent variables. They show minor but interesting mutual differences. They are sufficiently sensitive to the luminance contrast of the characters, their font, and their physical sharpness to be used as design criteria. Different subjects obtain quite comparable results, and representative standards can most likely be derived.

The results demonstrate that luminance contrast of the characters, bandwidth translated into physical sharpness, and character font are important parameters. More data are needed to allow conclusions to be drawn with any confidence on topical questions like whether dark characters on a bright background are better than light ones on a dark background. The results pose some intriguing questions about the processes causing the relations which are found.

Acknowledgement

This research project was supported by the Netherlands Technology Foundation granted to the first author under number EIP00.0024.

References

Allnatt J.W., Gleiss N., Kretz F., Sciarappa A. & Van der Zee E. (1983). Definition and validation of methods for the subjective assessment of visual telephone picture quality. *CSE2T Rapporti technici*, XI, pp. 59-65.

Blackwell H.R. (1946). Contrast thresholds of the human eye. *Journal of the Optical Society of America*, 36, pp. 624-643.

Blackwell H.R. (1959). Specification of interior illumination levels on the basis of performance data. *Health Engineering*, 54, pp. 317-353.

Blackwell H.R. (1972). *A unified framework of methods for evaluating visual performance aspects of lighting* (Technical Committee Report of the CIE. CIE publ. 19 (TC 3.1)), Paris.

Bouma H. (1978). Visual search and reading: Eye movement and functional visual field. A tutorial review. In: *Proceedings of Attention and Performance VII, Senanque 1976*, J.R. Requin, (Ed.), Hilsdale, Seebaum, N.J. pp.115-147.

Burkhardt D.A., Gottesman J., Kersten D. & Legge G.E. (1984). Symmetry and constancy in the perception of negative and positive luminance contrast. *Journal of the Optical Society of America*, 1, pp. 309-316.

Cakir A, Renter H.J., Schmude L. van & Ambruster A. (1978). *Untersuchungen zur Anpassung von Bildschirmarbeitsplätzen an die physische und psychische Funktionsweise des Menschen.* Bundesministerium für Arbeit und Soziale Ordnung, Referat Pressen und Offentlichkeitsarbeit, Bonn.

Cakir A., Hart D.J. & Stewart T.F.M. (1979). *The VDT manual: ergonomics, workplace design, health and safety, task organisation.* Darmstadt: IFRA.

Edwards A.L. (1957). *Techniques of attitude scale construction.* Appleton-Century-Crofts. N.Y.

Grandjean E. (1980). Ergonomics of VDU's: Review of present knowledge. In: *Ergonomic aspects of visual display terminals.* E. Greandjean and E. Vigliani (Eds.). Taylor and Francis, London, pp. 1-12.

Kelly D.H. (1961). Visual responses to time-dependent stimuli. I Amplitude sensitivity measurements. *Journal of the Optimal Society of America,* 51, pp. 422-429.

Lange H. de (1954). Relationship between critical flicker-frequency characteristics of the eye. *Journal of the Optical Society of America,* 44, pp. 380-389.

Matula R.A. (1981). *Effects of visual display units on the eyes: A bibliography (1972-1980).*

Nes F.L. van (1985). A new character set for TELETEXT with improved legibility. In: *International displays research conference, October 15-17, 1985*; Conference record. Piscataway, IEEE, N.J., pp. 114-117.

Nes F.L. van & Bouman M.A. (1967). Spatial modulation transfer in the human eye. *Journal of the Optical Society of America,* 57, pp. 401-406.

Padmos P. (1988). Visual fatigue with work on visual display Units - the current state of knowledge. In: *Human-Computer Interaction: Psychonomic aspects.* G.C.v.d. Veer and B. Mulder (Eds.) Springer. Heidelberg.

Rayner K. (1981). Visual cues in word recognition and reading: Introduction. *Visible Language,* XV (2), 1981, pp. 125-128.

Reulen J.P.H. (1984). Latency of visually evoked saccadic eye movements. I. Saccadic latency and the facilitation model. *Biological Cybernetics,* 50, pp. 251-262.

Roufs J.A.J. (1972). Dynamic properties of Vision-I Experimental relationship between flicker and flash thresholds. *Vision Research,* 12, pp. 261-278.

Roufs J.A.J. & Bouma H. (1986). Towards linking perception research and image quality. *Proceeding SID,* 21, pp. 247-270.

Roufs J.A.J., Soons A.A.G. & Eising R. (1982). Some experiments on sharpness in relation to contrast bearing on electronic optical imaging. *IPO Annual Progress Report,* 17, pp. 70-75.

Tinker M.A. (1965). *Bases for effective reading*. University of Minnesota Press, Minneapolis.

Torgerson W.S. (1958). *Theory and methods of scaling*. Wiley and Sons, New York.

The Presentation of Visual Information: Statistical Aspects

Chapter 5. Displaying Statistical Information - Ergonomic Considerations

Ivo W. Molenaar

Everyone spoke of an information overload, but what there was in fact was a non-information overload (R.S. Wurman, quoted in Tufte, 1983, p.90).

1. Introduction

Newspapers tell us that we live in a computer era, or information era. Computers have invaded everybody's life, in their function as information processors rather than in their older role of powerful calculators. Storing information has become cheap and simple. A century ago each transaction or observation was written down with pen and ink; now a sensor traced along an optical mark, a magnetic card inserted into a slot, or a finger touching the appropriate section of a personal computer screen suffices to register it in some computer memory. Advanced computer technology and the human need for more information have stimulated each other into an information explosion - this formulation avoids the tricky question of which caused which.

As is evident from the quote at the top of this page, the enormous increase in available data has stimulated an increased need for techniques to condense the information. The name of statistics stems from the desire of the State to have information on population characteristics and economic activity effectively condensed into a few characteristic numbers (like means, quartiles, or correlation coefficients), or into tables or graphs. Modern multivariate statistics similarly condense many observed variables into a few principal components, just as multidimensional scaling aims at a geometrical representation in a few dimensions. The power of computer graphics has led to many innovative methods for displaying multivariate data, reviewed in Wang (1978) and Barnett (1981).

All such condensations share the goal of a compact but faithful representation of information that, in its original form, transcends the processing capabilities of the human mind. Both the act of condensation and the subsequent processing are no longer the prerogative of a few experts: thousands of computer software packages incorporate standard condensation and display techniques, and millions of people look at the resulting summarized numbers, tables, or graphs, trying to perceive and understand the information condensed in them. Even before the large scale introduction of personal computers with their popular spreadsheet programs, Tufte (1983, p.10) estimated that about 10^{12} images of statistical graphics were printed each year. The number of copies of tables with statistical information produced per year must be at least several billion.

A substantial part of this vast amount of statistical information fails to reach its destination because of suboptimal layout. Traditional wisdom has led to many recommendations for the designers of graphs and tables, for example Chambers (1983), Schmid and Schmid (1979), Ehrenberg (1975), Cox (1978), Tukey (1977), and Tufte (1983). They deal with topics like clear labeling, choice of scales and grids, removal of unnecessary ink, and transformation to linearity. Some examples are discussed below. Titles like *How to lie with statistics* (Huff, 1954) and *How to display data badly* (Wainer, 1984) indicate some awareness of the risk of purposely or unintentionally misleading the consumer of statistical information. Yet none of these publications alludes to a psychological theory explaining the human perception and understanding of graphics and tables. What is even more remarkable, none of these sources quotes any experimental observations under controlled conditions that could motivate their recommendations for good displays. Their persuasive power lies mainly in their agreement with common sense. It would not be the first instance, however, in which common sense turned out to be deceptive.

It would be an exaggeration to state that absolutely no theory and no experiments have been published. Bertin (1983/1967) provides at least an orderly discussion of the concepts that play a role in the design of graphics, and bases his subsequent recommendations on his general principles. Tufte (1983) proposes some indices for the quality of a graphic display. Kosslyn (1985) brings some principles from perceptual psychology into his review of five major books on graphics, and experiments have been reported by Wainer (1974), Wainer and Francolini (1980), Wang (1978), Cleveland and McGill (1984), and Naveh-Benjamin and Pachella (1982), for example.

The present paper discusses the choice between various display techniques as well as the choice between variants within a display technique. It explores how cognitive task analysis and experiments can assist in making such choices. It would be an illusion to think that simple choice rules of universal validity lie ready to be unveiled: it will be argued that many factors should be taken into account in any specific choice. On the other hand, so many suboptimal or even misleading condensations of statistical information are still in regular use, that more theory and more experiments can be expected to yield important short term benefits, in the form of both improved software and improved training of human information processors. The computer not only increases the need for such developments, but simultaneously is an important tool for implementing them. Good software for computer graphics encourages the user to find the most suitable display method and layout for his data by trial and error, and facilitates controlled experiments that verify whether indeed a compact but faithful condensation has been obtained.

2. Some Comments on Principles from the Literature

Kosslyn (1985) presents a review from a psychologist's point of view, of five basic books on graphics written by statisticians and cartographers, taking as the central question: "How well do the recommendations offered by the books respect the strengths and weaknesses of the user?" Indeed, the effectiveness of charts and graphs can only be evaluated relative to the nature of the human information processing system: a good graph should take advantage of our perceptual and cognitive abilities. Kosslyn organizes his discussion around the three stages that occur when someone meets a graphical representation of information:

1. The light reaching the retina leads to neural impulses sent to the brain, where a presemantic visual pattern develops
2. A few perceptual units are formed and held in short term memory
3. The long-term memory is searched for knowledge about how charts and graphs convey information, as well as for information about the domain of this particular one, and comprehension of the input is attempted

In almost all cases, steps 2 and 3 have to be repeated several times before the comprehension leads to inferences being made.

In any of the three steps things may go wrong. For step 1 marks on the display must be discriminable, both in an absolute sense and from one another, in order to achieve an adequate visual pattern. Some variations in marks are more suitable for conveying information than others. There are processing priorities by which some characteristics are noticed and attended to more than others, and the visual system may lead to a distorted impression. In step 2 the organization into perceptual units may go wrong, or the display may require the simultaneous consideration of too many items. In step 3 ambiguity may result from the accessing of more than one stored memory, or a wrong inference may result when the display leads to the accessing of incorrect associations: the layout of such a display may invite the reader to draw unwarranted conclusions. Most of the "how to lie with statistics" examples fall into this class.

I believe that a more thorough understanding of the visual and cognitive processes involved will have a doubly beneficial effect. First, it will lead to better professional standards for the design of graphics, and secondly it will be essential for a long overdue educational program for "graphicacy," i.e., training the viewers of graphics to avoid being misled. In view of the frequent use of graphics and of the overwhelming evidence that they are frequently misunderstood, it is remarkable that the general school curriculum and even the training of scientists includes a negligible amount of time spent on teaching about graphical representations. There is a widespread but dangerous optimism that common sense should suffice to avoid the pitfalls. As observed by Schmid (1978, p.74): "Although statistical charts are often a more powerful and significant vehicle of communication than words, there is a strange tolerance for poorly constructed charts." Schmid contrasts this with the irritation caused by an ungrammatical sentence, an ambiguous statement, or even misplaced punctuation marks, and is amazed at the general indifference to "crudely designed, idiosyncratic, inappropriate or even confusing charts." The situation is rather similar with respect to statistical tables and with respect to summaries into means, medians, variances, correlation coefficients, and the like. Here too, better design standards and better education of consumers are essential for a compact but faithful transmission of information.

Bertin (1967) offers many useful taxonomies of graphical concepts. The number of variables to be simultaneously displayed, combined with their measurement level, leads him to a system of display methods. Cases like "paired observations of two ordinal variables," "three numerical variables per geographical district," or "frequencies for a nominal variable in two groups of persons" each ask for their own display method. His list of "visual variables" that can be used obviously starts with the two dimensions of the plane. At each position determined by the two coordinates one can choose between symbols (triangle, circle, star, rectangle), each of which can have different sizes, colors, shades of darkness, and density of hatching; for some symbols their orientation can also be meaningfully varied. The coordinate positions are best suited for information at the interval level of measurement. Sizes and shades lend themselves well to displaying a limited number of ordered classes. Color and form, for which no natural order is perceived, should be reserved for nominal categories. In a sequence of graphs or tables the assignment of display formats to variables should be kept constant. Violations of such simple rules at best force the viewer to repeated consultation of the legends, and at worst lead to totally wrong inferences triggered by the natural interpretation of the layout.

A few of Bertin's recommendations are based on the perceptual properties of the visual variables, like how different two marks or two angles must be for minimal discrimination. His treatment of the differential suitability of the variables remains rather abstract, however, and his abundance of good ideas is not organized to the needs of someone who wants to look up the best display method for a particular data set. The book is not based on the body of knowledge of perceptual psychology, and experiments are never mentioned.

The terminology is somewhat idiosyncratic, and the choice of illustrations has a strong bias towards the display of information about geographic units. Nevertheless, Bertin's work is a landmark on the road to a substantive theory of graphics.

The other books reviewed by Kosslyn share a more practical orientation. I found Tufte (1983) the most rewarding one, both for the beauty of his illustrations and for his attempts to provide numerical measures for some aspects of graph quality. The "data-ink ratio" (p.93) is defined as the proportion of a graphic display's ink devoted to the nonredundant display of data information. Obeying his exhortation to "erase non-data ink, within reason" does away with a lot of gratuitous decoration, or with too many and too heavy grid lines or labels, and thus helps the viewer to form and process the more meaningful perceptual units. "Data density" is the number of data entries in a graphic divided by its area; Tufte's plea for "shrunken, high density graphics" reflects his admiration for the art of cramming a vast amount of information into one small picture. A successful example is a dramatic map of Napoleon's defeat in Russia (Tufte, 1983, p.41), showing the geographical area, the steadily diminishing size of the army, the time scale, and the temperature. Frequently, however, Tufte's exhortations to maximize data ink ratio and data density will be incompatible with the more important goal of efficient interpretation. It is clear that some redundancy and a substantial data reduction often lead to improved information transmission. Wainer calls this "Less is More" : if you show less, then more information reaches its destination.

This is particularly true in tables (Ehrenberg, 1975; Boomsma, 1983), where reduction of the number of decimals and the use of blanks for unimportant entries facilitates the transmission of the important messages. Ehrenberg argues that only two-digit numbers can be easily held in short term memory during comparison, and that seeking outliers in a column of numbers is easier than in a row. Not too long ago the whims of computer programmers forced one to quickly seek the largest from a row like .770426E+0 .980375E-1 .213867E+0 .781815E+0 .834012E-2 .159318E-1. A brief task analysis shows that this requires sequentially locating all signed numbers behind the E symbols in order to establish their maximum (in our case +0). Within the numbers in the list that share this exponent the maximum of the fractions must be established. At each step one must thus locate the exponent, and compare it with the current maximum. If it is larger it replaces the current maximum and its first few decimals are stored. If it is equal its first few decimals are checked against the current maximum of the first few decimals thus far found combined with the maximum exponent, and when larger, replaces them. All this becomes easier when a column rather than a row is shown, facilitating the location of exponents and decimal positions. The task becomes much easier when the numbers are given with a fixed number of decimals, and even more when a small number of digits per entry is used, enabling the user to keep complete numbers in short term memory during comparison.

The other important tool for tables is reordering of rows and/or columns. Wainer "is not interested in Alabama first"; an alphabetic ordering helps to find the entries for one's own state, but ordering by population size or some other important variable is usually very helpful to spot the important main effects in a table. Bertin makes the same points for graphs.

Table 1. Accuracy of the Bolshev, Bomol, and Poisson approximations to cumulative binomial probabilities B for $n=20$ and $p=.2$

Event	B	Bolshev	Bomol	Poisson
$X<0$	.0115	.0117	.0114	.0183
$X<1$	.0692	.0700	.0689	.0916
$X<2$	.2061	.2073	.2056	.2381
$X<3$	.4114	.4120	.4108	.4334

Table 2. Relative error $(A-B)/B$ in per cent for approximations A (Poisson, Bolshev, and Bomol) to the cumulative binomial probabilities B

Event	B	Poisson	Bolshev	Bomol
$X<0$	.012	59%	2%	-1%
$X<1$	.069	32%	1%	
$X<2$	.206	16%	1%	
$X<3$	.411	5%		

Tables 1 and 2 illustrate the effect of table layout. Both present the same fragment from a set of tables with many more rows and columns in Molenaar (1970). In Table 1 it is very difficult to assess the quality of the three approximations to the cumulative binomial probabilitities. Re-expression, reordering, and avoiding "decimalitis" as in Table 2 removes the need for mental arithmetic, sacrificing only some information that is almost inessential. A blank means a relative error of less than 0.5%, and one can see at first glance which approximation has many blanks and thus performs well. Modern statistical packages, and even more some of the better spreadsheet programs, have made it very easy to try out different formats, different orders, different layouts, and different display methods. Previewing them on the screen and sending the best one to the printer is now so easy that one can only admire the ingenuity of William Playfair (1759-1823) who designed very effective graphs in an era when any alternative solution meant several hours of drawing work. Some problems remain. Even in the good packages the default solutions of the packages are sometimes suboptimal: LOTUS 1-2-3 and SuperCalc label each scale tick, and do not warn by a scale break when they use false origins. Moreover, many users who have to try and choose a display format are not well trained in discriminating between good and bad alternatives for a graphic display or a table. They will probably opt for too many numbers and for too many or ill chosen colors, as in the promotion leaflets of SAS/GRAPH; this arouses a feeling of "how wonderful that a computer can do this" rather than a feeling of "now I can see quickly what is important in these data." The availability of many alternatives after no more than a few keystrokes is thus an additional reason for teaching graphicacy: more people than before will be not only viewers but designers of graphics.

3. Investigation of the Box Plot

The results of a task analysis will now be illustrated in more detail for the case of the "box and whisker plot" proposed by Tukey (1977, p.39) for quick graphical presentation of a univariate frequency distribution. Table 3, taken from *Statistisch Zakboek* (1985, p.57), gives the distribution of height for all Dutch conscripts observed by the military medical board (at the age of 18.5 years until 1970, but 17.5 years from 1980 onward). This table can be compared with the box-plot presentation of the same data in Figure 1.

Table 3. Height of Dutch conscripts at year of medical inspection

Height (cm)	1950	1960	1970	1980	1984
< 160	1.5	0.7	0.3	0.2	0.1
160-164	6.0	3.4	1.5	1.0	0.8
165-169	17.3	12.2	6.8	4.4	3.7
170-174	28.3	25.5	18.6	13.9	12.1
175-179	27.0	30.0	29.0	25.9	23.9
180-184	14.4	19.1	25.8	28.0	28.8
185-189	4.5	7.2	12.9	17.7	19.9
190-194	0.9	1.7	4.2	6.8	8.2
195-199	0.1	0.2	0.8	1.7	2.1
200 and over	0.0	0.0	0.1	0.3	0.5
Population size	79 696	77 950	88 847	104 746	105 104
Mean height (cm)	174.0	175.8	178.5	180.3	181.1

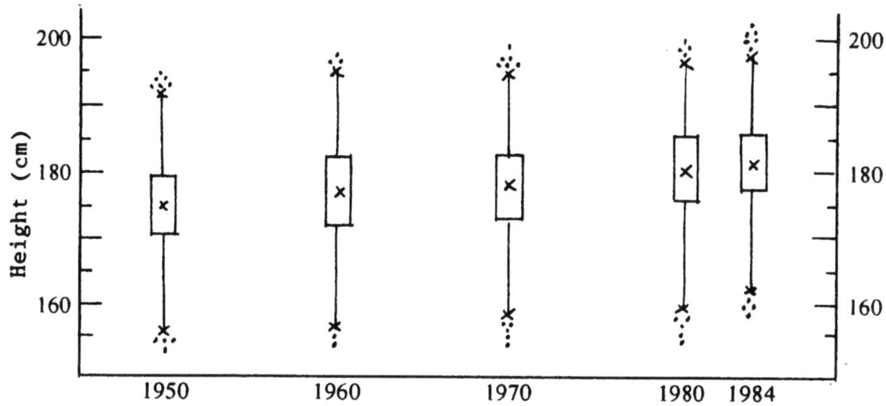

Figure 1. Box plot for the height distribution of Dutch conscripts. Each dot represents 0.1 % of the population, each box gives quartiles and median (see text)

The main goal must be to present and compare the frequency distributions of each year. Let us briefly explain how the box plot achieves this. In the horizontal dimension it shows the shorter time interval 1980-1984. For each year, a box has been drawn between the two quartiles of the length distribution (strictly speaking Tukey replaces quartiles by hinges, which are so similar to quartiles that the difference need not concern us here). The star in each box denotes the location of the median. From each box a "whisker" extends outward to the value which is the last observed value within 1.5 box lengths of the box endpoint. Values outside these so-called "inner fences" are somewhat stray and will be individually plotted in the display. Values at more than two box lengths away, not present in our example, would have been plotted with a more conspicuous symbol, and when desired individually labeled, to signal that they are unusually far from the other observed values. Our data have been treated as samples of size 1000 for easy plotting and comparison: each dot in Figure 1 thus represents 0.1 % of the conscripts of that year.

Let us now examine Tukey's claim that such box plots provide an adequate quick summarization of batches of numbers, comparing Figure 1 to Table 3 and occasionally to some other graphical or tabular presentation forms. Unfortunately, choosing an effective display form is a case of multi-attribute decision making. The adequacy of a display method depends not only on the nature of the data but also on the reasons for examining them. "Thus, we must not ask which of two displays is better but, rather, which is better for yielding the answer to a particular question" (Wainer and Reiser, 1978, p.83). An important question will be a shift in location. The designer of Table 3 has added the line of mean values to show the increase in mean length. Note that the percentages in the table itself provide no quick answer to the location question, although one can see after some effort that the modal category shifts from 170-174 via 175-179 to 180-184 as the years go by.

Do the distributions have the same spread? Here Table 3 has no answer, whereas the box plots show stable values both for the interquartile range and for the total range. If the distribution is normal, the standard deviation can be found as the box length divided by 1.35, because the standard normal quartiles lie at plus and minus 0.6745.

Are there deviations from a normal distribution? This is again a difficult question for Table 3. The box plots show that the median is close to the middle of the box, and exhibit no systematic differences in the number of observations outside of the two whiskers: both are indications of symmetry. For detecting heavy or light tails (kurtosis) the user must know that in any normal distributions 0.4 % of observations are expected to lie outside each whisker, as is easily derived from a table of cumulative normal probabilities. The number of dots per tail in Figure 1 varies from two to six and is close enough to the expected number of four to infer close adherence to the normal distribution.

What percentage of the conscripts are higher than x centimeters? Here Table 3 allows an answer by interpolation and cumulation, and for the special values $x = 199.5$ and $x = 159.5$ the answer can be directly read. The box plots allow an answer by counting of dots if x falls outside the whiskers, but in the middle they only give a rough answer via the quartiles and the median.

Other questions could be considered, but we shall close the section on box plots with some more general remarks. In the experiments of Lourens (1984, p.35) it became clear that a box plot is absolutely unsuitable to detect a bimodal distribution. Introductions to exploratory data analysis like Tukey (1977), McNeil (1977), and our favorite Velleman and Hoaglin (1981), contain examples supporting our claim that box plots are very good for offering a first glance comparison of a few distributions (say between two and ten) with respect to location, spread, and symmetry. Their performance in detecting deviations from the normal distribution is extensively discussed in Molenaar and Broersma (1984) in the form of a task analysis and an experiment with 33 students. For the task of specifying which of two displayed distributions had the highest standard deviation, skewness, and kurtosis, Broersma and Molenaar (1985) reported a task analysis and an experiment with 22 staff members specialized in methodology. In both cases the box plots were only moderately successful.

Readers who have no previous exposure to box plots may wonder why Tukey recommended this new tool, forcing the viewers to learn new terminology and new methodology. In a case like Table 3 we could have followed the standard practice of just reporting means and standard deviations. This would have hidden all information about the tails (which are surely of some interest in the case of heigth). For small or moderate sample sizes (say up to 500 or even 1000), means and standard deviations are very sensitive to the occurrence of an occasional outlying observation. A box plot not only plots such an outlier, but moreover its influence on quartiles and median is very limited. In many applications of statistics such robust estimates of location and spread are far superior to the mean and variance: the latter are optimal (so-called "sufficient statistics") as long as the distribution is normal, but their performance deteriorates rapidly when the assumption of normality is violated.

A display of five histograms side by side or one below the other would be more familiar to many viewers than the box plots. It would take more space than Figure 1. Moreover, the appearance of histograms is rather dependent on the class sizes and class boundaries (Bertin, 1983/1967, p.172; Molenaar and Broersma, 1985, p.228). Space does not permit the discussion of the performance of a display of five histograms for all the questions listed above: it is sometimes better and often worse than the box plots. Molenaar and Broersma (1985) extensively discuss the performance of many display methods for univariate frequency distributions when it has to be established whether the distribution is normal.

4. Discussion

In modern data registration and data proccssing the computer takes care of many tedious tasks. The human investigator is often satisfied with looking at summaries produced by the computer. In the old days the investigator registered his data one by one, warning signals for anomalous values were spontaneously generated, and appropriate action could be taken. Software for automatic processing should either use robust methods, or be equipped with automatic warning procedures for anomalies. The latter solution is problematic, because the boundary between "usual" and "anomalous" is dependent on many circumstances that cannot easily be incorporated into the software.

We have seen that the choice between various display methods often depends on the particular question that the viewer wants to see answered. Another disturbing factor is that the performance of a fixed display method depends on the variant that is chosen. One may reverse the roles of the horizontal and vertical dimension, choose a different scale unit, use symbols of different size, form, and color, and change the labeling. Such choices often have a substantial influence on the effectiveness of the display. In the case of box plots, their implementation in three well known statistical packages shows substantial differences. This has led Molenaar and Broersma (1985, p.235) to formulate desiderata for good box plots, based on task analysis and experiments. They recommend scale ticks at nice round values, clear documentation of the detailed display algorithm, horizontal boxes as default, and options for a user-defined scale unit, simultaneous display of several boxes on a common scale, vertical boxes, simplified Tufte boxes, and notches.

For the commonly occurring kinds of data, most books on graphics contain at least some recommendations for choosing a good display method as well as a good variant within a method. Frequently they are not based on task analysis or experiments. As the choice must depend on the nature of the data, the prior knowledge of the intended audience and the goal of the display, simple general rules cannot be given.

What can be done at this stage is to put forward some general procedures that should help to find a good method for transmitting statistical information in a particular situation. A task analysis should begin with establishing what types of question the persons looking at the display will probably seek the answer to. Next, the designer should assess the amount of statistical knowledge that can be assumed for the readers: a box plot or a quartile plot is very useful to well-trained data analysts, but should be either avoided or carefully explained when the readers are not familiar with such methods. Subsequently, some tentative choices of display method and format can be made. They should next be tested by establishing, for each important question, how observation of the display followed by reasoning can lead the reader to the desired answer. If difficulties are to be expected at the observation or reasoning stages, attempts should be made to modify the display in order to remove or mitigate the difficulties. It is very useful to validate the task analysis by asking a few persons representative of the future readers to look at the display and comment on it.

If additional information can be added to the table or graph without obstructing the essential observations and reasonings, this is desirable if it serves to answer important additional questions. The maximization of the data-ink ratio and data density is useful, if this is not carried to the point where it would hamper the process of answering the key questions. Here Bertin's distinction is useful between graphs and tables that "replace human memory," to be consulted like a telephone directory, and graphs that aim at "writing their message into human memory," where more simplification is imperative.

The future of statistical information and human-computer interaction is rather unpredictable because of the rapid technological changes. The battle between innovation and standardization will continue. We will have still cheaper and faster hardware and somewhat cheaper software by semi-automatic program generation in well-equipped programming environments. Work stations will allow easy shifts between many computers, many software packages, and many databases. As argued in Molenaar (1984), the anonymous and powerless user of these beautiful gadgets will have to fight in order to ensure that they become better adapted to the aims and the shortcomings of human perception and human cognition, and in order to obtain better training, documentation, and help facilities. If accidents at the human-computer interface were as visible as traffic accidents or fire accidents, legislative measures would long have been passed. Whether by legislation or by free enterprise, the next decade will see a growing cooperation between computer scientists and cognitive, behavioral, and social scientists.

References

Barnett V. (Ed.) (1981). *Interpreting multivariate data.* Wiley, Chichester.

Bertin J. (1983). *Semiology of Graphs.* (W.J.Berg, Trans.). University of Wisconsin Press, Madison WI. (Original work published 1967)

Boomsma A.(1983). *On the robustness of LISREL (maximum likelihood estimation) against small sample size and non-normality* (Thesis, University of Groningen). Sociometric Foundation, Amsterdam.

Broersma H.J. & Molenaar I.W. (1985). Graphical perception of distributional aspects of data. *Computational Statistics Quarterly,* 2, pp. 53-72.

Chambers J.M., Cleveland W.S., Kleiner B. & Tukey P.A. (1983). *Graphical methods for data analysis.* Wadsworth, Belmont, CA.

Cleveland W.S. & McGill R. (1984). Graphical perception: theory, experimentation and application to the development of graphical methods. *Journal of the American Statistical Association,* 79, pp. 531-554.

Cox D.R. (1978). Some remarks on the role in statistics of graphical methods. *Applied Statistics,* 27, pp. 4-9.

Ehrenberg A.S.C. (1975). *Data reduction.* Wiley, New York.

Huff D. (1954). *How to lie with statistics.* Gollancz, London.

Kosslyn S.M. (1985). Graphics and human information processing. *Journal of the American Statistical Association,* 80, pp. 499-512.

Lourens P.F. (1984). *The formalization of knowledge by specification of subjective probability distributions.* Thesis, University of Groningen.

McNeil D.R. (1977). *Interactive data analysis. a practical primer.* Wiley, New York.

Molenaar W. (1970). *Approximations to the Poisson, binomial and hypergeometric distribution functions* (Mathematical Centre Tract 31). Centrum voor Wiskunde en Informatica, Amsterdam.

Molenaar I.W. (1984). Behavioral studies of the software user. *Computational Statistics and Data Analysis,* 2, pp. 1-12.

Molenaar I.W. & Broersma H.J. (1984). Interpretation of statistical software output: some behavioral studies. In: *COMPSTAT 1984 Proceedings*, T.Havraek, Z. Sida and M. Nova, (Eds.), pp. 341-346. Physica Verlag, Wurzburg.

Molenaar I.W. & Broersma H.J. (1985). Exploratory data analysis: psychology applied to the presentation of statistical information. In: *Symposium Statistische Software*, P. Debets et al. (Eds.) pp. 227-240. Technisch Centrum FSW, University of Amsterdam.

Naveh-Benjamin M. & Pachella R.G. (1982). The effect of complexity on interpreting "Chernoff" faces. *Human Factors*, 24, pp. 11-18.

Schmid C. (1978). The role of standards in graphic presentation. In: *Graphic presentation of statistical information* (Technical Paper No 43). pp. 69-78. U.S. Bureau of the Census, Washington DC.

Schmid C.F. & Schmid S.E. (1979) *Handbook of graphic presentation* (2nd ed.). Wiley, New York.

Statistisch Zakboek (1985). Staatsuitgeverij, CBS-publicaties, The Hague.

Tufte E.R. (1983). *The visual display of quantitative information.* Graphics Press, Cheshire (CT).

Tukey J.W. (1977). *Exploratory data analysis.* Addison-Wesley, Reading (MA).

Velleman P.F. & Hoaglin D.C. (1981). *Applications, basics and computing of exploratory data analysis.* Duxbury Press, Belmont (CA).

Wainer H. (1974). The suspended rootogram and other visual displays. *American Statistician*, 28, pp. 143-145.

Wainer H. (1984). How to display data badly. *American Statistician*, *38*, pp. 137-147.

Wainer H. & Reiser M. (1978). Assessing the efficacy of visual displays. In: *Graphic presentation of visual information* (Technical Paper No 43). pp. 83-88. U.S. Bureau of the Census, Washington DC.

Wainer H. & Francolini C. (1980). An empirical inquiry concerning human understanding of two-variable color maps. *American Statistician*, *34*, pp. 81-93.

Wang P.C.C. (Ed) (1978). *Graphical representation of multivariate data.* Academic Press, New York.

Chapter 6. Factors Influencing the Detection of Trend Deviations on VDTs

Ted N. White and Paul van Schaik

1. Introduction

For human supervision of process operation, trend recorders are commonly used as graphical displays. From process information as a function of time, operators are able to predict future values of variables represented by those trends. Moreover, trend information promotes the detection of malfunctions in the measurement and control systems.

The new generation instrumentation systems are based on large computer systems. Conventional trend recorders have been replaced by presentation of trends on visual display terminals (VDTs). Compared with hard-wired recorders. VDTs are much more flexible for changing the layout as well as the location of trends on the VDT screen. This freedom of choice leads to a decision problem. When a layout can be choosen freely, the criteria for a choice should be specified; they may be aesthetic, technical or based on constraints given by the human capabilities and limitations.

The literature on this topic does not help much in selecting the appropriate criteria for the design of task-oriented trend displays. Therefore, the better trend layouts and trend scalings are still largely based on more or less satisfactory guesses or trial-and-error approaches. Published studies about the topic have focused on the prediction of future trend values (Rouse and Enstrom, 1976; Van Bussel, 1980; Van Heusden. 1980) or dealt with the control of a system based on trend presentation (Boesser and Melchior, 1984).

In contrast, the present study deals with the early detection of deviations in various trend presentations on VDTs. Early and correct detection is regarded a crucial step in the train of human information processing. When no deviations are detected, no further action is taken. A false detection, however, may lead to further upsetting the system under control.

The ultimate aim of this investigation is to formulate recommendations for trend layouts on VDTs. both for early detection of on-coming deviations (Van Schaik and Rijnsdorp, 1985) and for improving the accuracy of prediction of future values of process variables (White and Van Heusden, 1984; White and Van der Meijden, 1986a, b).

2. Hypotheses

When a trend signal deviates from the normal or expected range, such deviation has to be detected to initiate a procedure or strategy to return the signal to within the limits. A detection error then, is defined as a nondetected deviation. A falsely detected (nonexisting) deviation is kept out of the discussion because in previous research hardly any "false alarms" have occurred. Performance is expressed as a percentage of correctly identified deviations and the observation time required to detect deviations. It is assumed that relatively short detection times and a low rate of detection errors lead to better process supervision and contribute to better process operation. Based on that notion the following hypotheses were formulated:

H1: A larger slope of a trend deviation leads to an improvement of the detection performance and is subjectively rated as making the task easier

H2: A smaller range of the trend amplitude results in an improvement of the detection performance and a lower subjectively rated difficulty

H3: A longer-deviation time window, the length of time over which the deviation is visible, leads to a higher percentage of correctly identied deviations, a shorter observation time and a lower rated difficulty

3. Method

3.1. Trend Signal and Experimental Variables

In order to test the hypotheses, a well-defined experimental setting is required. A nonfiltered white noise was chosen as a trend signal. To simulate a trend deviation, a linear function was added to the signal at unpredictable moments (see Figure 1).

The VDT screen had a surface of 512× 256 pixels. The horizontally displayed time information consisted of 148 pixels. The maximum amplitude

Figure 1. Construction of a trend in deviation A=trend amplitude, W=time window, S=slope

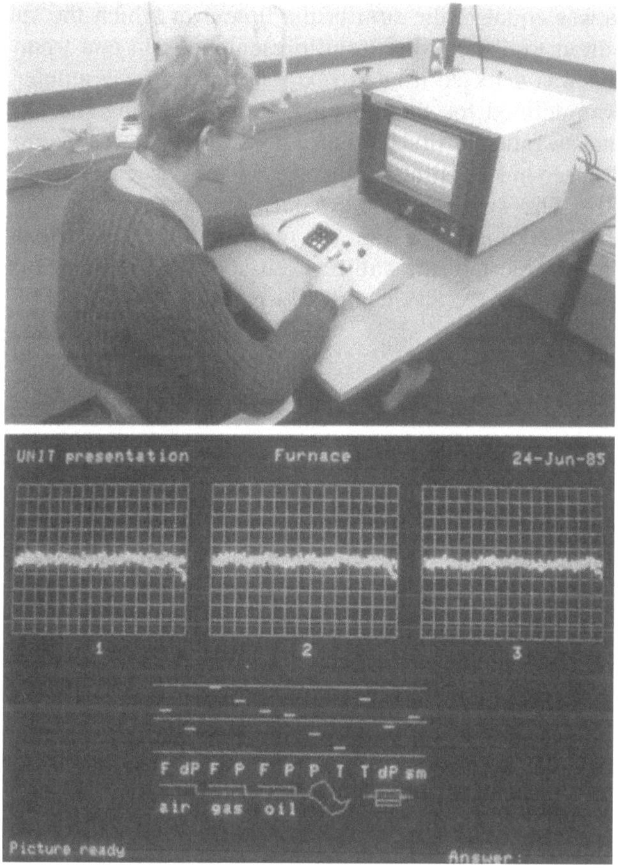

A

B

Figure 2. Operator task: experimental situation (A) and screen image of the three records (B)

scaling (*A*) of the noise had a range of 12, 15, or 18 pixels in a vertical direction (pv). The slope (*S*) or inclination of a deviation was 34 or 43 degrees (dg). The time window (*W*) over which the deviation stretched was 6, 9, 12, or 15 pixels in the horizontal direction (ph). The ratio $S \times W/A$ was defined as the rate of perceivability of a deviation (dg× ph/pv).

3.2. Operator Task

The task of the subjects was to detect deviations in color-coded trends which were presented on a VDT in three records of three trends each. In each record, the trends had the zero line in common (see Figure 2). Trends were shown as long as the operator pressed a LOOK-button on a keyboard. The total observation time was equal to the sum of the time over which the subject pressed the LOOK-button to observe the trend presentations in one trend picture. When a deviation was detected it had to be reported to the computer system. A set of keys was defined for this purpose. After releasing the LOOK-button the subjects had to indicate first in which trend record a deviation was found (1,2, or 3). The second keystroke indicated which particular trend was deviating (1, 2, or 3). The keys were color-coded to represent the color of the trends. The third action was a set of two or three keystrokes. It represented a rating of how certain the subjects felt about the existence of the trend deviation (20%, 40%, 60%, 80%, or 100% certain).

3.3. Experimental Setting

The experiments were carried out in a homogeneously lit room. Each subject was seated in an office chair behind a desk with a dedicated keyboard and a high-resolution monitor. An LSI 11/02 minicomputer was used for signal generation and data recording. For trend generation a Ramtek 9250 graphical system was used. The information on the subject's monitor was also available to the experimenter; computer and experimenter were in another room.

4. Experiment 1

4.1. Independent Variables

The slope was varied over two levels, 34 and 43 degrees (dg), and trend amplitude was varied over three levels, 12, 15, or 18 pixels vertical (pv). The time window was fixed at 12 pixels horizontal (ph). This resulted in a total of six experimental conditions and in four different rates of perceivability:

Condition	Perceivability	Condition	Perceivability
		(43dg,12pv,12ph)	43.0 dgx ph/pv
(34dg,12pv,12ph)	34.0 dgx ph/pv	(43dg,15pv,12ph)	34.0 dgx ph/pv
(34dg,15pv,12ph)	27.2 dgx ph/pv	(43dg,18pv,12ph)	28.7 dgx ph/pv
(34dg,18pv,12ph)	23.0 dgx ph/pv		

The conditions were presented to the subjects in a random order. In each of the six series, 20 detection trials were made. Prior to the experimental conditions, subjects were given a training session which could be lengthened on request. After each session a break was introduced in which subjects had to fill out a questionnaire. Subjects were students of Twente University of Technology, ($n = 15$). They were tested for normal colour vision (Ishihara test) and none was found to have any form of colour vision defect.

4.2. Dependent Variables

To test the hypotheses the following dependent variables were measured: percentage of missed deviations (MD), total observation time (OT), certainty estimate of a detection (CE), and subjectively rated difficulty of detecting a deviation (SRD).

In line with the working hypotheses, it was expected that the presentation of trends with a higher perceivability would lead to fewer MDs, a shorter OT, a higher CT, and a lower SRD.

4.3. Results

The experimental data were tested using the Wilcoxon matched-pairs signed-rank test. In the figures, conditions with equal perceivability are connected by dotted lines and marked are by *S** if differences between conditions are statistically significant ($p < .05$). The other conditions are connected by uninterrupted lines and are marked by *S* if statistically significant differences are found.

Figure 3 shows the percentage MDs for the three trend amplitudes and for the two angles of deviation. The results can be interpreted as showing that: (a) the smaller the amplitude and the larger the slope, the less deviations are missed by the subjects; in other words, higher perceivability leads to fewer MDs; and (b) equal perceivability does not lead to an equal percentage of MDs. In cases of equal perceivability a larger slope results in fewer MDs.

When total OT, i.e., the time the subject presses the LOOK-button, was analyzed, it was found (see Figure 4) that the smallest amplitudes (12pv) show the shortest total OT, that increasing the amplitude results in an increased OT, and that conditions with equal perceivability do not show significant differences in OTs. For the condition 34dg/18pv a drastically larger OT would have been found if the percentage of MDs (see Figure 3) had not been so high. The missed deviations are probably flattening the results.

The effects of the amplitude and slope of the deviation on the CE are presented in Figure 5. It appears that in the large slope conditions (43dg), the increase of the trend amplitude has no effect on the CE of perceiving a devia-

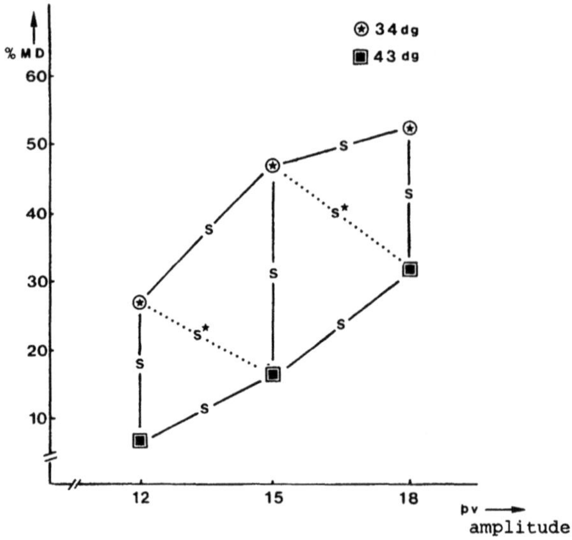

Figure 3. The percentage of missed deviations (*MD*) as a function of slope and trend amplitude

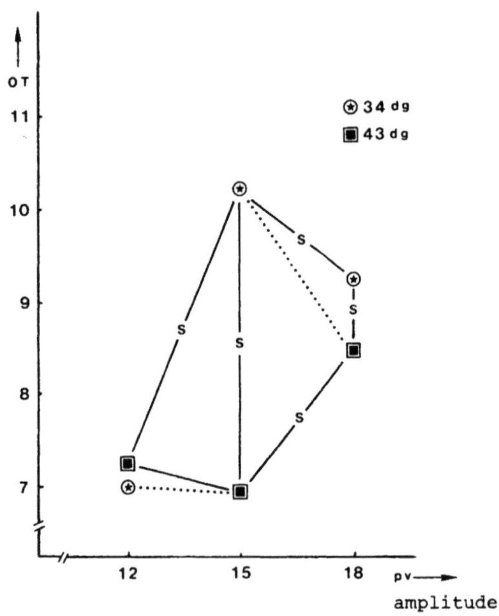

Figure 4. The observation time as a function of slope and trend amplitude

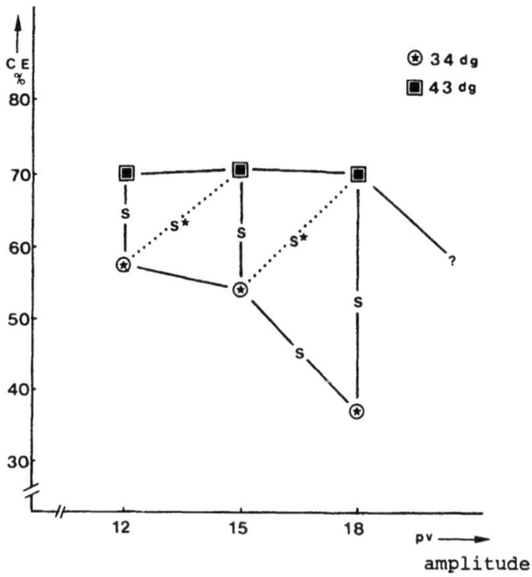

Figure 5. The certainty estimate (*CE*) as a function of slope and trend amplitude

tion. In addition, the CE in all large slope conditions is significantly better than in all small-slope conditions, and in the small-slope conditions, the difference between the CEs at trend amplitudes of 15 and 18 pixels is significant. For conditions of equal perceivability, CE is higher in cases of a large angle of deviation.

The last dependent variable to be considered was SRD. The subjects had to indicate the difficulty on a 7-point scale, varying from very easy (1) to very difficult (7). The results are presented in Figure 6. and show that increasing the trend amplitude results in an earlier increase of SRD for the small angle conditions compared with the large-angle conditions, that decreasing the rate of perceivability increases the SRD, and that equal perceivability conditions are rated as equally difficult.

4.4. Conclusions

Increasing the range of the amplitude decreases the number of MDs and increases OT. It also effects the subject's CE and SRD. The effect of the increased amplitude can be reduced by the application of a large angle. The quantity which expresses the perceivability does not contradict the subject's perceived difficulty when detecting deviations of trends; it is therefore regarded as a useful tool for the evaluation of trend presentations. When dealing with conditions of equal perceivability, the large-slope conditions lead

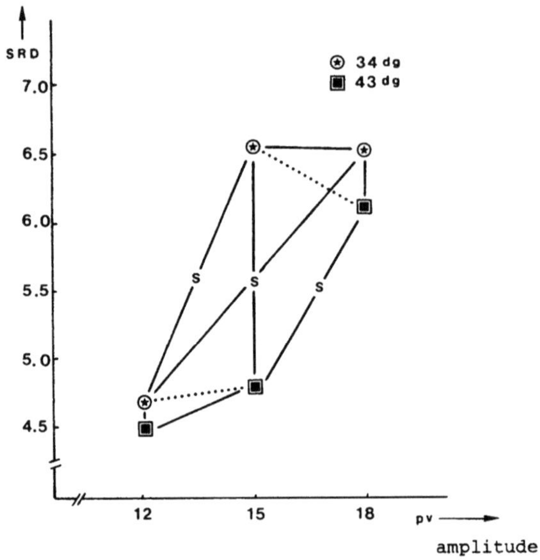

Figure 6. The subjectively rated difficulty (*SRD*) as a function of slope and trend amplitude

to better detection performance and an equal SRD. Depending on the variable under consideration, the concept of perceivability can be applied as a sensible quantity. The results obtained from the experiment therefore confirm the hypotheses to a large extent.

5. Experiment 2

In a second experiment the time window and the slope were investigated. The range of the trend amplitude was fixed at the level which gave the best results in Experiment 1.

5.1. Dependent Variables

The hypotheses were tested by means of the following dependent variables: percentage of missed deviations (MD), total observation time (OT), the certainty estimate of a detection (CE), and the subjectively rated difficulty of detecting a deviation (SRD).

It was expected that increasing the slope and/or increasing the size of the time window would give fewer MDs, shorter OTs, higher CEs, and lower SRDs.

5.2. Independent Variables

The experiment was run along the same lines as Experiment 1. The 12 subjects which participated were students of Twente University of Technology. None of the subjects had any kind of colour deficiency. Six combinations of slopes and time window apertures were used:

Condition	Perceivability	Condition	Perceivability
(34dg,12pv,6ph)	17.0 dgx ph/pv		
(34dg,12pv,9ph)	25.5 dgx ph/pv	(43dg,12pv,6ph)	22.0 dgx ph/pv
(34dg,12pv,12ph)	34.0 dgx ph/pv	(43dg,12pv,9ph)	32.0 dgx ph/pv
(34dg,12pv,15ph)	42.5 dgx ph/pv		

After each session a break was introduced in which subjects had to fill out questionnaires. The order of presentation of conditions was randomized.

5.3. Results

Data were analyzed with the Wilcoxon matched-pairs signed-rank test with a .05 significance level.

Figure 7 shows the percentage of MDs for the four window apertures and the two slopes of departure. Again *S* denotes a significant difference between conditions and *S** denotes a significant difference for equally perceivable conditions. The results can be interpreted as showing that increasing the slope leads to fewer MDs, enlarging the window aperture and increasing the rate of perceivability lead to a smaller percentage of MDs, and combinations of equal perceivability do not show statistical differences in percentage of MDs when perceivability is low. Statistical differences are present for the highly perceivable conditions and between conditions 43dg,9ph and 34dg,12ph. This latter aspect might indicate that when a trade-off has to be made a large slope is preferable to a large window.

It has to be remarked that detecting a deviation and formulating a CE requires more time than detecting a nondeviation. Moreover, the number of deviations occurring was not equally spread over the conditions. Therefore a correction was made to the rough OT data. The total OT per condition was divided by the number of deviations in that condition. The corrected observation times will be referred to as cOT.

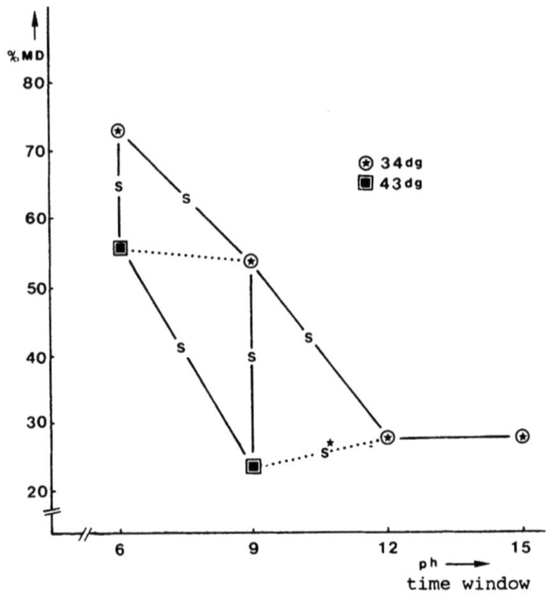

Figure 7. The percentage of missed deviations (*MD*) as a function of slope and trend amplitude

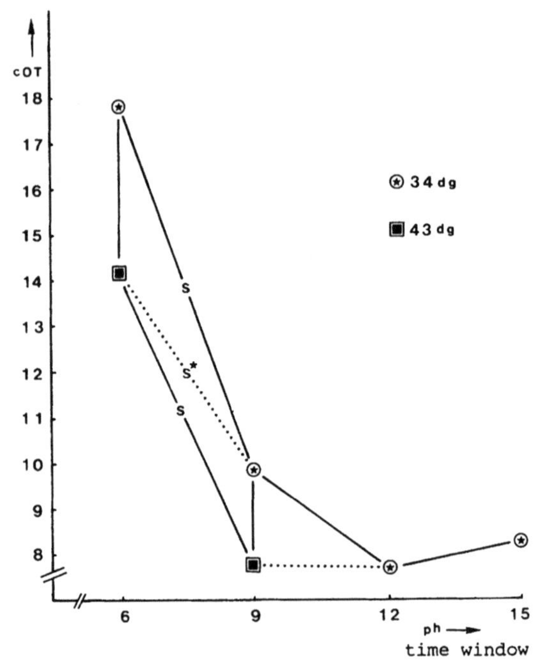

Figure 8. The corrected observation time (*cOT*) as a function of slope and time window

Figure 8 shows the numerical results obtained with the cOTs, as well as the results of statistical testing. Enlarging the slope has an effect in the predicted direction, but this is not significant. The larger the time window becomes, the shorter the cOTs found; the optimum is rapidly reached at the level of 9ph. No numerical and statistical differences are found when the time window increased above 9ph. Equal perceivability conditions only differ statistically when relatively small time windows are compared (cOT,34dg/9ph < cOT,43dg/6ph). Equally perceivable conditions do not differ near the optimum time window.

Figure 9 shows the results of testing CE. The data can be interpreted as showing that the larger the time window, the higher the CE of correct detections is. Again, an optimum is found for a time window aperture of 9ph, conditions with larger time windows not being statistically different. The CEs of equally perceivable conditions are statistically different up to the optimum of 9ph. The large time window condition leads to more certainty. In contrast to other results, the condition 34dg,9ph leads to a significantly higher CE than the condition 43dg,9ph.

Figure 10 shows the results for the SRD, which demonstrates that the slope does not influence the SRD, and that the larger the time window becomes the lower the difficulty is rated. The optimum time window is 12ph. Different SRDs between conditions 43dg,6ph and 43dg,9ph approach significance. The results also show that equally perceivable conditions lead to unequal SRDs; 43dg,9ph and 34dg,12ph are significantly different and the difference between 34dg,9ph and 43dg,6ph approaches significance. As postulated, the large time window conditions show lower SRDs.

5.4. Conclusions

With an increase in the time window up to a certain level (9 to 12ph), fewer missed deviations and lower cOTs are found. These objectively measured quantities are not contradicted by subjective measures, CE and SRD. The CE is highest for a window of about 9 to 12ph. The subjective rating of a window aperture of 12ph indicates the lowest perceived difficulty. From the results it is clear that a time window of more than 12ph does not lead to improved MDs, cOTs, CEs or SRDs. Increasing the slope results in fewer MDs and lower cOTs. The results of the subjective measures do not indicate a preference and if any preference is measured it is in favour of decreasing the slope. Conditions with an equal rate of perceivability show that MDs benefit from a large slope, while cOTs and CE benefit from a large time window. When one compares the condition 34dg,12pv,12ph in Experiment 1 with the same condition in Experiment 2, one finds a striking equality in the objective measures.

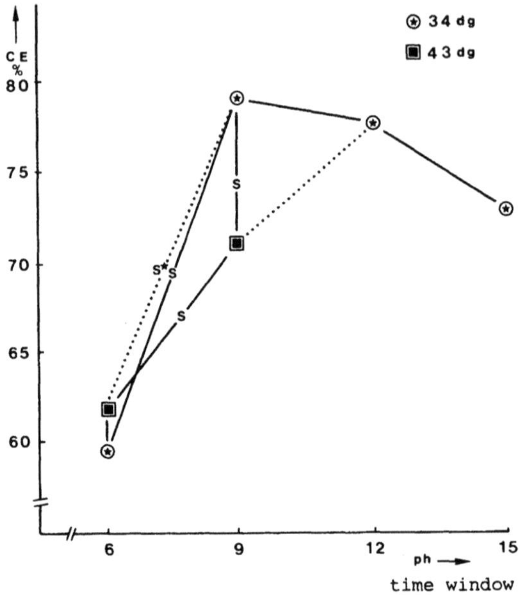

Figure 9. The certainty estimate (*CE*) as a function of slope and time window

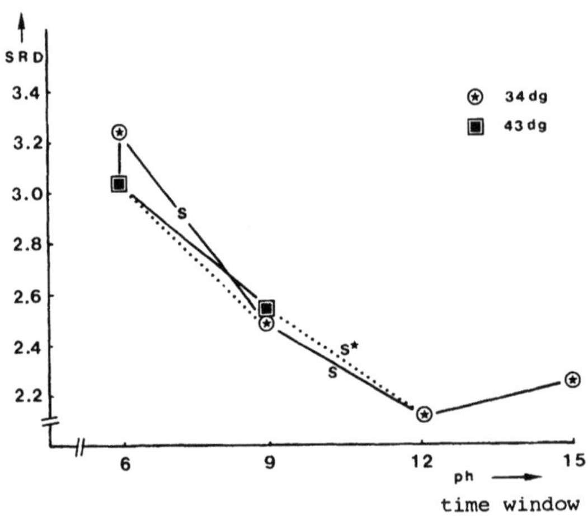

Figure 10. Subjectively rated difficulty (*SRD*) as a function of slope and time window

However, this does not occur for the subjective measures CE and SRD. The experimental context, variation of amplitude, or variation of time window might be influencing factors.

6. General Discussion

From the results of the objective and subjective measures of the two experiments several assertions can be made. The rate of perceivability as defined in the present study can be used as a sensible first approximation for judging VDT trends as far as early detection tasks are concerned. However, the formula representing the rate of preceivability should be further tuned to apply to those cases where the observable conditions appear the same but different results are obtained. Each of the parameters used to define trend formats has been found useful when dealing with early detection tasks (present study; Van Schaik and Rijnsdorp, 1985). For related tasks such as the prediction of future trend values, the parameters have also been found valuable (White and Van Heusden, 1984; White and Van der Meijden 1985a, b). Other studies on trend displays have suggested different parameters, but have investigated different tasks. To design generally applicable VDT trend displays, knowledge of both the task content and of the parameters suggested in the literature is essential. Few steps have been made to categorize and quantify the cognitive aspects involved in the observation of trends. Scaling does not influence the information content of the displayed signal, but does humans' detection and prediction performance.

References

Boesser T. & Melchior E.M. (1984). Utilization of time-series information in an optimization task. In: *Proceedings of the Fourth European Annual Conference on Human Decision-Making and Manual Control*, pp. 201-212. Institute for Perception TNO, Soesterberg.

Rouse W.B. & Enstrom K.D. (1976). Human perception of the statistical properties of discrete time series; effects of interpolation methods. *IEEE Transactions on Systems, Man, and Cybernetics*, 6 (7), pp. 466-473. Computer Society Press of the IEEE, Washington, D.C.

Van Bussel F.J.J. (1980). Human prediction of time series. *IEEE Transactions on Systems, Man, and Cybernetics*, 10 (7), pp. 410-414. Computer Society Press of the IEEE, Washington, D.C.

Van Heusden A.R. (1980). Human prediction of third-order autoregressive time series. *IEEE Transactions on Systems, Man, and Cybernetics*, 10 (1), pp. 38-43. Computer Society Press of the IEEE, Washington, D.C.

Van Schaik P. & Rijnsdorp J.E. (1985). Detection of on-coming off-normals in VDU trend presentation. *Ergonomics International 1985. Proceedings of the Ninth Congress of the International Ergonomics Association*, I.D. Brown, R. Goldsmith, K. Coombs and M.A. Sinclair, (Eds.). pp. 835-837. Taylor and Francis, London.

White T.N. & Van Heusden A.R. (1984). Various display scalings of trend information and human's predictability. *Proceedings of the Fourth European Annual Conference on Human Decision-Making and Manual Control*, pp. 263-275. Institute for Perception TNO, Soesterberg,

White T.N. & Van der Meijden P. (1986a). VDT trend representation affecting human prediction accuracy. *Proceedings of the Sixth European Annual Conference on Human Decision-Making and Manual Control*, J. Patrick and K.D. Duncan (Eds.), pp. 37-47. Dept. of applied Psychology, University of Wales, Institute of Science and Technology, Cardiff.

White T.N. and Van der Meijden P. (1986b). Trend presentation and human's predictability. In: *Proceedings of the International Federation of Automatic Control IFAC Workshop on Reliability of Instrumentation Systems for Safeguarding and Control.* Netherlands Association of Engineers (NIRIA) and Royal Institution of Engineers (KIvI) in the Netherlands. The Hague.

The Presentation of Visual Information: Linguistic Aspects

Chapter 7. Visual Presentation of Text: The Process of Reading from a Psycholinguistic Perspective

Leo G.M. Noordman

1. Introduction

The aim of this chapter is to give an insight into the reading process and an overview of the psycholinguistic research on reading. It will focus on the so-called higher-order processes that take place while the reader is reading a text; the cognitive aspects of information processing. Factors that affect these processes will be discussed. These include factors inherent in the text as well as factors external to the text. These issues are discussed in the first part of the chapter, an overview of visual perception in reading. The subsequent discussion of textual factors is organized from smaller units to larger units: words, sentences, texts. Finally, some extratextual factors in text processing are discussed. This order of discussion is selected only as a convenient way of presentation; it does not imply that the reading process takes place in this order.

The chapter does not pretend to give a complete overview of the reading process. Only some aspects of the different subprocesses in reading are discussed. A consideration in selecting the topics to be discussed has been to illustrate how the reading process is affected by textual and extratextual factors. The factors that are discussed no doubt have implications for the ergonomics of reading and text processing. This is particularly true for factors related to text characteristics and sentence constructions.

In the second part of this chapter some aspects of man-computer interaction in reading are discussed. The claim is made that the speed of reading and the quality of understanding is mainly determined by the higher-order processes discussed in the first part of the paper. The bottleneck in normal reading is not so much the perception of the visual information but the processing of the higher-order information. So, an important question with respect to man-computer interaction is whether the presentation of text on a computer screen can affect the higher-order processes discussed in the first part, so as to influence the speed of reading and the quality of understanding. This issue has been studied in research using the technique of rapid serial visual presentation. Research on this issue is presented in the second part of the chapter.

2. Overview of the Reading Process

Reading will be approached as an activity of information processing. The central topic of this chapter concerns the cognitive processes underlying text processing. The incoming information consists of scribbles on a piece of paper. This information is subject to all kinds of transformations until the end-result is reached, the understanding of the text. The semantic and textual information that is understood is ultimately derived from the scratches on the page. The vicissitudes of the incoming visual signs leading to the end-result of text understanding will be reviewed briefly.

Reading, so considered, is a complex process that consists of a number of component processes. On the basis of the characteristics of the letters, sometimes with the aid of letter-sound conversion, words are recognized and understood. This implies that the meanings of the words are looked up in a kind of mental dictionary. At the same time the word class of each word is determined, i.e., the syntactic function of the word in the sentence is established. On that basis different kinds of syntactic and semantic strategies enable the reader to determine the syntactic structure and the meaning of the sentence. The information in the sentence is then related to other information that may or may not be explicitly expressed in the sentence. The reader uses his general knowledge to attain a deeper understanding by inferring information that is not explicitly expressed in the text. The result is the comprehension of the text: the reader has derived an internal representation of the concepts and their relations.

In this chapter, the different processes are dealt with in an intuitively obvious order. First, the most peripheral process, namely the visual processing of the letters is discussed. Subsequently the more central, higher-order processes are described. The order of treatment might suggest the order of processing, i.e., the lower-order processes would seem to be perequisites for the higher-order processes. In the literature this approach is referred to as bottom-up or data-driven processing. However, empirical evidence suggests that the different processes do not necessarily occur in this order. It is possible that a word is understood before all the letters are identified. Similarly, a reader can construct the structure of a sentence before all the words have been identified. Moreover, knowledge of the subject matter of the text can facilitate word recognition. In these cases, the processes occur in reversed order. This is called top-down, or conceptually driven processing.

There is a theory of reading in which reading is considered as a top-down process: reading as a guessing game (Goodman, 1970). On the basis of higher-order information, hypotheses are generated with respect to the subsequent text and are then tested. Such a process would be rather inefficient and, with respect to cognitive resources, rather uneconomic. It is very unlikely that the reading process is such a top-down process. What is very likely, however, is that the different subprocesses can occur in different orders, and may affect each other in several ways.

Each component process requires the activation of particular kinds of knowledge: knowledge of characteristic features of letters, of letter-sound relations, of the regularity of the spelling of words, i.e., orthographic knowledge, of the morphological composition of words, of word meanings, of sentence structures and the syntactic function of words, of the ways in which particular texts are structured, and of the subject matter of the text. There is a certain relation between these kinds of knowledge and the different subprocesses, but this is not a one-to-one relationship. Syntactic knowledge, for example, can be used in understanding individual words as well as in understanding the structure of a sentence. In summary, the reading process is a complex interaction between component processes in which the different kinds of knowledge can be used in different ways. On top of that, both characteristics of the reader and characteristics of the task the reader sets himself greatly affect the reading processes. The intricacies of these processes in reading and the factors influencing the relations between these processes will no doubt be the object of a lot of research in the near future.

2.1. Visual Perception

Reading is done with our eyes but what do our eyes do while we are reading? We may have the impression that they perform a continuous movement over the page, but this is not the case. Our eyes go over a line in a stepwise fashion. The jumps performed by the eyes are called saccades. The size of the saccades is about 8-10 character positions. The duration of a saccade is on average 30 ms. After a saccade, the eyes remain for a while in a relatively fixed position. These periods of nonmovement are called fixations. The fixation duration is on average 200 - 300 ms. Apart from the saccades and the fixations there are also backward jumps, called regressions (Rayner, 1978).

It is only during fixations that information is extracted from the text. Research on eye movements has demonstrated that a particular piece information is perceived during only one fixation. McConkie (1978) presented a sentence, e.g., "Fred says that his old garage leaks so much that he will not store tools in it." During the reader's first saccade, the word *leaks* was changed into *leans*, and during the second saccade *leans* was changed into *leaks*. One striking finding was that the reader was not aware of the changes. Another result was that the reader had processed only one interpretation of the sentence, and so had read only one word at that location. The conclusion of this research was that a particular word is perceived during only a single fixation.

Now the question arises as to how the perceived information is processed. Several models have been put forward to account for this process (Rayner, 1977). According to one model, the information that is perceived during a fixation is stored in a buffer. Semantic processing of the information is delayed until enough information is available for deriving the interpretation of the sentence. According to another model, words are processed semantically as soon as they are fixated. In that case one would expect the fixation duration to correlate with the difficulty of the fixated words. This would imply, for example, that infrequent words, ambiguous words or, in general, words that require extra processing, are fixated for longer than other words. Most experimental evidence favors the latter model. There appears to be a clear relationship between the fixation duration and the cognitive processing of the fixated stimulus. That is the reason why the registration of eye movements and, in particular, fixation durations is a useful method in reading research.

2.2. Word Recognition

Word recognition takes place on the basis of the visual information. There are a great number of theories and models of the process of word recognition. Only two aspects will briefly be dealt with: the question of what the units in word processing are and the issue of letter-sound correspondence.

With respect to the units of processing, the question is whether word perception is based on a preceding letter perception, or whether words can be perceived directly. A third possibility is that word perception is a complex interaction between letter identification and word identification. It is impossible to discuss the different theories and their empirical support in a satisfactory way. Only one model will be discussed: the interactive model of McClelland and Rumelhart (1981). Apart from higher levels of information in word processing, they distinguish between three lower levels: the level of letter features, the letter level, and the word level. There is a continuous interaction between these levels. Essentially, this interaction consists of an increase or decrease of the activation of the information at a particular level. The information at each level is represented by nodes: feature nodes, letter nodes, and word nodes. Nodes at the same level can only decrease each other's activity. These nodes are in fact mutual competitors. Nodes at different levels can increase as well as decrease each other's activity. If a word is presented, particular letter features corresponding to each letter position in the word are detected. On the basis of these features, letters containing these features are activated and the activation of other letters is decreased. The activated letters at the different positions in a word increase the activation of words that contain those letters at the same positions and decrease the activity of words that do not contain those letters. Letter nodes that are candidates for a particular position in a word inhibit each other's activation. Similarly, activated word nodes inhibit each other's activity. There is also an interaction between levels: activated word nodes increase the activation of corresponding letter nodes. Finally, only those letters and words will be perceived that correspond with the nodes with the highest activation.

An interesting phenomenon that this model can explain is the word-superiority effect (Reicher, 1969): a letter is more easily recognised when presented in a word than when presented in an arbitrary string of letters, and also better than when presented in isolation. The explanation is that there is no node corresponding to an arbitrary string of letters and consequently no activation of such a string.

Factors that influence the speed of word recognition are, among others, word length and word frequency. The effect of these factors can easily be accounted for in McClelland and Rumelhart's model. The longer a word, the more elements have to be activated. The more frequently a word is used in the language, the higher the initial activation of the word is, and consequently the greater the activating effect on corresponding letters and deactivating effect on other letters.

Another object of research is the role of sounds in word recognition. Before children learn to read they know the relation between a spoken word and its meaning. Learning to read consists initially in learning the relation between the visual word and the sound, since the relation between the sound and the meaning of the word is already known. Learning to read is initially reading words aloud. In technical terms it is learning the correspondence between graphemes and phonemes. The question is whether after the stage of learning to read, reading is still accompanied by vocalizing the words in one way or another. Is the relation between visual signs and meaning established via the sounds or do the visual signs provide a direct access to the meanings in the mental lexicon? If word meanings are accessed through their sounds, then the code is, at least in part, phonological.

Support for phonological coding has been obtained by among others Meyer, Schvaneveldt, and Ruddy (1974). Subjects had to judge whether two strings of letters were both words or not. They found that the reaction time was shorter when both words rhymed (*mint, hint*) than when they did not rhyme (*mint, pint*). Evidence against a phonological coding was obtained in an experiment by Kleiman (1975) which will be reported here in a somewhat simplified way. Words had to be judged with respect to sound similarity (for example *tickle* and *pickle* rhyme, but *lemon* and *demon* do not), or with respect to letter similarity (for example *heard* and *beard*, apart from the initial letter, have the same letters, but *grace* and *price* do not). The judgments had to be given in a condition in which only the visual words were presented and also in a condition in which, simultaneously with the visual words, numbers were presented acoustically which the subjects had to say out loud (shadowing task). If phonological coding plays a role, one would expect the reaction times to be much smaller in the normal condition than in the shadowing condition. The reason is that the shadowing task, in which sounds are heard and produced, should interfere with the presumed phonological coding in reading. If, however, a phonological code is not required, one would expect the difference between the shadowing condition and the normal condition to be greater when the words have to be judged with respect to sound similarity than when they have to be judged with respect to letter similarity. This was indeed found to be the case.

On the basis of extensive research with respect to phonological coding, one most probably has to conclude that the mental lexicon can be accessed both directly and through a phonological code. In adult reading a phonological code in general does not play a role. If, however, the reading task requires extra memory load, phonological coding does play a role (Levy, 1978). In those cases a phonological coding would be instrumental in keeping the information in memory through rehearsing. The phonological code, then, probably does not play a prelexical but a postlexical role.

2.3. Analyzing the Structure and Meaning of Sentences

With the understanding of the words, the syntactic and semantic information of the words becomes available. That information is used to recover the structure and the meaning of a sentence. Syntactic and semantic strategies may be used in the process of deriving the structure and meaning of a sentence. These strategies give some insight into the linguistic factors affecting sentence processing and thereby into difficulties of sentence processing.

Some strategies concern the syntactic parsing of a sentence. An example is the interpretation of a noun-verb-noun sequence as actor-action-object. The effect of this strategy is illustrated in the following sentence: "The man offered a hundred dollars for the bottle of 1962 vintage Mouton Rothschild is my uncle" (Clark & Clark, 1977). The application of this strategy leads to a wrong parsing of the sentence. Another example is the function of the relative pronoun in a sentence: it indicates the beginning of a new clause. This can be illustrated nicely in English where the relative pronoun can be omitted: "The man [whom] the dog bit died". *Whom* indicates that the reader/listener has to make a segmentation. Moreover, *whom* gives information about the function of the subsequent words: *whom* + noun + verb has to be interpreted as direct object, actor, and action. These are two reasons why deleting the relative pronoun increases the difficulty of sentence processing (Fodor & Garrett, 1967).

If syntactic parsing is an important aspect of sentence processing, the processing should be easier as the syntactic structure is indicated more clearly. This is indeed the case. Graf and Torey (1966) had readers read sentences presented in one of two formats. In one format each line corresponded to a syntactic unit; in the other format syntactic units were split by the end of a line. The sentences in the former format were understood better than in the latter format. Consequently, the identification of syntactic constituents is an important part of sentence processing.

Besides information for syntactic analysis, the definite article contains semantic information. It is an indication for the reader to search for an entity in his memory that corresponds to the noun that follows the article. This can explain why the sequence "Mary got the picnic supplies out of the car. The beer was warm" is more difficult than "Mary got the beer out of the car. The beer was warm" (Haviland & Clark, 1974). *The beer* suggests that *beer* had already been introduced in the previous discourse. Consequently, an inference should be made that the picnic supplies contained beer. Owing to that inference, the reading time for the second sentence in the first sequence is longer than the reading time for the same sentence in the second sequence.

Processing strategies can also be based on the semantic content of the words. A single word can contain important information for the integration of parts of the sentence. Consider the word *convince*. The presence of this word presupposes that there is a person, and that there is something which that person is being convinced of. These functions are generally indicated by the term cases, such as actor, recipient, object. The cases are important integration devices (Just & Carpenter, 1980).

The syntactic and semantic strategies are important in determining the difficulty of a text. Actually, the question of whether a sentence allows the application of such a strategy affects the difficulty of processing. What is important in this respect is that the factors that have been discussed contribute to text difficulty since they determine the processes of text understanding. This is an important point, especially in the light of reading formulas.

Before discussing the processes at text level, two points will be treated briefly: the question of when the different processes take place in time and, secondly, how these processes relate to one another. With respect to the first question, there is quite a lot of evidence that the different processes take place as soon as possible. A reader does not delay the interpretation of a sentence until he has read the whole sentence. On the contrary, the information in a particular word is processed as soon as that word is perceived, even at the risk of a wrong interpretation (Carpenter & Daneman, 1981). This is illustrated by so-called garden-path sentences, e.g., "The granite rocks during the earthquake" (Milne, 1982) where *rocks* is initially interpreted in the most plausible way, namely as a noun, and not as an intransitive verb. Another illustration of the immediate application of a particular strategy is given in the following sentence: "The horse raced past the barn fell" where *raced* is initially interpreted as the main verb of the sentence, whereas it is the verb of a relative clause qualifying *horse*. In sum, the information is processed immediately. The research on eye movements discussed earlier supports the same conclusion.

The second issue concerns the relation between different processes. Sentence understanding requires the processing of letter forms, sounds, words, and syntactic and semantic information in the sentences as well as information inferred from the context. How do these processes relate to each other? There are two opposing views, the modular and the interactive theory of sentence processing. Modularity implies that a particular process corresponds to an independent module. Modules are autonomous in the sense that processes in a module are not affected by other processes. Fodor (1983) claims that the input system in the language user is a modular system: on the basis of the incoming perceptual information a linguistic representation is constructed. Contextual information such as syntactic and semantic constraints in the context do not play a role in the process. Only the output of this process is available for contextual interpretation. Modular models resemble a transformational generative grammar. The construction of a linguistic representation and the analysis of contextual information are seperate processes. An interactive model does not have independent modules or independent levels of processing that correspond to the different linguistic levels. On the contrary, graphemic, orthographic, lexical, syntactic, semantic, and contextual information is available simultaneously. Sentence processing is a continuous interaction between these sources of information.

As an illustration of the issue, only one study will be presented, a study that supports the interactive theory of language processing. The evidence presented is not enough to decide between the interactive view of sentence processing and the modular view. Marslen-Wilson and Tyler (1975) and Marslen-Wilson and Welsh (1978) demonstrated that a spoken word is recognized before all acoustic information is perceived. When the first sounds of a word are heard, all words that start with the same sounds are activated by the hearer. With the increasing number of sounds that are perceived, an increasing number of word candidates drops out until only one candidate is left over. The word is recognized at the point at which it diverges from all other words that start with the same sounds. Words in context are recognized even faster. Brown, Marslen-Wilson and Tyler (in preparation) demonstrated that syntactic and semantic information in the context can speed up the word recognition process, in the sense that the word can be recognized before the acoustic information is available on the basis of which the word could be recognised. Syntactic and semantic information is used so that less acoustic information is required for recognition. Subjects had to press a button as soon as they heard the word *guitar*. (This study dealt with spoken word recognition. Strictly speaking, the results may not be generalized to reading. But it seems rather unlikely for there to be an interaction between subprocesses only in listening and not in reading.) This word was used in the context of the following sentences:

1. John held the guitar.
2. John buried the guitar.
3. John drank the guitar.
4. John slept the guitar.

The first sentence is a normal sentence. In sentence 2 a pragmatic rule is violated: guitars are in general not buried. Sentence 3 violates a semantic selection restriction: drinking requires a fluid object, which a guitar is not. In sentence 4 a syntactic subcategorization rule is violated: to sleep is an intransitive verb, and does not have a direct object. In the first sentence there is no syntactic, semantic, or pragmatic violation. If these sources of information are used in understanding the sentence, the word *guitar* should be recognized more quickly in the first sentence than in the other sentences. That was indeed found to be the case. The conclusion is that the different kinds of context information affect word recognition. As soon as the verb is heard, the syntactic, semantic, and pragmatic information of the verb is available. On the basis of this information relations between the words in the sentence can be established. Consequently, successive words can be recognized with still less acoustic information. This result argues against a modular view of sentence processing.

2.4. Integration of Sentences and Understanding of Text

Text comprehension requires the construction of a coherent representation of the sentences. That representation cannot be described in terms of the semantic and syntactic properties of the sentences. In fact, these properties are not sufficient for constructing a coherent representation. Contextual information and knowledge of the world play an important role in this respect. Some research will be discussed that demonstrate how properties of the text at local and global levels affect the construction of a coherent representation.

What processes take place in the contruction of a coherent text representation? More concretely: what are the textual means to relate parts of the text to one another and how are these processed? One of the ways in which connections in a text are established is predicating new information on old information, i.e., information that is already available. This is expressed in linguistic terms as given and new information, or topic and comment (Halliday, 1967). Given information is information that is supposed by the speaker or writer to be known by the hearer or reader. New information is information that, in the opinion of the speaker/writer, the listener/reader does not yet have available. An illustration of the given-new structure as well as of its processing consequences was given earlier in the discussion of semantic strategies in sentence processing. One of the ways to express old information is the definite noun phrase. This presupposes that the referent of the noun has already been mentioned in the preceding discourse. If that referent is not explicitly mentioned, a search procedure should start to compute the appropriate referent. This kind of inference requires extra time.

Thus, text understanding implies a process of relating current information to preceding information. This means that a text should be easier to process if there are explicit references to other parts in the text. That this is indeed the case was demonstrated by Kintsch, Kozminsky, Streby, McKoon, and Keenan (1975). They used texts that were matched with respect to the number of words and number of propositions. In one text there were few different concepts that were repeatedly used as arguments in different propositions. In another text there were many different concepts with fewer repetitions. The question was whether the frequent occurrence of the same concepts would cause interference between the various uses of the concepts and consequently would slow down reading and decrease recall. Alternatively, it might be the case that texts with few different arguments would make it easier to connect the parts of the text to one another and, consequently, would increase recall performance. The results indicated that texts with a great number of different concepts were less well recalled than texts with a small number of different concepts. This is evidence for the occurrence of integration processes in reading.

That concepts occurring later in the text are related to concepts occurring earlier in the text has been demonstrated by McKoon and Ratcliff (1980). The first sentence of a text they presented to subjects was: "A burglar surveyed the garage set back from the street." The last sentence of the text was either:

1. The burglar slipped away from the streetlamp.
2. The criminal slipped away from the streetlamp.
3. A cat slipped away from the streetlamp.

Having read the text, the reader had to say whether the word *burglar* occurred in the text. This judgment was made more quickly if the last sentence had been 1 or 2 than if 3 had been the last sentence. Thus, the concept *criminal* in the last sentence, which refers to *burglar* in the first, does indeed activate this word. More interesting is that similar results were obtained for the target word garage. If the word *criminal* occurred in the last sentence, it is not only the word *burglar*, to which *criminal* refers, that is activated, but also the word *garage*, which in the first sentence is connected with *burglar*. McKoon and

Ratcliff also investigated the structure in memory that results from the processes of anaphoric reference. The question was whether the propositions containing the referent and the propositions containing the anaphor are connected together. After reading the text just described, readers had to judge whether particular words occurred in the text, e.g., the words *streetlamp* and *burglar*. When the last sentence had contained the word *criminal* (sentence 2) the judgement for *streetlamp* was facilitated much more strongly by a preceding judgement *burglar* than when the last sentence had contained the word *cat* (sentence 3). In the representation that results from the processing of the text, the concepts *burglar* and *streetlamp* are related to one another through the concept *criminal*. Although there is no reason, as far as the semantics of the words is concerned, why the presentation of the one should facilitate the recognition of the other, such facilitation is actually found. This suggests that the concepts are related in the representation that results from the processing of the text.

The text variables discussed so far concern the ways in which a word in a text refers to another word in the text. The research dealt with local coherence relations. Now, some global characteristics of the structure of text and their effect on text processing will be discussed. In general, the different parts of a text (sentences or sequences of sentences) correspond to a particular plan or structure. This structure has been worked out most clearly for stories. Stories have a particular regularity and different parts of a story have a well defined function. The structure of stories has been conceived of as analogous to the structure of sentences. This regularity has been described with the same formalism with which sentences are described. That formalism is called a story grammar. Just like a sentence grammar, a story grammar consists of rewrite rules. Some rules in the story grammar of Thorndyke (1977) are:

Story → Setting + Episode
Setting → Characters + Location + Time

The analogy between a sentence grammar and a story grammar should not be taken too strongly (Wilensky, 1983). The nodes in a sentence grammar are linguistic categories, whereas in a story grammar they are conceptual units. That sentences and stories are fundamentally different entities is clear from the fact that sentences are linguistic entities but stories can be nonlinguistic.

A story grammar is not only useful as a means to describe a particular kind of text: the description also has a psychological plausibility. The structure described by a story grammar has implications for the processing of the story. What people recall from a story depends on the structure of the story: information of a higher level in this structure is recalled better than information from a lower level. Similarly, what people reproduce as the summary of a story is in general information from the higher levels in the structure (Thorndyke, 1977). Finally, the hierarchical structure also has an effect on the encoding of the text: sentences from a higher level in the structure require a longer reading time than sentences from a lower level (Cirilo & Foss, 1980). Thus, the processing of a story shows what is called a levels effect. Several explanations of this levels effect can be put forward. One explanation is that readers are able to estimate the relative importance of the parts of the text they are processing and that the more important parts are processed more fully, which requires longer reading times and leads to better recall. The interesting question then is how readers are able immediately to evaluate the relative importance of the parts of the text and what cues they use in these evaluations. A more bottom-up explanation of the levels effect is that elements lower in the structure require fewer integration processes than information high in the structure. This could be argued for in several ways. First, information higher in the structure is claimed to contain more new concepts and ideas than information lower in the structure. Secondly, elements higher in the hierarchy may in general have more causal links to other elements than elements lower in the hierarchy, and causal relations are important determinants of the depth of processing (Reiser & Black, 1982; Van den Broek & Trabasso, 1986). That the structure of a text is an important factor in text processing is clear from other studies as well. Readers who are able to identify the most important structural relations in a text are better able to reproduce the text than readers who are less able to identify the text structure (Bartlett, 1978). Furthermore, it has been observed that children are less able to perceive the causal structure of a story than adults (Mandler & Johnson, 1977). Adults recall both the events and the results of the events. Children, however, predominantly recall the results and not the ways in which the results come about. Consequently, an important factor in the development of text processing skills is the development of schemata to organize text reproduction.

2.5. Extratextual Factors in Text Processing

The discussion so far has dealt with the impact of textual factors on text processing. They comprised factors at the word, sentence, and text levels. The reading process, however, also depends on factors outside the text. What the reader brings to the task greatly affects text processing. Two factors will be discussed: first, the reader's knowledge with respect to the subject of the text and, secondly, the reader's purpose.

2.5.1. Reader's Knowledge

Reader's knowledge was involved, of course, in the previous studies. They concerned knowledge with respect to words, syntactic structure, text organization, etc. What will be the issue now is not the linguistic knowledge of the reader but his knowledge about the subject matter of the text.

When reading a text, the reader constructs a coherent representation of the information in the text. That representation, however, contains more information than is explicitly stated in the text. Actually, a text can be very parsimonious because the reader adds a lot of information: the reader makes inferences. This is clear from a simple example: "There were elections yesterday. The majority of the inner city voted left. This caused a big shift in the city council." These sentences can be understood without any problem. But knowledge of the words and of the sentence structures is not enough to arrive at a coherent representation. All kinds of information are supplemented by the reader, for example that *inner city* does not refer to a part of the city but to its inhabitants; that the inner city constitutes a relatively large part of the city; that the right wing used to be better represented in the council.

The role of knowledge in reading is predominantly conceived of in terms of scripts and similar concepts (for example see Brown & Yale, 1983). Scripts refer to knowledge of more or less stereotypical situations and events. Most research on scripts has dealt with the retention and reproduction of information in texts. The results show that what is reproduced depends heavily on that knowledge.

Apart from the effect on the reproduction of text, one can ask whether the reader's knowledge affects the processes that occur during reading. Vonk, Noordman, and Kempff (1984) investigated whether the representation that is constructed during reading depends on the reader's knowledge. They conducted the following kind of experiments. A text about a sailing competition contained the sentence "Connors used Kevlar sails because he expected little wind." The concept *Kevlar* was unknown to the readers. A thorough understanding of the sentence requires the inference that *Kevlar* is advantageous when there is not much wind. The question was whether readers make that inference during reading. This was measured by presenting this sentence in two conditions to different groups of readers. In the one condition the sentence was preceded by the information that had to be inferred (Kevlar has advantages when there is not much wind) and in the other condition it was not. If the inference is made during reading, the reading time in the former condition should be shorter than in the latter condition. This was not observed systematically, however. The conclusion is that causal inferences related to issues that are not within the knowledge of the reader are not made during reading. These inferences were made, however, if the reader, after reading the text, was explicitly asked a question with respect to that information. These and some other studies suggest that inferences that contribute new knowledge are not made during reading, while inferences that are activations of available knowledge are.

2.5.2. Reader's Purpose

The second factor to be discussed is the reader's purpose. It is fairly obvious that the reader's purpose affects the reading process. If a reader wants to understand a text well and to capture the line of thought, he reads the text in a quite different way than when he wants to get information about a particular prespecified topic. The question is which processes are different in these cases.

A more or less classic study on the impact of the purpose on reading is the research by Anderson and Pichert (1978). They had subjects read a text under one of two different perspectives. The text gave a description of a house and contained elements that were relevant from the point of view of a possible buyer (e.g., a leak in the roof) as well as elements relevant from the point of view of a burglar (e.g., an expensive coin collection). The perspective under which the readers had to read the text largely determined what they recalled from the text. Even more interesting was the following. After the readers had read the text under the perspective of the burglar and, subsequently, had recalled the text, they were unexpectedly asked to recall the text once again but now under the perspective of the home buyer. It appeared that the readers were able to recall quite a lot of things relevant for a home buyer that they had not mentioned in their first recall. Similarly, they left out quite a lot of things relevant for a burglar that they had produced in their first recall. The conclusion is that the reader's perspective determines to a great extent what can be retrieved from memory. This study, however, does not demonstrate whether the reader's perspective on the text affects the encoding processes in reading. Anderson, Pichert, and Shirley (1983) tried to get evidence for a separate encoding effect of the perspective using a recall task. Borland and Flammer (1985) claimed that their recall task was not appropriate, and used a recognition task to establish encoding effects. More direct evidence for encoding effects were obtained by Vonk and Noordman (1984) who measured sentence reading times in combination with a recognition task. They found an effect of the reader's perspective both on the reading times and on the recognition. This research suggests that the influence of the reader's perspective on the recall can, at least partly, be attributed to selective processing during reading.

3. Some Aspects of Computer Presentation of Text

Having presented a global overview of the reading process, I will now discuss the question of what the effect is of the computer presentation of text on the reading process. The majority of the factors and processes that have been discussed in the preceding part of this chapter are relevant to reading, no matter how the text is presented, either on paper or on a computer terminal. In many laboratory studies on online text processing, texts are presented on a computer terminal. Consequently, many of the results apply to computer-controlled text presentation. In that sense, the research earlier discussed really dealt with man-computer interaction. Nevertheless, some more specific points should be made with respect to computer-controlled text presentation.

3.1. Reading from a Page vs. Reading from a Display

The first issue is how reading a printed text compares with reading a text on a display. Is reading from a computer display quicker or slower than reading from a real page? Muter, Latreouille, Treurniet, and Beam (1982) had subjects read text for 2 h. The text was presented either on a display or as pages in a book. Text comprehension was the same in both conditions, but reading from a display was 30% slower than reading from a book. Reading speed was measured in terms of words per minute. This disadvantage of a display did not disappear when proportional writing was used on the monitor. Factors that might cause the difference between the two conditions in this study are the number of characters per line (39 in the monitor and 60 in the book), the number of words per page (120 in the monitor and 400 in the book), the time necessary for filling the screen, and the difference in contrast between letters and background in the two conditions. Subsequent research (Kruk & Muter, 1984) pointed out that the distance from the screen, which was varied from 40 cm to 120 cm, did not affect the reading speed. The length of the time period necessary to fill the screen, which was varied from 0.5 s to 9 s, did not have an effect either. Two factors that did have an effect on the reading speed were related to the format of the text. When the number of characters per line increased from 39 to 60 the reading speed increased by 10%. The distance between the lines, affecting the number of lines per page, also had an effect. Reading speed was 15% greater with double spacing than with single spacing. All these conditions, however, had no effect on the comprehension of the text.

A second factor that may be relevant in comparing reading from a display and reading from print is fatigue. In the study by Muter et al. (1982) there was no appreciable fatigue after reading for 2 h. Gould and Grischkowsky (1984) investigated reading-induced fatigue over a longer time period. Subjects read for six periods of 45 min on each of two consecutive days. On one day they had to read from a book, and on the other from a computer screen. In both conditions the task was to identify spelling errors. In the book condition, they had to mark the spelling errors; in the display condition, they had to indicate them with a light pen. This research indicated again that reading from a book was about 20%-30% quicker than reading from a display. There were indeed symptoms of fatigue, but subjects showed the same level of fatigue when reading from a book as when reading from a display.

An obvious difference between reading from a book and from a display concerns the recollection of the place where particular information occurred in the text. This is very useful for making regressions as well as for looking up parts of the previous text. Reading from a display probably makes it much more difficult to identify and remember locations in a text. This difference may be very important for the speed of reading and text processing.

3.2. Effect of Computer Presentation on Higher-Order Processes

Having discussed some of the differences between reading from a computer display and reading print, I will now discuss a more fundamental aspect of man-computer interaction: the question of whether computer-controlled presentation can influence the reading process.

As far as the processing of the visual input is concerned, the reading process could go faster than it does. We can see a word in about 50 ms. This means that, as far as the visual input is concerned, we could read four times faster than we do. Two explanations for the slowness of reading can be conceived of. The first explanation is that the bottleneck in reading is the processing of the higher-order information and not the perception of the visual information. This does not mean that the visual perception is never a bottleneck; it certainly can be. But even in the case of optimal legibility of the visual input, the reading process is slowed down by higher-order processing. Most of the processes that have been discussed in the preceding section were higher-order cognitive processes. Are there any grounds for expecting that text presentation on a display affects the higher-order processes? Thus the question is whether there are methods of text presentation that facilitate the higher-order processes in text understanding.

The other explanation of the slowness of reading is that the perceptual processes during reading are not efficient. In this explanation the bottleneck is visual perception during reading. The argument then is that the way in which our eyes go through the text is inefficient. There are indeed several reasons to question the effectiveness of the eye movements in reading. It is quite conceivable that they just go through the text too slowly and that by speeding up the movements of the eyes the reading process can be speeded up. Speed reading courses are partly based on this idea. Another reason why eye movements in reading are supposedly inefficient is the fact that eye fixations are quite often inaccurate. This is particularly true for the first fixation on a new line.

Whatever the explanation of the alleged slowness of reading, the question is whether certain ways of presenting text can influence the reading process positively. This kind of question has been investigated with the rapid sequential visual presentation (RSVP) technique, used since Forster (1970) and Bouma and De Voog (1974). For an overview see Potter (1984). In this technique the visual information is presented quickly and at the same location on a screen. This can be done in several ways: one can, for example, show each word separately with a duration of 50 ms per word. When text is presented in this way eye movements are superfluous. One might argue that this method is not at all typical of normal reading, because we never read like that. This, however, is an open question. In fact, when reading a text attentively we fixate about every word. Furthermore, in normal text presentation the information is also processed as soon as it is fixated, as has been argued above. Whether the RSVP method is an ecologically valid method is an empirical question. In the following section, some studies will be discussed dealing with the question whether computer presentation of text affects higher-order processes in text understanding. Juola, Ward, and McNamara (1982) presented text either as a whole page on the screen, in which case eye movements were necessary, or in an RSVP procedure, in which case eye movements were not necessary. There were several reading speeds in the whole-page condition and corresponding reading speeds in the RSVP procedure. Text understanding was measured with comprehension questions. There was no difference in text understanding between the page condition and the RSVP condition. The conclusion was that eye movements are not necessary. The results suggest that there may be possibilities for the RSVP technique to positively influence the reading process, since text understanding was about equal even though readers had hardly any experience and training in RSVP.

One way to facilitate the reading process is to find out what is the best unit for the presentation of text. Cocklin, Ward, Chen, and Juola (1984) varied the size of the units that were presented from one word to about three or four words, the equivalent of about 20 characters. In this presentation words were not split into parts. Text comprehension was best when the texts were presented in units of about 12 characters. This was observed independently of the speed of presentation.

This leads to the question raised earlier: can one find a way of text presentation that facilitates the higher-order processes? An obvious candidate among these higher order processes is the syntactic analysis of the sentence. The research by Graf and Torrey (1966), discussed earlier in the context of the syntactic processing strategies, showed that the presentation of sentences in terms of syntactic units or clauses facilitates text understanding. These syntactic strategies concern the segmentation of the sentence. An example of such a strategy is: if you encounter a function word, start a new constituent. In a subsequent experiment Cocklin et al. (1984) compared the comprehension of text presented in two different ways. In one condition the units of presentation corresponded as exactly as possible to 12 character positions, without having split words. In the other condition, units of presentation corresponded as nearly as possible to idea units. The description of the material makes it clear that syntactic considerations played an important role in defining the idea units. Text comprehension was significantly better in the latter condition than in the former. The structural information in the presentation of the text facilitates the syntactic analysis of the sentence and frees mental capacity for the semantic analysis of the text. It may be expected, then, that especially poor readers will profit from training with such a RSVP presentation, which is what Juola, Haugh, Trast, Ferraro, and Liebhaver (1985) did indeed find. Text comprehension of poor readers was significantly better after training with the RSVP technique than after training with normal presentation on a display. Moreover, it appeared that good readers did not profit from RSVP presentation. The RSVP technique can probably be a useful means for the syntactic analysis of sentences.

The conclusion of this research is not that the RSVP technique is the method par excellence to increase text comprehension and reading speed. What might be concluded, however, is that insight into the syntactic and semantic processing of text may be of practical importance in determining the format of the presentation of information on a display. Furthermore, it seems worthwhile to investigate whether the RSVP technique can be of any help in learning to read, especially for children who have problems with the syntactic and semantic analysis of sentences.

References

Anderson R.C. & Pichert J.W. (1978). Recall of previous unrecallable information following a shift in perspective. *Journal of Verbal Learning and Verbal Behavior*, 17, pp. 1-12.

Anderson R.C., Pichert J.W. & Shirey L.L. (1983). Effects of the reader's schema at different points in time. *Journal of Educational Psychology*, 75, pp. 271-279.

Bartlett B.J. (1978). *Top-level structure as an organizational strategy for recall of classroom texts.* Unpublished doctoral dissertation, Arizona State University.

Borland R. & Flammer A. (1985). Encoding and retrieval processes in memory for prose. *Discourse Processes*, 8, pp. 305-317.

Bouma H. & de Voogd, A.H. (1974). On the control of eye saccades in reading. *Vision Research*, 14, pp. 273-284.

Broek P. van den & Trabasso T. (1986). Causal networks versus goal hierarchies in summarizing text. *Discourse Processes*, 9, pp. 1-15.

Brown G. & Yale G. (1983). *Discourse analysis.* Cambridge University Press, Cambridge.

Brown C.M., Marslen-Wilson W.D. & Tyler L.K. (in preparation). Contextual factors in word recognition.

Carpenter P.A. & Daneman M. (1981). Lexical retrieval and error recovery in reading: A model based on eye fixations. *Journal of Verbal Learning and Verbal Behaviour*, 20, pp. 137-160.

Cirilo R.K. & Foss D.J. (1980). Text structure and reading time for sentences. *Journal of Verbal Learning and Verbal Behaviour*, 19, pp. 96-109.

Clark H.H. & Clark E.V. (1977). *Psychology and language.* Harcourt, Brace, Jovanovich, New York.

Cocklin T.G., Ward N.J., Chen H.C. & Juola J.F. (1984). Factors influencing readability of rapidly presented text segments. *Memory and Cognition*, 12, pp. 431-442.

Fodor J.A. (1983). *Modularity of mind.* M.I.T. Press, Cambrigde, MA.

Fodor J.A. & Garrett M.F. (1967). Some syntactic determinants of sentential complexity. *Perception and Psychophysics*, 3, pp. 453-461.

Forster K.I. (1970). Visual perception of rapidly presented word sequences of varying complexity. *Perception and Psychophysics*, 8, pp. 215-221.

Goodman K.S. (1970). Reading: a psycholinguistic guessing game. In: *Theoretical models and processes of reading.* H. Singer & R.R. Ruddle (Eds.). International Reading Association, Newark.

Gould J.D. & Grischkowsky N. (1984). Doing the same work with hard copy and with cathode-ray-tube (CRT) computer terminals. *Human Factors*, 26, pp. 323-337.

Graf R. & Torrey J.W. (1966). Perception of phrase structure in written language. *American Psycological Association Convention Proceedings*, pp 83-84.

Halliday M.A.K. (1967). Notes on transitivity and theme in English: II. *Journal of Linguistics*, 3, pp. 199-244.

Haviland S.E. & Clark H.H. (1974). What's new? Acquiring new information as a process in comprehension. *Journal of Verbal Learning and Verbal Behaviour*, 13, pp. 512-521.

Juola J.F., Haugh D., Trast S., Ferraro F.R. & Liebhaber M. (1985). *Reading with and without eye movements.* Paper presented at the third European conference on eye movement, Dourdan, France.

Juola J.F., Ward N.J. & McNamara T. (1982). Visual search and reading of rapid serial presentation of letter strings, words and text. *Journal of Experimental Psychology, General*, 11, pp. 208-227.

Just M.A. & Carpenter P.A. (1980). A theory of reading: From eye fixations to comprehension. *Psychological Review*, 87, pp. 329-354.

Kintsch W., Kozminsky E., Streby W.J., McKoon G. & Keenan J.M. (1975). Comprehension and recall of text as a function of content variables. *Journal of Verbal Learning and Verbal Behaviour*, 14, pp. 196-214.

Kleiman G.M. (1975). Speech recoding in reading. *Journal of Verbal Language and Verbal Behaviour*, 14, pp. 323-339.

Kruk R. & Muter P. (1984). Reading of continuous text on video screens. *Human Factors*, 26, pp. 339-345.

Levy B.A. (1978). Speech processes during reading. In: *Cognitive psychology and instruction*. A.M. Lesgold, J.W. Pellegrino, S.D. Fokkema & R. Glaser (Eds.), Plenum Press, New York.

Mandler J.M. & Johnson N.S. (1977). Remembrance of things parsed: story structure and recall. *Cognitive Psychology*, 9, pp. 111-151.

Marslen-Wilson W.D. & Tyler L.K. (1975). Processing structure of sentence perception. *Nature*, 257, pp. 784-786.

Marslen-Wilson W.D. & Welsh A. (1978). Processing interactions and lexical access during word recognition in continuous speech. *Cognitive Psychology*, 10, pp. 29-63.

McClelland J.L. & Rumelhart D.E. (1981). An interactive activation model of content effects in letter perception: Part 1. An account of basic findings. *Psychological Review*, 88, pp. 375-407.

McConkie G.W. (1978). *Where do we read?* Paper presented at the Psychonomic Society meetings, San Antonio.

McKoon G. & Ratcliff R. (1980). The comprehension processes and memory structures involved in anaphoric reference. *Journal of Verbal Learning and Verbal Behaviour*, 19, pp. 668-682.

Meyer D.E., Schvaneveldt R.W. & Ruddy M.G. (1974) Functions of graphemic and phonemic codes in visual word recognition. *Memory and Cognition*, 2, pp. 309-321.

Milne R.W. (1982). Predicting garden path sentences. *Cognitive Science*, 6, pp. 349-373.

Muter P., Latremouille S.A., Treurniet W.C. & Beam P. (1982). Extended reading from continuous text on television screens. *Human Factors*, 24, pp. 501-508.

Potter M.C. (1984). Rapid serial visual presentation (RSVP): A method for studying language processing. In: *New methods in reading comprehension research*. D.E. Kieras & M.A. Just (Eds.).

Rayner K. (1977). Visual attention in reading: Eye movements reflect cognitive processes. *Memory and Cognition*, 4, pp. 443-448.

Rayner K. (1978). Eye movements in reading and information processing. *Psychological Bulletin*, 85, pp. 618-660.

Reicher G.M. (1969). Perceptual recognition as a function of meaningfulness of stimulus material. *Journal of Experimental Psychology*, 81, pp. 274-280.

Reiser B.J. & Black J.B. (1982). Processing and structural models of comprehension. *Text*, 2, pp. 225-252.

Thorndyke P.W. (1977). Cognitive structures in comprehension and memory of narrative discourse. *Cognitive Psychology*, 9, pp. 77-110.

Thorndyke P.W. (1979). Toward a model of text comprehension and production. *Cognitive Psychology*, 9, pp. 77-110.

Vonk W. & Noordman L.G.M. (1984). *Reader's perspective and encoding of text*. Paper presented at the 26. Tagung experimentell-arbeitender Psychologen, Nürnberg.

Vonk W., Noordman L.G.M. & Kempff H.J. (1984). Tekstbegrip en inferenties: wordt tijdens het lezen meer begrepen dan dat er staat? In: *Het Leesproces*. A.J.W.M. Thomassen, L.G.M. Noordman & P.A.T.M. Eling (Eds.), Swets and Zeitlinger, Lisse.

Wilensky R. (1983). Story grammars versus story points. *Behavioral and Brain Science*, 6, pp. 579-623.

Chapter 8. The Effect on Reading Speed of Word Divisions at the End of a Line

Gerard L.J. Nas

1. Introduction

The more comprehensive software for text processing usually includes a facility which automatically breaks words at the end of a line printed on the screen of a monitor or on paper. The ergonomic qualities of this facility can be examined from two points of view. It can be evaluated on its user friendliness from the point of view of a typist, or it can be evaluated from the perspective of a reader. In this study the latter point of view was taken.

In some books, newspaper articles, and television news programs breaking words at the end of a line of print is consistently avoided. The reason for this policy seems to be that it is assumed to be kind to readers if words are only printed in their undivided format. In most newspaper articles and books, however, words are broken whenever the end of a line is reached. The question then arises which policy is more closely related to word recognition processes taking place in readers. In the former case it is apparently assumed that decomposing a word, as is done when a word is broken at the end of a line, does not match any similar procedure in the reading process. This assumption is supported by the view that both morphologically complex and simple words are fully represented in the mental lexicon (Jackendoff, 1975). Hence, any decomposition, such as takes place in word division, makes it necessary for a reader to add an extra procedure to his/her reading process in which the decomposed word is put together again before access is gained to the mental lexicon. For example, if it is assumed that the word *decision* is represented fully in the mental lexicon (Jackendoff, 1975), breaking this word at the end of a line would have to result in the additional coupling procedure discussed above. Otherwise, how could effective matching take place between the two separate parts of the word being read and its undivided representation in the mental lexicon? In this view the assumption is correct that breaking words at the end of a line is not reader friendly.

Jackendoff does not discuss the representation of orthographic information in the mental lexicon. However, in psychological models of lexical access (Forster, 1976; Morton, 1979) it is assumed that this information is represented at the same level of specification as the phonological representation of a word. However, if it is assumed that the stems of morphologically complex words are represented as separate units in the mental lexicon (referred to as the impoverished entry theory by Jackendoff, 1975), and if it is assumed that during reading words are decomposed into morphemic units before access is gained to the mental lexicon (Taft and Forster, 1975), word division could be regarded as a service to readers. The necessary decomposition of structurally complex words has already been performed in the text and hence need not be carried out by the reader himself.

The latter views of an impoverished representation of morphologically complex words in the mental lexicon and of a corresponding procedure of morphological decomposition before lexical access are reflected more in (British) English word division than in the Dutch rules for breaking words at the end of a line. While rules for British English mainly take the morpheme as the unit of division (Quirk, Greenbaum, Leech & Svartvik, 1972, p. 1057), Dutch rules rely more on the syllable as a unit of word division (Kruyskamp, 1976). This means that in many Dutch words the appropriate points at which a word may be broken off do not coincide with their morpheme boundaries. For example, in the Dutch word *denken* (think) syllable division results in *den ken*, thus separating the *k* from the morpheme to which it belongs, *denk*. If the view of morphological decomposition before access to the mental lexicon is taken, word divisions at syllable boundaries cannot be considered a helpful practice as long as they do not coincide with morpheme boundaries.

If the effect of word divisions on reading is to be investigated, the above accounts of word recognition, of lexical storage and of word division rules make it clear that not only the practice of breaking words but also the rules governing that practice have to be taken into consideration. This applies especially to the Dutch rules of word division in which syllabic rather than morphemic principles prevail. Below, four experiments are reported addressing these problems both for silent reading and for reading aloud

2. Silent Reading

2.1. Experiment 1

2.1.1. Material

In this experiment reading times for a text with word divisions were compared with reading times for the same text without any word divisions. It was a narrative text of 50 lines (344 words) adapted from a story taken from a periodical. For reasons explained later, this text was divided into two parts of 25 lines each. Each part in turn was subdivided into seven. For the experimental condition in which word divisions were to be tested, a word was broken at the end of each available line. For the two halves together this amounted to 48 word divisions. The following examples show the first part of the text for both experimental conditions:

1. Als gewoonlijk kom ik nogal laat het
   gebouw binnen. Een zwaai naar de portier,
   die met haar collega aan de koffie
   zit.
2. Als gewoonlijk kom ik nogal laat het ge-
   bouw binnen. Een zwaai naar de por-
   tier, die met haar collega aan de kof-
   fie zit.

2.1.2. Design

Figure 1 shows that the two text halves and the two experimental conditions were arranged in a split-plot design (Winer, 1971, pp. 366-371) with two reading sessions and an intervening word identification experiment which will be discussed later. The split-plot design ensured that each subject was tested in both experimental conditions and that the same text was involved in these conditions. Moreover, dividing each text-half into seven parts ensured that the reading times of the two conditions could be compared at seven points, which was thought to contribute to a reliable comparison of the data. The second

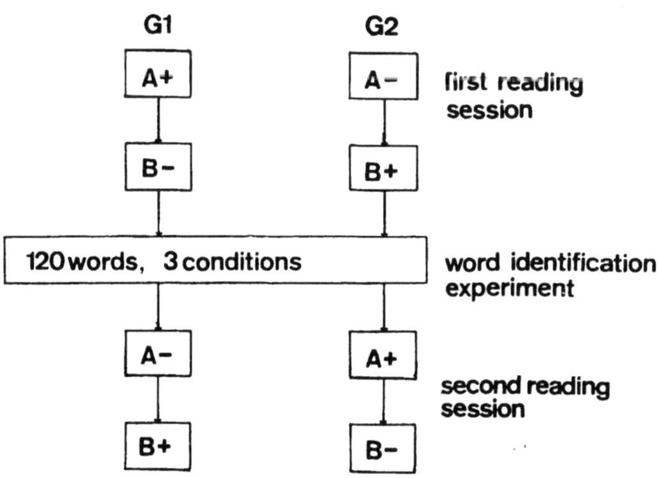

Figure 1. Order in which the two text halves (A and B) and the two experimental conditions (+ word divisions and − word divisions) appeared in the design. The subjects were divided into two groups (G1 and G2)

part of the design was a replication of the first, but with the order of the text conditions reversed. It was meant to see if the results of the first part of the experiment remained the same if the subjects were already familiar with the semantic content of the story.

The separate word identification experiment was put in between the two parts of the text reading experiment in order to ensure that the subjects would only recall the events described in the text but not the exact wording. Although research has shown that the exact words that have been read are soon lost from memory (Sachs, 1967; Wanner, 1974), the distracting influence of the word identification experiment was thought to ensure that this loss indeed occurred. Thus, in the second half of the experiment it would be possible to confront subjects with new versions of both text-halves in which word divisions had been introduced or left out, and to expect these subjects to read the words of the text in much the same way as they had done the first time. Thus, it would be possible to compare the data of the first part of the experiment with those of the second.

2.1.3. Procedure

In the written instructions the subjects were introduced to the relevant aspects of the design and to the purpose of the experiment. They were asked to read carefully the text which appeared on a monitor and to press the space bar on the keyboard in front of them as soon as they had finished reading the part of the text that was visible on the screen. Speed and accuracy were equally stressed and the procedure was repeated with a separate text until both the experimenter and the subject were satisfied with the result. The subjects were told that they would have to answer questions about the contents of the story after each text-half.

The entire experiment was computer-controlled. To begin the experiment subjects pressed the space bar. For 250 ms an asterisk appeared on a monitor indicating where the first word of part one of the text would appear. The computer measured the time from the appearance of the first word until the moment the space bar was pressed indicating that the subject had finished reading the part of the text on the screen. The asterisk reappeared and the procedure was repeated until a text-half had been read. Then some questions were asked about the contents of the story. After that the procedure was repeated for the second half of the text.

The text was in upper case for greater legibility. Pretesting had shown that the lower-case character set used by the computer was confusing to some readers. This was not the case with capital letters.

Before the subjects read the text for a second time, in the third part of the experiment, they again received written instructions informing them about the changes in the experimental conditions. They were asked to read the text in the same way as they had done the first time. Again they were asked questions about the contents after having read a text half. Of course, these questions were not the same as before. The questions were only to ensure that the subjects would pay attention to the contents of the text.

2.1.4. Subjects

After rejecting the subjects whose data could not be used because of irregularities in the registration of their reading times, a total of 17 subjects contributed to the results of the experiment. Nine of them read the text halves in the order A+, B− during the first reading session and A−, B+ during the second. Most of the subjects were language students at the University of Utrecht, and some were members of the academic staff of the Institute of Phonetics. The students were paid for their services.

2.1.5. Data Treatment and Analysis

In the analysis, mean reading times were calculated for each of the 14 parts of the text, for both text conditions and for both reading sessions. Then a three way analysis of variance (ANOVA) was done in which "text condition" and "reading session" were taken as fixed factors and "part of text" as a random factor (Keppel, 1973, p. 425ff).

2.1.6. Results and Discussion

The mean reading times for the entire text, for both text conditions and for both reading sessions are shown in Figure 2. From the figure it appears that results were similar for both reading sessions. It took subjects longer to read the text versions with word divisions than those without. Analysis of variance of the reading times per part of the text supports this observation ($F(1,13)=13.22$, $p<.005$). In the first reading session the mean difference between the two text conditions was 6 s. This amounts to a mean extra reading time of 125 ms per word division. For the second reading session this extra time is 133 ms per word division.

Figure 2 also shows that reading the same text for a second time resulted in lower means for both conditions. The mean difference was 15 s for both experimental conditions. This observation is supported by an ANOVA ($F(1,13)=13.34, p<.005$). Finally, there was no interaction between the factors "text condition" and "reading session" ($F<1$).

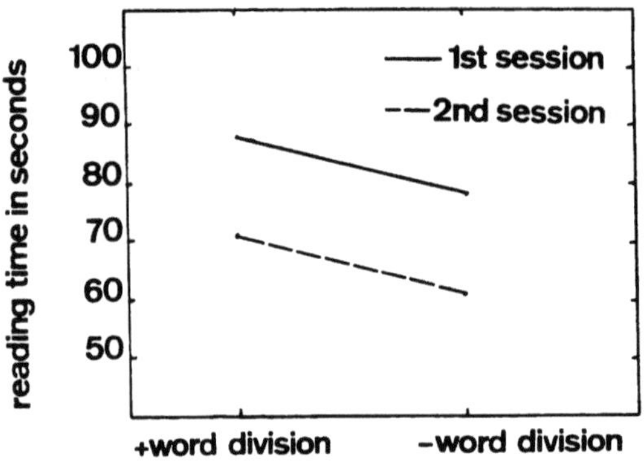

Figure 2. Mean reading times for two text conditions and for two sessions of silent reading

How far these results can be attributed to the design of the experiment, to the subjects, and to the Dutch rules of word division, will be considered in the following discussion.

The experiment was self-paced, i.e., the subjects were not put under any time pressure during reading. Therefore the differences in reading times for the different text conditions are unlikely to be the result of some time artifact.

The subjects had to press the space bar when they wanted to read the next part of the text. This may have slowed down their reading rate but it is unlikely to have affected their reading strategy. Moreover, this factor affected all conditions equally. Therefore, the direction of the results, slower reading times for the text versions with words broken at the end of a line and faster reading times for the second reading session, is not thought to have been affected by this extra task. However, it is likely to have resulted in longer reading times than would have been found if real-time measurement of their reading had been possible.

In the text condition in which words were broken at the end of each line the number of word divisions of course far exceeded that found in normal texts. This is thought to be a quantitative difference only and is therefore not considered to have influenced the reading behaviour of the subjects. This view is based on the fact that the subjects were prepared for the word divisions in the instructions for the experiment.

In the experiment the subjects read the texts on a monitor in front of them. Therefore their angle of vision is likely to have been different from the angle that would have been adopted if the texts had appeared in the format of newspaper columns. Likewise, the angle may have differed from the one taken when reading a text on a television screen at home. These differences in angle of vision would be particularly important if they affected the speed with which readers could move their eyes from the first part of a divided word to the second. This would limit conclusions based on the results of this experiment to reading a text on a monitor. The eye-movement literature that I have consulted did not offer any information on a possible effect of the angle of vision on reading speed.

As for a possible effect of the reading skill of the subjects who took part in the experiment, they were all considered to be skilled readers. Yet their reading speed decreased when they had to read text in which words were broken off at the end of a line. It seems likely that this result would also appear if subjects with a lower degree of reading skill were used. Otherwise it would have to be assumed that a lower degree of skill is associated with a more effective procedure to deal with word division. Therefore it is assumed that the results of this experiment extend to readers with a lesser degree of skill as well.

Finally, it has to be considered whether the word division rules of the language of the experiment, Dutch, could have affected the results. This may have been the case. As mentioned in the Introduction, Dutch rules for word division are based on the syllable as the unit of division. It was also mentioned that from a theoretical point of view, the syllable need not be the unit which is most effective for word recognition. Instead the most effective unit may be the morpheme. Therefore, it could be that the slower reading times found in the text versions with word divisions were the result of some delay in the process of word recognition caused by the wrong unit of lexical access, viz. the syllable. This interpretation is supported by the fact that in 25 cases in the text word divisions coincided with syllable boundaries. Consequently, it could be that word divisions falling only on morpheme boundaries would result in lexical access without any delay, and hence result in the same reading times for text versions with word divisions and without. In order to test this hypothesis Experiment 2 was done.

2.2. Experiment 2

2.2.1. Material

In order to test the hypothesis discussed above, the obvious solution seems to be to use the same text as for Experiment 1. However, creating two versions of that text, one with words broken at syllable boundaries and the other with the same words broken at morpheme boundaries, is unnatural. It either results in word divisions that are not permitted according to Dutch rules or in no word divisions at all, if the word concerned has two syllables but is at the same time monomorphematic. Therefore, a solution was sought using isolated words that could be matched on features that were likely to affect their reading times such as word frequency, word length, number of syllables, and word class.

Although reading isolated words cannot easily be compared to reading a text it has the advantage of allowing for a clear comparison between the effect of syllable and morpheme divisions on the recognition of words broken at the end of a line of print. And this was exactly what was needed if the hypothesis of a superiority of morpheme divisions over syllable divisions were to be tested. Therefore isolated words were considered to be suitable for this experiment.

In order to create the necessary experimental conditions, i.e., words broken at syllable boundaries and matching words broken at a morpheme boundary, advantage can be taken of the fact that in Dutch spelling syllable and morpheme boundaries often coincide. This applies to all words that have a closed vowel in their stem, which has to be preserved in a single consonant. For example, the verb stem *val* (fall) is given a double *l* if a suffix is added to the stem, as in *vallen*. When this word is divided the boundary occurs between the two *l* s, *val-len*. As far as the verb stem *val* is concerned, this boundary is both the syllable and the morpheme boundary. If on the other hand the matching verb *denken* is considered (see above for the definition of matching that applies here) its stem *denk* ends in two consonants. Consequently, Dutch rules of word division state that the boundary occurs in between *n* and *k*, so that the word has to be broken off after the *n* into *den-ken*. In this case the syllable boundary, after *den*, does not coincide with the morpheme boundary, after *denk*. By selecting word pairs that all match on the points mentioned above but at the same time differ in their word divisions in the same way as the otherwise matching verbs *denken* and *vallen*, the effects of word divisions at syllable boundaries can be compared with divisions at morpheme boundaries.

For reasons to be explained, threesomes were selected of words that were matched on the features mentioned above. They were all taken from a Dutch frequency count (Uit den Boogaart, 1975), and all three members belonged to the same frequency class, had the same number of letters (±1), the same number of syllables, and belonged to the same word class. Altogether 40 threesomes were selected. The following are some examples:

niemand, el-kaar, zo-veel
verdedigen, verbe-teren, terug-keren
herinnering, geschie-denis, burge-meester
tevreden, vre-selijk, on-bekend

2.2.2. Design

This experiment was performed between the two text reading sessions, for reasons already explained. The 40 threesomes were mixed in a random order.

2.2.3. Procedure and Subjects

After an introduction to the purpose and character of the experiment, written instructions informed the subjects that they had to press the space bar in order to start the experiment. An asterisk followed by a row of dots appeared on the screen for 250 ms to indicate the spot on which either the first half of a word would become visible together with a hyphen, or an entire word. If only one half of a word was visible on the right side of the screen the subjects were to move their heads to the left to read the second half which appeared one line down 40 ms after the first half of the word had appeared on the screen. In a pretest it had been established that the movement of the head necessary to direct the eyes from the right side of the screen to the left took up sufficient time for this 40 ms delay to go unnoticed. Yet the time span was sufficiently long to create a noticeably longer latency if a subject started reading at the left side of the screen instead of the right. By means of this longer latency, and by the fact that the wrong starting position of the head would be visible to the experimenter, procedural errors on the part of a subject would be clearly indicated and the responses involved could be marked as wrong. Such incorrect responses could then be excluded from data analysis.

The task of the subjects was to read the word on the screen and to press the space bar as soon as they had identified it. This manual identification task was considered to be prefarable to a vocal one because it resulted in faster latencies and posed fewer measurement problems. When a subject pressed the space bar the stimulus disappeared from the screen and there was a 2s period in which the subject could report the word he had identified. The computer measured the time elapsing between the appearance of a stimulus on the screen and the moment the space bar was pressed by a subject. The vocal report was marked as correct or incorrect by the experimenter. The incorrect responses were not considered during data analysis. Before the experiment started the subjects were trained until both subject and experimenter were satisfied with the result. The same 17 subjects that took part in Experiment 1 participated in this experiment.

2.2.4. Data Treatment and Analysis

As mentioned above only the correct answers were included in the analysis. As recommended by Clark (1973) both "subjects" and "words" were treated

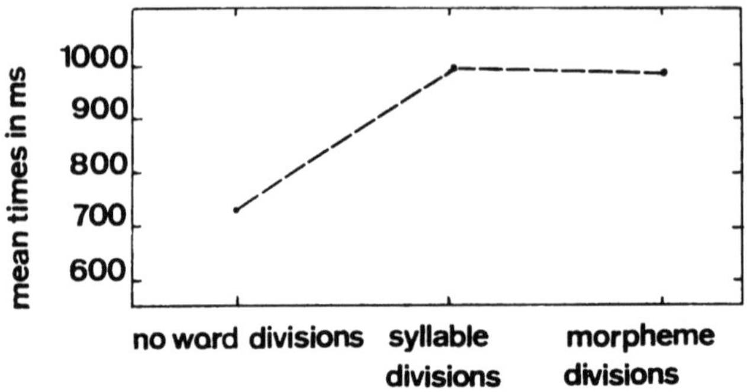

Figure 3. Mean word identification times for three word conditions

as random factors in an ANOVA. As also recommended by Clark (1973), the result of this ANOVA will be expressed in min F'.

2.2.5. Results and Discussion

The mean word identification times are given in Figure 3. This shows that there is a large difference between the mean of the undivided words on the one hand and the means of the two word-division conditions on the other. The difference with the word-division by syllable condition is 271 ms, and with the word-division by morpheme condition it is 255 ms. This is much larger than the differences of 125 and 133 ms that were calculated for Experiment 1. However, it has to be taken into account that in this experiment the subjects had to move their heads from right to left in order to read the divided words. This was not the case with the undivided words. This factor is thought to explain why the difference between the means for the undivided and divided words is quite large. In the first experiment such a difference in head movements did not occur because there the subjects had to move their heads in both conditions. Therefore the differences found in Experiment 1 are thought to be a better estimate of the extra reading time needed for words that are broken than the times that were registered for this experiment. The data on the undivided words will be left out of the discussion because they are not relevant to the hypothesis to be tested.

It remains to be discussed that the means for the two word-division conditions (944 and 928 ms) are rather high compared with the means that are usually reported for experiments using a comparable task like lexical decision. Consequently, it could be argued that the data on the two types of word-division do not tell us anything useful about much faster processes like reading words. However, in this case essentially the same argument as above is thought to apply when discussing the difference between the means for the divided and the undivided words. First of all, the mean of 673 ms for the undivided condition is well within the range of the means to be found in reports on reaction time experiments. Secondly, the slower times for the two types of word division were obtained with the same task and could be attributed, as above, to head and eye movements. Consequently, the task used in this experiment is thought to be sufficiently sensitive to differences in processing time to tell us something about the reading of the two types of word division.

The data on the two types of word division suggest that word divisions that only coincided with syllable boundaries were identified more slowly than those in which syllable and morpheme boundaries occurred together. However, the difference of 16 ms between the two means was not statistically significant (min $F' = 1.71$). The percentage of errors by the subjects for all 120 words ranged from 0 to 2.9%. The mean percentage was 0.84%. This low percentage of errors indicates that the task did not present any special problems to the subjects.

Before any conclusions are drawn, it must be considered how far the results may have to be attributed to factors other than the experimental variables. As was argued in the discussion of the results of Experiment 1, the subjects were skilled readers. Yet, it was argued, there is no reason to assume that readers with a lower degree of skill would have produced a different pattern of results. This is also thought to apply to the results of this experiment.

Another variable that may have influenced the results of the experiments is the uniqueness point of the words used in the syllable and morpheme conditions. The concept of the uniqueness point of a word has been developed as part of the cohort model of spoken word recognition (Marslen-Wilson & Welsh, 1978). According to this model, the process of word recognition can be characterized as follows: the first few phonemes of a word activate in memory the representations of words that begin with these phonemes. These activated representations constitute a cohort. As more phonemes become available to the word recognition mechanism, representations remove themselves from the cohort if their features do not match the incoming information. In a short time all representations but one have removed themselves from the cohort on account of their diverging features. The point where only one candidate remains for recognition is called the uniqueness point of that word.

Reading divided words may be similar to listening to spoken words in the sense that word representations in memory are activated on the basis of incoming information about that word. In the case of reading divided words this would mean the activation of word candidates by the first part of a divided word while the eyes move from the right side of the page to the beginning of the next line on the left. In that case it would be advantageous if the first half of a divided word already contained the uniqueness point of that word.

If the concept of the uniqueness point is applied to the results of this experiment it could be that all or nearly all of the words that were used both in the syllable and in the morpheme conditions were broken off on or after their uniqueness points. In that case divisions on syllable or morpheme boundaries would not make any difference to the time needed for their recognition. Hence the concept of the uniqueness point would explain why no effect was found in this experiment.

Inspection of the words showed that in only three words was the uniqueness point passed when these words were broken. The word divisions concerned are: afschu-welijk, aankij-ken and eenvou-dig. Out of a total of 80 word divisions these three words cannot have brought about the results of this experiment. Moreover, a comparison of the means of these three words with the means of their counterparts in the experiment by means of a sign test showed that no significant differences in response times had occurred. In summary, this shows that the results of this experiment cannot be attributed to the uniqueness points of the words used in the experiment.

If the results of Experiment 2 can only be attributed to the two variables of syllable and morpheme word divisions, the conclusion can only be that no support has been found for the hypothesis that word divisions at morpheme boundaries result in faster word recognition times than do divisions at syllable boundaries. Hence, there is no reason to expect that the results of Experiment 1 would have been any different if only word divisions at morpheme boundaries had occurred in the text.

In the Introduction the hypothesis of faster recognition times for word divisions at morpheme boundaries in Dutch words was based on the theory that morphological decomposition occurs as part of the process of word recognition. The fact that the hypothesis was not supported by the results of this experiment implies that, at least for Dutch word divisions, no evidence has been found for such decomposition. This applies to both Experiments 1 and 2. Instead, the results support the alternative hypothesis, also discussed in the introduction, that decomposed words, such as divided words, have to be restored by readers to their undivided format in an additional coupling procedure before access can be gained to the mental representations of these words. This restoration procedure would explain why, in Experiment 1, reading times for the text with word divisions were slower than those in the text without any word divisions.

3. Reading Aloud

3.1. Introduction

There are many occasions on which professional or nonprofessional readers have to read a text aloud. Often such texts are typewritten. In typing, words are regularly broken. Therefore, it is relevant to ask if the results of the first two experiments also apply to reading aloud. Reviews of research into the process of reading aloud show that the answer is by no means clear (Henderson, 1982). Yet this answer could be of importance to all those who have to do their reading aloud within a certain time. It may be assumed that in general this is the case with news readers and with those who have to read out a spoken comment upon a filmed event.

It is particularly relevant to see if words that are broken and that have to be read aloud are subject to the same constraints as those that are read silently, and thus show the same results as were found in the first two experiments. In order to determine this, two similar experiments were performed, but with a different task.

3.2. Experiment 3

3.2.1. Subjects and Procedure

The two aspects in which this experiment differed from Experiment 1 were the subjects and the task. Seventeen subjects took part in this experiment. Although they were also students or staff members none of them had taken part in the first two experiments. Their task was to read the text aloud and press the space-bar at the moment they had finished speaking. The computer measured the time elapsing from the moment a piece of text appeared on the screen until the moment the space bar was pressed. This time span was chosen in order to be certain that hesitations in reading aloud the second part of a divided word, which might occur because the second part had not yet been fully processed when reading that part aloud was to begin, would be included in the measurement. Moreover, this procedure was thought to be a more adequate representation of real-time processes during reading aloud than the more usual latency measurements, which do not include the last phase of the process, vocalization. The task was practised until the experimenter was satisfied with the accuracy of the performance of the subject.

3.2.2. Results and Discussion

The mean reading times for the entire text, for both reading sessions and for both text conditions, are shown in Figure 4. This shows that the results of

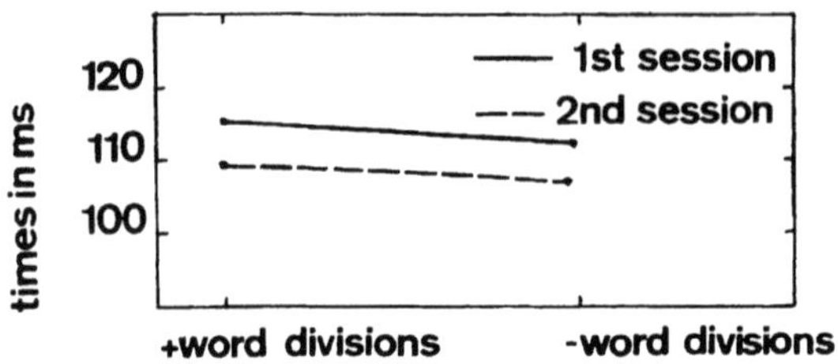

Figure 4. Mean reading times for two text conditions and for two sessions of reading aloud

Experiment 1 are essentially replicated. This time too, it took the subjects longer to read the text version with words broken at the end of each line than the version without any word divisions. There was a difference of 4 s between the two means. The ANOVA shows that this difference is significant ($F(1,13)=14.20, p<.005$). Likewise, reading the text a second time resulted in lower reading times. The difference between the two means was 4 s for the text containing word divisons and 5 s for the condition without any word divisions. This difference was significant ($F(1,13)=34.58, p<.001$). Finally, as in Experiment 1, there was no interaction between text condition and reading session ($F<1$). This indicates that while reading aloud the text for the second time, the subjects did not benefit from their previous experience with the text when dealing with words that were broken.

Not surprisingly, this experiment shows slower reading times than Experiment 1. However, the interesting finding is that otherwise the results are the same for both experiments. This seems to indicate that the processes of silent reading and of reading aloud have some part of the word recognition system in common, the most obvious common part being the procedure of access to the mental lexicon.

The difference in time gain between silent reading and reading aloud when dealing with the same text for a second time (in Experiment 1 this gain was on average 15 s, in Experiment 3 it was reduced to an average of 4.5 s) could be explained by a difference in the kind and detail of information needed for the two reading modes. When reading silently the emphasis is on meaning. On the other hand, when reading aloud, pronunciation is emphasized. The former kind of information remained available to the subjects for long enough and in sufficient detail for them to be able to benefit from it when reading the same text again silently. Hence the relatively large time gain in the second reading session of Experiment 1. On the other hand, the phonological information needed for the pronunciation of the individual words was lost from memory soon after the subjects of Experiment 3 had read the text aloud for the first time (see the Introduction, where this early loss of information about the individual words of a text has already been discussed for both reading modes). Therefore. this information had to be retrieved again. Consequently. the subjects of Experiment 3 could not benefit from their previous experience with the text to the same extent as the subjects of Experiment 1.

For the results for the two text conditions, which were the same for reading aloud as they were for silent reading, the obvious conclusion seems to be that word divisions slow down readers to a comparable extent when reading aloud and when reading silently. In other words, in neither reading mode can word divisions be considered reader friendly.

3.3. Experiment 4

3.3.1. Procedure

In this experiment the same material, apparatus, and design were used as for Experiment 2, but again task and subjects were different. The subjects were the same 17 students and staff members that had taken part in Experiment 3. The task was the same as for the previous experiment, i.e., the subjects had to read aloud the word that appeared on the screen and they had to press the space bar as soon as they had finished pronouncing that word. For this experiment practice also continued until the experimenter was satisfied with the accuracy of the performance of a subject.

3.3.2. Results and Discussion

The mean reading times for the three word conditions are shown in Figure 5. As before, only correct responses were included in the analysis. Apart from the slower reading times the results of this experiment are essentially the same

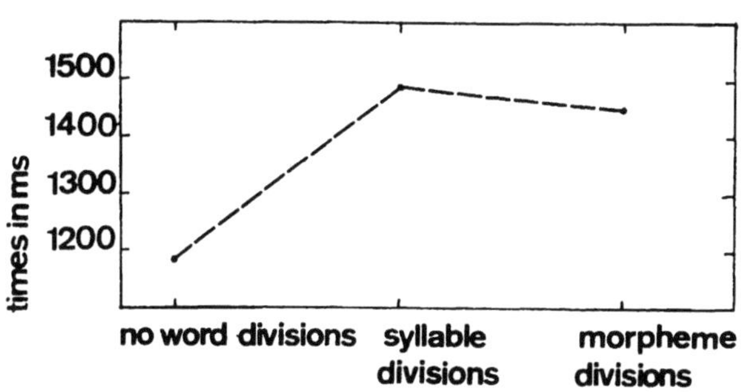

Figure 5. Mean reading times for three word conditions

as those of Experiment 2. Again, the mean for the syllable condition is somewhat higher than the mean for the morpheme condition (43 ms), but again the difference is not statistically reliable (min $F' = 1.80$). The percentage of incorrect responses ranged from 0 to 4%. The mean was 0.6%, which indicates that this task again presented no problem to the subjects. As the results of this experiment replicate those of Experiment 2, the same conclusions apply to both. Again, no support was found for the hypothesis that the morpheme is a better unit of word division than the syllable.

From a theoretical point of view there is again the interesting result that a difference in reading times is the only factor that distinguishes the results of Experiments 2 and 4. This strengthens the interpretation put forward when discussing the results of the previous experiment, i.e., that the mental lexicon was consulted both for silent reading and for reading aloud. At the same time this result does not support the view that reading aloud could be characterized as a process in which only grapheme-phoneme conversion takes place.

4. Summary

Now that the results of the four experiments have been discussed, it is appropriate to bring to the fore again the perspective from which the research questions were formulated. This is the perspective of reading ergonomics. It is relevant to ask what the effect on reading is if words are broken at the end of a line of print. This question is particularly relevant if it is taken into account that it seems to be the policy of some printers, or others who are responsible for the lay-out of printed texts, to avoid breaking words altogether.

These two opposite policies could be based on opposing views of the effect of word divisions on reading. If breaking words is avoided it would seem to relate to the view that reading is somehow hampered if breaks occur. On the other hand, if the more prevalent practice of word division is followed, this would relate to the view that reading is a process which allows readers to deal with words both in their divided and undivided formats equally effectively. Clearly, such opposing assumptions about the reading process had to be taken into account in this research. The next paragraph deals with this aspect.

In the Introduction two opposing theoretical views of the mental representation of words were discussed that can be brought to bear on the two ways of ending a line of print. One view states that all words, including those consisting of two or more morphemes, are fully represented in the mental lexicon. This view was thought to be incompatible with the practice of word division because it requires readers to put both parts of divided words together again before matching can take place with their representations in the mental lexicon.

The theoretical view to which the policy of word division can be related is that of a mental lexicon in which the morpheme or morphemes of which a word consists is/are stored separately. The process of gaining access to these mental representations is described in a psychological model of morphological decomposition that was also discussed in the Introduction. According to this model, words consisting of two or more morphemes are decomposed into their respective morphemic units before the mental lexicon is consulted. The words that are thus decomposed are then matched with their representations in the mental lexicon.

In two experiments, Experiments 1 and 3, the above views were tested both for silent reading and reading aloud. The results showed that reading a text with word divisions took longer than reading the same text without any word divisions. In the two other experiments, 2 and 4, the hypothesis was tested that word divisions at morpheme boundaries would result in faster identification (Experiment 2) or faster reading times (Experiment 4) than word divisions at syllable boundaries. No support was found for this hypothesis. This result was interpreted as evidence against morphological decomposition. Since the result was identical for both experiments, this interpretation was thought to apply both to silent reading and to reading aloud. An explanation of the results of the experiments was attempted in terms of an additional coupling procedure needed to restore word divisions to their undivided format. The extra processing time taken up by this coupling procedure would explain why it took longer to read the texts of Experiments 1 and 3 in their versions with word divisions than in their versions without.

As mentioned in the Introduction, this research is not only meant to address a theoretial problem. At the same time its purpose is to answer a question about the reader friendliness of the practice of breaking words at the end of a line. As far as silent reading is concerned the results of the two experiments have clearly shown that word divisions slow readers down. In the discussion of the results of Experiment 1 it was estimated that the extra time needed to read word divisions is between 125 and 133 ms. If this is compared with the average time it takes to recognise an undivided word in print, which is generally estimated to be about 250 ms, it is clear that word divisions result in about 50% extra word recognition time. For reading aloud these differences are smaller, since the difference in mean reading times of the two text conditions of Experiment 3 was smaller than that in Experiment 1.

Another aspect of reader friendliness that was investigated in these experiments was the basis on which Dutch rules of word division are formulated. As explained in the Introduction, the syllable is the unit of word division for Dutch. In Experiment 2 it was investigated whether the morpheme would be preferable to the syllable. No statistically reliable evidence was found for this. This implies that there is no reason to propose changing Dutch rules of word division. As the above will have made clear it seems, on the other hand, more appropriate to propose avoiding word divisions altogether, especially if readers are given only limited time in which to read the text concerned.

However, at this moment this recommendation cannot be made without qualifications. These concern two possible negative effects of avoiding word division altogether in a manuscript. The first negative effect of avoiding word divisions altogether could be the indentations appearing on the right side of a page in their place. It could be argued that these indentations slow readers down more than do divided words because there is no fixed point on the page at which the eyes, and the head, have to be moved to the beginning of the next line. This situation prevailed in Experiments 1 and 3, in the condition without any word divisions. However, in spite of the indentations reading times were faster in this condition than they were in the condition with word divisions. Therefore no support was found in this research for the view that indentations at the right-hand side of a line of print could slow readers down to the same extent as word divisions.

The second, possibly negative effect may occur in the more advanced word processing software in which right justification sometimes results in gaps between words that are considerably larger than the usual space. If this right justification replaces word- division in text processing it could result in slower reading, because every time right justification occurs an eye-span encompasses a gap as well as text and consequently contains less information than would have been the case otherwise. Hence the slower reading rate. This research does not offer any information on this issue. Therefore the above recommendation to avoid using word divisions will be have to qualified for the moment and further research remains to be done to clear up this matter.

References

Clark H.H. (1973). The language-as-fixed-effect fallacy: a critique of language statistics in psychological research. *Journal of Verbal Learning and Verbal Behavior*, 12, pp. 335-59.

Forster K.I. (1976). Accessing the mental lexicon. In: *New approaches to language mechanisms.* R.J. Wales & E. Walker (Eds.) pp. 257-287. North Holland Publishing Company, Amsterdam.

Henderson L. (1982). *Orthography and word recognition in reading.* Academic Press, London.

Jackendoff R.S. (1975). Morphological and semantic regularities in the lexicon. *Language*, 51, pp. 639-671.

Keppel G. (1973). *Design and analysis: a researcher's handbook.* Prentice Hall, Englewood Cliffs, NJ.

Kruyskamp C. (1976). Beginselen van de Nederlandse spelling. In: *Groot Woordenboek der Nederlandse Taal, van Dale, IX-XXIX*, Martinus Nijhoff, Den Haag.

Marslen-Wilson W.D. & Welsh A. (1978). Processing interactions and lexical access during word recognition in continuous speech. *Cognitive Psychology*, 10, pp. 20-63.

Morton J. (1979). Word recognition. In: *Psycolinguistic structures and processes.* J. Morton & J.C. Marshall (Eds.) pp.107-156. Elek, London.

Quirk R., Greenbaum S., Leech G. & Svartvik J.A. (1972). *A grammar of contemporay English.* Seminar Press, London.

Sachs J.S. (1967). Recognition memory for semantic and syntactic aspects of connected discourse. *Perception and Psychophysics*, 2, pp. 437-442.

Taft M. & Forster K.I. (1975). Lexical storage and retrieval of prefixed words. *Journal of Verbal Learning and Verbal Behavior*, 14, pp. 638-647.

Uit den Boogaart P.C. (1975). *Woordfrequenties in gesproken en geschreven Nederlands.* Oosthoek, Scheltema & Holkema, Utrecht.

Wanner E. (1974). *On remembering, forgetting and understanding sentences.* Mouton, The Hague.

Winer B.J. (1971). *Statistical principles in experimental design.* McGraw-Hill Kogakusha, Tokyo.

Chapter 9. Document Processing

Louis G.Bouma, Jeroen Bruijning and Johannes C. van Vliet

Processing of documents using screen displays and computers is increasing greatly. Systems for processing documents vary from simple programs for drawing up letters and memos, to very advanced systems for producing books whose contents are complex. In this article an overview of important developments in this area is given. A glance into the office of the future is also given, in which advanced workstations will make it possible to manipulate and process texts (including formulas, tables, and drawings) interactively.

1. Introduction

Conveying information via writing is not new. In the south of France rock drawings have been found dating from 30000 B.C. Picture writing, in which pictograms are used (small drawings), is from a later period, and is also used today on traffic signs, on direction signs in stations, and so on. Hieroglyphic writing is a sort of intermediate form in which, besides pictograms, syllable marks and phonetic symbols appear. The last step in development is phonetic writing, which can be alphabetic or syllabic. Our writing is alphabetic, every letter representing a sound, while the Japanese Katakana is syllabic.

Hieroglyphic writing led, via Sinai writing, to the Phoenician system which used 22 consonants. The Phoenician system was made into a complete alphabet by the Greeks. Initially it was written from right to left, but later was written first one way and then the other, from left to right and then from right to left, as a farmer ploughs a field. Finally, the Romans developed the alphabet further. The Roman alphabet initially comprised 20 letters, to which at a later stage, the letters *G*, *Y*, and *Z* were added. In the 10th century a distinction was made between *U* and *V*, while only in the 17th century were the *I* and *J* separated; the *W* completed our present alphabet. Initially, an additive system was used for numbers as is found in Roman numbering. About 500 AD the 0 was "discovered" in India and a pure position system could arise in which the value of a cipher depends on its position in the number. The Indian ciphers were introduced into Europe by the Arabs in about 1000 A.D. For more detailed information about the origin and development of our writing, see Treebus (1983), Barthel (1972), and Diringer (1977).

Printed text also has a long history. The discovery of the art of book printing is generally attributed to Gutenberg (approx. 1440), who made loose type from metal. Because printed text had to resemble handwritten text as much as possible he had different versions of each letter, as well as a number of combinations (ligatures), and used about 300 characters.

Much earlier, prints were made using figures cut out of wood. In Europe this technique was used from the 6th century onwards for textile printing. In China in about 1000 A.D. prints were made from wooden blocks and loose symbols from baked clay. This discovery was not really of great importance because there was no alphabet and therefore many molds had to be kept. The oldest way of setting type is by hand. Standing behind "buck," a wooden piece of furniture with a slanting top, the hand-setter took lead letters from a type case with one hand and placed them in a small rack in the other hand. The lines were then filled up with blanks to make them all of the same length, and after that bound together in a mold. Hand-setting is now an almost extinct trade and a few of the type cases can be found as wall decorations in living rooms.

In the second half of the 19th century mechanical setting was developed. In Linotype, molds (thin copper plates with an engraved letter image) are assembled by hitting a keyboard. When a line is complete, lead is sprayed on a casting mold and a lead line of type is made. For corrections the whole line has to be re-set. With Monotype machines, the casting machine is used in a similar manner, but here the cast consists of loose type so there is more flexibility in correction. After the second world war phototypesetting was developed whereby characters were recorded on photographic film. Presently, phototypesetting machines are attached to computers. Text is input and stored using a terminal. Formatting is often a separate phase, and during this process the text is cast into paragraphs which are then sent to the phototypesetting machine. The formatting of the text is ruled by commands entered together with the text.

Since the rise of the art of book printing many fonts - sets of characters in a particular style - have been developed. Development of these is partially determined by technology: lead casting has different requirements for the precise formation of characters from photographic setting. For the reproduction of text on a display screen there are yet more constraints. Very often the text on a display screen is typographically far from perfect. This is to a large degree caused by the limited resolution of displays, current graphic displays often having a resolution of 70-100 bits (pixels) per inch. Phototypesetting machines have a resolution in the order of 1500 pixels per inch. Add to this the fact that ink flows, so the contours of the characters have a flowing form of their own. Special techniques have to be used to develop good legible fonts on displays (Bigelow & Day, 1983; Bigelow, 1985). One of the possibilities is to offer for each pixel a number of grey values as well as the "black" and "white." The design of type fonts is a separate trade, into which the computer can also be brought. IMP (Carter, 1984), LIP (Flowers, 1984) and Metafont (Knuth, 1979) are state-of-the-art examples of (interactive) systems for the design of letter shapes. For more detailed information on typography and the different setting methods, see Treebus (1983) and Groenendaal (1975).

In this article an overview will be given of the different systems that have been developed for the electronic processing of documents. In the following section a division is proposed between systems for processing texts in which use is made of simple graphic possibilities, such as letters and memos, and systems for processing complex material. In Sects. 3 and 4 a few important examples from both categories are discussed. There is a growing interest in interactive systems for processing documents. In the office of the future a lot of information will be exchanged via displays, and one may expect systems that will bring about even better reproduction of documents with varied contents. Section 5 goes deeper into this development. An extensive overview of different systems for processing documents is to be found in Furuta et al. (1982); Sigplan (1981) and Miller (1984) collected conference papers on this subject; and finally, Nievergelt et al. (1982) present a number of previously published articles.

2. Word Processing vs Document Processing

A typewriter is an excellent medium for producing simple documents with straight text such as letters or reports. With this approach however, it is awkward to make nontrivial corrections. When a computer is used it is a lot simpler. A letter is composed with the help of a text editor, and can then be printed using a printer connected to the computer. Using this approach it is also possible to automate simple text lay-out. The text can be compressed automatically so that as many words as possible are put onto a line, it can be justified, which results in a straight margin, and a routine can be built which endeavors to hyphenate words that do not fit on the line (van Vliet, 1972; Boot & Koppelaar, 1982). There are a large number of systems on the market for this type of application. In a number of cases these program packages are intended for general purpose microcomputers, but in other cases they are used in special word processing configurations. In the latter case there is often a keyboard available with function keys adapted to the application. In many of these systems the editor commands are dedicated to the special use. The output generally takes place via a typewriter-style printer or a dot matrix printer. With the latter there are more possibilities; text can for example be printed in italics or bold, even if the result is not always typographically appealing. Systems of this class are referred to in this article by the term "word processing" and are discussed further in Sect. 3.

At the other end of the spectrum systems can be found which produce output for a phototypesetting machine or laser printer. These allow text to be set in different fonts and sizes. There are also often fonts available with special symbols such as those used in mathematics. Finally, these systems sometimes have graphic capabilities, so drawings can be made, thus enabling complex documents to be produced. The accompanying formatting programs often have extensive facilities for laying out text, such as:

- Automatic production of running heads, in which, for example, the title of a chapter or section is repeated at the top of each page
- Automatic setting of footnotes at bottom of the page
- Automatic production of an index or table of contents
- Resolving cross references, such as "see page $A," whereby the system exchanges the text "$A" for the correct page number
- Moving drawings or tables, within certain limits, so that these are not placed across page boundaries or outside of the edges of the page

Section 4 goes more deeply into a few systems in this category and an idea of their possibilities is given by means of examples. In these systems, again, the input is done via text editors. Most display screens are not good enough to give a true picture of the output, and as the formatting process is rather complicated and time-consuming it generally occurs off-line.

In this article we will not go any futher into the characteristics of the different text editors. Meyrowitz and van Dam (1982) offer an excellent overview of this subject. In Table 1 the most important differences between the two categories of systems are summed up. It is obvious that there is no clear boundary between word processing and document processing systems, as there are relatively simple and cheap systems that are attached to a small phototypesetting machine. However, we still consider it important to make this distinction. Many of the current systems for document processing have only limited facilities. but there are also professional systems which enable the user to process complex documents in a most desirable way. We expect a certain

Table 1. Global classification of systems for document and word processing

Word processing	Document processing
Interactive	Batch
Simple documents	Complex documents
Matrix printer	Phototypesetting machine/laser printer

shift here, so that in the future texts can be processed at the normal availabl workstations in a flexible and attractive way.

3. Word Processing

Here, we will elaborate on the concept of word processing. Characteristics o the systems concerned are:

- The text to be processed is presented full-screen: the screen represents window on part of a complete document
- The user has a cursor at his disposal with which in principle ever position in the text can be reached
- The system is directed at processing straight text (no graphics or drawings
- The system contains (almost) no knowledge of different type fonts
- The system has no knowledge of the construction of more complicate documents such as a whole book (table of contents, index, chapte numbers)
- The system is designed for working with a simple output apparatus (daisy wheel printer, dot-matrix printer; not for an advanced laser printer or pho totypesetting machine)

The systems that we will consider here have been in use for a number o years, especially in offices, but increasingly in the home. We distinguish tw categories: word processing on personal computers and that using "dedicated word processors. In the following a few examples of both categories are men tioned. We are definitely not aiming to give a market survey, and do not pre tend that the systems mentioned by us are necessarily the best in thei category. However, they are characteristic of a whole family.

3.1. Word Processors on Personal Computers

The personal computer was, due to its flexibility, promptly used for word pro cessing. It does not seem an exaggeration to say that for many users the possi bility of word processing is the most important reason for the purchase o such an apparatus. There are few grounds for supposing that a dedicated wor processor will produce better work than a personal computer with a good pro gram. In this section we will consider one of the well-known word processor available for personal computers: WordStar from MicroPro. WordStar cam on the market at quite an early stage. Over the years facilities have bee

```
                         editing no file

   D=create or edit a Document file            H=set Help level
   N=create or edit a Non-document file        X=eXit to system
   M=Merge-print a file                        P=Print a file
   F=File directory off (on)                  Y=delete a file
   L=change Logged disk drive                  O=cOpy a file
   R=Run a program                             E=rEname a file

DIRECTORY of disk B:
 ARTIKEL1.DOC PIP.COM     EXAMPLE
```

Figure 1. WordStar options menu

added for personalized standard letters ("Mail merge"), entry into databases, arithmetic ("Spreadsheet"). etc. WordStar is now generally available for CP/M computers, and MS-DOS systems (CP/M is the de facto industry standard for operating systems for 8-bit microcomputers; the IBM PC, a 16-bit machine, also works under MS-DOS). The package is full-screen oriented but a true picture of the final output is not always shown. When this program is started up, a menu screen appears with a number of options (Figure 1). This screen allows the user to carry out the most important file-oriented commands: copy, rename, and delete. It is thus possible for a user who is only interested in word processing to settle everything within WordStar.

The most obvious option is "D," editing of a "document file." When the user chooses this option, he is asked for a file name, after which "edit" appears on the screen. On the line at the top of the screen the title of the document is shown, and the position of the cursor, expressed by the line number and character position within the line. Below this appears the "ruler line," on which are given the positions of the left and right margin stops and the tabulator positions. Figure 2 shows a screen display during a session with WordStar. Within WordStar the cursor can be directed to any position on the screen (at least within that part of the screen that is reserved for the reproduction of the document). For commands, including cursor movements, on most machines WordStar does not make use of special function keys, but of a combination of the "control" key (^) and a normal letter key. So ^E, ^S, ^D and ^X will move the cursor upwards, to the left, to the right, and downwards, respectively. This appears at first sight to be illogical and difficult to remember, but a glance at the keyboard shows that the relative positions of the keys concerned have been taken into account. Moreover the "control" key is usually within reach of the left little finger, so the cursor direction can be completely controlled by the left hand. Once learnt, this arrangement turns out to be ergonomically successful.

In the normal state, the text that is input by the user is inserted in the existing text. If necessary, a word that no longer fits on the line is moved completely

```
    B:EXAMPLE    PAGE 1 LINE 8 COL09              INSERT ON
L----!----!----!----!----!----!----!----!----!----!----!--------------------R
This  is an  example of an  Edit  screen.  On the  status line at the  top the
present  position of  the cursor is given, and whether typed text is  inserted
(INSERT ON) or written over the  existing text (INSERT OFF).  The  second line
gives the left and right margins and the positions of the tabulator stops.
Closed paragraphs  are noted in  the right margin by the sign "<".  The closed
lines are justified by adding spaces in between words._
```

Figure 2. Display screen during a session with WordStar

Table 2. A few layout commands

.pl N	page length is N lines
.pa	force turn over of page
.he '...'	define running head with text '...'
.pn N	begin page numbering with N
.op	do not number pages
.cw N	character width is N dots (for daisy wheel printers)
.lh N	distance between lines is N dots (for daisy wheel printers)

to the next one. The finished line is justified immediately. When the user does not want to justify a line, e.g., when he wants to begin a new paragraph, this is done by pressing the "return" key. WordStar then positions the cursor at the beginning of the next line. In addition, the "window" that WordStar places on the document is adjusted if necessary.

WordStar also allows the user to create subscripts and superscripts, an alternative letter type, boldface and underlined text. To this purpose the pieces of text concerned must be surrounded with so-called control characters, and most implementations of WordStar cannot show real underlining or bold text on the screen. Documents built up in this way can be printed under control of WordStar, and usually the added attributes such as underlining will then be made visible. WordStar "knows" a large number of printers and endeavors to achieve the desired effect in the most efficient way possible. With printers capable of proportional spacing, use is made of this in justifying lines. WordStar knows yet another way to influence the layout of the printed document. This occurs by means of commands embedded in the text at the beginning of a line, starting with a full stop. One can direct the number of lines on a page, cause skipping a page, define the running head, direct the page numbering, etc. (see Table 2). These commands are not shown on the display screen. This is part of the price one pays for terminal and printer independence, and it is partly the result of the relatively simple hardware on which the system runs. In spite of this WordStar can be called a user friendly product. More extensive systems such as Wang and IBM provide additional facilities, especially with regard to the administration of all documents, somcthing that can be very important in a setting with several users.

3.2. Dedicated Word Processors

Because the user interface of configurations directed at word processing does not differ in principle from that of WordStar, we suffice by mentioning a few points. Wang word processors are to be found in many offices. They are in principle microcomputers that have been specially equipped for word processing. Characteristic aspects are:

- Appearance of a classic terminal with screen and keyboard, provided with a few special keys
- Selection of pieces of text by means of highlighting
- Function keys for copy, move, delete, etc.
- Each command must be confirmed
- Menu-guided selection of files and facilities such as backup
- An extended index containing information about the files, such as time of creation, time of last change, author, typist, size

4. Document Processing

In this section four systems for processing documents with complex contents will be considered. The output of these systems is generally processed by a phototypesetting machine or laser printer. Troff and T_EX are well-known batch-oriented systems. Both have extensive facilities, which require an expert user to fully exploit them. However, by using the macro facilities, the layout of documents with a standard structure can be greatly simplified. This approach is carried further in Scribe. Scribe makes use of a database in which, for each type of document, the structure and the way the structure leads to a specific layout is determined. The user only has to give this structure in the input text. Standardization in the field of word processing is taking place within the International Standards Organization. In the system chosen to this end, called SGML, the user states the structure of the document in the input. It is important that SGML offer facilities to define the syntactic form of input commands, so that it is possible to connect to systems already in existence.

4.1. Troff

Under the UNIX operating system a number of programs are available for document processing. The central component of these is the program Troff which was developed in about 1973 (Ossanna, 1976). Troff is a text formatter that gives output for a phototypesetting machine. The most recent version is known by the name Ditroff (Kernighan, 1982a); the output from Ditroff is machine-independent, so that coupling with different phototypesetting machines is relatively simple. There is also a program, largely compatible

Table 3. A few Troff commands with their meanings

Command	Initial value	Meaning
.ps N	10 points	Change the letter size to N points
.vs N	12 points	Change the vertical distance between lines; distance can be in points, inches or centimeters
.ft F	Roman	Change to type font coded F
.pl N	11 inch	Set the page length to N (centimeters, inches, points)
.ll N	6.5 inch	Set the line length
.bp	1	Go to a new page. The present page is closed. The (internal) page number is increased by 1
.ne N	-	Indicates that a vertical space of height N is needed. If this space is not available on the current page a transfer to a new page is generated
.nf	fill up	The text following this command is copied to output unaltered; in other words new lines in the input lead to new lines in the output
.fi	fill up	From this point as much text as possible is again put on each line
.na	justify	From this point the lines are not justified; in other words the right margin is ragged
.ce N	-	The following N output lines are centered

Table 4. A few ms commands with their meanings

Command	Meaning
.TL	Below this follows the title of the document
.AU	Below this follows the name of the authors
.AB	Start abstract
.AE	End abstract
.NH N	Start a new section at level N
.PP	Begin a new paragraph
.FS	Now follows a footnote

Input text:

```
.TL
Software engineering
.AU
J.C. van Vliet
.AB
It is argued in this article that Software Engineering
must be brought in as compulsary subject
at Univertities.
.AE
.NH
INTRODUCTION
.LP
Programs are often delivered too late, do not meet the specifications
and beyond this include mistakes.
.NH 2
Why Software Engineering is also a nice subject
.LP
As opposed to Function Theorie, Software Engineering is a
subject whereby one
```

Output:

Software engineering

J.C. van Vliet

ABSTRACT

It is argued in this article that Software Engineering must be brought in as compulsary subject at Univertities.

1. INTRODUCTION

Programs are often delivered too late, do not meet the specifications and beyond this include mistakes.

1.1. Why Software Engineering is also a nice subject

As opposed to Function Theorie, Software Engineering is a subject whereby one

Figure 3. Use of the ms package

with Troff, called Nroff, that produces output for a line printer or typewriter. In the following we will limit the discussion to Troff. The input to Troff is a standard UNIX text file. Lines in the input that begin with a "." are understood as special commands for the formatter. In Table 3 a number of the commands are given together with their meanings. The input lines that do not begin with a "." are, under the direction of the applicable Troff commands, copied to the output. The basic commands from Troff are relatively primitive. The user can select fonts, set the height and width of pages, give low level layout instructions, etc. Besides this, Troff allows a series of layout instruction to be combined in macro functions, after which these "macros" can be used as commands. One can in this way define a series of macros that together determine the style of the document. The standard macro package is known by the name *ms* (Lesk, 1978). In Table 4 a few often used ms macros have been listed with their meanings. Figure 3 shows an example of the use of this package. Using macros is preferable to using primitive commands, as one can define a collection of macros once, and subsequently use them for a series of documents, such as a report series. Troff thus allows us to process straight text in a flexible way. In addition, there are under UNIX separate programs available for processing formulas (EQN), tables (TBL), and drawings (PIC). These programs all work as preprocessors for Troff. A program like EQN (Kernighan & Cherry, 1975) filters from an input text those parts in which formulas are described and edits these to a text (low-level and illegible to the user) which is then further processed by Troff.

In Figure 4 an example is given of a text in which formulas appear. A formula is surrounded by the commands .EQ and .EN. EQN only processes the

Input text:

```
After integration we get
.EQ
W(t) = 1 - exp ( - int to t p ( alpha ) d alpha )
.EN
Suppose p(t) = at.
The progress is then given by a Raleigh distribution
.EQ
dW over dt = ate sup { -at sup 2 / 2 }
.EN
```

Output:

After integration we get

$$W(t) = 1 - \exp(-\int^{t} p(\alpha) d\alpha)$$

Suppose p(t) = at. The progress is then given by a Raleigh distribution

$$\frac{dW}{dt} = ate^{-at^2/2}$$

Figure 4. Use of EQN formulas

text between these two commands and copies the rest of the input directly to the output.

Between the commands .EQ and .EN is found text that deviates in structure from the normal Troff input. Formulas are described in a language that looks quite natural. The EQN program reacts to words such as *sum*, *int*, and *over*. The remaining text is set in italics unless it consists of words with a standard mathematical meaning, such as sin, log, max. TBL (Lesk, 1979) reacts in a similar way to the input between the commands .TS and .TE. For each table, the options, format, and data have to be input by the user, in this order. Among other things the options can be used to state whether the table is to be centered on the page and whether lines are to be drawn around the whole table. In the format section the layout of the table is specified. Each line in this section gives the layout of one output line, with the exception of the last, which gives the layout of all following lines. The user indicates for each column, layout details such as:

- Whether the text is to be justified to the left or to the right, or centered (codes *l*, *r* or *c*)
- Whether the text should run from the previous column through to this column (code *s*)
- How much space must be left open between the columns
- How wide a column must be (minimal)
- Whether columns have the same width

Then the contents of the table are given. In Figure 5 is shown an example of a simple table. The different columns are separated by a special symbol, which in Figure 5 is "@".

The program PIC (Kernighan, 1982b) is used to produce drawings. The structure of input for PIC is very similar to that of EQN. The user specifies, in what appears to be a relatively natural language, the structure of the picture. To assist him standard components are available such as boxes, circles, ellipses, and lines, from which the drawing can be constructed. Figure 6 shows a simple example of the use of PIC.

The programs discussed briefly above offer far more possibilities than have been mentioned here. They offer so much that an expert is quickly needed; this is particularly true for formulas, pictures, and so forth, where it is sometimes difficult to see from the input how the output will appear.

A second problem is that the different programs do not know anything about each other. EQN expects the text to be set with 10 point letters as standard. In a similar way the program PIC does not know the size of the possible text that is put in drawings. This can lead to results such as are shown in Figure 7.

Input text:

```
.TS
center, box, tab(@);
cfB s s
c c c
^c c
l n n.
Size of programs
Name@Lines@Object bytes
@source code@(text+data)
_
Troff@8681@73136
EQN@1821@34164
TBL@2581@39936
PIC@3760@83968
.TE
```

Output:

Size of programs		
Name	Lines source code	Object bytes (text+data)
Troff	8681	73136
EQN	1821	34164
TBL	2581	39936
PIC	3760	83968

Figure 5. Example of the use of TBL (Source: Kernighan, 1984)

Troff is already more than 10 years old. In the course of time various preprocessors have been added and this has not been of help to the structure as a whole. The system offers many possibilities to the experienced user. Less experienced users can limit themselves to the use of macro packages and with little effort can produce documents of reasonable quality. For further details, see Akkerhuis (1984a, b) and the above-mentioned literature.

4.2. $\mathrm{T_EX}$

$\mathrm{T_EX}$ (Knuth, 1979, 1984) was developed in the second half of the 1970's by D.E. Knuth, author of the monumental work *The art of computer programming*, of which the first 3 volumes have appeared. The story is, that when a revision of volume 2 had to appear, the publisher announced that this could not be as well presented as the first print, because the existing computer programs for the setting of texts were not capable to do so. Knuth would not accept this and developed $\mathrm{T_EX}$ to prove the contrary. $\mathrm{T_EX}$ stands for *Tau epsilon chi* and is pronounced as "tech"; the letters $\tau\epsilon\chi$ are the first letters

Input text:

```
.PS
B0: box ht 0.4i wid 1.5i "initialize" "iteration"
arrow down 0.5i from B0.s
box ht 0.4 wid 1.2 "x:= f(i)"
arrow down 0.5i

BI: box invis "x > eps"
line from BI.n to BI.e
line from BI.e to BI.s
line from BI.s to BI.w
line from BI.w to BI.n
arrow down 0.5 from BI.s " no" ljust
box ht 0.4i wid 1.2i "zero" "found"
arrow right 1.0i from BI.e "yes" above

B: box ht 0.4i wid 1.2i "i:= next(i)"
line up 0.95i from B.n
arc
arrow left 1.725i
.PE
```

Output:

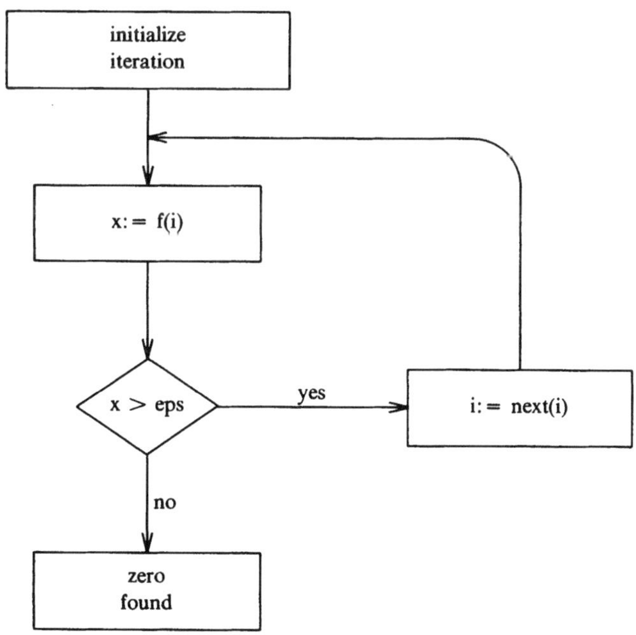

Figure 6. Example of the use of PIC

Input text:

```
.nr PS 16
.nr VS 20
This text is set large, but the formula
.EQ
FP = sum from i TC sub i * log sub 2 TC sub i
.EN
unfortunately not.
```

Output:

This text is set large, but the formula

$$FP = \sum TC_i * \log_2 TC_i$$

unfortunately not.

Input text:

```
.PS
box "with a text somewhat too wide"
.PE
```

Output:

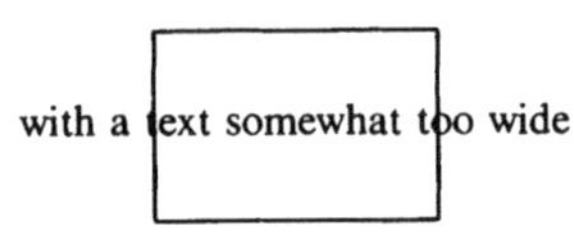

Figure 7. Two unexpected results

of the Greek word that means knowledge; this stem also appears in words such as "technology". TEX is, in Knuth's words, meant to produce beautiful books. In TEX much attention is paid to techniques to process mathematical and tabular material. In contrast to Troff, this is not done by means of preprocessors. One of the noticeable attributes of TEX is the way in which normal text is treated. The "box" plays a central role in TEX. A "box" indicates something that can be set. This can be a separate character, a whole word, a mathematical formula, and so forth. These boxes are placed below and next to each other in order to fill up a line, paragraph or page. When filling them only the height and width of these boxes plays a role and not the contents. Boxes are connected to each other by "glue"; there is a certain amount of freedom here so an optimal composition can be sought. In straight text those boxes represent the words of a paragraph, and the glue the variable spaces between the words. Between successive words there is a nominal white space. This can be made a little smaller or larger depending on how the lines can be best filled. As little deviation as possible from the nominal space between the words is preferred. The greater the deviation, the worse the text is set. One can also see this in terms of "penalty." The penalty for a paragraph set in a particular manner is a measure of the degree to which the word spacing in this paragraph deviates from the nominal word spacing. The best way to set a piece of text is then the distribution over lines that results in the lowest total penalty. Knuth and Plass (1981) developed a very elegant algorithm for this which also takes a number of other aspects into account:

- hyphenating words must be avoided as much as possible
- the last line of a paragraph should preferably contain more than one word
- it is desirable that there should be an approximately equal amount of space between the words in successive lines (a line with a lot of space between the words followed by a line with little space between the words is disturbing to the eye)

These types of consideration can also be formulated precisely in terms of penalties and are then processed further automatically by Knuth's algorithm. The way in which TEX text is divided within paragraphs is nicer than the way in which this occurs in Troff. In Troff as much text as possible is put on a line. If the line is full, then it is carried on to a new line. In TEX the whole paragraph is taken into consideration and this gives on the whole a more balanced-looking text (Brown, 1984). Just as in Troff, with TEX one often makes use of a macro package in which the standard structure of a document is defined. Figure 8 shows the input of the text shown in Fig. 3, making use of the AMS-TEX package (Spivak, 1983). The name of the package used is given here in the first line, while in the second line a specific format is

Input text

```
\input amstex
\documentstyle{amsppt}
\title Software engineering \endtitle
\author J.C. van Vliet \endauthor
\abstract{It is argued in this article that Software Engineering
 must be brought in as a compulsory subject at
 Universities.}
\heading 1. INTRODUCTION \endheading
 Programs are often delivered too late, do not meet the specifications
 and beyond this include errors.
\subheading {1.1. Why Software Engineering is also a nice subject}
 As opposed to Function Theory, Software Engineering is a
 subject whereby one ...
```

Figure 8. Example of AMS-TEX-input

Input text:

```
After integration we get
$$ W(t) = 1 - \exp {(- \int↑ t p( \alpha)d \alpha)}$$
Suppose p(t)=at. The progress is then given by a Raleigh
distribution:
$$ dW \frac dt = ate ↑ {-at↑ 2 /2}$$
```

Figure 9. Example of formulas in TEX

chosen from the possibilities offered in the package. The rest of the input speaks for itself. The output is comparable with that of the previously discussed ms package.

In TEX much attention is paid to the setting of formulas, and dealing with formulas is integrated in the system. Formulas are placed between $ symbols (or, should they have to be put on a separate line, between double $ symbols). In specifying formulas use is made of a language similar to that of EQN. There are no reserved words as in EQN; instead this type of symbol always begins with '\'. The repertoire is very extensive. As an example, in Fig. 9 the TEX input is given for the text of Fig. 4. Finally, TEX can also produce tables. Here one makes use of relatively low-level commands, which results in the input text for tables quickly becoming complex. TEX thus offers many possibilities of producing handsome documents. The use of basic commands is, as with Troff, quite complicated, and here too macro packages are being developed which can greatly simplify the processing of documents with a standard layout. An excellent discription of TEX is given in Knuth (1984), and there is also a users group which provides a newsletter (*TUGboat*).

4.3. Scribe

In Troff, TEX, and comparable systems the input consists of a mixture of text and commands. The commands are often of a low level and take the form of specific layout instructions: "now indent 3 spaces," "change to font 7." Users are forced to be occupied with this if they want to get what's in front of them precisely on paper. The author of the documents does not traditionally have this knowledge, and should limit himself to giving the text and indicating the (logical) structure of the document. Further processing is best left to an expert in text make-up and layout.

It is a step in the right direction when one makes use of macro packages with systems such as Troff and TEX. The make-up of a specific type of document is defined in such a package and one then makes use of commands such as "begin a new paragraph," and "a footnote now follows." In Scribe this design

```
@Make (article)
@Heading (Software engineering)
@Center (J.C. van Vliet)
@PrefaceSection (Abstract)
It is argued in this article that Software Engineering
must be brought in as a compulsary subject at
Universities.
@Section (INTRODUCTION)
Programs are often delivered too late, do not meet the
specifications and beyond this include errors.
@Subsection (Why Software Engineering is also a nice subject)
As opposed to Function Theory, Software Engineering is
a subject whereby one
```

Figure 10. An input text for Scribe

is carried much further (Reid, 1980). In Scribe use is made of a database in which for different *document types*, such as a business letter, an internal memo, an article for magazine X, a description is given of how a marked-up document is to be transformed into a typeset version. It is intended that modifications and additions to this database be made only by experts.

Figure 10 illustrates how the output in Fig. 3 could be obtained via Scribe. Scribe enables the user to give the logical structure of a document in a simple way, after which all further layout details are taken care of by the system. On the other hand, only those objects for which descriptions of the structure and layout are entered in the database can be processed. In the version Reid (1980) describes, no complex formulas and tables can be processed.

4.4. SGML

Within ISO, standardization in the domain of text processing takes place in the committee TC97/SC18. One of the most important parts of the developing standard is SGML "standard generalized mark-up language" (ISO, 1986). In SGML the emphasis is firmly placed on giving the logical structure of a document. The system can be informed as to the precise structure and the type of each text element that may be used. In a *document type definition* all possible correct forms of a certain type of text element are given. Figure 11 shows a simplified version of the declaration of an element *fig*.

The first line states that a figure contains a *body*, possibly followed by a *caption*. The "?" shows that the *caption* is optional. A figure has an attribute *id*

```
<!    ELEMENT     CONTENT                     ATTRIBUTE
1     fig         (body, caption?)            id
2     body        (artwork | (p | ol)+)
3     artwork     NONE                        depth
4     caption     (#CDATA)
>
```

Figure 11. SGML declaration of a "figure"

in which an identification can be given. The next line defines that the *body* consists of *artwork*, of a series of paragraphs (*p*) and/or ordered lists (*ol*). The elements *p* and *ol* must be entered elsewhere in the definition of the document type. In the formalism used one reads "or" for "|", and "repeated at least once" for "+". After this *artwork* is defined. Content is stated to be none - the drawing is stuck in later - and there is an attribute *depth* by which the height can be given. Finally, it is specified that the *caption* consists of a row of 0 or more characters. Essentially, a grammer is given for the structure of the element concerned, in a BNF-type notation. With this formal definition the make-up of a drawing such as that in Figure 12 is now allowed. The different labels (tags) are placed between the symbols "<" and ">". Each part is started with a begin label (as "<fig"). An end label takes the form "<\fig>". In places where this cannot lead to ambiguities the end label may be left out.

Such a declaration can be given for each text element. Together they offer a precise description of a certain type of document, and a given text can then subsequently be analyzed on the basis of the description. Should the description not allow a drawing to contain another drawing, such an appearance is detected in an input text. This is analogous to the manner in which, for programming languages based on a grammar, a parser is generated with the help of a parser-generator such as Yacc (Johnson 1978). Programs in the language concerned are subsequently analyzed using this parser. Through the facilities offered for the definition of the syntactic form of the make-up commands in SGML, connection with existing systems is possible.

```
<fig id=diagram1>
<body>
<artwork depth=20>
<caption> a flowchart
<\fig>
```

Figure 12. Correct make-up of a drawing

5. Interactive Processing of Documents

Implementations of the systems discussed in the previous section are batch-oriented: an input file is created and, without the intervention of the user, is formed into (type set) pages. In sharp contrast to this are the interactive text processing systems, in which text make-up and graphic design facilities are integrated. That is to say, it is possible for the user in one session to make straight text as well as graphics and formulas which can easily be manipulated. A document is in this view no longer a linear row of characters, but an object with its own structure and subobjects such as text, drawings, and formulas. A second important aspect of interactive text processing is the so-called WYSIWYG principle: what you see is what you get. For the user this means that all changes made in the document must be immediately visible. This is where interactive systems differ from systems like Troff and $\TeX$. Thirdly, we will go into what is meant by the fashionable phrase "user friendliness." One must not forget that the most important market for this type of system is the automated office, from which it follows that a mixed group of users must be able to work in such an environment with relatively little effort.

Before we go on to discuss two examples we will give a short explanation of the philosophy behind the development of an environment that is currently quickly becoming popular. The necessary hardware and software for this type of environment (graphic screen displays with high resolution, mouse devices, ergonomic, friendly keyboards, and so forth) have existed for some time, but in recent years have just come within the reach of the less financially strong consumer. The desktop paradigm is central. An important part of the professional world for the classic office worker is a desk on which there are a number of documents (arranged more or less orderly), in- and out trays for mail, etc. A modern workstation offers in fact an image that is modelled on this as far as possible: objects in the system (files, programs, and so forth) are presented on the display screen by means of drawings called icons. The user can manipulate these icons, whereby one must think of manipulations such as opening, moving, sending to and storing in an archive. This manipulation is done with a so-called mouse: a little box with one or more push-buttons that can be moved over the table. A little ball rolls within the box over the worksheet: these movements are translated into movements of a small arrow on the display. In this manner icons are selected (by pointing) and activated (by using one or more of the push-buttons). Commands that work on an icon once it is selected are given in "popup" menus. It must be remarked here that uniformity and consistency of the command structure are explicitly strived for: commands are given the same meaning in different contexts as far as possible. The analogy with the desk is further maintained by the "window" concept: the user obtains a view of a once-activated object through a window.

This window is, as it were, laid over previous windows (that then also remain visible in as far as they do not overlap the now active window). In this way the impression of a desk strewn with papers is strengthened further. It is of course possible to change the relative positions of these windows with the usual selection principles, to move them, to change their size, and so on. Finally, the file system is organized like a filing cabinet: files are stored in drawers, named "folders." This filing system often has a treelike structure: folders can in turn also contain folders, etc. We will illustrate the use of interactive systems with a short discussion of two which are currently operational, the Xerox 8010 and the Edimath system.

5.1. Xerox 8010

The Xerox 8010 is part of an extensive family of products that together cover many requirements of the automated office: the Xerox 8000 family. These include among other things, word processors, file servers for data storage, a laser printer and communication facilities, both local (Ethernet interface) and global (inclusion of local Ethernet networks in an international Internet network). Apart from the normal components such as a CPU, memory and so on, the Xerox 8010 has a high-resolution (1024 × 809 pixels) bit-mapped display screen, a 29 Mbite hard disk and a mouse. For hard copy and communication facilities the Ethernet and the laser printer (300 dots/inch) can be called upon.

The user interface is to a large extent as described above. A document for example is created by activating a blank document; similarly an existing document can be changed. The user is offered control in the text editor over text attributes such as font, type size, underlining, sub- and superscripts. These attributes are brought together in a "property sheet." The user can select an arbitrary piece of text and ask for its attributes; these then appear in a separate window in which the desired changes can be made. The new collection of attributes can be declared to be applicable, which has the result that the previously selected text is modified. A similar editor is offered for drawings: complex objects can be built up out of basic forms, with which there are choices of, among others, filling with different patterns, different frames and form changing. Furthermore, there is a graphics generator that is driven by a table supplied by the user. With this pie and bar charts can be generated. More than one document can be handled at the same time on the screen, and there are extensive facilities for the integration of text and graphics. Finally, the 8010 also allows processing of formulas. With this one makes use of, among other things, "virtual" keyboards: the user can let the keys on the keyboard correspond to for example Greek letters, or signs that are used in mathematical formulas. The OPS-2000 is a system comparable to the 8010 that runs on a SUN workstation (Markoff and Robinson, 1985). Many facilities that are included can be traced back to research undertaken by Xerox PARC (Smalltalk, Alto, Star).

5.2. Edimath

Our second exmple is the Edimath system, developed by the IMAG laboratories, under the direction of V. Quint. This concerns an extensive research project that is only partly realized. The system is based on an abstract view of document processing. The document is seen as an object with a subobject structure and a formally defined syntax. Examples of objects are text, drawings, and formulas. An aim is that the design be independent of specific hardware. As a prototype an editor for mathematical formulas has been designed, which has now been implemented on different systems. For two of these implementations modern hardware such as a display screen and a mouse is available, for the rest use is made of standard alphanumeric terminals. The formula editor is interactive and has a uniform command structure: commands are given by function keys or menu selection, and a certain key (menu choice) has a fixed meaning that is independent of time and context. Creation and changing of formulas is completely syntax directed and one always finds oneself in a well-defined construct. The basic constructs are: fractions, roots, integrals, sums, vectors, blocks, exponents, and character strings. When changing parts of these constructs, the surrounding constructs are immediately changed in the same way; when, for example, the denominator of a fraction is made longer, then the dividing line is also lengthened and the numerator and denominator recentered. The complete formula is stored in a treelike structure and one can move (syntax directed) through this tree. A fixed number of commands are available for changing constructs (delete, replace, insert before, insert after). In Figure 13 part of an interactive session with Edimath is given as an example. In the left-hand column are the commands given by the user, in the right-hand column is the formula as shown on the screen. The bold characters indicate that a function key has been used: "Fraction", "End", "Integral", "Root", "Block", "Power", etc. The summation sign is given by a triple indicated by *T*. The *H* shows that it is a high symbol, the *S* indicates the summation sign. The position of the cursor is given in the right column by the dot. The system has many interesting implementation details which we cannot go into further (see also Quint, 1983); here we will only mention that the lay-out of the formulas is based on Knuth's approach.

6. Conclusion

The Edimath system described in sect. 5.2 is a good example of how a system for the processing of complex material could appear. Greatly improved user

F	$\frac{\bullet}{}$
1	$\frac{1\bullet}{}$
E	$\frac{1}{\bullet}$
2 n	$\frac{1}{2n\bullet}$
E	$\frac{1}{2n}\bullet$
I	$\frac{1}{2n}\int_{\bullet}$
0	$\frac{1}{2n}\int_{0\bullet}$
E	$\frac{1}{2n}\int_{0}^{\bullet}$
R	$\frac{1}{2n}\int_{0}^{\sqrt{\bullet}}$
y	$\frac{1}{2n}\int_{0}^{\sqrt{y\bullet}}$
E	$\frac{1}{2n}\int_{0}^{\sqrt{y}\bullet}$
E	$\frac{1}{2n}\int_{0}^{\sqrt{y}}\bullet$
B (	$\frac{1}{2n}\int_{0}^{\sqrt{y}}(\bullet$
T H S	$\frac{1}{2n}\int_{0}^{\sqrt{y}}\left(\sum_{\bullet}\right.$
k=1 **E**	$\frac{1}{2n}\int_{0}^{\sqrt{y}}\left(\sum_{k=1}^{\bullet}\right.$
n **E**	$\frac{1}{2n}\int_{0}^{\sqrt{y}}\left(\sum_{k=1}^{n}\bullet\right.$
sin **P**	$\frac{1}{2n}\int_{0}^{\sqrt{y}}\left(\sum_{k=1}^{n}\sin^{\bullet}\right.$
etc...	

Figure 13. Example of a session with Edimath

When correcting printing proofs by hand all sorts of correction signs are used: examples are signs to put words together, to remove letters, or to show that no break of a particular word should take place. One can also show that a line should be indented.
The system can recognize such movements of the mouse and translate them into the correct command for the text processor.

Figure 14. The indication of corrections

interfaces can be found in, for example, the Xerox 8010, the Macintosh and the OPS-2000 systems. The time is ripe for systems that go further than imitating a typewriter on a display screen (Lemmons, 1984). Investigations in the area of interactive text processing are currently being carried out by us. Characteristics of the system that we envisage, are:

1. Text, drawings, formulas, etc., should be integrated in one system, in which the user has available a uniform collection of commands
2. The user should only see the text as it will be set, and the operations conform with this image
3. The system should be interactive, and operations should have an immediate effect on what is shown on the display screen
4. The assignments given by the user should concern the (logical) structure of the document and not the layout
5. The user should be able to direct the justification algorithm (for example by indicating how bad frequent interruption of words is relative to the inclusion of extra space)
6. The system should allow correction of text in a simple way

Concerning this last point, the following could be considered: in correction of proofs much use is made of a number of signs with a fixed meaning, like the standard set recommended by the Nederlands Normalisatie Instituut (n.d.). Marked texts appear as in Figure 14. One can also "draw" these symbols with a mouse on a display screen. It would be interesting to investigate whether this leads to an ergonomically attractive way of correcting text.

References

Akkerhuis J. (1984a). Typesetting at the CWI, part I. *CWI Newsletter*, 3, pp. 15-24.

Akkerhuis J. (1984b). Typesetting at the CWI, part II. *CWI Newsletter*, 4, pp. 21-32.

Barthel G. (1972). *Konnte Adam schreiben? Weltgeschichte der Schrift.* M. DuMont Schauberg, Cologne.

Bigelow C. (1985). Font design for personal workstations. *BYTE, 10* (1), pp. 255-270.

Bigelow C. & Day D. (1983). Digital typography. *Scientific American, 249* (2), pp. 94-112.

Boot M. & Koppelaar H. (1982). *De tekstmachine.* Academic Service, The Hague.

Brown H. (1984). From text formatter to printer. In: PROTEXT 1, *Proceedings of the first international conference on text processing systems*, J.J.H. Miller (Ed.). Boole Press, Dublin, pp. 98-107.

Carter K.A. (1984). IMP - a system for computer-aided typeface design. In: *Proceedings of the first international conference on text processing systems* J.J.H. Miller (Ed.), Boole Press, Dublin, pp. 114-119.

Diringer D. (1977). *A history of the alphabet.* Unwin Brothers Ltd., Old Woking.

Flowers J. (1984). Digital type manufacture: an interactive approach. *IEEE Transactions on Computers, 17* (5), pp. 40-49.

Furuta R., Scofield J. & Shaw, A. (1982). Document formatting systems: survey, concepts, and issues, *ACM Computing Surveys, 14*, pp. 417-472.

Groenendaal M.H. (1975). *Drukletters. Hun ontstaan en hun gebruik.* Technische Uitgeverij H. Stam, Culemborg.

International Standards Organization (1986). *Information processing - Text and office systems - Standard Generalized Markup Language (SGML)*, ISO 8879-1986.

Johnson S.C. (1978). *YACC: Yet Another Compiler Compiler.* Bell Laboratories, Murray Hill, NJ.

Kernighan B.W. (1982a). *A typesetter-independent Troff.* (Computing Science Technical Report 97). Bell Laboratories, Murray Hill, NJ.

Kernighan B.W. (1982b). PIC - A language for typesetting graphics. *Software Practice & Experience, 12*, pp. 1-20.

Kernighan B.W. (1984). The UNIX document preparation tools - a retrospective. In: *PROTEXT 1, Proceedings of the first international conference on text processing systems*, J.J.H. Miller (Ed.), Boole Press, Dublin, pp. 12-25.

Kernighan B.W. & Cherry L.L. (1975). A system for typesetting mathematics. *Communications of the ACM, 18* (3), pp. 151-157.

Knuth D.E. (1979). *T_EX and METAFONT, new directions in typeseting.* Digital Press, Bedford, MA.

Knuth D.E. (1984). *The TEXbook.* Addison-Wesley, Reading, MA.

Knuth D.E. & Plass M.F. (1981). Breaking paragraphs into lines. *Software Practice & Experience, 11*, pp. 1119-1184.

Lemmons Ph. (1984). Beyond the word processor. *BYTE, 9* (1), pp. 53-56.

Lesk, M.E. (1978). *Typing documents on the UNIX system: using the -ms macros with Troff and Nroff.* Bell Laboratories, Murray Hill, NJ.

Lesk, M.E. (1979). *TBL - A program to format tables.* Bell Laboratories, Murray Hill, NJ.

Markoff J. & Robinson P. (1985). Lasers, office publishing, and more. *BYTE, 10* (4), pp. 379-384.

Meyrowitz N. & van Dam A. (1982). Interactive editing systems, Parts I, II. *ACM Computing Surveys, 14*, pp. 321-416.

Miller J.J.H. (Ed.) (1984). *PROTEXT 1, Proceedings of the first international conference on text processing systems.* Boole Press, Dublin.

Nederlands Normalisatie Instituut (n.d.). *Correctietekens voor drukproeven* (NEN 632).

Nievergelt J., Coray G., Nicoud J.-D. & Shaw A.C. (1982). *Document preparation systems.* North-Holland Publishing Cy., Amsterdam.

Ossanna J.F. (1976). *Nroff/Troff user's manual.* Bell Laboratories, Murray Hill, NJ.

Quint V. (1983). An interactive system for mathematical text processing. *Technology & Science of Informatics, 2* (3), pp.169-179.

Reid B.K. (1980). *Scribe: a document specification language and its compiler.* PhD Thesis, Department of Computer Science, Carnegie-Mellon University.

Sigplan (1981). Proceedings of the ACM SIGPLAN SIGOA symposium on text manipulation. *ACM SIGPLAN Notices 16* (6).

Spivak M. (1983). Summary of AMS-TEX. *TUGboat, 4*, (2), pp.103-126. (Newsletter of the TEX Users group, American Mathematical Society, PO Box 5248, Providence, RI 02940, USA)

Treebus K.F. (1983). *Tekstwijzer, een gids voor het grafisch verwerken van tekst.* Staatsuitgeverij, The Hague.

van Vliet J.C. (1972). *Bestesplits I, een procedure voor het automatisch afbreken van Nederlandse woorden.* (*Report IN28/72*). Centrum voor Wiskunde en Informatica, Amsterdam.

The Representation of Knowledge

Chapter 10. A Comparison of Presentation and Representation: Linguistic and Pictorial

René Jorna

1. Introduction

In his book *Brainstorms* (1978) Daniel Dennett makes some very important remarks about man and computers. The main theme of the book is that computers lack intentions, whereas we, humans, can understand each other because we have and use intentions. In the chapter "Conditions of Personhood" Dennett puts the following question:

> Do we communicate with computers in Fortran? Fortran seems to be a language; it has a grammar, a vocabulaire, a semantics. The transactions in Fortran between man and machine are often viewed as cases of *man communicating with machine*, but such transactions are pale copies of human verbal communication precisely because the Gricean conditions for nonnatural meaning have been bypassed. There is no room for them to apply. Achieving's one's end in transmitting a bit of Fortran to the machine does not hinge on getting the machine to recognize one's *intentions*. This does not mean that all communications with computers in the future will have this short-coming (or strength, depending on your purposes), but just that we do not now communicate, in the strong (Gricean) sense, with computers. (p. 280)

The strong (Gricean) sense of communication is totally based on first and higher order intentions. Grice (1957) has stated that two persons A and B are communicating if A by uttering a sentence intends B to give a certain answer or to do something. Furthermore, B has to recognize the intention of A and finally has the intention to fulfill the intention of A. According to Dennett this is something computers can't do; computers don't have intentions, although, as some people may assert, computers can fulfill the intentions of humans.

So. if we agree with Dennett and Grice, there is a problem in defining the so called interaction between man and computer. One way of solving a problem is to reformulate it. Instead of defining interaction again, I would like to wonder whether psychology could offer us a way out. If we consider man and computers as natural and artificial information processing systems, we could ask two questions.

The first question is about the sort of psychological approach we need. Are we dealing with instructional psychology if a human being learns to "communicate" with a computer or are we talking about cognitive psychology because of a confrontation of two representational systems? Why is this a problem? In my opinion instructional psychology tries to study task demands, whereas cognitive psychology studies the human mind, in other words the representational system. In this respect the computer has two faces. On the one hand we have to deal with the task demands of the computer system; that is to say, we have to know which modes of presentation (on the screen) are available and what their effect will be on the (human) user. This is the instructional point of view. On the other hand the computer is a representational system; a system that works with and operates upon representations, that can present and represent information. In this respect cognitive psychology supposes that a comparison between humans and computers is fruitful, precisely because human beings also present and represent information.

The second question concerns the nature of and the conditions for information-processing; what do we mean by (mental) representations? what are the constraints and the requirements? I will not go into the details of this question now, but in the following sections I want to try to answer these two questions. In the first place I want to pay attention to problems a novice faces when trying to work with (micro)computers. In this case not only the presentation (on the screen), but also the representation that the user has of the computer or task, plays a very important role. In the second place I will try to answer the question of in what respect modes of presentation could differ from each other and in what respect computer-representations are essentially different from human mental representations. For that reason I will discuss some theories of mental representation that cognitive psychology has formulated in the past 20 years.

The problem we then face is how to compare presentations with mental and computer representations as well as theories of mental representation with one another? I think that one way of handling this problem is to assert that presentations and mental and computer representations can be seen as symbol systems. In the final section I will use the technical and psychological features of symbols that have been analyzed by Goodman (1968, 1984) to compare pictorial and verbal (propositional) presentations. In my opinion this way of comparing presentations can be extended to mental representations.

2. Presentation and Representation of Novice and Expert

Let me start with an example of two different modes of presentations of information with the Micro Soft-Disk Operating System (MS-DOS). The commands in MS-DOS can be presented in text and in icons. The normal way

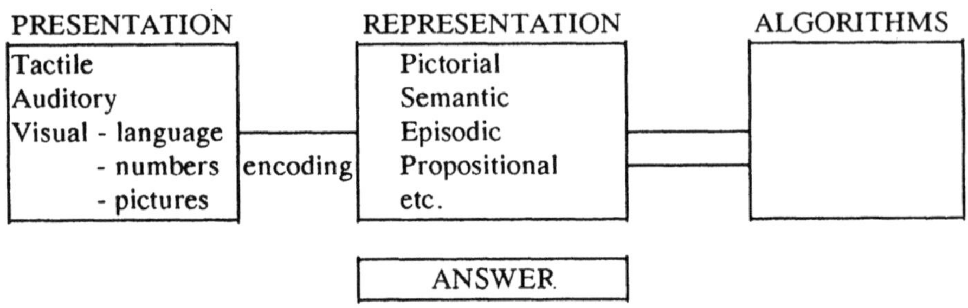

Figure 1. Scheme of the processing of information.

one learns to work with MS-DOS is by text; that is to say, in a languagelike manner one learns how to copy, delete, check, make, etc. files. But there is another way to work with MS-DOS and that is by using a pictorial presentation of the commands in the program GEM-DESKTOP (or MS-Windows). This program uses a mouse (or a cursor) and windows provided with icons to manipulate files. With the help of this program people can easily learn to do things on a personal computer

The very simple scheme in Figure 1. shows the relationships between presentation, representation, and problem-solving algorithms. First I want to discuss the notion of presentation. Everyone knows that information has to be presented before it can be mentally represented and processed, but, in my opinion, the psychological relevance of the modes of presentation is widely underestimated. Two factors can be distinguished in the modes of presentation.

The first factor is related to the sense modalities. Music, for example, can be presented auditorily as performance of a concerto, but it can also be presented visually as notes in a musical score. Language can be presented visually, that is to say on paper or on a screen, but it can also be presented in a tactile manner, such as in the form of signs of braille. Even "spoken" language, which normally has an auditory presentation, can also be visually presented when one tries to lip-read.

The other factor concerns a subdivision within the sense modalities, for example within the visual modality. Characters and words of natural and artificial languages as well as pictures, figures, and numbers are visually perceived. Everyone who has taught arithmetic or mathematics knows that the way of presenting a problem is strongly related to the ease with which it is solved; for example, a complex linguistic statement may be transformed into a symbolic expression. Suppose one asserts that it does not matter whether a 5% reduction is received first and then 18% tax is paid after that, or 18% tax is paid first and then a 5% reduction is received; the correctness of this assertion can clearly be shown by presenting it as an example of the commutativity of multiplications (Treffers, 1984).

The distinction between novice and expert can be used to illustrate this point on the relevance of modes of presentation (and of course mental representation) further. Starting from presentation and representation an expert can be defined as someone whose problem-solving strategies are independent of the mode of presentation of the problem and whose mental representations can change accordingly. This definition allows that experts may have different opinions about solving the same problems and transforming information, which, as we know, often happens. This also makes it clear why it is so difficult to build expert systems on protocols of different and sometimes conflicting experts. By habit and education an expert will prefer one presentation above another and use one mental representation rather than another.

The definition of a novice is as follows: a novice is someone who either does not have an "articulated" mental representation concerning the problem space or uses a "rigid" mental representation. In contrast with an expert a novice is dependent upon the elements used in the presentation. A novice does not know which the individual elements in the presentation are, or know which operations are allowed on the elements. This is not to say that an expert explicitly knows what he is doing in solving problems. Examining what the important aspects of the presentation are in the case of experts and in the case of novices is a task for instructional psychologists. In my opinion this is an important part of studies on human-computer interaction. People have to learn how to cope with (personal) computers, and because computers can rapidly change their presentation (on the screen, etc.) more options for instruction are available than in a normal learning environment.

In a discussion about the modes of presentation two aspects are very important, the elements used in the presentation and representation, and the equivalence of presentations and representations. Concerning the elements in the presentation the question is which elements constitute, for example, pictures, which constitute the sentences in languages, and which are components of other presentations? I propose to call the elements of presentation (or information) symbols.

In the second place there is the question of the value (the equivalence) of the different presentations. Is information in braille, where the symbols consist of configurations of bubbles on paper, equivalent to information in the form of sentences and words, where the symbols consist of characters of the alphabet? And what about the equivalence of information in the case of a performance of a concerto and the notes in a musical score? For some people the value (quality) of information is the same for both presentations of music. As a first step in answering the question about the equivalence of presentations and representations Simon (1978, p.4) distinguished two sorts of equivalence. The first he called informational equivalence:

> Two representations are informationally equivalent if the transformation from one to the other entails no loss of information, i.e. if each can be constructed from the other.

As an example of informational equivalence Simon mentions "distance equals average velocity times time" and "$S = w \times T$". I think that in this example it will be clear that the expressions are informationally equivalent, but I wonder whether cognitive psychologists would call the notes in a musical score and the tones in a performance informationally equivalent.

Simon (1978, p.5) also mentions another sort of equivalence, computational equivalence:

> Two representations are computationally equivalent if the same information can be extracted from each (the same inferences drawn) with about the same amount of computation.

This notion of computational equivalence presupposes a computational theory of information processing, which seems to be no problem in the case of computers, but is according to some psychologists and philosophers (Dreyfus, 1982; Searle, 1984) problematic in the case of human beings. One consequence of computational equivalence is that we do not have to worry about the hardware of the information processing systems. I will not go into the details of the equivalence of presentations now, because I think a greater part of the solution of the problem depends on what can be said about the features of symbols.

The reason why I treat the modes of presentation at some length is that a (personal) computer has the possibility to change its mode of presentation. As mentioned earlier, in MS-DOS commands can be presented in the form of icons and in the form of propositions, and the time will come when a computer will use a voice-analogon and an ear-analogon. Except for hardware and memory facilities, the mode of presentation is not of great importance for the computer. But the mode of presentation is very important for the user: the human information processing system. For some people icons will be easier, for others propositions (Kolers & Smythe, 1979). This brings me to the second aspect of the scheme in Figure 1 the mental representation.

In brief, representation means that one state of affairs stands for another state of affairs. According to Palmer (1978, p.262) a representation is completely defined if the following five demands are fulfilled.

> ..., one must state: (1) what the represented world is; (2) what the representing world is: (3) what aspects of the represented world are

being modeled: (4) what aspects of the representing world are doing the modeling; and (5) what are the correspondences between the two worlds. A representation is really a *representational system* that includes all five aspects.

I think the computer and the human being differ very strongly in respect to these five aspects. The difference is related to the difficulty in defining the worlds or domains and the elements within them in the case of mental or cognitive states. One should not forget that in the case of human information processing we are talking about the mental representation, which cannot (yet) be formulated in terms of hardware, software, or firmware. I will return to mental representations in the next section.

The third aspect in the scheme concerns the "algorithms", although it would perhaps be better to say the repertory of solutions. This repertory is closely connected to mental representations and as far as cognitive psychologists have found, also consists of mental representations; the difference between them appears to relate to the difference between declarative and procedural representations.

3. Theories of Mental Representation

Until now I have discussed the distinction between instructional and cognitive psychology and between presentation and representation. Furthermore, I have stated that the elements in the presentation consist of symbols. In this section I will look at some aspects of representations, that is to say at theories of mental representation in cognitive psychology.

The first question we have to ask is whether mental representations also consist of symbols. A rhetorical answer could be, what else can mental representations consist of? Newell (1980, p.38) has said:

> The notion of symbol that it [computer science and artificial intelligence] defines is internal to this concept of a system. Thus, it is a hypothesis that these symbols are in fact the same symbols that we humans have and use everyday of our lives. Stated another way, the hypothesis is that humans are instances of physical symbol systems, and, by virtue of this, mind enters into the physical universe.

In the same way, Pylyshyn (1984, p. 51) defended a strong equivalence between natural and artificial information processing systems. Concerning symbols he stated:

> The notion of a discrete atomic symbol is the basis of all formal understanding. Indeed, it is the basis of all systems of thought, expression, or calculation for which a *notation* is available.

So, according to Newell and Phylyshyn, and many other cognitive psychologists and workers in artificial intelligence as well, the units of information processing are symbols.

In this section I will give a short summary of some of the theories of mental representation that can be found in the literature of cognitive psychology (see also Rumelhart & Norman, 1983). In the next section I will go into the details of symbols, considered as the units of presentation and mental representation.

It is rather confusing that in cognitive psychology internal symbol systems as well as internal mechanisms are conceived as mental representations. This confusion is mentioned in the top of the scheme (Figure 2), but it exists also in the distinction between declarative and procedural representations. Let me start by giving a brief description of the various mental representations conceived as mental elements. Semantic representations presuppose that meanings of mental elements consist of sets of verbal associations structured in the form of networks. Several semantic systems have been formulated for this purpose. Episodic representations (Tulving, 1983) consist of events or episodes, which are stored in memory along the temporal dimension. Furthermore, the structure of events has an internal hierarchy. This feature distinguishes them from temporal string representations (Anderson, 1983) which only have a sequential ordering. These three types of representations can be considered as instances of propositional representations. Propositional representations consist of statements with a truth value, to which the rules of logical calculus are applicable (Fodor, 1975).

Pictorial representations in contrast to propositional representations do not have a truth value. Pictorial representations are considered as rather similar to images in visual perception (Kosslyn, 1981; Johnson-Laird, 1983). As indicated in Figure 2, propositional and pictorial representations are both conceived as instances of declarative representations.

Declarative representations are explicit; that is to say the knowledge-structure consists of symbols, which are directly accessible. This is not so in the case of procedural representations. Procedural representations are related to operations in the mental system. Procedures are not directly accessible; as Pylyshyn (1984) has said, they are cognitively impenetrable. In fact the distinction between declarative and procedural representations is on a different level to the distinction between semantic and pictorial representations. The

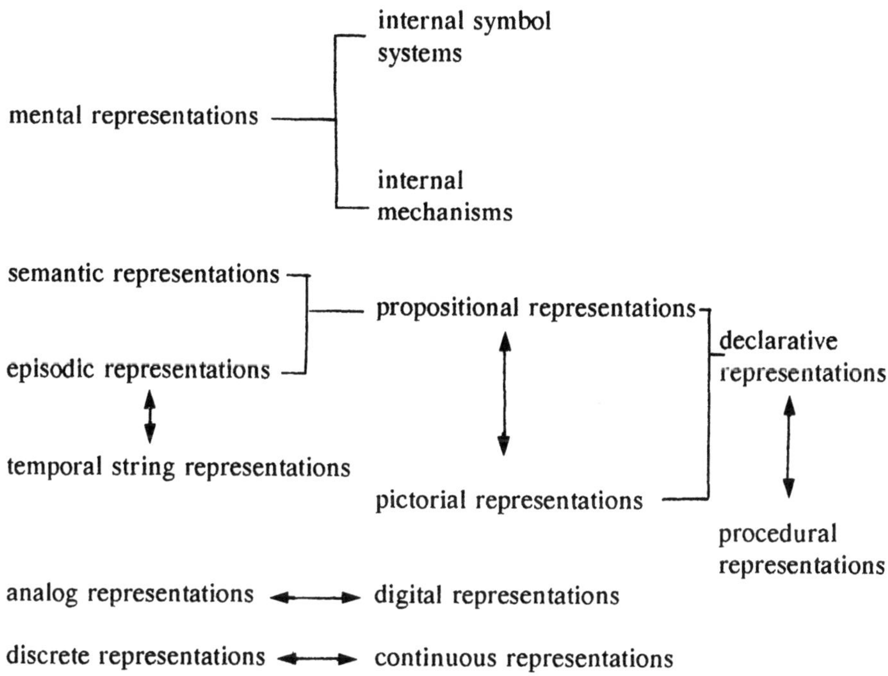

Figure 2. An overview of the interrelatedness of mental representations.

situation is still more complicated however, when we realize that declarative representations can change into procedural representations (Rumelhart & Norman, 1983).

In Figure 2 two further distinctions are illustrated, one between analog and digital representations and the other between discrete and continuous representations. The former distinction is based on a criterion of similarity between the representing and the represented elements, whereas the latter regards the continuity of physical reality, whether or not this is adopted in the represented world (Palmer, 1978), as crucial. Finally, there is a lot of overlap between analog, continuous, and pictorial representations and between digital, discrete, and propositional representations.

To introduce the concept of symbols, common in my opinion to presentation and to mental representation, I want to elaborate two theories of mental representation: semantic and pictorial representations. Psychological research has shown that human individuals use pictorial and semantic representations. The existence of semantic representations can be demonstrated in the following way. It takes more time to answer the question of whether a canary is an animal then the question of whether a canary is a bird. This fact can be explained by assuming that we have an internal semantic network consisting of nodes for concepts and paths for relations; this network is structured hierarchically. In answering the question of whether a canary is a bird two nodes and one path have to be activated, whereas in the other case three nodes and two paths must be activated. This explains the different latencies (Anderson & Bower, 1973; Vonk, 1977).

Many experiments have been done concerning pictorial representations (for an overview see Kosslyn, 1981). One was that by Shepard and Metzler (1971) who demonstrated that in order to say whether two pictures were congruent, subjects had to mentally rotate one of the pictures. The result of the experiment was that the greater the angular separation of the congruent figures, the longer it took subjects to respond. So, it seems that people do have and rotate pictorial representations. In cognitive psychology the discussion of whether pictorial representations can be reduced to semantic representations is still going on (Johnson-Laird, 1983).

If we assume that mental representations consist of symbol systems and operations on symbols, then we have to look for a theory of symbols. A comparison of several mental representations can only succeed if mental representations have something in common. So, what can we say about the technical and psychological features of symbols?

4. Technical and Psychological Aspects of Symbols

The first person to make an approach to a theory of symbols, is, as far as I know, Nelson Goodman (1968, 1972, 1984). According to Goodman (1968,p.XI):

> 'Symbol' is used ... as a very general and colorless term. It covers letters, words, texts, pictures, diagrams, maps, models, and more, but carries no implication of the oblique or the occult. The most literal portrait and the most prosaic passage are as much symbols, and as 'highly symbolic', as the most fanciful and figurative.

Although pictures, words, etc. can be considered as symbols, the sets of symbols differ because of the technical and psychological aspects that fix symbols and strings of symbols.

The technical features that Goodman distinguishes refer to syntactic and semantic aspects of symbols. The syntactic aspects relate to the well-formedness of symbols, and are syntactic disjointness and syntactic finite differentiation. The former relates to the question of whether symbols are real copies of each other, whereas the latter has something to do with the decision about whether a character belongs to one or the other symbol.

The semantic features relate to the domain of reference of symbols, but one has to keep in mind that symbols do not necessarily refer. Symbols not only symbolize, but can also classify (Goodman, 1968, p. 27). Instances of semantic features are semantic unambiguity, semantic disjointness, and semantic finite differentiation. In the case of semantic unambiguity a symbol refers to one object, "but in some cases syntactic replicas differ in extension" (Elgin, 1983, p. 102). Furthermore, symbols in a symbol system may not be semantically disjoint. For example, a dog belongs to the extensions of *mammal, faster than a human*, and *larger than a beatle.* "Given an object, we cannot derive a unique compliance class to which it belongs, for the object complies with a host of expressions whose extensions diverge." (Elgin, 1983, p.102). Semantic finite differentiation relates to the fact that determination of whether an object belongs to the one or to the other symbol is possible (Goodman, 1968). This is not so in the case of natural language; for example take an unripe banana. We cannot ultimately decide a symbol for the color of the banana. We can take two shades of yellow, for example greenish-yellow and yellowish-green. But it could be the case that the color is something like halfway between yellowish-green and greenish-yellow, or halfway between halfway, etc. Only if a symbol system is syntactically disjoint and finitely differentiated, and semantically unambiguous, disjoint, and finitely differentiated, can we call it a notational system.

Table 1. Technical and psychological features of symbols in two descriptions of commands in MS-DOS (icons and languagelike structure)

	Icons or pictorial presentation	Language or semantic presentation
Technical features		
Syntactic		
Disjointness	no	yes
Finite differentiation	no	yes
Semantic		
Unambiguity	yes	no
Disjointness	yes	no
Finite differentiation	yes	no
Psychological features		
Size of symbol set	small?	large (words)?
Clarity	?	?
Graphic suggestiveness	high?	low?
Mnemonic efficacy	high?	low?
Performability	difficult?	easy?

Table 1 indicates the technical and psychological features that GEMDESK-TOP (consisting of icons, windows, etc.) and the languagelike command structure of MS-DOS (consisting of letters and words) have. For the sake of completeness, the technical features are also included, but will not be discussed. Instead, I want to consider the psychological features and try to give some suggestions for further research.

Goodman does not treat the psychological features extensively, and in fact only mentions them. However, if the presentation and (mental) representation of information consist of symbols (and I have argued here in favor of this view), instructional psychology with reference to presentation, and cognitive psychology with reference to mental representation, have to find out whether for example size of the symbol set or mnemonic efficacy have any effect on the processing of information. To the best of my knowledge no psychonomic or ergonomic research has been done concerning the psychological features of any symbol system, and so I have formulated a few preliminary expectations for the symbol systems of icons and language-like commands (the question-marks in Table 1).

The set of symbols is large for languagelike commands compared with icon symbols. This can be important because the larger the symbol set the more difficult it will be to learn the symbols. The clarity of the symbol systems depends on the circumstances and the material the symbols are presented on. There does not have to be any difference in clarity between the two presentations, although it could be that in the case of icons more information can be presented in the same time. Both the graphic suggestiveness and the mnemonic efficacy of icon symbols seem to be high compared with language-like symbols, but it remains a task for psychological and ergonomic research to give operational definitions of mnemonic efficacy and graphic suggestiveness. As an illustration of the performability of symbols one only has to look at the characters in the Roman alphabet and Japanese ideograms. The symbol set of the former is small and easily performable, whereas the symbol set of the latter is large and not so easily performable. In our example of the presentation of MS-DOS commands the performability of languagelike symbols seems to be easy compared to icon symbols.

I will not say anything here about the comparison of symbols in mental representations, because I think the same can be done in this case as in the case of symbols in the modes of presentation, and also because in this case we have to look at the foundations of cognitive psychology (Palmer, 1978; Phylyshyn, 1984).

For the same reason it is very difficult to say anything about the comparison of mental representations and computer representations. If humans "interact" with computers, they mostly see icons or propositions on the screen; these are the screen presentations. They are the last step in a complex processing of internal representations in the computer. On several levels in the computer codes, i.e., symbol systems, are translated.

The important question in respect to human-computer interaction is whether mental representations in the human are coextensive with representations (symbolic codes) in the computer. In my opininion the answer to this question is negative, at least for the time being. This is because coextensiveness requires that extensions be defined. In the case of computer representations the domains and the elements within them are defined. Icon presentations on the screen are defined by the screen matrices as are the symbol systems (the machine-language and the programming languages) of which the icons are the representations.

The situation is unclear in the case of mental representations. The characteristic features of pictorial and propositional (mental) representations, although they consist of symbols and symbol systems (Newell, 1980; Pylyshyn, 1984), cannot be defined easily. But if we suppose that computers and humans are symbol-manipulating-systems, further psychonomic and ergonomic research should uncover the features of the mental symbol systems humans use. I think that an analysis of the features of symbols in general is an essential part of this enterprise.

5. Conclusions and Questions

In this last section I will reconsider the main themes of this chapter. Concerning human-computer interaction one has to make the very important assumption that information in information-processing systems (humans and computers) consists of symbols, in the sense of Goodman or Newell, and that processing is of symbols. That is to say, presentations as well as (mental) representations consist of symbols.

Furthermore, I have suggested that instructional psychology and cognitive psychology can both make contributions to problems concerning the interaction of humans and computers. Cognitive psychology has to find out more about the five aspects of mental representations that Palmer (1978) mentioned. For example, at present it is very unclear in what respect the elements in episodic representations really differ from the elements in temporal string representations. And if we agree with the above-mentioned assumption about symbols and operations on symbols, cognitive psychology has to investigate what I have called the technical and psychological features of icon symbols, alphabet symbols, diagrams, models, etc. Perhaps even the list of psychological features has to be extended. This research is important, because we have to know more about the human mind in order to facilitate human-computer interactions.

Instructional psychology has to concentrate on the relation between presentation and representation (in Figure 1 this relation is called encoding). As we know from research in problem solving, modes of presentation do influence subjects. Physical characteristics (providing a case for research in ergonomics and human factors) as well as psychological characteristics may facilitate or hinder problem solving. Also, the symbols used in presentations influence the mental representations, which in turn give meaning to presentations. This complex situation has to be elucidated in order to improve the interaction of humans and computers.

Acknowledgements.

I would like to thank H. Bogers, J.A. Michon and G. Mulder for the comments they have made on an earlier draft. Preparation of this paper was aided by Grant 56-202 form the Nederlandse Organisatie voor Zuiver Wetenschappelijk Onderzoek (Z.W.O.).

References

Anderson J.R. (1983). *The Architecture of cognition.* Harvard University Press, Cambridge, MA.

Anderson J.R.& Bower G.H. (1973). *Human associative memory.* Winston Washington DC.

Dennett D.C.(1978). *Brainstorms.* Harvester Press, Hassocks, Sussex.

Dreyfus H.L. (Ed.). (1982). *Husserl, intentionality and cognitive science* M.I.T. Press. Cambridge, MA.

Elgin C.Z.(1983). *With reference to reference.* Hackett, Indianapolis.

Fodor J.A. (1975). *The language of thought.* Harvester Press. Hassocks Sussex.

Goodman N.(1968). *Languages of art.* Bobbs-Merrill, Indianapolis.

Goodman N. (1972). *Problems and Projects.* Bobbs-Merrill, Indianapolis.

Goodman N. (1984). *Of mind and other matters.* Harvard University Press Cambridge, MA.

Grice H.P. (1957). Meaning. *Philosophical Review*, *LXVI*, pp. 377-88.

Johnson-Laird P.N. (1983). *Mental models.* Cambridge University Press, Cambridge.

Kolers P.A. & Smythe W.E. (1979). Images, symbols and skills. *Canadian Journal of Psychology*, 33 (3), pp. 158-184.

Kosslyn S.M. (1981). *Image and mind.* Harvard University Press, Cambridge, MA.

Newell A. (1980). Physical symbol systems. *Cognitive Science*, 4, 2, pp. 135-183.

Palmer S.F. (1978). Fundamental aspects of cognitive representation. In: *Cognition and categorization.* E.H. Rosch & B.B. Lloyd (Eds.). Erlbaum, Hillsdale, NJ.

Pylyshyn Z.W. (1984). *Computation and cognition.* M.I.T. Press, Cambridge, MA.

Rumelhart D.E. & Norman D.A. (1983). *Representation in memory.* Cognitive Science Laboratory, La Jolla, CA.

Searle J.R. (1984). *Intentionality.* Cambridge University Press, Cambridge.

Shepard R.N. & Metzler J. (1971). Mental rotation of three-dimensional objects. *Science*, 171, pp. 701-703.

Simon H.A. (1978). On the forms of mental representation. In: *Perception and cognition.* (Minnesota Studies in the Philosophy of Science Vol. IX.) C. Wade Savage (Ed.), University of Minnesota Press, Minneapolis.

Treffers A. (1984). Mathematisch-didactische Stromingen en Onderzoek van Wiskunde-onderwijs. In: *Rekenen.* P.G. Vos, K.B. Koster & J. Kingma, (Eds.). Swets and Zeitlinger, Lisse.

Tulving E. (1983). *Elements of episodic memory.* Oxford. University Press, Oxford.

Vonk W. (1977). *Retrieval from semantic memory.* Academisch Proefschrift, Groningen.

Chapter 11. Structuring Knowledge in a Graph

Frans N. Stokman and Pieter H. de Vries

1. Introduction

The idea that knowledge is a commodity that can be used by machines in various ways forms the entry to our discussion of knowledge based systems. We will limit ourselves to those systems that are in an active dialogue with their human user. As a consequence, the use and structuring of knowledge in autonomous systems, like robots or visual pattern recognizers, will not be discussed. In general, knowledge-based systems cannot be considered as models of human cognition. Rather, they should provide an extension of the user's cognitive abilities.

The emergence of knowledge-based systems showed that within a limited domain of expertise it is possible to construct computer programs that give intelligent advice to professional users. These systems, however, are still used on a rather small scale. Two obstacles seem to prevent a more widespread use. The first is the inconvenience that a knowledge based system is generally constructed in view of one type of task. However, one would like to use the same knowledge base for different purposes, e.g., a knowledge base in the medical domain should not only be applicable to diagnosis but also to other tasks such as therapy selection, explanation of results to the user, instruction to students, and information retrieval for planning new research. The second factor that stands in the way of more frequent use of knowledge-based systems is the scope of their expertise. Typically, the scope is limited to the knowledge of one expert. For more advanced applications, however, this will not be sufficient and the problem arises of under which conditions the representations of different experts can be integrated. In particular, the question arises as to what contribution a "new" expert can make to an already existing body of knowledge.

The research project on procedures and concepts for the construction and analysis of knowledge graphs of the Technology University of Twente and the University of Groningen aims to develop a system for the representation of scientific theories in (at least) medical and social sciences. The structuring of knowledge in a graph can be seen as the construction of a knowledge-based system integrating knowledge from different sources. In this paper we will give a short overview of knowledge-based systems, and subsequently will justify the representation of empirical scientific knowledge in a graph. We will then outline the procedures for structuring knowledge in a graph, and finally will elaborate the role of textual analysis in the knowledge-acquisition phase.

2. Exploitation and Structuring of Knowledge

The way in which knowledge is used may to a certain extent influence the form in which it is stored in a machine. A model specifying the organization of this storage is referred to as a representation of knowledge. The application of a knowledge representation for a specific task is referred to as exploitation. The process of obtaining and adapting such a representation will be called the structuring of knowledge.

A typical example of exploitation of knowledge is decision support in its various forms. An example can be drawn from medicine where we have a task, diagnosis, that is executed on a representation of a generic patient. The task requires an initial specification of a particular patient, i.e., his symptoms. On the basis of the inferences defined for the representation a specific model for that patient is computed. This kind of inference can be generalized to other forms of decision support. For instance, one not only wants to have a correct diagnosis for the abnormal behaviour of an object but also a description of the behaviour when certain courses of action are taken. Apart from decision support, information retrieval and instruction are important forms of exploiting knowledge. We will not discuss all varieties of exploitation here.

Knowledge-based systems are faced with the problem of acquiring their knowledge. The knowledge acquisition comprises both the collection of knowledge elements in a given domain and their integration in a common representation. The knowledge elements as they are collected do not in themselves suggest a valid representation. It is in the process of their integration that a representation emerges. Because of the role of active integration we will use the concept of "structuring of knowledge" rather than the more passive "acquisition of knowledge."

Learning is a typical form of structuring knowledge. Here, the question is how a representation is organized in a way that permits continuous updating and integration of knowledge. Of course this description of learning leaves many psychological aspects untouched. However, it is sufficient to separate exploitation from structuring of knowledge and we will outline some models for machine learning in the next section. Learning can also be seen as a form of structuring knowledge in which representations from different cognitive systems are compared and integrated. We can regard cognitive systems as a set of experts (either human or artificial) that each have a representation of a common domain. A question that arises in this context is how the knowledge of a common domain is extracted from its carrier, i.e., from its text, and organized into an integrated representation. A second question concerns what effective procedures can give the relations between representations of different individuals. These and other questions will be dealt with in our discussion of knowledge graphs.

3. An Overview of Knowledge Representation

When talking of knowledge representation we can distinguish between procedural and declarative knowledge. This distinction was elaborated in philosophy when Ryle (1949) distinguished between "knowing how" and "knowing that." In the context of this discussion we can describe procedural knowledge as a set of prescriptions for actions. Generally, these prescriptions are referred to as situation-action rules. In a given system the set of rules, and therefore its knowledge, is tuned toward the task for which the system is designed. In a declarative representation, knowledge is not given as a set of rules but as a set of assertions about a certain subject. Conclusions can then be drawn from these assertions by inference methods. These inference methods can be based on formal systems like logic (e.g. the principle of resolution; Robinson, 1965), or, as in our case, graph theory. An important property of a declarative representation is that the same knowledge base can be used in different tasks. For each task an inference mechanism is defined that interprets the same set of assertions. Within a declarative approach to knowledge representation we face the problem of distinguishing among various types of relations that are specified in the assertions about a domain of interest. We will refer to conceptual knowledge as a declarative representation. Furthermore, the core of conceptual knowledge consists of explicitly defined types of relations between concepts. Various types can be distinguished, e.g., they can express definitional as well as empirical relations between concepts. For the selection of the types of relations it is difficult to give general criteria. We note here, however, that if the type of relation is left open an important distinction between a procedural and a conceptual representation vanishes. A relation then merely has the function of an association (possibly directed) between two concepts. Such a neutral relation can adequately be formalized by either a production rule, logical implication or associative link in a graph.

In Table 1 forms of knowledge are contrasted with uses of knowledge to form a four-field table of knowledge based activities. The table should not be considered as a classification of systems, as systems exist that unite activities belonging to different fields in this table. The table only enables a systematic evaluation of systems in this vigorous field of research.

Table 1. Classification of knowledge-based activities

	Form of knowledge	
Use of knowledge	Procedural knowledge	Conceptual knowledge
Exploitation	Decision-support and information retrieval on the basis of chaining of rules	Decision-support on the basis of detection of causality, information retrieval on the basis of definition relations
Structuring	Verification of rules Induction of rules	Integration of definitions and causal models

The procedural knowledge is generally represented as a set of *if-then* rules, such as the following:

if heart-attack *then* conclude high blood pressure
if x is a bird *then* conclude x has wings and x can sing

The *if* part of a rule contains a description of a situation that can be observed in the data-base of a rule-based system. The *then* part contains an action. In the example the action is a conclusion. Note that the nature of the inference made in a rule cannot be obtained from the rule itself. The first rule in the above example for instance, embodies an inference based on a causal relation: the high blood presssure is the cause of the heart-attack. In the second rule, however, the inference is of a purely definitional nature. The fact that rules are neutral with respect to the type of relation they specify between antecedent and consequent terms brought about the term shallow reasoning for this use of knowledge.

The exploitation of procedural knowledge is accomplished by the chaining of rules. Rules can be chained in a forward or backward direction. The former occurs when a situation provides enough evidence for executing an action. This is the case, for example, in a design-task like configuring a computer with its peripherals (McDermott, 1982). In backward chaining the execution of the action has to provide evidence for a postulated situation. This kind of reasoning is found in a diagnosis task. Here we postulate a certain situation, i.e., a disease, and carry out an action to obtain evidence for it (Davis,

Buchanan & Shortliffe, 1977). The logical scheme behind both kinds of reasoning is identical.

A relatively simple method of structuring procedural knowledge is the inspection and updating of a chain of rules triggered by a particular problem presented to a rule-based system. The expert system MYCIN has such a complementary system for structuring rules, namely TEIRESIAS (Davis, 1982). In a dialogue the user can see what the consequences are of deleting or inserting a rule in the the knowledge base. A more complicated method of structuring procedural knowledge is the induction of situation-action rules given a set of examples. Winston (1975) describes a program that, on the basis of examples, identifies correctly the geometrical shape of an arch.

An example of the exploitation of conceptual knowledge is the application of inference procedures to semantic networks for the retrieval of information. In semantic networks many types and even sub-types of relations are distinguished (see Brachman, 1983). In every network, however, two types of relations play a central role: the relation indicating class membership and the relation giving a property of a class. An example of the former is the assertion "a canary is a bird," in which the concept of canary is linked to the class of birds. An example of the latter is the linking of the property "wings" to the concept of bird, i.e., the assertion "a bird has wings." These two types of relations are basic for the retrieval of information: when a particular property cannot be directly retrieved from a concept it is inherited from a concept higher in the class hierarchy. Retrieval from new generations of databases will draw heavily on a conceptual representation of knowledge (Riet, 1983). Conceptual networks can also be generalized to express relations between subnetworks, also referred to as partitions (Winograd, 1980).

Another form of exploitation of conceptual knowledge is causal reasoning. Various forms of causality can be detected, e.g., the so-called minimal cause (Vries Robbe, 1978). In the research on knowledge representation there is a tendency to refine the notion of causality. In Kuipers (1984) a distinction is made between the functional dependencies between quantities and the causal dependencies between the state-changes manifested by these quantities. For a further discussion of the refinement of the notion of causality in knowledge based systems the reader is referred to Vries Robbé and Vries (1985). The term deep reasoning refers to the inferences that are performed on a representation making explicit the relations giving the structure and function of a mechanism.

An example of a program structuring conceptual knowledge is EURISKO (Lenat, 1983). It contains a large network of concepts connected by various types of links such as generalization and specification links and so-called suggestion links. The program has several procedures of a heuristic nature that explore the network. It has been shown that these procedures can integrate existing definitions of concepts to form new meaningful concepts. For instance, the concept of length was "discovered," starting from the elementary concepts of equality, list, and set. The comparison of representations of different individuals and their integration is another form of structuring conceptual knowledge. These topics will be treated in the discussion on knowledge graphs.

4. Representation of Scientific Knowledge in a Graph

As was stated in the introduction, the research group on procedures and concepts for the construction and analysis of knowledge graphs of the Technology University of Twente and the University of Groningen aims to develop a system for the representation of scientific theories in (at least) medical and social sciences. Theories in these sciences are empirically oriented, rather than deductive systems built upon a small number of premises as in, for example, physics. Scientific knowledge in the former sciences is oriented towards explanation and prediction of empirical phenomena by means of theories, in which covariations between classes of phenomena are ordered in a logically consistent and coherent system. The building stones of these theories are concepts of which at least some should be related to empirical phenomena. In order to test a scientific theory (in experimental designs as well as in non-experimental settings) two submodels can be distinguished: a *measurement model* that specifies the relation between manifest (experimental) behaviour and latent (theoretical) concepts; and a *structural* model that specifies the direction and type of association between the different concepts and that, as a consequence, specifies the structure of the phenomena to which these concepts refer.

As such the scientific process can be seen as a process in which, for a class of objects, relations between these objects and their properties are specified and estimated by means of structural models. These properties are related to behavior manifested by measurement models. The estimation of parameters is restricted to the set of variables that is considered in a structural model. Consequently, representation of these parameters with the object of using them in inferences in a knowledge-based system integrating several models would be misleading. Therefore, only the presence or absence of structural relations (possibly extended with a measure of their likelihood of existence) will be used in the designed inferential procedures. The user, however, is given the opportunity to specify all kinds of information for the relations he thinks useful.

Let us start the discussion on the chosen knowledge representation with the elements that constitute the basic parts of any measurement process. Measurement can be seen as the process in which properties are instantiated for a given object (Pfanzagl, 1968; Krantz, Luce, Suppes & Tversky, 1971). Such an instantiation is denoted a value. *Objects, properties* and *values* are therefore essential building stones of empirically oriented scientific theories, and therefore of systems that represent scientific knowledge. Symbols and concepts (including subsets of natural language, logic, and mathematics) are the linguistic elements to denote these building stones. Objects, properties and values are related to concepts by a realization or projection of the linguistic concept or symbol into an empirical, "real-world," system. Objects, properties and values must have been defined on a linguistic level to enable one to speak about empirical elements. Within the empirical system a property is the result of the identification of an aspect of an object, and a value is produced by the measurement of a property.

Structural dependencies between properties of an object (i.e., the structural models) can be considered the core of scientific knowledge because they refer to relations between empirical phenomena that are corroborated in empirical research and are assumed to be more generally valid. Such structural dependencies can be represented by arcs between vertices in which the arc denotes a structural dependence relation (denoted CAU) and the vertices denote properties. Such a CAU relation is directed from "cause" to "effect." It should have at least a sign to denote whether the relation between the properties is positive of negative. Taking this perspective on causality, we follow Simon's definition of causality as "an asymmetrical relation among certain variables, or subsets of variables, in a self-contained structure" (Simon, 1977). This definition corresponds to the intuitive use of causality in scientific discussions, in contrast to definitions in terms of logical implications which have the counterintuitive implication that *A causes B* implies *not B causes not A*.

According to the definition of measurement, properties should be related to a generic object. To represent this, the relation *is part of* (denoted PAR) is introduced and represented in the knowledge base by an arc from property to object. A third type of relation - indispensable for purposes of integration and structuring of scientific knowledge from different sources - is used in the knowledge base to represent the relation *is a kind of* between two concepts (denoted AKO). This type of relation is introduced in order to represent that structural relations between properties of a certain class of objects can be considered a special case of those of another class of objects.

Values are not represented as vertices, but as information associated with vertices in their role as properties. In the current representation only presence and absence can be attached to a property if it is a dichotomy, or positive/neutral/negative when the property is a continuum. These values are not relevant in the structuring process, but only in the exploitation phase. In decision support for example, values can be assigned to certain properties by the user. The consequences of this assignment are computed for other properties of an instantiation of an object on the basis of the signs of the CAU relations.

The above three relations, CAU, PAR, and AKO, are the three fundamental relations in the knowledge base, CAU being defined between properties, AKO between objects, and PAR relating properties to an object (see Figure 1). The three relations are represented by arcs simply because they are asymmetric relations. The direction of an arc does not prevent its use in the opposite direction in searching and inferential procedures such as path algebras. In the opposite direction, arcs represent respectively the relations *is caused by* (denoted CBY), *has as part* (denoted HAP), and *has as kind* (denoted HAK). The restriction of the system to the above mentioned types of arcs is not fundamental and the number of types of arc can be gradually extended. In the present stage of the project the restriction is warranted because of the very fundamental problems that are to be solved precisely in the field of integrating and structuring pieces of information and knowledge from different sources. This area is often avoided in artificial intelligence by restricting the knowledge represented in a system to that of one expert or source. Whether a vertex takes the role of object, property, or both, in the knowledge base is determined by its relations with other vertices. If a vertex is involved in AKO relations or is the head of a PAR relation, it takes the role of object; otherwise it takes the role of property.

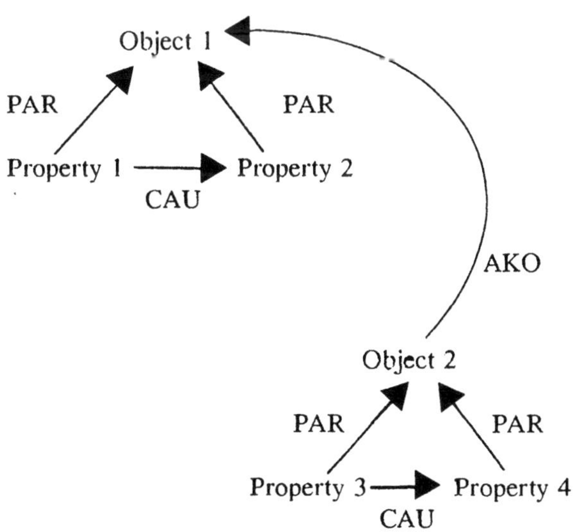

Figure 1. Types of relations in the knowledge base

The above representation, however, is not yet sophisticated enough to represent scientific knowledge. Quite often concepts are introduced to denote relations between concepts and these are subsequently used as part of a relation with other concepts. An example is contained in the following sentence:

> The syndrome, in which renewed contact with allergens leads to bronchial obstruction, is an example of extrinsic asthma (Example a)

Such a relation on a relation might have been represented by an arc on an arc, but this was rejected because it can be considered as a special case of a more general phenomenon in which concepts are introduced to denote a whole process consisting of a set of relations and concepts. This can be illustrated with the following example:

> Atopic patients have a familial tendency towards a sensitivity for known inhalation allergens (like dust, molds and pollens). Hereby IgE antibodies are created. The renewed contact with the allergen leads to

a

b

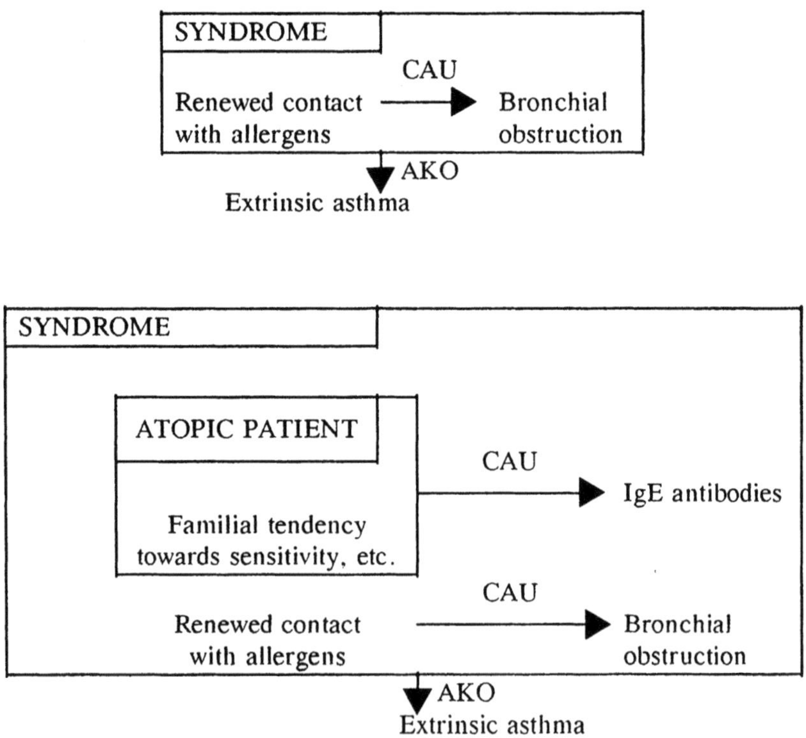

Figure 2. The representation of the text examples a and b using frameworks

a bronchial obstruction. This syndrome is an example of extrinsic asthma (Example b)

Therefore, a general solution was sought, and consisted of the introduction of a new primitive into the knowledge representation: the framework. A framework represents a whole set of concepts and relations. A new relation, the FPAR relation, represents the relations between a framework and its constituent concepts and relations. Figure 2 shows the representations of the above examples with frameworks. The main features of a procedure for text analysis that has been developed within the context of the present project are given later.

Frameworks and the FPAR relation make it possible to represent relations between whole processes. But the FPAR relation can also be seen as a generalization and an alternative representation of the PAR relation: all PAR relations are replaced by frameworks. The framework then represents an object and the vertices within the framework its properties (see Figure 3). When a knowledge graph is constructed for a certain class of objects, e.g., a class of patients in a medical application, the whole graph can be considered as a framework. A PAR relation connects the arcs and vertices of a graph (representing medical processes in this case) to a framework (in this example the patient). The introduction of the framework makes it possible to represent explicitly the class of objects considered.

A representation with frameworks is no longer a graph-theoretical representation and consequently precludes the application of the full variety of graph-theoretical concepts and procedures that was the main reason to search for that type of representation. The above representation can be transformed into a strictly equivalent representation in which all the above-mentioned elements (vertices, frameworks and arcs) are represented as the vertices of the new graph. When a vertex or arc is contained in a framework, this is represented in the new graph by arcs from the constituent elements of a framework to the vertex representing the framework. The other arcs in the new graph represent

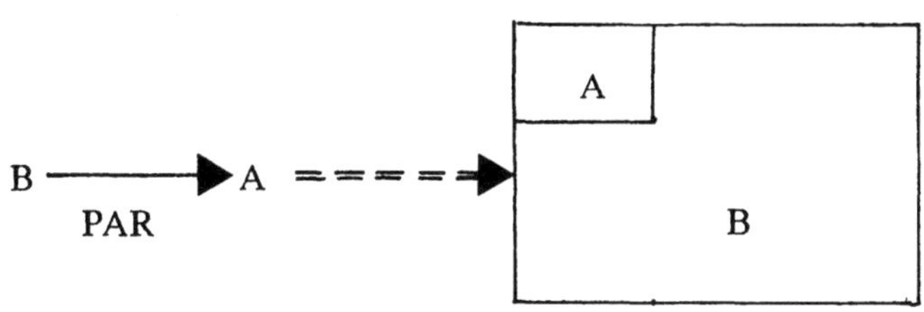

Figure 3. Alternative representations of the PAR-relation

the incidence relations between the vertices and arcs in the original representation. The chosen representation is known as the total graph.

A graph-theoretical representation has major advantages above other representations because of the large number of graph-theoretical procedures and concepts that can be applied meaningfully to graphs representing (scientific) knowledge. These procedures and concepts concern such aspects as features of the overall structure of the graph, the (relative) centrality of arcs and vertices within a graph, and the detection of subgraphs with certain characteristics. These aspects may be less important for systems that are restricted to the representation of the knowledge of one expert or (scientific) scource, but they are highly important in the light of the aims of the present project that is oriented towards comparing, structuring, and integrating scientific knowledge obtained from different sources.

5. Procedures for Structuring Knowledge in a Graph

The flow diagram given in Figure 4 specifies the system for the manipulation of knowledge graphs. It contains the basic classes of procedures for structuring and integrating knowledge into an integrated graph and the class of procedures to use the integrated knowledge base for exploitation. To represent the main knowledge in a particular field of science the first basic problem consists of the selection of sources from which the knowledge can best be collected. Several recommendations might well be proposed by the system, but no explicit procedures will be developed to support the decisions of the researcher in this respect. Formally, however, it can be seen as a first step in the structuring of knowledge in an integrated knowledge base. More important for us are the other four classes of structuring procedures, because our project aims to develop well-defined procedures to support knowledge engineering in those respects. Extraction of the relevant concepts and relations from a text is the first major class of structuring procedures that is considered in the project. This extraction through *textual analysis* should result in a representation of all relevant parts of a text in a so-called *author graph*. This class of procedures is elaborated in the next section.

Three classes of structuring procedures aim to integrate the different pieces of knowledge as they are represented within the different author graphs. Integration of author graphs requires first of all *identification of concepts* belonging to different graphs. On the basis of the names of the concepts, but also on the basis of structural equivalence of concepts and subsets of concepts in the graphs, concepts that are identical should be identified. In the context of con-

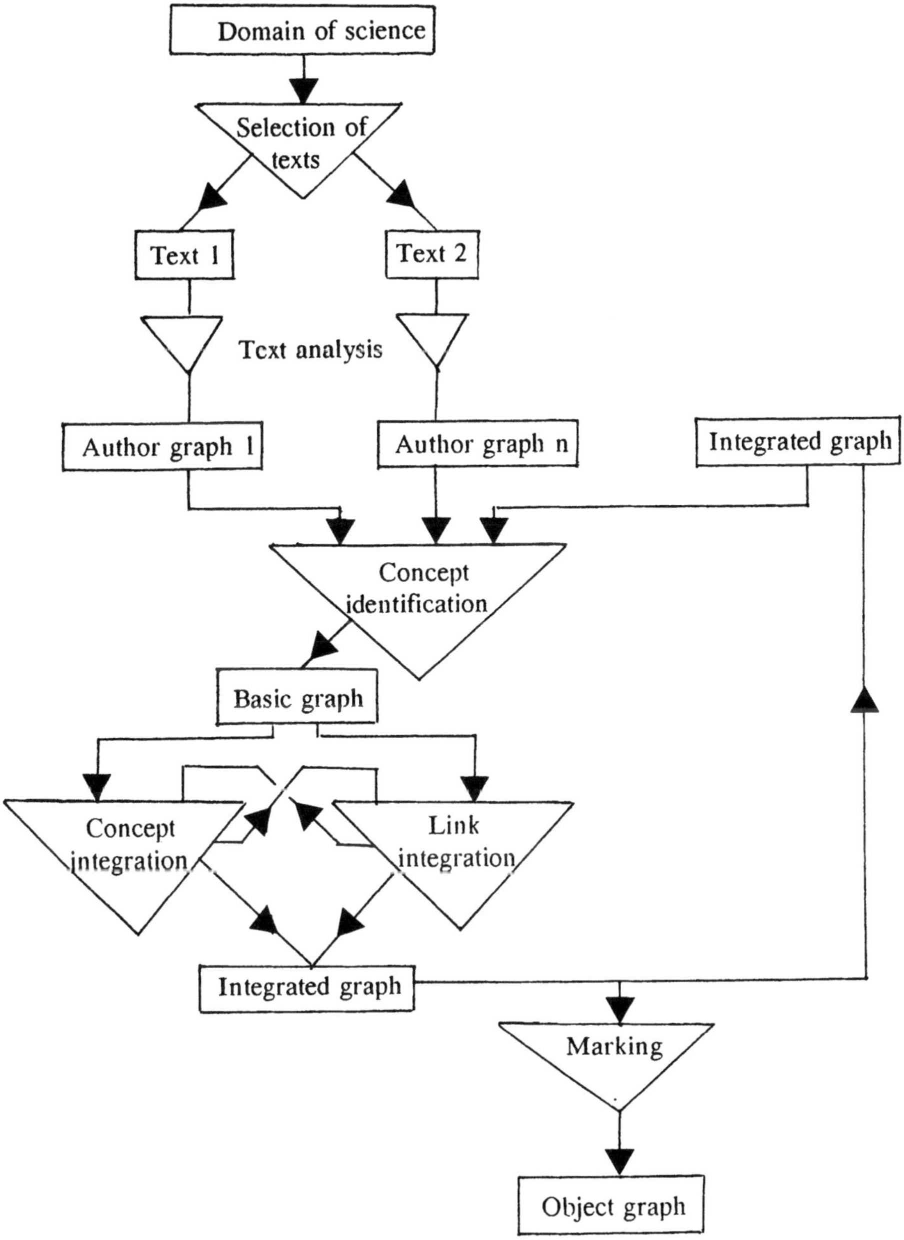

Figure 4. Flow diagram for the structuring of knowledge in a graph

cept identification a number of graph theoretical algorithms have been developed to facilitate the identification process for the user (Hoede, 1986). The detected structural equivalences can be represented by contracting vertices or by adding AKO and PAR relations to the knowledge graph. The author graphs, together with these additional definitive relations, form the *basic graph*. To transform the basic graph into an *integrated graph*, first of all concepts that form a modular unit, a construct, are detected (Bakker, 1984). In the chosen representation these constructs are implemented as frameworks. Such an integration may result in several parallel relations between concepts when the user replaces the framework representing a construct by a simple vertex. Procedures of *line integration* aim to integrate such relations to one new relation with a minimal loss of information. A path algebra has been developed that can be used to determine the relation that results from a set of relations combined either in parallel or serially (By, 1985).

As the flow diagram shows, the process of structuring and integrating knowledge can be repeated several times. Of course, an integrated graph can itself again be used for concept identification and concept and line integration with new author graphs to obtain a higher-order integration, as is also shown in the flow diagram. Such structuring processes may be done on the basis of complete equality of the different author graphs, but also on the basis of a target graph (which may or may not be an earlier integrated graph). The main aims of the structuring processes are, then, to show the overlap, additional information, and the contradictions of one or more author graphs with respect to the target graph.

6. From Text to Knowledge Graph

The first stage in the construction of a knowledge graph concerns the translation of knowledge "at large" into the arcs and points of an author graph. By knowledge at large we mean knowledge that is not formatted in a way that permits manipulation by an automaton. A subset of this knowledge resides in the head of human experts. One of the reasons rule based systems are used is the ease of creating and maintaining a knowledge bank of rules. When collecting the knowledge elements in a domain, rules lend themselves easily to representing the knowledge obtained in an interview with an expert. However, the fact that the knowledge obtained in this way is procedural in nature may turn out to be a disadvantage. A procedural representation cannot be used for generating adequate explanations, as was outlined in the overview of knowledge representation. This inadequacy follows directly from the way in which the representation was constructed. Often, experts can only say how they solve a problem but not what model they use. This model gives the conceptual knowledge necessary for explaining a solution of a problem.

Given the aim of the system, for knowledge graphs the representation of conceptual knowledge is crucial. Therefore, the conversion of knowledge in the head of a human expert into a formal representation is not sufficient. Rather, the knowledge at large that is selected for representation should be extracted from handbooks, articles, and other scientific documents. These documents are of an explanatory nature and contain the conceptual knowledge left implicit in the protocols obtained from interviewing experts. The role of the human expert in the construction of a knowledge graph is thus situated in two places, first as the selector of the texts to be translated into author graphs, and secondly as a judge of the results obtained from the knowledge-structuring process, i.e., an integrated graph.

A procedure for text analysis for cognitive maps is given by Wrightson (1976). Cognitive maps are conceptual representations strongly resembling knowledge graphs. Taking this procedure as a starting point, Buissink (1982) developed a text-analysis procedure for knowledge graphs. This procedure was applied and validated for texts in the domain of social dentistry. The procedure of text analysis discussed below follows from these earlier studies. The texts are drawn from the domain of obstructive lung diseases. This domain was selected because the integrated graph can then be exploited as a knowledge base for medical decision making. Furthermore, obstructive lung diseases are one of the most frequently occurring complaints in a physician's practice, and local expertise is available for selection of texts and validation of the obtained knowledge graphs.

Essentially the method for text analysis is based on two assumptions, the first of which is that *there exists a set of base sentences onto which virtually all sentences in a text can be mapped.* Some of these base sentences are the expression in natural language of the types of arcs defined for a knowledge graph, or their attributes, an example of the latter being the sign of a causal relation. Other base sentences express knowledge that is not (yet) represented in a knowledge graph. The introduction of base sentences permits a gradual decomposition of a text. In the first stage only those text sentences are identified that contain at the functional center a base sentence defined for a knowledge graph. When assembling these base sentences into a knowledge graph a further decomposition of the parts of these sentences may be necessary in order to assure a correct linkage of the arcs and vertices in the knowledge graph.

The second assumption in the method of text analysis concerns the information conveyed by base sentences, and is that *The object for which the knowledge graph is constructed is defined.* The object, (see the overview) acts as a context in which base sentences are evaluated. We assume that in a scientific text at least two objects are described, the object investigated and the object conducting the investigation, i.e., one or more scientists. The description of the former gives a structural model of the observed object, which the scientist claims is, at least to some extent, independent of his observation. A scientist does not claim such an objective status for the sentences describing the second object, i.e, him- or herself. These sentences express the motives that led to the investigation of the first object. Although these sentences might contain base sentences expressing a type of arc defined for a knowledge graph they must be skipped because they are not a part of the structural model of the predefined object of investigation.

The decomposition of a text sentence into a set of base sentences is accomplished by means of a so-called *dependency grammar.* A dependency grammar is based on the concepts of argument, operator, and modifier. We speak of dependency because in this grammar an argument is defined as dependent on an operator and an operator as dependent on a modifier. The grammar gives an instrument for determining the functional center of a sentence, i.e., the main operator in a sentence. Dependency grammars have been analysed by Harris (1982) for their application to natural language. Their implementation in a computer program is described by Sager (1981) .

The concepts involved in a dependency grammar can be defined as follows:

Arguments are words on which other words do not depend. Typically, these words are (non-relational) nouns denoting "static" objects like box, chair, etc.

Operators are words of which other words depend as arguments. Examples of operators are verbs, adjectives, and relational nouns (e.g., father of, example of). Operators differ in the number of arguments they bind. In a knowledge graph all relations, including frameworks, are modelled as binary relations. For this reason we assume that the maximum number of arguments bound by an operator is two. Operators that may seem to bind more arguments can be handled by adding modifiers to a two-placed operator.

Modifiers are words on which an operator or other modifier is dependent. Adverbs are examples of one-placed modifiers. Modifiers can also be two-placed, in which case they relate an object to an action, or an action to another action. Prepositions are examples of the former. Examples of the latter are conjunctions like *while* and *because.*

The concepts of argument, operator, and modifier can be applied recursively to decompose a sentence. This decomposition is recursive because the arguments dependent on an operator can be considered as constituents that can again be decomposed into operators, arguments, or modifiers. An example of

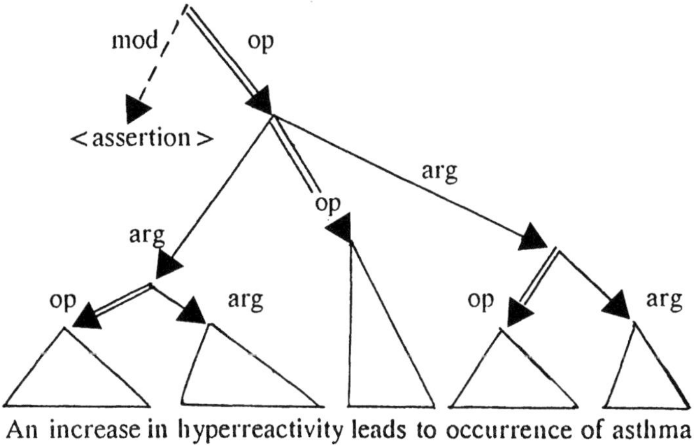

Figure 5. Decomposition of a sentence in arguments (*arg*), operators (*op*) and modifiers (*mod*)

a recursive definition of a sentence is given in Figure 5. Note from Figure 5 that the fact that the sentence in this example is an assertion is represented as a modifier of the central operator. In a knowledge graph only sentences that are assertions are represented. Sometimes an assertion is itself the main operator, as in a sentence like "We emphasize that bronchial obstruction is an important characteristic of asthma." In these cases the message, i.e., that which is asserted (which is the second argument of the central operator), is further decomposed. Dependency grammars permit an operator to be not explicitly stated in a sentence because it does not contribute to the informativeness of that sentence. For instance, it is in general not informative to state explicitly that a sentence is an assertion. Likewise, some operators that are indicated by the verb *to be* are sometimes left out due to their noninformativeness. Examples of such a form of operator reduction are sentences like "Asthma is a disease." Reintroducing the full operator into this sentence gives "Asthma is an example of a disease".

In order to decompose a text adequately we have extensively defined the operators that stand for the types of relations in a knowledge graph. The sentences giving these operators can be described as follows:

Causal sentences are sentences where a change in one property is described as structurally dependent of that in another property (e.g., "An increase in hyperreactivity leads to the occurrence of asthma")

Composition sentences are sentences that identify a property of an object. (e.g., "Obstruction of the bronchus is a property of asthma")

Generalization sentences are sentences where an object is described as a special case of another object. (e.g., "Asthma is a special case of a disease")

Note that a causal sentence in its complete form is composed of three operators, one expressing the change in the cause (e.g., "an increase in hypereactivity"), one expressing the change in the effect (e.g., "the occurrence of asthma"), and one that attributes the change in the effect to the change in the cause (e.g., "leads to"). On the basis of the direction of the changes of cause and effect a sign for the causal relation in the knowledge graph can be computed.

The steps in the procedure for text analysis can be summarized as follows:

1. Search for operators, arguments and modifiers in sentence
2. Identify message in assertion
3. Classify main operator in message as a relation-type
4. Identify corresponding arguments as nodes or frameworks
5. Classify main operator in modifier as a relation type
6. Identify corresponding arguments as nodes or frameworks

It is worth noting that in a message both the operator and its modifier have to be inspected. The reason is that the causal relation can occur as a combination of an operator and a modifier. Generally, the causation is expressed by the main operator in the message and the changes of the properties are contained in its arguments. An example of such a sentence was shown in figure 5. However, it is also possible that the main operator in the message expresses a change and that its modifier reflects the causation (see Figure 6).

The method of text analysis described here is still under development. With respect to the decomposition of sentences into arguments, operators, and modifiers, we have examined to what extent automatic procedures can support the detection of central operators that express a type of relation defined for a knowledge graph. Furthermore, reliability studies will be undertaken to estimate the agreement among several lay human analysers of a text. These studies will show the variability that occurs due to text phenomena that are hard to formalize. Basically these phenomena concern two issues, namely, the identification of the appropriate context (i.e., the object of investigation), and the correct resolution of references occuring in sentences describing this object. Both issues still are an important bottleneck for an automatic analysis of text. The results of reliability studies will show to what extent a knowledge graph correctly represents the central assertions in a text.

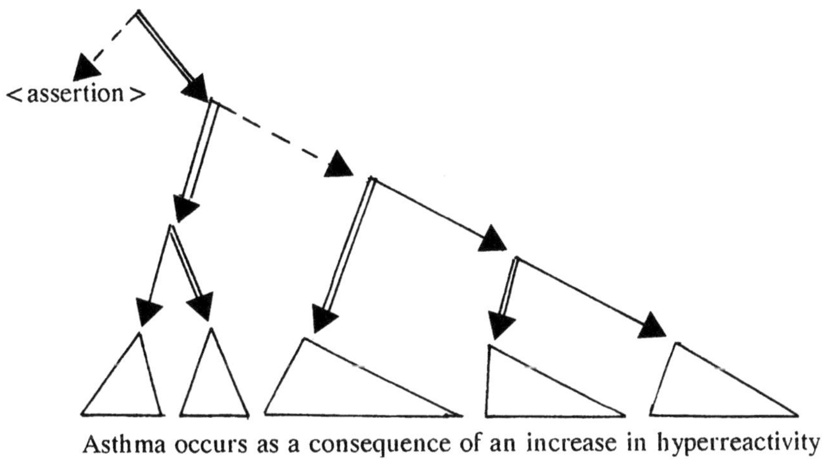

Figure 6. Causal sentence with main operator of the message reflecting change

7. Summary

In the preceding discussion we have elaborated the view that knowledge is a commodity that can exploited in various ways. Examples of such exploitations are decision making, information retrieval, and instruction. In order to exploit a knowledge base to its full extent it is necessary to seperate the knowledge in a certain area of interest from the task-specific inferences defined on it. In an overview of knowledge-based systems we have observed that such a seperation of domain and control knowledge is realized in systems based on a conceptual knowledge representation. Procedural representations, by contrast, are fixed with respect to a predefined task. Here, control and domain knowledge are merged into a knowledge base of rules. An important restriction of most knowledge-based systems is that their knowledge is typically limited to that of one expert. In general, few procedures are provided to evaluate the effect of "new" knowledge on an existing knowledge base.

The central issue in the discussion has been how conceptual knowledge from different sources can be obtained and organized in a coherent representation. Within the domain of theories from medicine and the social sciences a representation in the form of a knowledge graph is given. Given the aim of integrating knowledge from different sources, a small set of types of relations is taken as a starting point. These types are a minimal requirement for representing the knowledge embodied in theories in medicine and the social sciences. The structural relations specified in a theory are represented by arcs labeled by a causal type. These structural relations are given for the properties belonging to one object. The relation connecting a property to an object is represented by an arc labeled by a composition type. In order to transpose the properties of one class of objects to another, arcs labeled by a generalization type are included in the representation. Objects, together with their properties and relations, are represented as frameworks. The inclusion of a framework in a graph is accomplished by a representation in the form of a so-called total graph.

Texts are the most widespread and accessible carriers of empirical theories. Extraction of the relevant concepts and relations from a text is the first major class of procedure for structuring knowledge in a graph. The extraction through textual analysis results in a so-called author graph. Procedures for concept identification transform a set of author graphs into a basic graph. Within a basic graph, concepts as well as relations can be integrated. In order to reason with different types of relations a path algebra was defined. The structuring of knowledge in a graph is a cyclic process that can take place on the basis of complete equality among author graphs, but also on the basis of a target graph.

For the extraction of an author graph from a text a dependency grammar is defined. According to this grammar, a sentence in a text is parsed into a structure of operators, arguments, and modifiers. Only sentences expressing an assertion are accepted as building blocks for a knowledge graph. In the asserted message the main operator and the operator in the modifier are provisionally classified as one of the three defined relation types. Their arguments coincide with vertices or frameworks, that may appear in the role of object or property (or both). A dependency grammar permits scanning of only the surface of a text. The outcome of the text analysis, i.e., the author graph, is only an approximative model of the knowledge in a text. It is sufficient, however, with respect to the structuring of knowledge obtained from different sources, such as the empirical domains mentioned above.

Acknowledgements

The research group on knowledge graphs consists of C. Hoede, R.R. Bakker, H.J. Smit (Twente University of Technology), F.N. Stokman, and P.H. de Vries (University of Groningen). The research is funded by the Dutch Organization for Scientific Research under grant no. 40-029. The research is done in cooperation with the MEDES project of the University Hospital Groningen under the direction P.F. de Vries Robbé. We thank Kees Hoede for comments on this chapter.

References

Bakker R.R. (1984). *Construct analysis as a method of knowledge integration of Cognitive Graphs.* (Memorandum no. 463), University of Technology, Enschede.

Brachman R.J. (1983). What ISA is and isn't: An analysis of taxonomic links in semantic networks. *IEEE Transactions on Computers, Special Issue on Knowledge Representation*, 16 (10), pp. 30-35.

Buissink J.V. (1982). *De kennisgraaf als instrument voor de opslag van kennis en de vorming van theorieën.* Sociological Institute, University of Groningen.

By R. de (1985). *Semantische aspekten van paden in kennisgrafen.* Univ. of Technology, Enschede.

Davis R. (1982). Teiresias: Applications of meta-level knowledge. In: *Knowledge-based Systems in Artificial Intelligence.* R. Davis & D.B. Lenat (Ed.), McGraw-Hill, New York. pp. 227-490.

Davis R., Buchanan B. & Shortliffe E. (1977). Production rules as a representation for a knowledge-based consultation program. *Artificial Intelligence*, 8, pp. 15-45.

Harris Z. (1982). *A grammar of English on mathematical principles.* Wiley, New York.

Hoede C. (1986). *Similarity in knowledge graphs.* Department of Applied Mathematics, Twente University of Technology, Enschede.

Krantz D.H., Luce R.D., Suppes P. & Tversky A. (1971). *Foundations of measurement: Vol. I Additive and polynomial representations*, Academic Press, New York.

Kuipers B. (1984). Commonsense reasoning about causality: Deriving behavior from structure. *Artificial Intelligence*, 19, pp. 39-88.

Lenat D.B. (1983). EURISKO: a program that learns new heuristics and domain concepts. *Artificial Intelligence*, 21, pp. 61-98.

McDermott J. (1982). R1: A rule-based configurer of computer systems. *Artificial Intelligence*, 19, pp. 39-88.

Pfanzagl, J. (1968). *Theory of measurement.* Physica-Verlag, Wurzburg.

Riet R.P. van (1983). Knowledge bases - de databanken van de toekomst. *Informatie*, 25, pp. 16-23.

Robinson J.A. (1965). A machine-oriented logic based on the resolution principle. *Journal of the ACM*, 12 (1), p. 23.

Ryle G. (1949). *The Concept of Mind.* Hutchinson, London.

Sager N. (1981). *Natural language information processing: A computer grammar of english and its applications.* Addison-Wesley, Reading, MA.

Simon H.A. (1977). *Models of discovery and other topics in the methods of science.* Reidel, Dordrecht.

Vries Robbé P.F. de (1978). *Medische besluitvorming: een aanzet tot formele besluitvorming.* Dissertation. University of Groningen.

Vries Robbé P.F. de & Vries P.H. de (1985). Epistemology of medical expert systems. In: *Medical decision making, diagnostic strategies and expert systems.* J.H. v. Bemmel, S. Grèmy & J. Zvárová, (Eds.), North-Holland, Amsterdam. pp. 89-94.

Winograd T. (1980). Extended inference modes in reasoning by computer systems. *Artificial Intelligence*, 13, pp. 5-26.

Winston P.H. (1975). Learning structural descriptions from examples. In: *The Psychology of Computer Vision.* P. Winston (Ed.). McGraw-Hill, New York. pp. 157-209.

Wrightson M. (1976). The documentary coding method. In: *The Structure of Decision.* R. Axelrod (Ed.). Princeton University Press, Princeton. pp. 291-332

Chapter 12. Knowledge Representation Techniques in Artificial Intelligence: An Overview

Koenraad De Smedt

1. Introduction

1.1. Knowledge Engineering

The way in which humans use computers is rapidly moving towards the delegation of increasingly complex problem-solving tasks to computers. At the same time the interaction between a human and a computer is becoming increasingly refined so as to allow a richer exchange of information. Both trends require the computer to be able to use a large amount of knowledge. Researchers in the field of artificial intelligence (AI) have been investigating how knowledge can be expressed in a computer system. The term which is used nowadays for the development of knowledge-intensive computer systems is *knowledge engineering.*

The knowledge which is applied in tasks like the recognition of visual images, the understanding of a natural language, medical diagnosis, or robot arm control is very different. Yet the different kinds of knowledge have some common traits:

1. The knowledge is largely qualitatively (symbolically) expressed, consisting mainly of rules (*if x then y*), relations (*x is a y*), procedures (*do x then y*) and properties with values along a qualitative scale (*the person x is severely ill* vs. *the variable x has the value 8.5*)
2. The knowledge includes abstract concepts. A simple collection of data is not considered to be knowledge. Knowledge implies the capacity of generalization (*all x are like y*)
3. The knowledge is closely related to the process which uses it. Because of the qualitative nature of knowledge, the processes which use it will be based on inference rather than on arithmetic

1.2. Requirements for Human-Machine Interaction

In the context of the interaction between humans and computers, an adequate representation is extremely important, because the knowledge has to be represented in such a way as to be useful to the program as well as comprehensible to a human.

Some requirements that can be made with respect to human-computer interaction are:

1. *Understandability.* A knowledge processing system should be able to represent its knowledge in such a way that people can understand it. This can be realized by natural language or graphical communication, but also by structuring knowledge in a way which feels natural to people
2. *Expressive Power.* A representation formalism should be powerful enough to absorb all the knowledge that a person wants to express. This criterion does not seem to be realized by any current formalism. Moreover, people often have to express their knowledge in a formalism which is different from the way they normally express it
3. *Modularity.* Knowledge should be structured in a modular way, so that the system is flexible enough to add or change knowledge at any point. This is especially important in environments dealing with rapidly changing knowledge bases, for example in office systems

The overview presented in this article will be confined to a brief discussion of four major groups of formalisms for the symbolic representation of knowledge. An indication of how well they realize the above requirements will be given.

In addition to work on representation formalisms, there is some AI research on knowledge representation from a more content-oriented perspective. One of the questions here is how one can choose a set of knowledge elements to form the base of a conceptual system. Although such questions are of great importance for knowledge engineering, they fall outside the scope of this article.

1.3. Diversity in Representation

Many formalisms for knowledge representation have been developed by AI researchers. Most of them are quite specific in the sense that they can express knowledge only in one particular way, for example as "if-then rules." Some formalisms are geared towards the representation of declarative knowledge (*what?* knowledge) while others are geared towards the representation of procedural knowledge (*how?* knowledge). So the programmer's choice of formalism must depend on how the knowledge involved in his application can best be expressed.

2. Four Main Styles of Knowledge Representation

In the present section, an overview is given of four main styles of symbolic knowledge representation used in AI: (a) logic, (b) production rules, (c) procedures, and (d) semantic networks and frames. Within each style, there are more subtle differences between individual formalisms. A discussion of these falls outside the scope of the present paper. The chapter by Jameson in this volume elaborates on variations within the production system paradigm.

2.1. Logic

Knowledge can be expressed as a set of propositions (facts), for example, expressions in predicate calculus notation. Predicate calculus was developed by philosophers and mathematicians in order to have a formal base for making inferences from propositions. A sentence like

A whale is a mammal

can be expressed in predicate calculus as follows:

ALL x: whale(x) → mammal(x).

Knowledge engineering with logic has two interlocking components. The first is purely declarative knowledge, a database of propositions expressed in logical notation. The second is a theorem prover which is able to prove that there are solutions to a problem described in logical notation by generating all the solutions. For example, when given an additional proposition expressing the fact that Wally is a whale,

whale(Wally),

we want the system to infer correctly that the proposition

mammal(y)

is true, because there is at least one instantiation of y (i.e. Wally) for which it can be proved that the proposition is true.

The best known example of logic programming is the PROLOG language (Clocksin & Mellish, 1981; Kowalski, 1974), which is considered to be the most important computer language in the Japanese project for building intelligent computers (Moto-Oka, 1982). In PROLOG, the program consists of a sequence of propositions in the form of Horn clauses, that is

$A0$:– $A1$, $A2$ ..., An.

which means "if $A1$ and $A2$ etc. and An then $A0$". If there are no elements following the ":–" sign, this sign can be omitted.

Each A in a Horn clause is an atomic formula representing the application of a predicate to a number of arguments (as in predicate calculus), as shown in the following clause:

mammal(X) :– whale(X).

The PROLOG interpreter is a mechanism which tries to find whether a given proposition is true or not. It does so by searching the database sequentially for a clause which proves the proposition in question. A clause proves a proposition if its left hand side (before the ":-" sign) matches the proposition, and the formulas on its right hand side can all be proved.

Variables (written in uppercase) occuring as arguments to predicates are instantiated during the pattern matching process. A proposition may match with more than one clause in the database, and then all possibilities for the value of a variable will be given. For example, given the following sequence of clauses:

```
king_of_belgium(leopold_I,1830,1865).
king_of_belgium(leopold_II,1865,1909).
king_of_belgium(albert_I,1909,1934).
king_of_belgium(leopold_III,1934,1951).
king_of_belgium(boudewijn_I,1951,1986).
is_king_of_belgium(M,Y) :-
    king_of_belgium(M,A,B),
    Y>=A,
    Y=<B.
```

then the query:

```
?- is_king_of_belgium(M,1909).
```

will produce the following possible bindings for the variable M and will yield a positive result:

```
M=leopold_II
M=albert_I
yes
```

PROLOG is a powerful knowledge engineering tool. Its most attractive feature is that the specification of knowledge in predicate logic is at the same time the implementation of a program because the interpreter can use the logical expressions to solve a particular problem. An interesting feature of logic programming is that knowledge given in a declarative way can be used for different purposes; it can be applied in recognition tasks as well as in production tasks. Some problems with PROLOG are that its interpreter has only one way of searching the database and that it is hard to implement certain kinds of procedural knowledge, because the classical program control structures are missing.

2.2. Production Rules

Production systems were developed during the seventies by A. Newell and H. Simon, among others, as a model for human problem solving (Newell &

Simon, 1972). The characteristic form of knowledge representation in production systems is the production rule, or condition-action rule. Such a rule consists of (a) a condition side, which specifies certain conditions which may or may not be fulfilled at any moment and (b) an action side which specifies one or more actions which may be performed if all the conditions are fulfilled simultaneously. Since they specify actions to be performed, production rules represent procedural knowledge. Which conditions are fulfilled is determined by checking the (continually changing) contents of a declarative store, commonly referred to as working memory.

The following is an English paraphrase of a production rule which appears in Anderson, Farrell and Sauers' (1982) simulation of the behavior of beginners who are learning the language LISP. The learner's task is to write and test a LISP function to satisfy a given specification.

If

the current goal is to compare the result obtained
when testing your LISP function with the correct result
and the result of the test was an error message,

Then

set as subgoals to fix the bug revealed by the error
message and to test the function again.

A production system typically consists of a few dozen to a few thousand rules of this general form. The rules can only produce actual behavior with the help of a so-called production system interpreter, which usually has the basic structure shown in Figure 1.

The interpreter performs a cyclical process where each cycle consists of three phases:

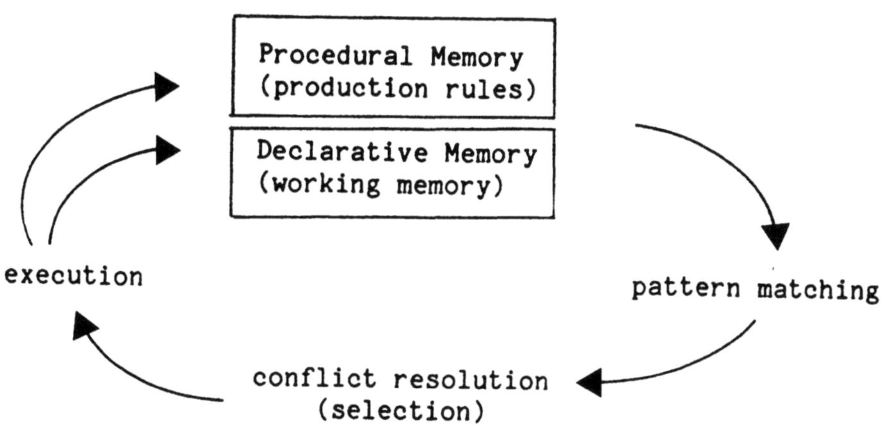

Figure 1. Production system interpreter

1. *Pattern Matching.* This phase determines for which rules the condition sides are currently satisfied. Each such case is called an instantiation of a rule
2. *Conflict Resolution.* It will often happen that more than one instantiation will be found by the pattern matcher. Since it is in general not considered desirable for all applicable rules to fire on each cycle, certain criteria are applied to select one or more instantiations
3. *Execution.* The actions of the chosen rule are executed. Although such actions can take many forms, the most typical ones involve the addition or deletion of certain facts from working memory or of rules from the procedural memory. Such changes will in general result in other rules becoming instantiated on the following cycle

Many variants on this general scheme have been designed. The chapter by Jameson in this volume discusses some of the dimensions of variation in production system architecture, and Davis and King (1977) gave an overview of the issues which arise in designing production systems.

Most of the appeal of production rules as a technique for knowledge representation stems from the modularity with which procedural knowledge is expressed. Each production rule typically expresses a small nugget of knowledge which can (ideally) be understood independently of the other specific rules. The practical usefulness of production rules is demonstrated by the fact that most successful expert systems in commercial use today express their knowledge in this kind of representation. An example of such a system is R1 (McDermott, 1981), a system to configure computer systems.

However, considering the whole set of rules, a number of disadvantages may become apparent. Since the flow of control is not specified by the rules themselves, but the rules are used in a cyclical control mechanism, it may be difficult for a user, or even a person who writes the production rules, to anticipate how the system will behave. Also, the problem of matching a large number of conditions against a large number of working memory elements is a challenging one, for which a number of solutions have been proposed (see the chapter by Jameson in this volume).

2.3. Procedures

Procedural knowledge is knowledge about how to do things. In a procedural representation, there is no general inference mechanism which is carefully kept separated from a database of propositions or rules. Rather, a procedural representation is a program which performs a specific process and has a specific control structure for doing so, sometimes implemented as a database of facts complemented by a set of plans to perform a certain action.

Procedural representation is often useful for the simulation of processes which require no explicit reasoning. An example of such "automatic behavior" is the use of linguistic knowledge; people process language in specific ways (for example, production, parsing, translation), yet they can rarely explain why they do so. In other words, people cannot formulate explicit rules or facts about many aspects of language but they are able to use their procedural knowledge.

One way of expressing knowledge in a procedural representation is to view structural elements in the problem domain as active procedures with a specific control structure. For example, in the procedural grammar of Kempen and Hoenkamp (1982), syntactic constituents and functions are viewed as active procedures, and a syntactic tree structure is viewed as a representation of a hierarchy of procedure calls. An example of such a hierarchy is shown in Figure 2.

The top of the tree is the main procedure and lower nodes are successive subprocedures. The procedural representation of linguistic knowledge has a number of advantages. Among the most obvious advantages are the possibility of executing "sister" branches in parallel and the representation of coordinate structures as iteration. Another way of representing knowledge as procedures is to express knowledge in a special procedural language like PLANNER (Hewitt, 1972), part of which was implemented as MICRO-PLANNER (Sussman, Winograd & Charniak, 1970). In these LISP-like languages, knowledge about how to do things is represented as a plan to achieve a certain goal. In the famous blocks world programs, the knowledge about the manipulation of blocks is represented as a set of plans to achieve goals concerning the relative positions of the blocks. Given the situation in Figure 3, for example, the fol-

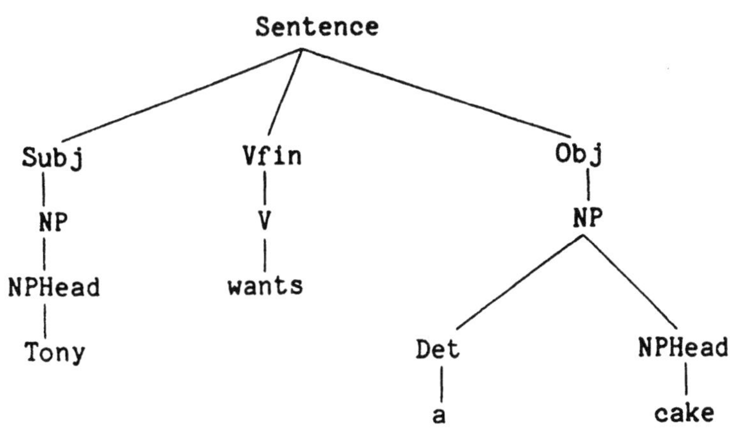

Figure 2. A hierarchy of syntactic procedures

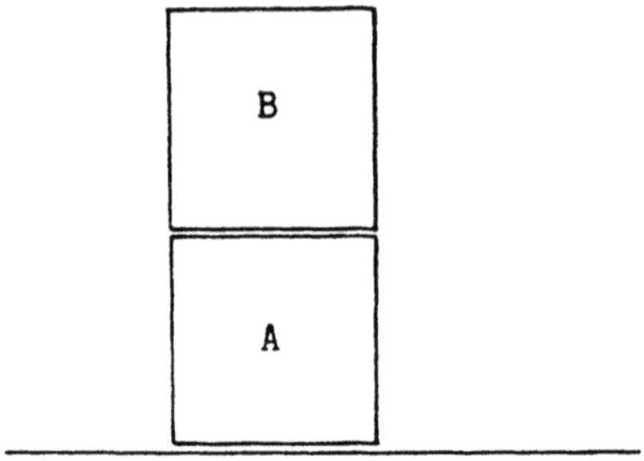

Figure 3. A blocks world situation

lowing plan might be used in order to achieve the goal that block A is on block B:

> To put a block X on a block Y,
> do the following sequentially:
> clear the top of X;
> clear the top of Y;
> grasp X;
> move the center of X above the center of Y;
> lower X.

MICRO-PLANNER has been used in work on theorem proving. If one views the proof of a theorem as a goal for which there may be a number of plans, a procedural representation may have the advantage that it helps to guide the inference process, in contrast to the "blind" search of a PROLOG interpreter. PLANNER and MICRO-PLANNER provide special constructs to direct the inference process or to restrict the search, for example by using filters on possible plans.

However, the directedness of the inference process can also prove to be a disadvantage. Specifically, mixing domain knowledge and control knowledge prevents abstraction. For example, the MICRO-PLANNER expression

(THAND A B)

does not only express that A and B have to be proved, but it really means "first prove A and then prove B". If under certain condition it were more feasible to prove B first, a procedural system would not be very flexible in modifying its knowledge to do so. Recent work (Van Releghem, 1984) is moving towards a separation of domain knowledge and control knowledge.

2.4. Semantic Networks and Frames

Semantic networks, frames and frame-related systems such as scripts and object-oriented languages provide a modular way to organize knowledge. In these formalisms, knowledge is organized in units which represent objects or events in the real world or abstract concepts. All information relevant to the entity in question is kept together as a whole in order to make it directly accessible when needed. Frame-based systems have been called the database approach to knowledge representation because in principle they provide an organization of knowledge which is independent of the control structure of the processes using that knowledge.

2.4.1. Semantic Networks

Semantic networks were first used during the sixties by Quillian (1968) at the Carnegie-Mellon University and by Frijda (1972) at the University of Amsterdam. They were seen as a psychological model of human associative memory. A network consists of nodes and of arcs or links (indicated by arrows) between the nodes. The nodes represent concepts, things, events, etc. The arcs represent semantic relations between the nodes. In Figure 4, for example, the fact that a whale is a mammal is expressed by two nodes representing the concepts "whale" and "mammal" and an *is a* relation between them. As already discussed above, such propositions can also be expressed in a logical representation. The difference between a representation based on logic (such as PROLOG) and a semantic network is that in logic, knowledge is represented as a sequence of propositions, whereas in a semantic network all relevant facts are grouped around the nodes, thus forming a structure resembling a net rather than a one-dimensional sequence. An example of such a net is shown in Figure 5. This network shows how inferences can be performed. Given that properties are inherited along *is a* links, Robert has a whalebone and his reproduction is viviparous.

The knowledge in a semantic network and the inference by means of *is a* links can equally well be expressed in a logical representation or in a production system. However, the advantage here is in the organization of the information: all relevant information about a thing, concept, or event can staightforwardly be reached from the node representing it. In this way the search for information can often be reduced significantly. A disadvantage of semantic networks is that it is not straightforward to express things other than objects or concepts and relations between them. Among the difficulties are procedural knowledge and logical operators such as negation and disjunction.

Figure 4. An *is a* link between two nodes

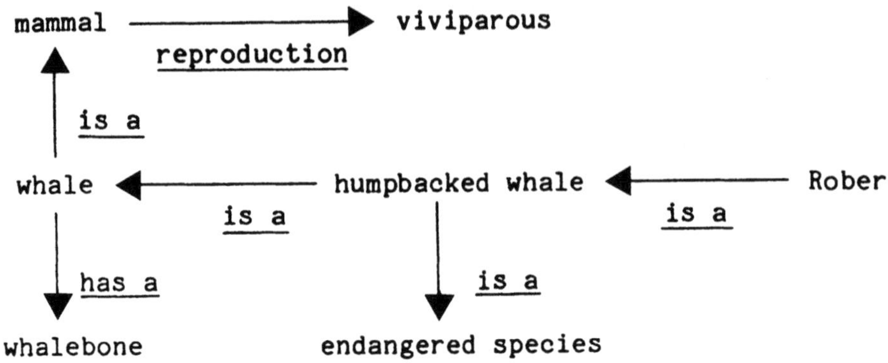

Figure 5. A semantic network

2.4.2. Frames and Framelike Systems

In frames, which were first proposed by Minsky (1975), knowledge is grouped in units resembling nodes in a semantic network. *Is a* relations are often treated specially in order to organize frames in an explicit specialization hierarchy, as exemplified in Figure 6. A frame has a number of aspects (or slots) which contribute knowledge. For example:

MAMMAL frame
specialization of VERTEBRATE
reproduction: viviparous
habitat: (restriction: land, water, or air)
(default: land)

WHALE frame
specialization of MAMMAL
habitat: water

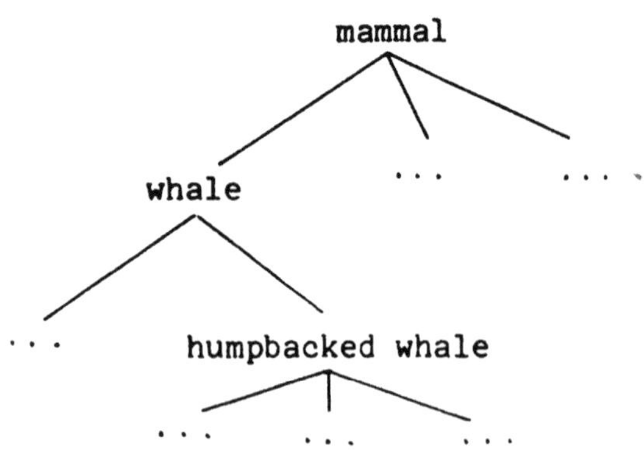

Figure 6. A partial specialization hierarchy of mammals

As shown in the mammal frame, aspects may not only contain references to concepts but they may contain restrictions on the possible fillers of the aspects. They may also contain a default filler which indicates what is normally the case unless some exception is given. For example, the habitat of a mammal is normally land, but for a whale it happens to be water.

Frame systems have a powerful mechanism called inheritance to deduce the contents of the aspects in a frame from that in other frames. Because a whale is a mammal, its reproduction is also viviparous. The inheritance mechanism follows the lines of the specialization hierarchy upwards until an answer is found. In some frame-based systems a multiple inheritance mechanism allows inheritance from more than one frame. In that case it is a quite complex mechanism, because inheritance will have to be selective. A frame for "toy truck," for example, may inherit from "toy" as well as from "truck": the shape will have to be inherited from "truck" but the price and the size from "toy truck".

In object-oriented programming languages, such as ORBIT (De Smedt, 1984), SMALLTALK (Goldberg & Robson, 1983), or the FLAVORS system (Weinreb & Moon, 1980), knowledge is grouped in frame-like objects. From object-oriented programming stems the idea that not only declarative knowledge, but also procedural knowledge can be organized around objects. This idea has been incorporated to a certain extent in frame-based languages, where it is called procedural attachment. Suppose that we would like to define a procedure which will compute the age of a person in years. We attach this procedure to the "age" slot of the "person" frame. However, for other objects we may need different procedures which for example compute the age in months or weeks:

PERSON frame
age: (procedure to compute age in years)

BABY frame
specialization of PERSON
age: (procedure to compute age in months)

INFANT frame
specialization of BABY
age: (procedure to compute age in weeks)

With the help of the specialization hierarchy, the correct procedure will be selected when the age of a certain entity is requested. A number of programming systems have been developed specifically for frame-based knowledge representation, including KRL (Bobrow & Winograd, 1977), FRL (Goldstein & Roberts, 1977), and KL-ONE (Brachman, 1978).

In object-oriented programming, there are two ways for objects to share common behavior using a specialization hierarchy, inheritance and delegation.

Lieberman (1986) distinguishes the two in the following way. Using inheritance, behavior common to a group of objects is encoded in a class object, which may have a number of instances. The analogy used here is that of a set and its elements. Delegation, on the other hand, does not need classes, only objects, and views each object as a possible prototype for other objects which are extensions. The idea here is that one can say "This object behaves like that one (with possible exceptions)."

In terms of modularity, delegation is more powerful than inheritance, because delegation means that a request for information is passed whenever it is needed, whereas in inheritance systems an instance is shaped after its class, and then becomes a self-contained knowledge unit. This means that in delegation systems it is easier to update and add knowledge which is to be shared by several objects.

A script (Schank & Abelson, 1977) is a variant of a frame which is used for the representation of stereotypical sequences of events and actions. The "restaurant" script is an example of a script which contains the knowledge that a person visiting a restaurant is expected to have. Semantic networks, frames and frame-like systems offer considerable advantages. Fikes and Kehler (1985) point out that "they capture the way experts typically think about much of their knowledge, provide a concise structural representation of useful relations, and support a concise definition-by-specialization technique that is easy for most domain experts to use." The grouping of information around objects has some computational advantages as well. First, information is quickly accessible. Secondly, if objects are provided with their own computational resources, they become active objects which can process knowledge in parallel (Lieberman, 1981; Theriault, 1982). What frame-based systems lack is a representation of rules and an inference mechanism which extends beyond the inheritance mechanism. Frame-based systems provide no special way of representing how the knowledge in a frame is to be used, and the attachment of procedures to frames to solve some specific problem is not meant as a systematic inference method.

3. Summary

Of the four main styles of knowledge representation discussed above, only some general properties were given and a few examples of existing representation languages were mentioned. More detailed discussions of knowledge representation languages for AI can be found in Barr and Feigenbaum (1981), Winston (1984), and Nilsson (1981).

The different styles discussed in the present paper each have advantages and disadvantages. Logic programming, for example, provides powerful inference on declarative knowledge, but it is hard to represent some kinds of procedural knowledge. Semantic networks model associative memory but don't represent rules. In a procedural representation, domain knowledge is not separated from control knowledge. Logic programming languages and production systems have a built-in interpreter to perform reasoning, whereas in procedural and frame based representations there is no predefined way of using the knowledge. Within each style, there is a lot of variation and a trend towards finely tuning the representation to the needs of an application. Representation languages are often adapted to suit specific needs and new formalisms are often designed for specific knowledge based systems. The chapter by Jameson in this volume discusses these points in the context of production systems.

If we look beyond the four main styles of knowledge representation which were presented here, we see that other, very different formalisms are emerging. Among those, a group of constraint languages, for example in the work of Kuipers (1984) and others (Bobrow, 1984), should be mentioned briefly. These formalisms offer possibilities for a description of mechanisms and processes in a qualitative, declarative manner, and are particularly suitable for causal reasoning. However, they are still very much in the research stage, whereas other formalisms, especially logic, production rules and frames, have grown towards fully developed, commercially available systems.

No formalism which is currently used seems to have an expressive power that allows all kinds of knowledge to be expressed in a convenient and usable way. Therefore, the question of which formalism is best can perhaps be replaced by the question of whether it is possible to design an open system where different representations co-exist. There are already a number of representation systems which provide a combination of frames and production rules: LOOPS, KEE, and CENTAUR are discussed in more detail by Fikes and Kehler (1985), who see production rules as a valuable addition to frames, which lack a representation of domain-dependent inference rules. Also worth mentioning in this context is recent work on object-oriented languages based on logic (Gallaire, 1986; Shapiro & Takeuchi, 1983).

A general recommendation for future research is that different styles be integrated within one knowledge engineering environment, or even better, that an open-ended knowledge representation system be created where predefined formalisms can be complemented by new, user-defined ones.

Knowledge representation deserves to be recognized as a separate programming level. Computer applications depend on a series of levels, of which the higher ones become increasingly important as the applications become more and more complex. Underneath the so-called complexity barrier one can write a computer application using the lower levels, but beyond this barrier this is almost impossible. If knowledge is to be used effectively, it has to be managed properly. The complexity and the sheer size of the knowledge needed in intelligent systems call for a management system on the knowledge level. The programming levels can be listed as follows:

Application
\
Knowledge representation: management of the knowledge base
\
System software: operating system and programming language
\
Architecture: a computer

The separate level for knowledge representation has been recognized in the AI community (Newell, 1981) and will allow a qualitative leap toward higher levels of intelligent computer applications.

References

Anderson J.R. (1983). Learning to program. In: *Proceedings of the Eighth International Joint Conference on Artificial Intelligence.* Karlsruhe, A. Bundy (Ed.), W. Kaufmann, Los Altos. pp. 57-62.

Anderson J.R., Farrell R. & Sauers R. (1982). *Learning to plan in LISP (interim report).* Carnegie-Mellon University, Dept. of Psychology, Pittsburgh.

Barr A. & Feigenbaum E.A. (Eds.) (1981). *The handbook of artificial intelligence.* (Vol. I). Heuristech Press, Stanford.

Bobrow D.G. (Ed.) (1984). Special volume on qualitative reasoning about physical systems. *Artificial Intelligence*, 24, (1-3).

Bobrow D.G. & Winograd T. (1977). An overview of KRL, a knowledge representation language. *Cognitive Science*, 1, pp. 3-46.

Brachman R.J. (1978). *A structural paradigm for representing knowledge.* Report No. 3605, Bolt, Beranek and Newman Inc., Cambridge, MA.

Clocksin W.F. & Mellish C.S. (1981). *Programming in PROLOG.* Springer, Berlin.

Davis R. & King J. (1977). An overview of production systems. In: *Machine Intelligence.* E.W. Elcock & D. Michie (Eds.) Wiley, New York. Vol.8, pp. 300-332.

De Smedt K. (1984). *ORBIT: an object-oriented extension of LISP.* (Internal Report 84-FU-13). Psychology Laboratory, University of Nijmegen.

Fikes R. & Kehler T. (1985). The role of frame-based representation in reasoning. *Communications of the ACM*, 28 (9), pp. 904-920.

Frijda N.H. (1972). Simulation of Human Long-term Memory. *Psychological Bulletin*, 77 (1), pp. 1-31.

Gallaire H. (1986). Merging objects and logic programming: relational semantics. In: *Proceedings of the 5th National Conference on AI. AAAI-86*, Morgan Kauffmann, Los Altos, CA. pp. 754-758.

Goldberg A. & Robson D. (1983). Smalltalk-80. Addison-Wesley, Reading, MA.

Goldstein I.P. & Roberts R.B. (1977). Nudge, a knowledge-based scheduling program. In: *Proceedings of the Fifth International Joint Conference on Artificial Intelligence*. R. Reddy (Ed.), Carnegie-Mellon University, Pittsburgh. pp. 257-263.

Hewitt C. (1972). *Description and theoretical analysis (using schemata) of PLANNER, a language for proving theorems and manipulating models in a robot* (Technical Report No. TR-258). AI Laboratory, Massachusetts Institute of Technology, Cambridge, MA.

Kempen G. & Hoenkamp E. (1982). *An incremental procedural grammar for sentence formulation* (Internal Report No. 82-FU-14). Psychology Laboratory, University of Nijmegen.

Kowalski R.A. (1979). *Logic for problem solving*. North-Holland, Amsterdam.

Kuipers B. (1986). Qualitative simulation. *Artificial Intelligence*, 29, pp. 289-338.

Lieberman H. (1981). *A preview of Act-1*. (Memo AIM-625). AI Laboratory, Massachusetts Institute of Technology, Cambridge, MA.

Lieberman H. (1986). Using Prototypical Objects to Represent Shared Behavior in Object-Oriented Systems. In: *Proceedings of the first ACM Conference on Object Oriented Programming Systems, Languages, and Applications. Portland, Oregon*. SigPlan Notices, 21 (11), pp. 214-223.

McDermott J. (1981 summer). R1: the formative years. *AI Magazine*, pp. 21-29.

Minsky M. (1975). A framework for representing knowledge. In: *The psychology of computer vision*. P. Winston (Ed.), McGraw-Hill, New York. pp. 211-277.

Moto-Oka T. (1982). *Fifth generation computer systems*. North-Holland, Amsterdam.

Newell A. (1981 summer). The knowledge level. *AI Magazine*, pp. 1-20.

Newell A. & Simon H.A. (1972). *Human problem solving*. Prentice-Hall, Englewood Cliffs.

Nilsson N. (1981). *Principles of artificial intelligence.* Fioga, Palo Alto.

Quillian M.R. (1968). Semantic memory. In: *Semantic information processing.* M. Minsky (Ed.), MIT Press, Cambridge, MA.

Schank R.C. & Abelson R.P. (1977). *Scripts, plans, goals, and understanding.* L. Erlbaum, Hillsdale, N.J.

Shapiro E. & Takeuchi A. (1983). *Object oriented programming in concurrent prolog.* Technical Report TR-004, Institute for New Generation Computer Technology, Tokyo.

Sussman G., Winograd T. & Charniak E. (1970). *MICRO-PLANNER reference manual* (AI Memo 203). AI Laboratory, Massachussets Institute of Technology, Cambridge, MA.

Theriault D. (1982). *A primer for the ACT-1 language* (Memo AIM-672). AI Laboratory, Massachussets Institute of Technology, Cambridge, MA.

Van Releghem E. (1984). Separating control knowledge from domain knowledge. In: *ECAI-84. Proceedings of the Sixth European Conference on Artificial Intelligence,* T. O'Shea (Ed.), Elsevier, Amsterdam. p. 354.

Weinreb D. & Moon D. (1980). *Flavors: message passing in the Lisp Machine* (Memo AIM-602). Massachusetts Institute of Technology, Cambridge, MA.

Winston P.H. (1984). *Artificial intelligence* (2nd ed). Addison-Wesley, Reading, MA.

Chapter 13. Tree Doctor, a Software Package for Graphical Manipulation and Animation of Tree Structures

Peter Desain

1. Introduction

User interfaces are increasingly relying on graphical facilities. Since the introduction of the Apple Macintosh, dragging icons seems to have become a popular method for user interfaces on personal computers. In the so-called *direct manipulation* method (Shneiderman, 1982), the graphical screen and a pointing device (e.g., a mouse, digitizer, or lightpen) are used to simulate the manipulation of real objects. This hands-on approach enables actions like grabbing, dragging, deforming, etc. In computer-aided design technology, where models of real objects are handled, this technique is common practice. But also when the objects are of an abstract kind and exist only within a formal theory, graphical representations may be available which permit the user to treat them in similar ways. In systems like the Macintosh operating system, the potential of the direct manipulation approach is realized to a very limited extent. For instance, files are organized in a well-defined structure (a hierarchical system of directories), which might be graphically represented as a tree. However, users are only allowed to act directly upon files, represented by icons. They cannot handle the stucture itself and are forced to edit it through possibly long sequences of selecting menu items and isolated objects on the screen.

We estimate that graphical layouts of hierarchical structures in the form of trees are ergonomically superior to other ways of presentation like indenting and nesting. Direct manipulation of tree structures is probably less error prone and more user-friendly than typing complex formulae. In our opinion this is true for both naive and expert users. However, the design of direct manipulation interaction is not a trivial matter. An excellent review of graphical user interface methods is given by Foley et al. (1984).

Interfaces between an application program and the user must be capable of handling a double communication problem. In addition to the interaction with the user, they must take care of a smooth interplay with the application program. The latter is of special importance to the programmers of the application.

2. Organizational Context

In the Language Technology Group of the Experimental Psychology Unit of the University of Nijmegen, many programs were developed which used tree structures. Koenraad De Smedt designed a tree drawing program. It transformed a logical description of a tree into a good looking picture. This program was limited in scope. It could not display transformations to trees dynamically, nor did it provide facilities for tree editing. As we needed a fully fledged tree editor and animator, I started to work on Tree Doctor in August 1985. All programming was done in Zetalisp on a Symbolics 3670 Lisp Machine.

3. Design Considerations

The design of Tree Doctor was guided by the following objectives:

- *Direct manipulation* should be the general method used for interfacing with the human user.
- *Absolute consistency* is required between the internal logical structure and the external graphical one ("what you see is what you get").
- *Universal tool*: The program should allow any sort of tree (it should be "empty", i.e., without domain knowledge).
- *Supervision*: The program should have a small and simple but high-level interface to the application program. This interface should also provide the functions for assisting and monitoring the user while he is editing trees. Thus the user can profit from any domain knowledge residing in the application program.
- *Animation*: It should be possible to display modifications to trees in animation mode, i.e., as continuous changes. This will help the user to keep track of complex operations on complex structures.

4. Examples

I will illustrate the capabilies of Tree Doctor with some examples from the lingustic domain. The two main modes of Tree Doctor, animating and editing, are treated here separately. However, in many applications, e.g., computer-aided instruction, they will be used in combination.

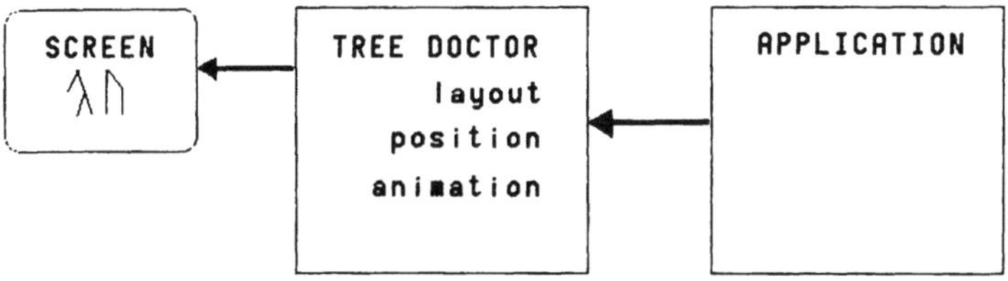

Figure 1. Information flow in animation mode

4.1. Tree Doctor as Tree Animator

When used as an animator Tree Doctor acts as an output device. The information flow is illustrated in Figure 1, which also shows the most important modules. This configuration can be used for making movies or for tracing processes. Figure 2 gives some "snapshots" of a sentence production process. The sentence generator, which was faked in this example, sends messages to Tree Doctor. These messages instruct Tree Doctor to make new nodes and branches but need not provide any graphical details. When the tree grows it reformats itself continually in order to keep enough space for new nodes. Terminal nodes can optionally be kept on the same horizontal line. The systematic alternation of "functional" and "categorial" nodes (as prescribed by the incremental procedural grammar of Kempen & Hoenkamp: 1984) is represented by different fonts. The application program can specify any number of node types and their associated fonts.

4.2. Tree Doctor as Tree Editor

The information flow and the most important subsystems when Tree Doctor acts as an editor are shown in Figure 3. In this mode a small pointing hand icon appears (see Figure 4). Nodes or branches can be selected by pointing. Selected objects are marked clearly. By pointing to the center of a node the user selects the whole subtree having this node as its root. When no other object is being pointed to, selection of the whole sheet is assumed by default. After an object has been selected, the three mouse buttons become associated with special functions as explained in a mouse status line at the bottom of the screen. Each function acts upon the selected object when the corresponding button is pushed.

One button is used for grabbing objects, moving them around and leaving them at a new position. Of course the logical and graphical structure of the tree is kept intact while nodes or subtrees are being moved. When a branch is grabbed it is detached from one of the nodes at its end, and can be attached to another node. The sheet itself can also be grabbed and moved. Its size is inde-

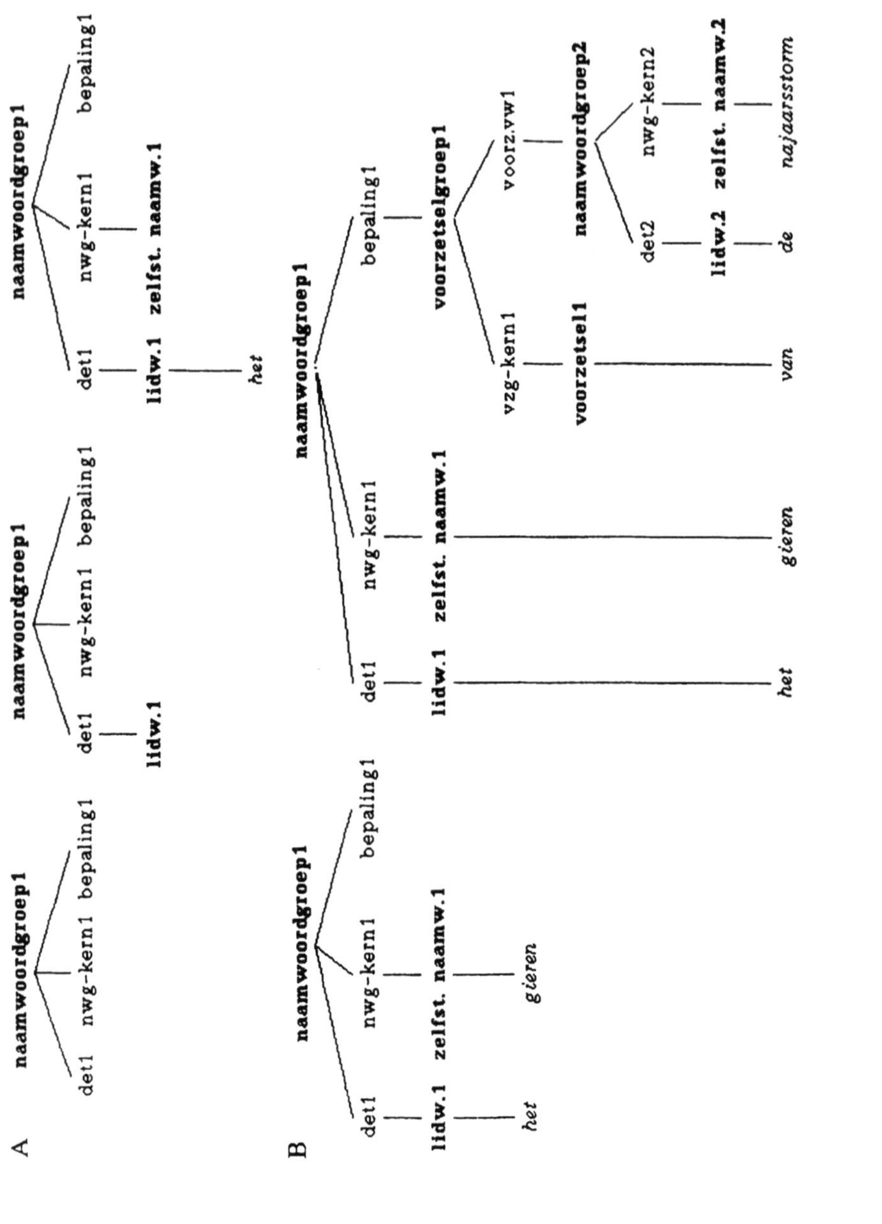

Figure 2. Trace of sentence production (A) and sentence generator (B). The following Dutch words and abbreviations are used in the examples in this and subsequent figures: *bepaling*, modifier; *det*, determiner; *kern*, nucleus; *lidw.*, article; *naamw.*, noun; *naamwoordgroep*/*nwg*, nounphrase; *voorzetsel*/*voorz.*, prepositional; *voorzetselgroep*/*vzg*, prepositional phrase; *vw*, object; *zelfst.*, independent.

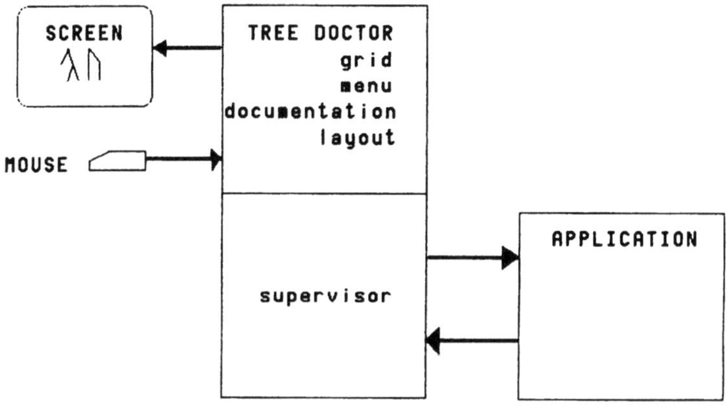

Figure 3. Information flow in edit mode.

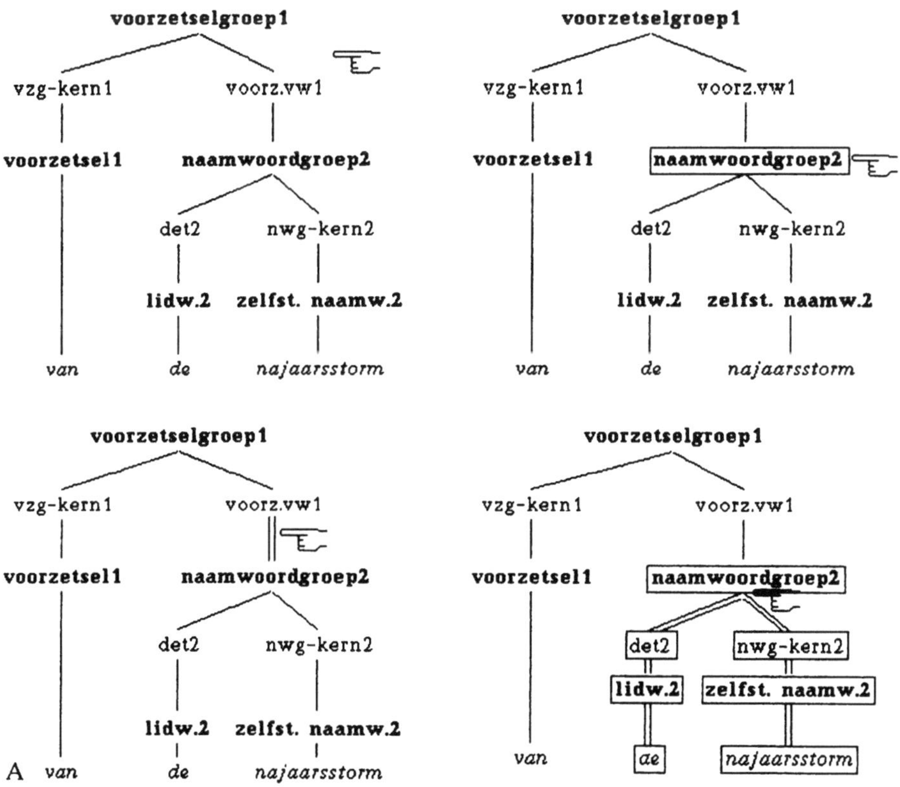

Figure 4. A, Selection of sheet, node, branch, and tree. B, Dragging nodes and trees. C, Creating branches.

voorzetselgroep1
vzg-kern1
voorz.vw1
voorzetsel1
naamwoordgroep2
det2
nwg-kern2
lidw.2
zelfst. naamw.2
van
de
najaarsstorm

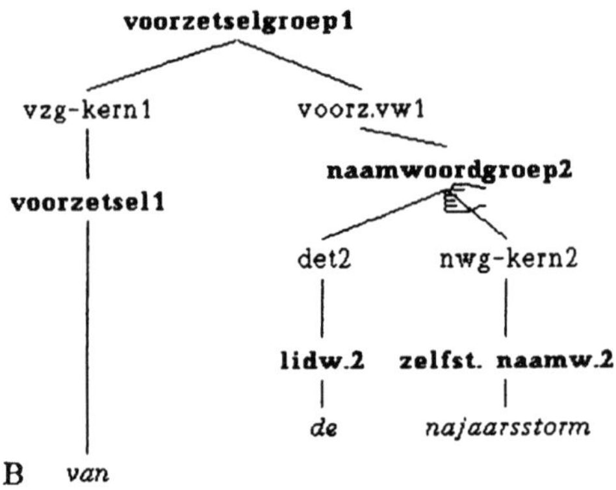
voorzetselgroep1
vzg-kern1
voorz.vw1
naamwoordgroep2
voorzetsel1
det2
nwg-kern2
lidw.2
zelfst. naamw.2
de
najaarsstorm
van

B

voorzetselgroep1
vzg-kern1
voorz.vw1
voorzetsel1
naamwoordgroep2
det2
nwg-kern2
lidw.2
zelfst. naamw.2
van
de
najaarsstorm

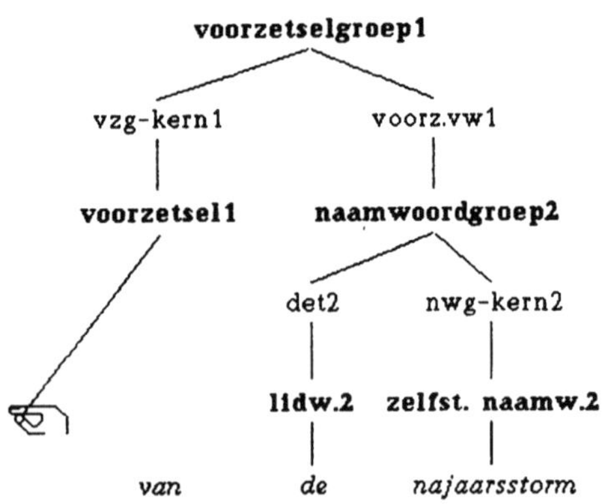
voorzetselgroep1
vzg-kern1
voorz.vw1
voorzetsel1
naamwoordgroep2
det2
nwg-kern2
lidw.2
zelfst. naamw.2
van
de
najaarsstorm

C

finite: any number of trees can be written on one sheet. Another button is used to start the creation of a new branch to or from the selected node. A third button calls a menu of further actions. Each object has a menu, listing in addition to the standard edit actions like copy and delete any number of domain-dependent operations. One such action which is useful in the liguistic domain is closing a (sub)tree. When too many details are visible in a tree it can be represented as a triangle. The terminals of a closed tree can optionally be shown underneath the triangle (Figure 5). List representations of trees can be sent to or read from a file. Tree diagrams can be saved, hard copied or sent to a picture editor for further treatment.

The application program can supply a "stock" of special objects to be displayed continuously (Figure 6). These objects copy themselves after being selected. The user can pick up such nodes (or even predefined subtrees) for constructing new trees. This method is more flexible and simpler to use than a menu.

The module called Supervisor continually informs the application program about what the user is doing. The application program may prohibit certain actions or cause certain events to happen, as prescribed within the domain.

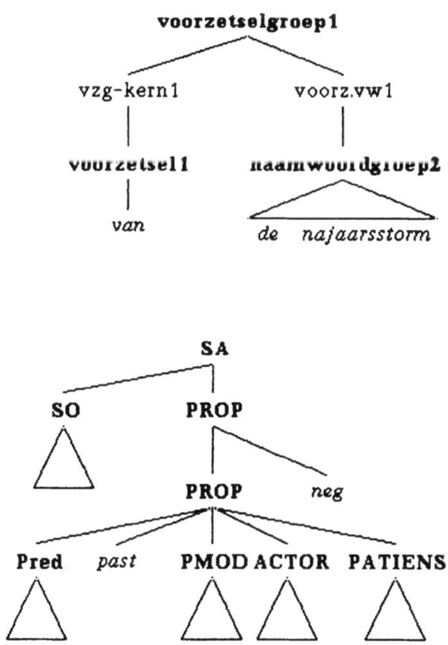

Figure 5. Closed subtrees.

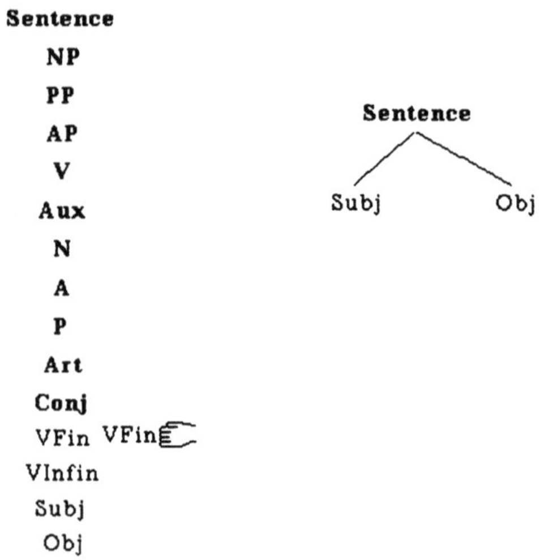

Figure 6. Use of a stock of predefined nodes.

Thus the application program is capable of limiting the editing actions of the user to "sensible" ones, and the trees are kept well formed. Another module of Tree Doctor helps the user to align objects on the screen very accurately, both horizonally or vertically (see section on the grid).

5. Modules

The components of Tree Doctor are interconnected in a heterarchical way. They can be viewed as a collection of experts, each knowledgeable in its own domain and able to ask the others for help.

5.1. Position Specification

In animation the application program can shift objects along the screen without having to calculate sizes of trees and coordinates. Positions can be specified in a small formal language rather than in terms of coordinates. A few examples are as follows (see also Figure 7):

- *Send tree 1 :animated-change-position* (*to left-of tree 2*) moves tree 1 to the left-hand side of tree 2
- *Send node 4 :change-position* (*to right bottom*) places node 4 at the right-hand bottom corner of the screen

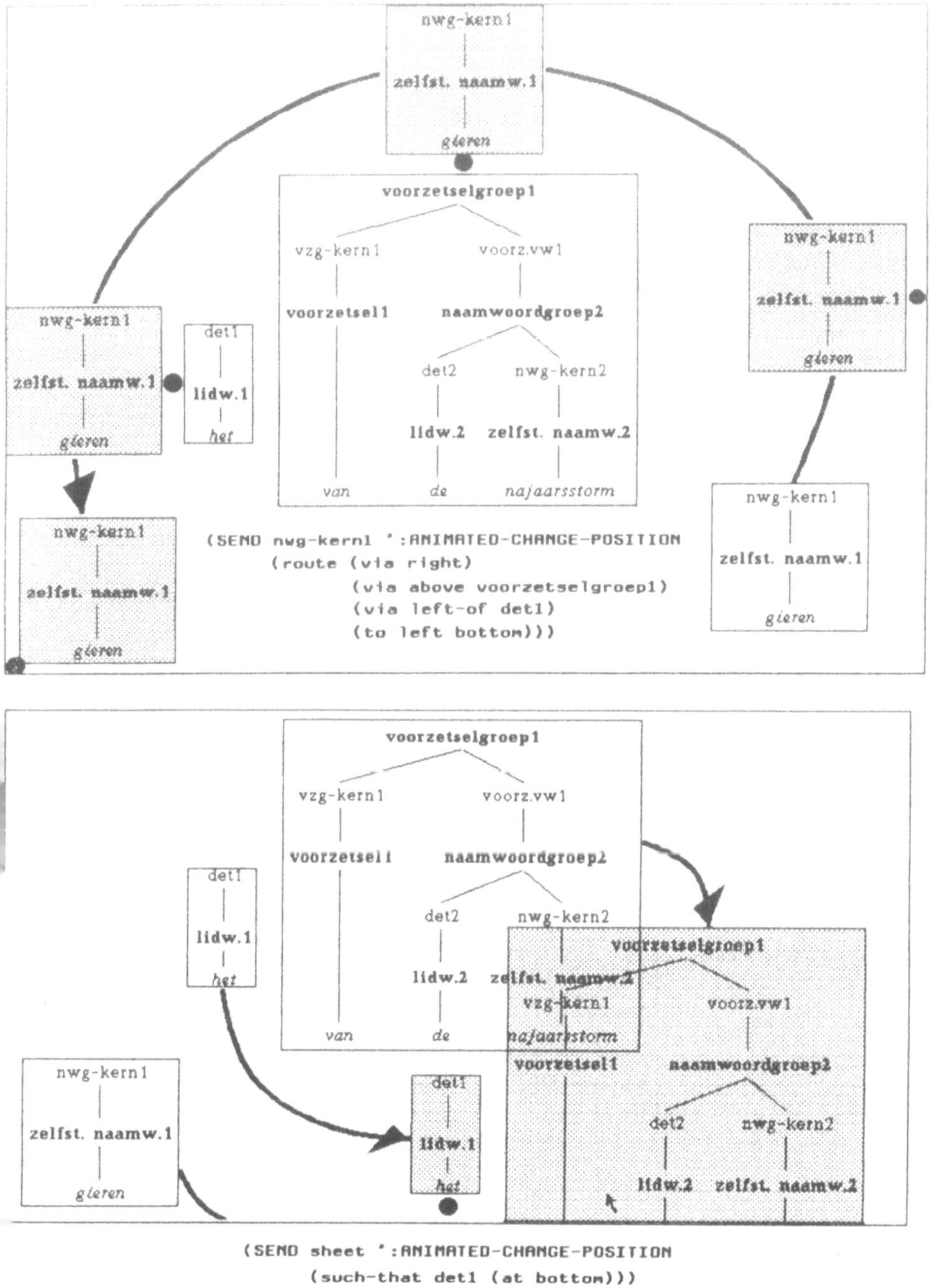

Figure 7. Position specification and animation.

- *Send tree 2 :copy (to above node 4)* produces a copy of tree 2 above node 4
- *Send tree 3 :animated-change-position (route (via below tree 2) (to top))* moves tree 3 along the terminals of tree 2 to the top of the screen
- *Send sheet :change-position (such-that node 4 (at center))* moves the whole sheet such that node 4 will be located in the middle of the screen

Relative position specifications, like *to above node 4* evaluate *to a* functions which, when applied to a screen object, yield the displacements needed to satisfy the specifications.

5.2. Tree Layout

Formalizing general methods of constructing good screen layouts is a difficult problem. We use the following computation. The width of a tree is calculated as the sum of the widths of the subtrees or, if this is greater, the width of the label of the root. In the latter case the remaining space is divided equally among the subtrees. Then the positions of the nodes are calculated by centering a subtree below its root (see Figure 8). This algorithm, although it is space consuming, gives a reasonable lay-out in most cases.

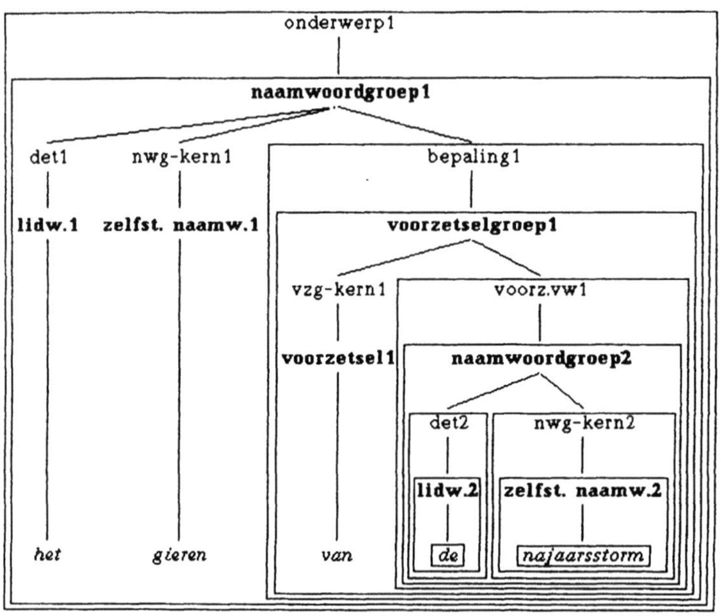

Figure 8. Calculation of tree layout.

5.3. Grid

As soon as a dragged object is released, a new grid is calculated by separately clustering the horizontal and vertical coordinates of the other objects on the screen. The dragged object is then forced into a gridpoint if it is already near one (Figure 9). This dynamic grid is easier to use than a simple fixed grid. It is adapting itself to the situation on the screen, and no explicit adjustment is needed.

5.4. Supervision

The supervisor takes care of the information flow to and from the application program. The latter can configure a supervisor reporting back just the information needed. So the application program can decide in how much detail it wishes to know about the edit actions of the user. If, for example, left-to-right order of subtrees is irrelevant to the application, the supervisor should not send messages indicating that the user has changed the order of subtrees. In another domain this information might be of vital importance. The application program can also delegate some tasks to the supervisor itself. For instance,

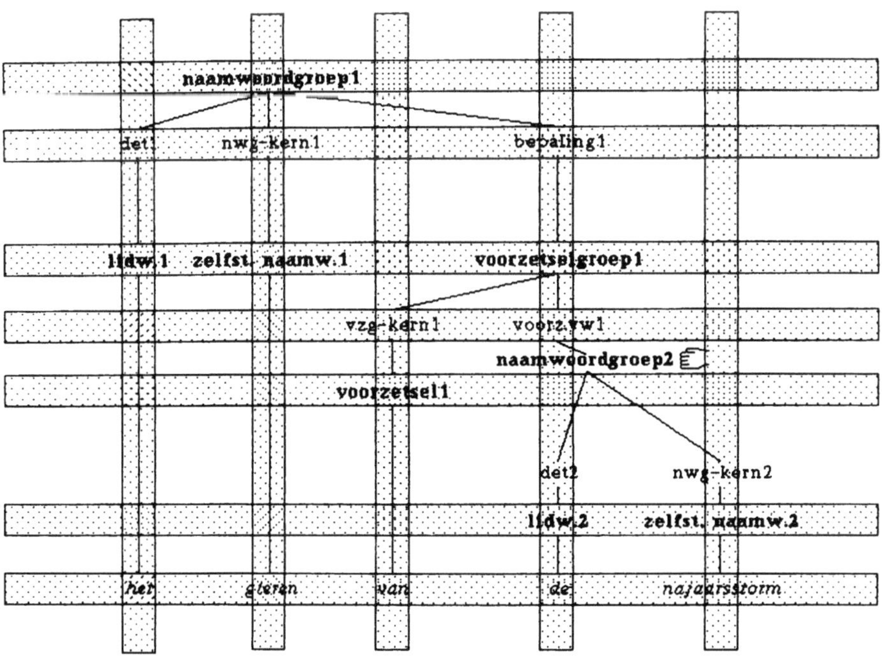

Figure 9. Grid.

the division of nodes into separate classes, and the rule determining whether two nodes of specific classes can be connected by a branch, can be handled by the supervisor, thus freeing the application program from this low-level task. This "type checking" is applicable in any domain where rules of "well-formedness" exists.

5.5. Animation

When given a starting position, a desired end position, and possibly intermediate points, the animator attaches to each node a trajectory (Figure 7). This is calculated by means of a cubic spline interpolation method with parameters for the general acuteness of angles and changes of speed. This key-frame animation method was adapted from Kochanec and Bartels (1984).

5.6. Parameter Adjustment

All graphical parameters (sizes, speeds, etc.) are defaulted to reasonable values. The user can change them by means of a menu. For instance, for children or people suffering from motor handicaps the clustering of coordinates in the grid can be made less fine.

5.7. Dynamic Menus

Domain-specific actions will be needed in most applications. Each object, be it a node, branch, tree, or sheet, carries its own menu of actions. This menu can be updated by adding or removing alternatives. Thus the set of permitted actions can be made dependent on the momentary context of the object.

5.8. On-Line Documentation

When an object is selected by pointing it can display some documentation in the status line. This feature is typically used to describe the object itself and the associated functions of the mouse buttons.

6. Applications

We have already mentioned the linguistic domain. We are currently working on an application of Tree Doctor to grammar teaching, building upon work by

Schotel and Pijls (1986). We are also planning to use Tree Doctor as an "outliner" to organize text fragments in paragraphs, chapters, etc. Because trees are widely used as formal models, numerous applications in other fields can be envisaged, although only mention the domain of operating systems. Hierarchical file systems, which are ubiquitous in modern operating systems, can easily be maintained with the help of a program like Tree Doctor (see Introduction).

7. Implementation

The package has been implemented in an object-oriented style on a Symbolics 3670 Lisp Machine (in Zetalisp, using the Flavors system). Functional objects and higher-order functions to handle them (Desain, 1983) served to implement position specifications and animation trajectories. Several preliminary prototypes were needed to test different user interaction models. In the programming environment of the Lisp Machine we were able to construct a clean final program (4000 lines of source code, including comments) in about four man-months. Animation is Tree Doctor's most critical component with respect to machine performance. In implementations on less powerful machines this feature may have to be left out.

8. Future Research

A program using the direct manipulation approach for the adjustment of layout parameters is still under construction. This program will extract the parameters from a hand-made layout example. Writing a stripped version of Tree Doctor for a powerful microcomputer with mouse and graphical screen is straightforward. We are planning an implementation in C or Pascal. Because graphs (networks, diagrams) in general have an even more widespread use, the next project aims at the construction of a network editor along the same lines. The nodes will be displayed in the form of user definable icons.

References

Desain P.W.M. (1983). *Representatie van inductief gedefinieerde objecten en recursie in een tweede orde getypeerde lambda-calculus.* Thesis, University of Twente.

Foley J.D., Wallace V.L. & Chan P. (1984). The human factors of computer graphics Interaction techniques. *IEEE Transactions on Computer Graphics and Applications*, 4, pp. 13-48.

Kempen G. & Hoenkamp E. (1984). *An incremental procedural grammar for sentence formulation.* Report, Department of Psychology, University of Nijmegen.

Kochanec D.H.U. & Bartels R.H. (1984). Interpolating splines with local tension, continuity, and bias control. *Computer Graphics*, 18, pp. 33-41.

Schotel H. & Pijls J. (1986). Een prototype van grammaticaonderwijs op een Lisp Machine. *Informatie*, 28, pp. 48-50.

Shneiderman B. (1982). The future of interactive systems and the emergence of direct manipulation. *Behaviour and Information Technology*, 1, pp. 237-256.

Chapter 14. Textvision: Elicitation and Acquisition of Conceptual Knowledge by Graphic Representation and Multiwindowing

Piet A.M. Kommers

1. Introduction

Knowledge engineering can be considered as an influential paradigm for the design of complex information systems. Moreover, it will ultimately be of importance in all those situations where humans are to be taught and are supposed to be learning by means of computers at their own pace and using their own style of learning. Expert systems which are designed to help in human tasks such as diagnostics and to interpret patterns of data, are expected to tackle complex material and may even change the frontiers of cognitive psychology. Because knowledge-based systems can assist the mental operations of humans, it will be important to preserve the opacity and comprehensibility of their knowledge bases and the mechanisms they use to infer new facts from it. In the last decade several computer-based instructional systems were predicated as being "intelligent": Bip, programming in basic (1976); Excheck, logic and set theory (1981); Spade, programming in Logo (1982); LMS, algebraic procedures (1982); Quadratic, quadratic equations (1982); Guidon, diagnostics of infectious diseases (1982); Algebra, applied algebra (1983). Since the main purpose of these systems was prototype development, they rely mainly on rule-based knowledge, particularly in the algorithmic components. Once there is a variety of software tools for the development of expert systems in several areas we will we able to elaborate on the more fuzzy and associative types of knowledge (Hofstaedter, 1985). Now we are only at the beginning of a new era in which unforeseen aspects of the human mind can be touched by means of "knowledge devices." Wilson and Welsh (1986) speculated about the impact of knowledge based-systems for educational use:

> The important point is what those packages represent to the field of instruction. They represent the opening of a door. It is now possible to find ways to use small knowledge-based systems to teach and support human performance. By analogy, the importance of Apple computers during the 70s was not that they represented the final destination of a technology, but instead they represented the beginning of a vast technological change in society.

Textvision is a conceptual tool the development of which was based on the question of how computers can help in the acquisition of new knowledge during the comprehensive reading of study texts. It is mainly based upon cognitive psychological theories originating from Ausubel (1963), Norman (1973), and Pask (1976). Besides the proposal of Textvision itself I will discuss two educational aspects of knowledge representation:

1. Conceptual analysis by means of graph representation in order to explicate the main ideas in a subject matter domain; current experiments try to determine the way teachers explore conceptual networks before they actually start teaching the topic
2. Conceptual representation as a tool during the acquisition of textual information; 22 college students were investigated and tested on their knowledge before and after instruction.

2. A Computer Program for the Representation of Concepts in Text

Interactive use of text is often approached as a search in hierarchically ordered sets and subsets of keywords. Users will start with the most general node of a tree structure and will only arrive at the target information if the right alternatives are chosen in the levels below. As can be observed with videotext retrieval systems like Prestel, Antiope, Telidon, Viditel, and Teletekst, much effort is wasted by switching levels and because of the impossibility of visualizing the map of connections between the main concepts in the available information. It is exactly this restrictive "local" view which obliges the user to make a more or less thrifty trip through the paragraphs of text (Kommers, 1982, 1986). By making use of a dedicated microcomputer like the SmallTalk-based Apple Macintosh it was possible to design a new graphic-based user interface. Five main principles underlie Textvision:

1. Both text and graphic levels should be accessible to the user in a very quick and easily switchable way
2. On the text level it should be possible to display several paragraphs in parallel
3. The relations between main and "help" concepts assigned on the textual level should automatically be matched to those on the graphic level and vice versa
4. The centrality of each concept in the structure should be reflected in a direct, eye-catching way, so that the user is immediately aware of the structural importance of the various concepts in question
5. Moving from the text to the graphic level and vice versa should be as natural as possible. This means that both representations should fit in one quasiphysical environment which stays constant for the user, which implies no changes of mode in the interaction (This last requirement is difficult to meet)

2.1. Intrinsic Presentation Strategy in the Program

Because of recent theories about how presentation of new information should be adapted to the actual state of knowledge of the user, we decided to start the interaction sequence by displaying the graphic level. In the actual network (Figure 1) 10 concepts which are connected by lines can be seen. The direction of a connection is shown not by arrows but by starting the line in the middle of the root concept, and by pointing up to the rim of the receiving node (e.g., *pop music* points to *rock 'n' roll*, and *rock 'n' roll* points to *rhythm and blues* (and vice versa). Every node can be selected (black or gray). In this example *pop music* (gray) has been selected as well as opened, which means that the user took out the relevant text paragraph before. This text still remains behind the network window, and can be seen by simply moving the network aside. The nodes representing the concepts have different sizes. As you see, *rock 'n' roll*, *rhythm and blues*, and *pop music* are the three most important at the moment. Importance in this example is defined in terms of "outdegree" which refers to "abstraction" (see later). The silhouette of *rock 'n' roll*, in a potentially new position in the network can be seen in the lower right-hand corner.

Figure 2 shows the effect of this movement, which is not an improvement of the transparency of the whole pattern. Figure 3 shows a rearrangement of

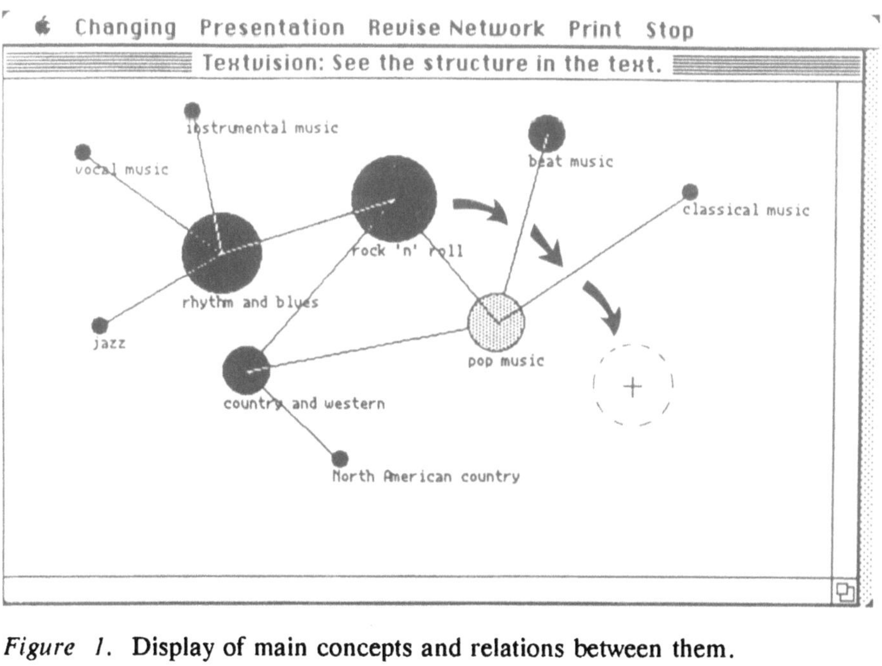

Figure 1. Display of main concepts and relations between them.

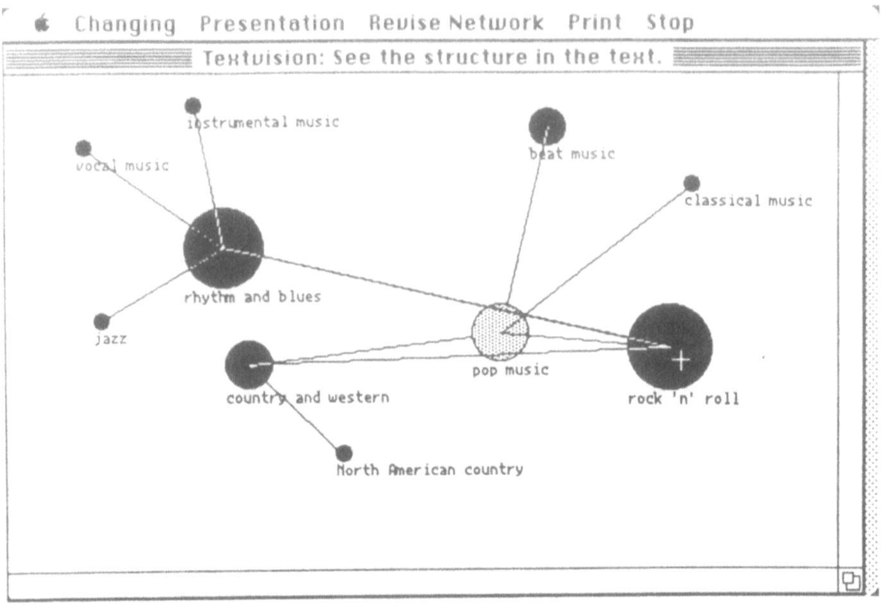

Figure 2. Display of rearranged network after replacing *rock 'n' roll.*

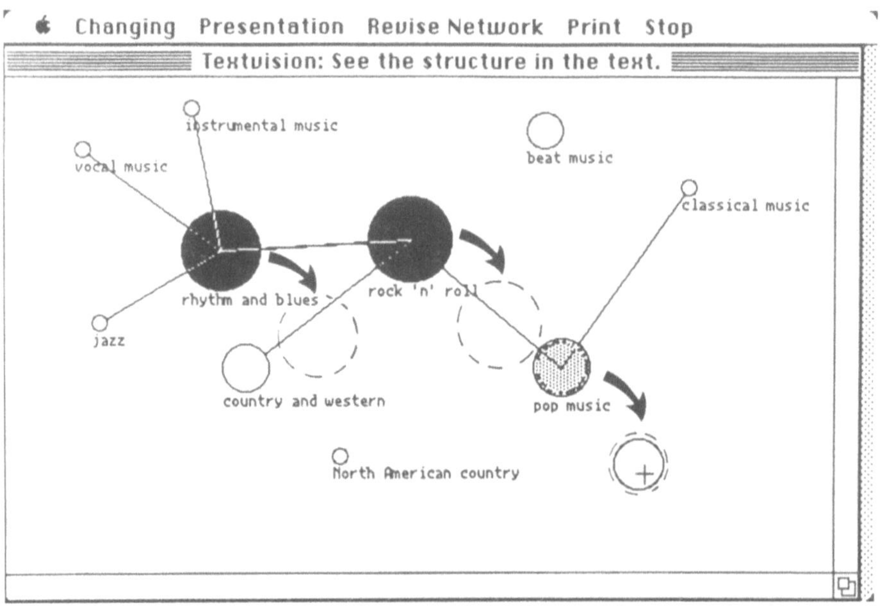

Figure 3. Simultaneous replacement of three concepts.

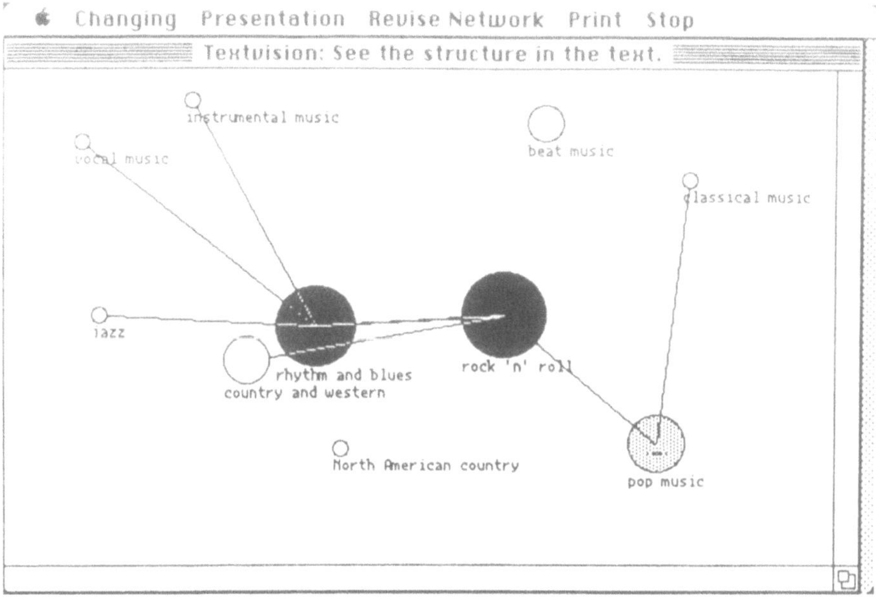

Figure 4. Display of network after replacing three concepts.

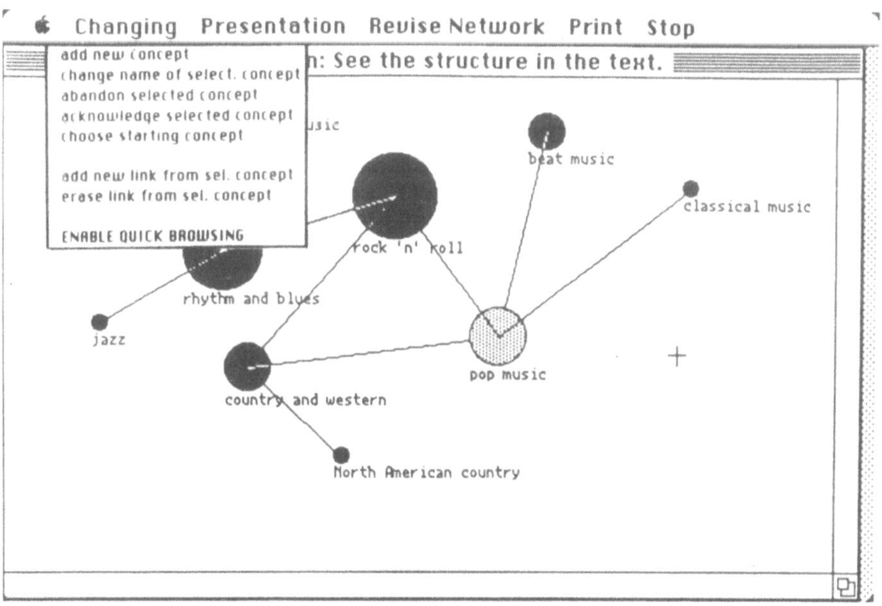

Figure 5. Pull-down menue with editing operations on network.

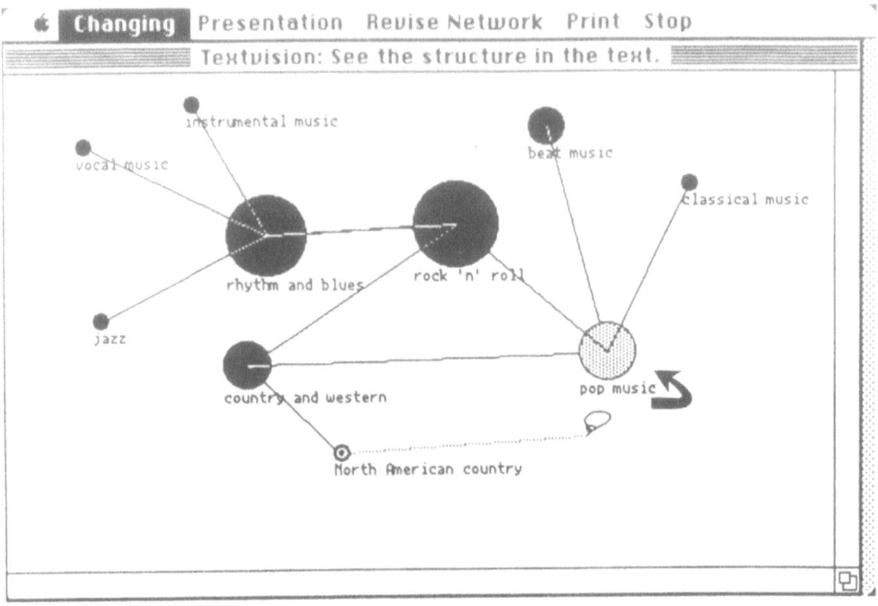

Figure 6. Establishing a new relation between two main concepts.

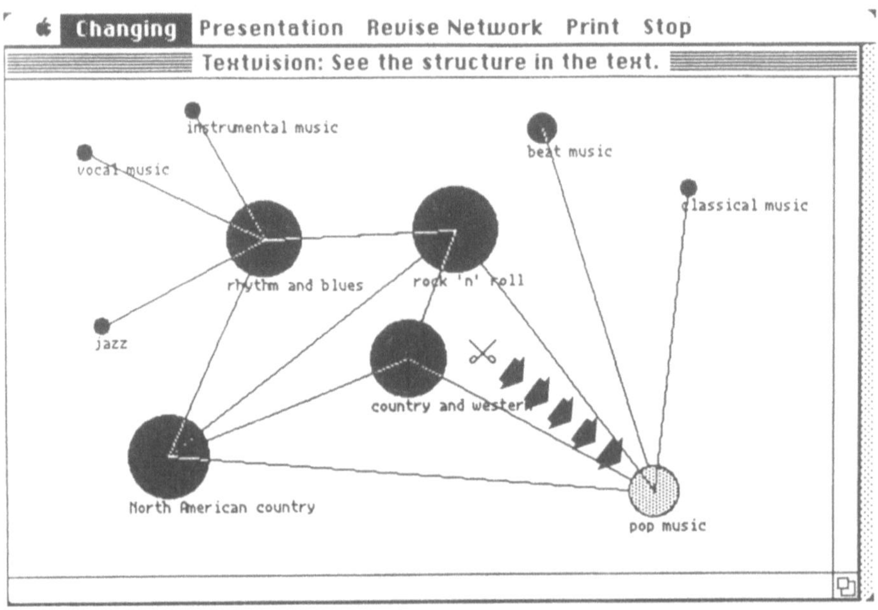

Figure 7. Removing an existing relation by using a pair of scissors.

three nodes. If the network needs a total redesign it is possible to replace multiple nodes in parallel. This can be done by means of a so called *extended select*. In this example the nodes *rock 'n' roll*, *rhythm and blues*, and *pop music* are to be dragged to the lower part of the network. Figure 4 displays the effect of the replacement. In this example the user has also stated that at this moment only three of the nine concepts should be selected. As a consequence, the outward relationships alone can been seen so the attention is focused mainly on the spot of action.

As many so-called "implicit functions" of the Macintosh *User Interface Guidelines* serve many self-supporting facilities which need not to be explained here I shall restrict myself to the more specific functions of Textvision. In Figure 5 on the top line can be seen the pull-down menus for different kinds of actions for text(s) or network. The first menu is for changing the network on a graphic level. Adding and removing concepts and links can be done by using a lasso and a pair of scissors which can be operated by the mouse and its push button (Figures 6 and 7).

2.2. Conceptual Structure Matched on Graphic and Textual Levels

Textvision mediates between the construction of global ideas as shown in a network visualization and the actual use of concepts in the texts themselves. Display of the text in a node is requested by clicking the mouse's push button twice. The text is displayed in a window which supports replacement of text, enlarging, and scrolling. Each time the user asks for a new paragraph, all the opened windows reappear in the same (opened) state as they were left before, and a pile of paragraphs results which is ordered like a stack: first in, first out. The user can bring one of the partly covered paragraphs to the front of the stack immediately so that it is ready to be controlled again, by means of the mouse's push button.

Figure 8 shows a state were four paragraphs are open and can be addressed immediately. *North American country* is in the scope of action. In this mode (*help*) the user can define several help concepts by selecting a string of text and assigning it to the list of help concepts in the lower window. At this moment *folk music* has become a helping concept. That means that from now on there exists a link from *North American country* to *folk music*. This new relationship also manifests itself on the graphic level. As *folk music* has not been included in the network yet, it is now created and is placed at a default spot in the upper left-hand corner of the network window (Figure 9). As *folk music* is embraced by square brackets, the user immediately knows that *folk music* was not one of the concepts in the network before. In this case one should still acknowledge this new concept on the graphic level before it can be used for further elaborations. In order to acknowledge a newly created con-

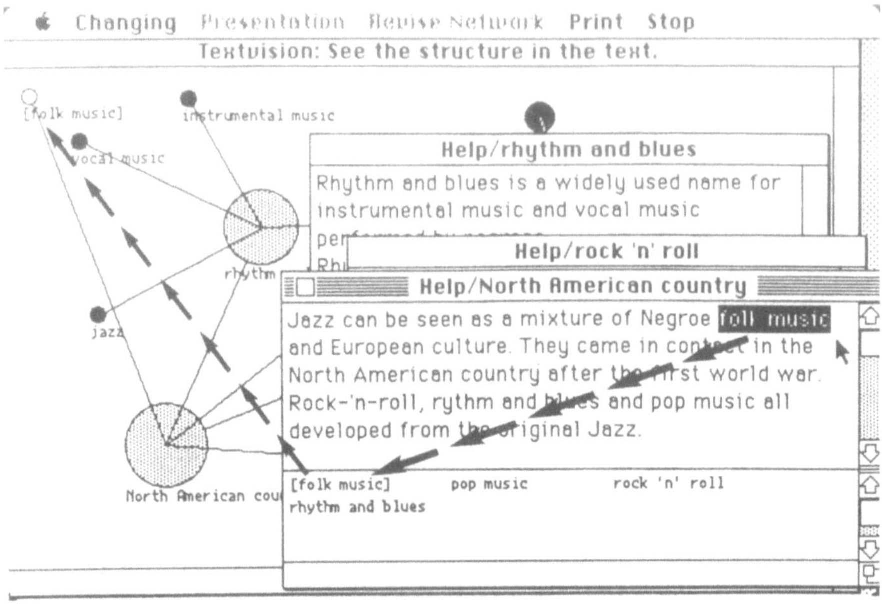

Figure 8. Several text windows can be opened simultaneously, and words or strings of words can be appointed to a main concept.

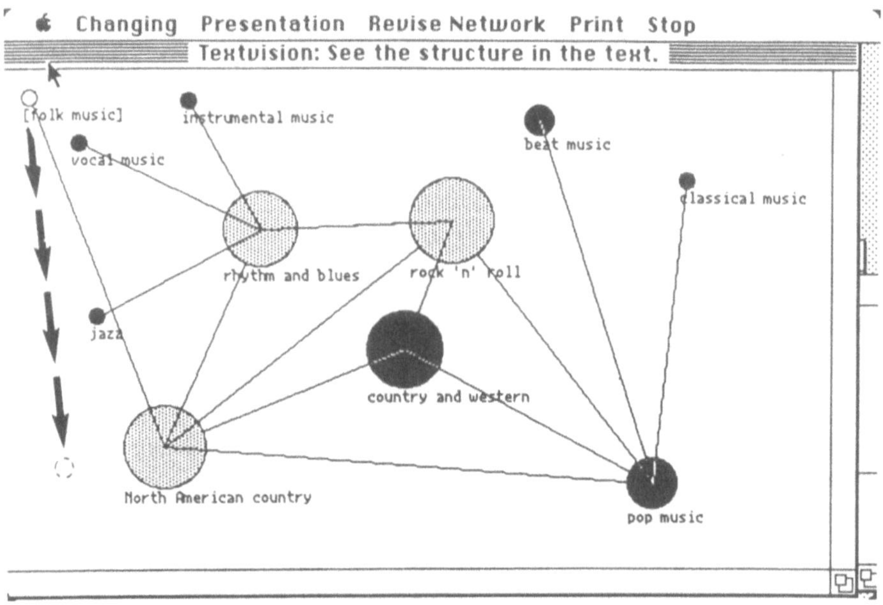

Figure 9. Graphic representation after a new main concept has been appointed on the text level.

cept, the user should select the concept node in the network, and select the "acknowledge" subcommand under the "Changing" pull-down menu.

2.3. Abstraction and Reachability as Two Criteria for Centrality

Visualization of conceptual structures may be thought of as a paradox because concepts are essentially mental constructs and not perceptual. Because real knowledge is quite extensive and complex to describe completely, we have to reduce the graphical representation to those parts which are essential for the task concerned. As the display of conceptual relationships in our program serves as an orientation map, we used graph analysis techniques in order to do this. One major question concerns how central or peripheral the position of a certain concept in the total graph is. The entire graph has to be taken account of before we can know the centrality of one particular node. Based on Hoede (1978), we can define the centrality of a node as the sum of the influences of its neighbors. This is a recursive definition, because the centrality of the neighbors is also dependent on their neighbors. Hoede proposed a "status index" which reflected a measure of centrality. Each successive step in the recursion had a smaller influence on the centrality score, in order to prevent endless cyclic influences of a node on itself. The index was calculated as follows:

$$s(i) = \sum_{j=1}^{n} w(i,j) + \sum_{j=1}^{n} w^2(i,j) + \sum_{j=1}^{n} w^3(i,j) + \ldots$$

An element $w^k(i,j)$ represents all sequences of length k from node i to node j, with a factor which is determined by the products of the weights of the arcs in the sequence. Without displaying the exact numerical values of the centralities thus derived, we decided to show it in a graphic way; the larger the centrality, the bigger the node. This has the advantage that important concepts will immediately catch the eye of the user so that the primary attention can be directed towards the structural aspects of the graph.

In Figures 10 and 11 can be seen the outcome of the centrality computation. The first computation is according to indegree, i.e., concepts gain importance by being indicated by important neighbor concepts. The second computation stresses those concepts which indicate other concepts which themselves indicate other important concepts. Striking differences occur such as the increase in relevance of *rhythm and blues* and *beat music*. Conspicuous differences can also be seen in the decline of centrality of *classical music*, *pop music*, and *North American country*. *Classical music* seems to be the most sensitive to the shift in criterion. It merely derives its high indegree status from *pop music*, which in turn relies heavily on *rock 'n' roll*.

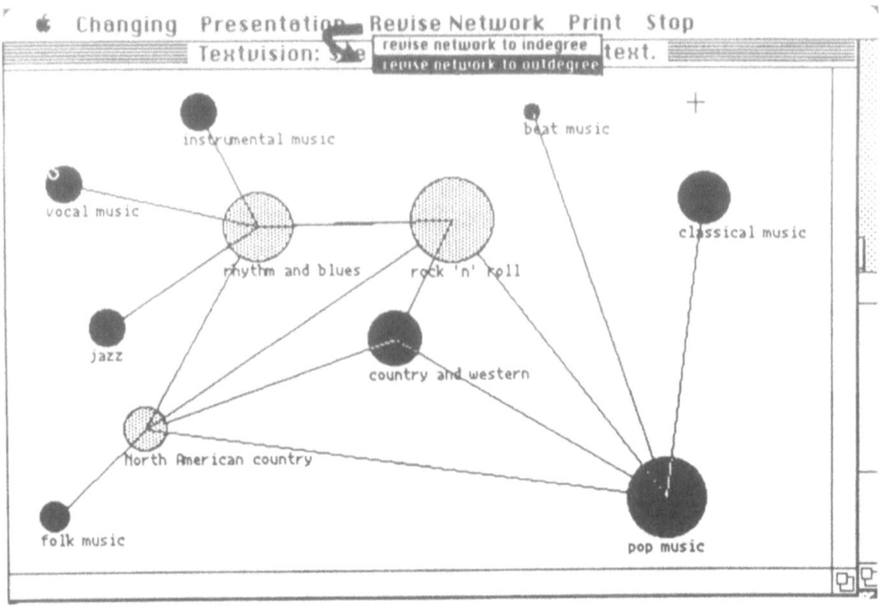

Figure 10. Sizes of nodes reflecting the centrality. The more important the coming relations the bigger the node.

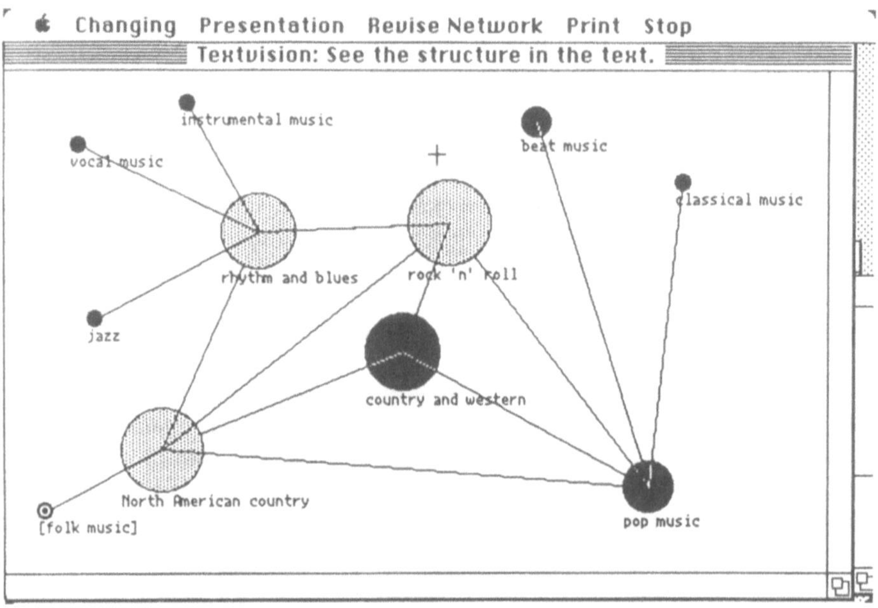

Figure 11. Size of nodes reflecting the centrality after recomputing the centralities to take account of outgoing relations.

2.4. Interpretation of Indegree and Outdegree as Criteria for Centrality

From Figure 8 it can be seen that in addition to the textual description in the paragraphs the user can assign help concepts which appear in the so called "declaration window." Defining *jazz* as a helping concept for *rhythm and blues* means that *rhythm and blues* is a concept necessary to explain the meaning of *jazz*. Those concepts which heavily rely on "remote descriptions" can be called abstract in the hierarchical meaning of the word; i.e., they stand at the top of a taxonomy. Looking to the reverse relationship we can state that those concepts which are mentioned frequently in the descriptions of other concepts have a high relevance on the basis of attainability. This latter criterion has a striking analogy with the notorious citation index which implies that the relevance of a text is raised if many other relevant publications refer to it. In our particular application, centrality based on indegree is equivalent to attainability, i.e., how often a concept is mentioned in describing other concepts. Finally, it can be seen that indegree and outdegree are two different criteria that can be used to get a quick idea of where the center of the information is. Graphic feedback can be used to maintain the elicitation of human knowledge and can also give some orientation to the novice who is not sure of what are main points and what are details.

2.5. Preliminary Experimental Results

In order to get detailed information on how Textvision might be used, we set up three experiments:

1. Seven secondary school teachers started from scratch and designed a conceptual network with its texts. The main investigation was to determine if Textvision helped them to prepare and display a didactically relevant piece of knowledge.
2. Twenty-four college students had two sessions of 45 min to elaborate an existing network about Dutch state government. The first question was how much of the existing information was remembered by the students. The second question was which parts of the existing network they changed and/or extended because of their own views on the topic and related areas.
3. Sixty-four primary school pupils worked with Textvision, mainly with the goal of studying the topic in an intensive way, so that they could answer questions about it later.

All three groups were trained to use the different actions in the program. After 30 min they proved to be at a basic level of skill such that they could work without help.

As the main purpose of this chapter is to introduce the user interface, I will restrict myself to the most salient conclusions. Teachers mainly focus on the didactic aspects of their subject matter, i.e., how to tell it to their pupils. Structuring and visualization of complex relationships are not new for them but can cause a shift from the procedural towards the declarative side of knowledge. Using the first version of Textvision the teachers made many valuable remarks about improving the current program. One central point was the suggestion to add a "help" window in which the author of a network could bridge the gap between the textual and graphic levels. Secondly, some of the teachers asked for different tools to represent rule-based versus more associative knowledge like geography, history, or literature. Thirdly, they questioned the mode of presentation to pupils. Should it be a free-browsing system without implicit or explicit instructional strategy, or should it encourage a more algorithmic searching behavior? All these questions seem to be highly relevant for successful use in educational settings, and will be examined in the future. Apart from these reservations all teachers considered Textvision an appropriate tool for consulting a large amount of text, that reduced the risk of serendipity (the finding of useful information while other information is actually being sought).

Both in the second and the third experiments we found strong indications that students and pupils tended to shift from a more receptive learning mode to a more productive use of information. In both groups we found that only 20% of the factual information was remembered. Detailed analysis is still required to answer the questions of in which particular learning phases pupils acquire new facts, and of whether there is a particular strategic pattern which is responsible for this acquisition.

3. Conclusion

The development of new human-computer interfaces will reveal new ways to help cognitive activities during complex mental tasks. In order to match the perceptual aspects of these interfaces to the user's conceptual problems, a lot of creativity in system design is needed, as is feed back from successful solutions to the psychologist's model of the user.

References

Ausubel D.P. (1963). *The psychology of meaningful verbal learning: An introduction to school learning.* Grune and Stratton, New York.

Hoede C. (1978). *A new status score for actors in a social network.* Internal report, Twente University of Technology, Department of Applied Mathematics, Enschede.

Hofstaedter D.R. (1985). *Metamagical themas: Questioning for the essence of mind and pattern.* Basic Books, New York.

Kommers P.A.M. (1982). *Design of an adaptive program for the presentation of textual information.* Swets and Zeitlinger, Lisse.

Kommers P.A.M. (1986). Adaptive presentation of text: Multi-windowing and network display for the acquisition of knowledge. In: *Programmatuur naar menselijke maat - cognitieve ergonomie van mens-computer systemen.* G.C. v.d. Veer & E. Lammers (Eds.) Stichting Informatica Congressen, Amsterdam.

Norman D.A. (1973). Memory, knowledge and the answering of questions. In: *Contemporary issues in cognitive psychology.* R. Solso (Ed.). Winston, New York.

Pask G. (1976). Conversational techniques in the study and practice of education. *British Journal of Educational Psychology,* 46, pp. 12-25.

Wilson B.G. & Welsh J.R. (1986). Something new under the instructional sun: Small knowledge-based systems as job aids. Paper at AERA 1986, San Francisco.

Chapter 15. Development of Mental Models of an Office System: A Field Study on an Introductory Course

Gerrit C. van der Veer and Michael A.M. Felt

1. Introduction

Users of a computer application need a clear and consistent structure of knowledge of the system with which they interact. This knowledge only concerns that part of the machine that is directly relevant to the delegation of tasks by the user to the system, the *virtual machine* or *user interface*. The cognitive ergonomic approach that will be illustrated combines methods for the representation of the user interface or virtual machine, with the concept of mental model. Our basic ideas are:

1. The mental model is an important aspect of human-computer interaction (Norman, 1983)
2. Specifying the virtual machine means defining explicitly the conceptual model for the user interface in a knowledge based way
3. The conceptual model can be described using a multilevel approach derived from Moran (1981), which should also apply to the user's mental model
4. This conceptual model should be presented to the user, taking into account relevant characteristics of human learning and user variables

These ideas will be illustrated in a field study of managers who had to learn the basic principles of an office system.

1.1. System and Models of the System

Norman (1983) made a clear distinction between a system, the conceptual model of the system, the mental model of the system and the scientist's conceptualization of the mental model:

1. *Target system.* This is the actual thing, e.g., a computer system
2. *The conceptual model.* This is a correct description of the system, as far as the human-machine interface is concerned; it is an accurate and consistent representation that is invented or developed by the teacher and/or designer. This includes both hardware effects of screen and keyboard, and application software, as far as the user interacts with these. The aim of teaching a novice is to transmit this model

3. *The mental model.* This concept denotes the knowledge structure the user applies in interacting with the computer. The user predicts reactions of the system to his own behavior. Decisions and planning are based on the mental model, as is explanation of unexpected system behavior. This model evolves during interaction with the target system, especially in the initial learning phase. A user "understands" a system if predictions based on his mental model are consistent with the behavior of the user interface of the target system. Unexpected effects and errors point to inconsistency between the mental model and the conceptual model
4. *The scientist's conceptualization of the mental model.* This is the idea the psychologist or researcher has about the mental model of the user.

1.2. Development of Mental Models

The development of cognitive representations of computing systems or user interfaces is a process in which structures in semantic memory are built or changed. The process of acquisition or change of mental representations is generally considered to be strongly based on analogies, and known concepts and structures are related to the new situation. This process can be activated if the teacher refers to existing semantic knowledge and schemes. Metaphors may be used to activate knowledge and act as analogies. These metaphors should be presented as such, not as actual representations of the new system (Simons, 1980). The choice of appropriate metaphors is crucial for the development of adequate mental models (Carroll & Thomas, 1982; Carroll, 1983; Clanton, 1983; Houston, 1983). In generating metaphors it should be kept in mind that the capacity of working memory is restricted to a limited number of "chuncks" (units of meaning that may be handled as one item and are only to be expanded when necessary, Lindsay & Norman, 1977). Metaphors that are too rich in composition distract too much attention and may obstruct the learning process. They must be broken down into manageable substructures when presented to the student.

Halasz and Moran (1982) pointed to dangerous aspects of this approach, especially when leaving the student alone and encouraging him to reason analogically. In using a single analogy, the teacher will soon discover that he has to adjust the metaphor, adding new (and often bizarre) features to it or, alternatively, combining various metaphors that are not normally associated. Galambos, Wiklere, Black and Sebrechts (1983) and Douglas and Moran (1983) presented examples of difficulties with the typewriter metaphor for the purpose of introducing text editing systems. On the other hand metaphors might still be useful as analogies to the conceptual models to be taught, according to Halasz and Moran, *if* the student is clearly aware of the fact the metaphors are only valid in respect to certain aspects of the system or process to be modeled. In that case, several distinct metaphors might be referred to for the same conceptual model. each illustrating a few aspects of the new system to be learned. The teacher has to be active in directing the associations of the students and in drawing the analogies, at the same time pointing to the limits of applicability of each metaphor.

1.3. Individual Differences in the Acquisition of Mental Models

Novice users of a system differ in two main relevant features. The first of these is *a priori knowledge*. Users who possess adequate mental models of systems that are relevant in task domains that are the same as or analogous to the system being learnt, have a good base for analogical reasoning (Waern, 1983). These may be computer systems, but for a lot of task domains computerless systems (e.g. office systems) exist that cover the same tasks.

The second relevant difference is in *style of information processing*. Individual styles of information processing not only result in preferences for different modes of presentation of learning material and of metaphors, but also lead to individual differences in the organization of semantic knowledge. In that respect the contrast between verbal and image representation may be relevant (van der Veer, van Muylwijk & van de Wolde, 1978; van Muylwijk, van der Veer & Waern, 1983).

Other individual differences that might be relevant in the way novice users acquire a mental model, such as field dependancy, analytical vs holistic structuring of information, general intelligence, etc., are not taken into account in this study.

1.4. The User Interface

The central point in teaching people about a human-machine system is the definition and representation of the interface (van der Veer, Tauber, Waern and van Muylwijk, 1985). There are many different points of view about exactly what the interface is, but a useful view is that an interface connects two communicating actors (independent system components) and can be regarded as the set of mutual suppositions, between the first actor (the user) and the second actor (the application).

When the computer is used as a tool for performing a set of well defined tasks (a task space), the user needs a set of assumptions about the virtual machine, virtual meaning that the machine must be seen only in respect to the defined task space, in the way in which the machine is able to perform these tasks, and in the way in which the user can specify the delegation of tasks to the system. Therefore, the user interface must be regarded as a whole in a conceptual sense, as the representation of the virtuality of the machine. The specification of the user interface can be regarded as a conceptual model, intended to be a feasible complement to the intended mental model of the user (Rohr & Tauber, 1984).

1.5. Representation of Conceptual Models

Moran (1981) proposed a representational framework in his Command Language Grammar (CLG) that enabled the description of the conceptual model of the user interface on the one hand and the intended mental model of the user on the other. An important aspect in CLG is the layering of knowledge about the system:

1. *Task level.* The taks level concerns the actual tasks for which the system may be used, their relations, and the integration of subtasks to be delegated to the system and subtasks delegated to other instances or completed by the human user. Tasks delegated to the computer system are defined by an object world (containing objects, object structures, and the state of the world) and a set of operations working on the object world (producing new objects, changing the state of the object world). All tasks of the virtual machine may be defined in the task space.
2. *Semantic level.* The semantic level of the man-machine interaction is based on the task space. It consists of the representation of the object world in the interface, the representation of the operations provided by the system to manipulate the system's object world. and the relations between the relevant objects. The semantic level is the description of the functions of the system regarding the task space. Semantics may be generalized to different systems for the same task domain or different implementations or releases of one system. Singley and Anderson (1985) showed there is strong positive transfer in learning a new editor with the same semantics as a known one. There is a problem about the relation between task level and semantic level however. The virtual machine's objects and their relations cannot always be consistently analogous to the objects and relations in the user's task space. If the system is designed without sufficient consideration of the user's problems in developing a mental model, the structure of the semantic level may be incongruent with the structure of the task level.
3. *Syntactic level.* System objects must be described and system operations must be evoked by the user. This linguistic component of the interface is captured by the syntactic level. It defines the command names and their parameters (procedures or operations triggered by the command). the context in which commands are valid. the descriptors for the objects. the

"state" variables (remembered by the system between two commands) and the organization of the output devices. The syntactic level is strongly system dependent. If the communication is not in a kind of "natural language" it is useless to define the syntax in analogy to human language. However, if one has to use different systems, negative transfer may result if the different syntaxes are built upon different kinds of structure, or lack any kind of consistency. The conceptual integration of knowledge on the semantic and syntactic levels is also increased by consistency in syntactic rules. Inconsistency in systems for different commands with related semantics leads to a disadvantage for the user (Green, 1984).

4. *Key-stroke level.* In Moran's terminology the key-stroke level is called the interaction level, but we prefer the label key-stroke, since interaction is often used in other contexts to denote the entire human-computer interaction. On this level the commands must be specified by actions like key strokes or pointing activities, and are followed by perceptible system behavior (e.g., sounds to indicate "illegal" commands, locking keys in certain contexts, changes on the screen, reaction time of the system, and attention-provoking cues like blinking of screen messages). This level of the user interface is always (terminal) hardware dependent.

2. A Field Study

In a field study we collected observations and generated ideas on the relation between course structure (the kind of metaphors used, the modes of presentation), relevant student characteristics (knowledge and experience with related tasks and systems, styles of information processing), and the resulting mental models of the system.

2.1. Hypotheses for the Study

The formulation and testing of statistical hypotheses was not sensible in this situation because of the small number of observations and the lack of control of environmental and personal influences. The expectations derived from a theoretical background we will call our hypotheses. The measurements we collected and the observations during and after the course may give some support for these hypotheses, or an impression of either the incorrectness or incompleteness of the theoretical notions, or of the importance of factors we neglected in this study. The theoretical notions we intended to investigate were derived from Norman's analysis of systems and models of systems (Norman, 1983), from Moran's analysis of the user interface in different levels

(Moran, 1981), from our analysis of individual differences and the appliction of metaphors for teaching, and from the analysis by van der Veer et al. (1985) of the virtual machine and the role of teaching about the user interface. Relating these notions we derived the following hypotheses:

1. Application of Moran's levels of representing the user interface results in a description of the virtual machine or user interface. This discription may be transformed into a teacher's conceptual model, tuned to a certain task domain and user group
2. Metaphors may be designed for teaching, consistent with the different levels of the conceptual model
3. A method may be developed to acquire a scientist's conceptualization of the mental models that result from teaching, in particular concerning the quality of the mental model, and of the user's way of representation
4. Users will differ in their mental models, depending on their a priori knowledge of the external task domain and of related systems, and depending on their preferred style of representation of information (verbalizing or imaging)

2.2. Design of the Study

We had the opportunity to collect observations in a real life environment during an internal course in a large insurance company, in which the participating students were managers. These students were all well acquainted with traditional office environments and the course was intended to draw upon this experience. The students needed to know the general principles of the new system in order to take decisions about the implementation of this or a comparable system in the work structure in their group, or in the group they advised. Most of them considered using such a system themselves, although the actual need varied. For all participants time was very scarce (in fact most would have preferred to take the course during the evenings) so the investment of 3 days was an indication of their motivation.

An interview took place some days before the start of the course to collect an impression of the students' prior knowledge, of their intentions in joining the course, and of some aspects of their style of information processing (imaging or verbalizing). On the same occasion, the students were told of the observations to be recorded during the course, of the questionnaire that would be handed out at the end, and of the aim of this evaluation. Students were asked to choose an identification number, and were told that the teacher would never know the identity of the individual from whom data were collected.

There were 10 students (the maximum number that could be accommodated in the course room). The arangement of the hardware allowed for five pairs of students who had to share one desk with a personal computer. The students were assigned to pairs, and matched as far as possible, on type and amount of prior knowledge in order to prevent one from dominating the other. During the course observations were made of the student-teacher interaction and of the students' cooperation. The final questionnaire was designed to get an impression of the type of representations students used in their mental models.

In order to design the course a specification of the conceptual model had to be developed. The only documentation available was an installation manual (a heavy set of books that could only be read by expert users) and a quick reference guide (a small booklet containing lists of tools, functions, commands, etc., each with a two- or three-line description). The manual contained introductory descriptions and the same type of lists as presented in the guide. The teacher relied heavily on one of the authors for the analysis of the user interface and the definition of the conceptual model, but shared responsibility for the design of the educational metaphors. The teacher agreed not to be informed about the differences in prior knowledge that were measured for the individual students, but was aware of the general level and the diversity of quality.

3. Conceptual Model of the Office System

We will only briefly mention the general structure of the target system, or to be more precise of the virtual machine, and the most important concepts of the user interface, restricting ourselves mainly to the task level and semantic level.

The system is composed of an integrated set of interactive sub-systems ("tools") for office management tasks. The package consists of seven tools (spreadsheet, [relational] database manipulation, graphics, editor [text entry and formatting], record manager and information retrieval, emulator for communication with a mainframe, generator for individual system profile [colors, names, configuration, passwords]) of which the first four are the primary tools, related directly to office tasks. The other three tools concern administration and communication between the tasks. Integration is realized by enabling the exchange of information between the tools in the way of transportable objects with attributes (documents, tables).

The user interface may be in a number of different modes, each enabling a different set of user actions. The *input* mode allows the input of information.

The *command* mode, allowing the issuing of commands by menu selection or typing in the command names, is automatically changed into the *edit* mode when an incorrect command is issued. In the same way an automatic change to the *point* mode occurs if that is feasible in case of certain commands. Procedures are defined by example.

There is a series of commands which may be used in all tools (e.g., COPY, DELETE, FORMAT, GOTO, HELP, INFO, INPUT, PRINT, OPEN, SAVE), but the syntax is not always uniform. Some of these commands communicate between the tools, others between a tool and different types of objects (like documents, pictures, graph ranges, and data tables). The commands may be typed, chosen from a menu or in some cases issued with a function key. In the spreadsheet and database tools the use of arithmetic functions is possible.

Metacommunication consists of error and warning messages from the system, and the HELP command from the user. The system tells the user to "wait" when an action takes more than fraction of a second. Only some of the tools display feedback like information about what percentage of a time-consuming action is accomplished.

3.1. The Teacher's Conceptual Model

The analysis and description of the virtual machine revealed a number of inconsistencies in the user interface, aparently due to the fact that the system seems to be assembled from a set of originally independant tools, combined with new facilities that were designed for the integration. The inconsistencies were especially noticeable in the syntax of commands with the same name and globally the same functions within different tools, and in attributes of tool-specific objects with similar meaning. It was decided to solve this problem by deliberately defining a consistent teacher's conceptual model that deviated from the target system. The teacher pointed to the exceptions, and called them bugs in the design of the system (it was in fact the first release of this product, for which criticism and comments from the teacher's compagny were actually welcomed).

The core concept for integration was, for this combination of users and task domains, decided to be the notion of constructing a report. Later on, after a lot of hands on experience with the system, we decided that for (other) user groups who have to use the facility themselves heavily for their daily work, the concept of administration would be a better core for the conceptual model. This difference will affect the formulation of metaphors at task level, the order of teaching the different tools, and the choice of examples.

3.2. Educational Metaphors of the Virtual Machine

In order to induce an adequate mental model, association with existing knowledge was the goal of the metaphors that were constructed. The metaphors appealed to the available schemes and knowledge of traditional office tasks and office structure. Since the teacher was well aware of the individual differences between verbalizers and imagers, metaphors were developed that combined verbal and pictoral elements. In fact, this development went on parallel with the formation of the conceptual model. The final metaphors will be described along with some remarks about their evolution.

3.2.1. A Metaphor of the Internal Task Space

This metaphor was designed to induce a mental model of the interaction with the virtual machine at the task level. The central theme of the metaphor was chosen to correspond to a knowledge domain that all students were expected to share prior to the course. The core of the metaphor was the management of an office comparable to the kind of situation in which the students practice their daily work, with delegation of subtasks to different functionaries. The most important among these (the chief of the typing pool, the draughtsman, the accountand, and the records officer) were referred to as individuals. Apart from this there were people from the communication services, from the safety department (with strange side-tasks like painting parts of the building in different colors), people from the record office and a group of elderly men nicknamed "Decent Old Style" (DOS), who did almost anything for you, provided you ask them precisely.

Originally the intention was not to refer to the different functionaries, but to the rooms in which the subtasks take place. It turned out that it was much more natural to refer to persons about the delegation of subtasks, rather than sending and receiving messages from the typing pool or drawing office. In some cases the delegation of subtasks was quite different from the normal way in an office, e.g., dealing with modes. This problem could not be solved in time for the development of the conceptual model, and the metaphor accordingly was incomplete at these aspects. Although the metaphor was mainly verbally presented, some visual elements were deliberately included, such as pictures of the most important functionaries (in fact representing actors in a well-known television series). Imagery was called on by referring to the spatial structure of the concern's main building, and the transportation of task-related objects (drawings, typescripts) between places.

3.2.2. A Visual-Spatial Metaphor of Semantics

The goal of this metaphor was to present an image representing the semantic structure of the virtual machine during interaction with the user. Starting with several trials of abstract overall schemes portraying data flow or communication channels within the package, and of figures representing parts that were analogous to other parts, the final solution consisted of one total view of the system (see Figure 1), consisting of a structure composed of a small number of visual metaphors or icons. Closed boxes depicted tools, cards in card-trays represented transportable objects with variable information content, and the origin or most obvious location of these objects was suggested by placing the card-trays adjacent to a certain tool icon. In the original pictures, colors gave some redundant information about the difference between tools and different types of objects. Communication channels that may be chosen with the commands were represented by tubes, and valves depicted choices of destination associated with some of the commands (attributes of the objects to be transported, in the sense of the semantics). The command names and the names of the tools and objects were indicated in the picture.

The image constructed was too complex for a novice to be comprehensible in any detail. Therefore, four subpictures were constructed (e.g., Figure 2), each representing a view of the system from the reference point of one tool: that is, the tool actually activated at that moment. These separate representations may be interpreted in a single view, since the number of chuncks does not exeed human attention capacity.

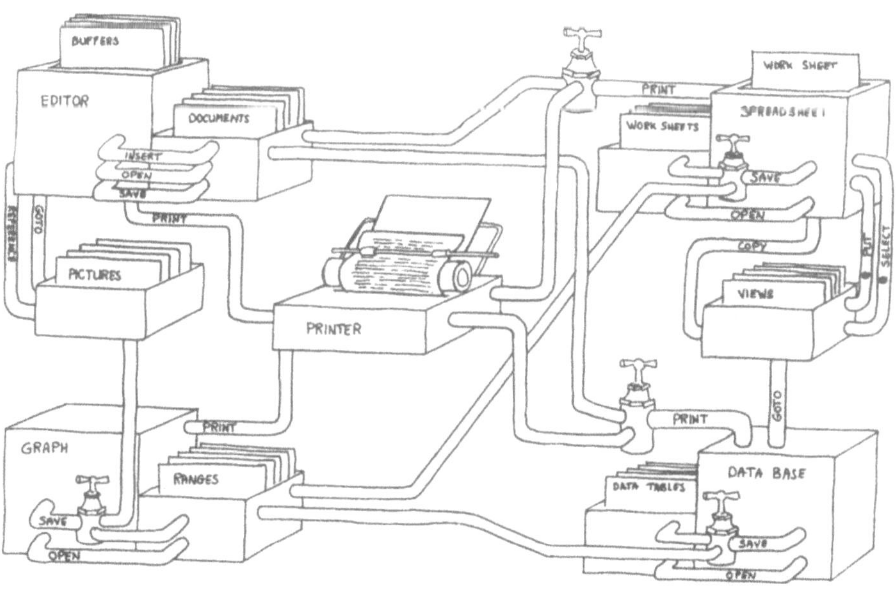

Figure 1. Visual-spatial metaphor of the semantics of the whole system

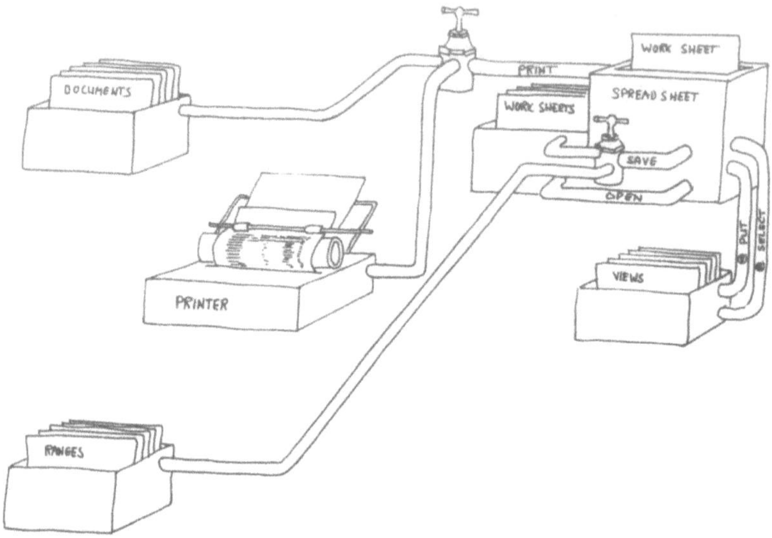

Figure 2. Visual-spatial metaphor of the semantics of a single tool

4. Structure of the Course

The course was scheduled to take 3 days in a row. One half day was intended for the introduction of the metaphors and the presentation of an overview of the system, each of the main tools was allocated another half-day, and the last afternoon was dedicated to an example of the use of the total system.

4.1. Introduction of the Metaphors

The course started by making the students aware of the fact that the introduction was to be in the form of metaphors. The task metaphor was introduced with a general question so that the students mentioned the different tasks that are normally performed in an office. After the list of functions was considered complete by the teacher, the story of a very large office in a large building was told, referring to the head office of the firm in question as an analogy. The students were asked to comment on the organization and its efficiency from their own point of view as managers, which gave the teacher the occasion to adjust the metaphor at places where the wrong associations turned out to be called upon. The students were told that they themselves would have to operate as a manager, and were advised to be autocratic in their behavior, and to know to exactly which person a certain task must be delegated.

After this discourse at task level the metaphor of the semantic structure of the system was introduced. The graphic representation and the icons were declared, and the general overview was superficially treated. It was immediately made clear that it was of no use to memorize all connections from this image. The fact that the same commands are available at the different tools was pointed out, and the functions of some of them were explained as examples.

4.2. The Tools

Each of the tools (subsystems) was introduced by the help of the appropriate image. Objects and commands were explained, as were the functions. For the first tool this took more time than for the others, since most of the commands have analogous meanings, as have some of the objects. The different modes, when applicable, were covered as well. The concepts treated were illustrated by a demonstration of their actual use with a video projector connected to the teacher's terminal. After some of the most important concepts were covered, the students were asked to explore the tool, guided by rather global tasks. After about an hour these explorations were concluded by a group session intended to evaluate the mental model of the tool as it had developed.

The last morning of the course was partly devoted to the possibility of creating procedures; these were explained and demonstrated but not actually practiced by the students.

4.3. An Integrated Case Study

For the last afternoon a set of data was prepared, consisting of a number of different tables about the capacity and attainability of the firm's telephone exchange and network. These data had previously been downloaded from a mainframe. The instruction was to construct some relevant tables, calculate some functions, display these in an annotated figure, and insert this in a piece of text describing the relations that were revealed. In the end the result had to be "printed," first on the screen and afterwards on a printer.

5. Observations

5.1. Description of the Students

The structured interview, held before the actual start of the course, was directed at the relevant aspects of the background and intentions of the students. We learned that all students either had personal experience with batch oriented systems, or had staff menbers that used these. Most of them were responsible for the integration of information processing into the work of their group, and some of them designed the allocation of tasks between human resources and computers for their own office. Experience with interactive systems was less general. A few had used them to different extents. All had some knowledge of the functions of personal computer applications, like text editing or spreadsheet programs, but none had any experience with an integrated system like the one being taught about in the course. Some had learned one or more computer languages, but most had not used them during recent years. All students had at least some typing skill.

In order to establish the individual style of information processing relevant to the mode of the metaphors presented we applied a procedure described by van der Veer, et al. (1978), that gives an indication of the extent to which a subject prefers to store an image representation, an abstract representation, or a verbal episodic representation. These representations are in general evenly distributed in investigations on adult groups. In this group, five students turned out to have a prefererence for image representations, and the other five displayed a mixture of the other possibilities. Since the group was so small, we decided to group the latter category together and label them nonimagers.

5.2. Observations on the Course

The course took place in a specially equiped room. The students were seated in pairs at a large desk with sufficient room for handling paper, and with one personal computer (PC) for each pair. The teacher used a large video projector to project the display of his PC, and an overhead projector for displaying material like the visual metaphor.

The introduction of the system as a whole and of the different tools always took the form of conversation and the task metaphor was elaborated first. Then, the image representing the semantics was projected, and a (black and white) copy of it was handed out. After this, and after some examples were displayed on the video screen, the students were asked to explore the possibilities that had been mentioned. At the first session this turned out to be somewhat difficult, as they had no clear idea of how to get started, and also because there were some fundamental misconceptions that were revealed during the discussion after this exploration phase. During the exploration of the tools in later sessions it was observed that the pairs started by discussing an exploration strategy, finding out which would be the interesting problems to attack and what would be a reasonable exercise. The integrated case study at the end of the course turned out to be very difficult on this first occasion.

Although all students succeeded in transporting information between the tools, converting the objects, and manipulating the content with the help of commands and functions, half of them did not have enough time to reach the ultimate goal of combining the constructed graph with a piece of text. Only one pair actually printed their product.

5.3. Impressions of Mental Models

At the end of the course a questionnaire was handed out by the experimenter who had taken the interviews and been present to record observations. He told the students that he wanted to know what kind of knowledge they had gathered about the system, and asked them to interpret the questions in this way. They were asked to mail the questionnaires, marked with their identification number, to the experimenter's institute. They were not allowed to take any official documentation about the system with them, but the experimenter promised to send them the quick reference guide as soon as he received their responses.

The topics covered by the questions can be grouped into four aspects: the use of analogies of existing knowledge, the quality at the semantic level of the resulting model, the preference for modes, and the kind of representation. For each of these aspects we will give an indication of any differences we found between the imagers and the non-imagers among the students. This is solely an indication of potentially interesting relations, as the small number of participants does not allow any statistically significant assertions to be made.

5.3.1. Analogies of Semantics

The analogy between one of the possible ways of installation of tabulations and margins in an editor, and the actions on a conventional typewriter, was correctly perceived by all imagers but by only two of the five nonimagers. The analogy of the a priori semantics of the concept *undelete* and the command UNDELETE was perceived by all but one (a nonimager) correctly. In fact this command could be used for other things apart from undoing an error, such as copying and transport of fragments within an object by first deleting these fragments and then transporting the content of the buffer to one or more places.

5.3.2. Correctness of Semantics

One of the questions asked for the difference between some related format commands. The responses contained the correct semantic distinctions in the case of all imagers, and of one nonimager. An example of a subject's semantic representation of three different format commands is as follows:

```
    This    is       verbatim.
This is fill.
This          is             justify.
```

Table 1. Example of a subject's semantic representation of relations between commands and tools

	function	where/when/which tool
OPEN	"open" file, worksheet, etc., for input, other modifications, joining, etc. It is put into internal memory	EDITOR SPREADSHEET DATABASE GRAPH
SAVE	write a file to hard disk or floppy	idem
PRINT	information to printer for printing on paper or to the screen	SPREADSHEET GRAPHICS EDITOR
COPY	copy data from a cell or range to another location	SPREADSHEET EDITOR
INSERT	insert of one or more rows or columns	SPREADSHEET EDITOR
GOTO	"jump" with the cursor to another location	SPREADSHEET

A question about the function of a list of commands and their relations to the different tools resulted in a reasonable description at the semantic level (e.g. Table 1) for all students except one nonimager. The representation of the relations between the objects and the modules or tools varied. Only some nonimagers were able to demonstrate (in a very fragmentary way) any relations, whereas all imagers could give either an indication of any relation (Figure 3) or a semantically annotated structure (Table 2).

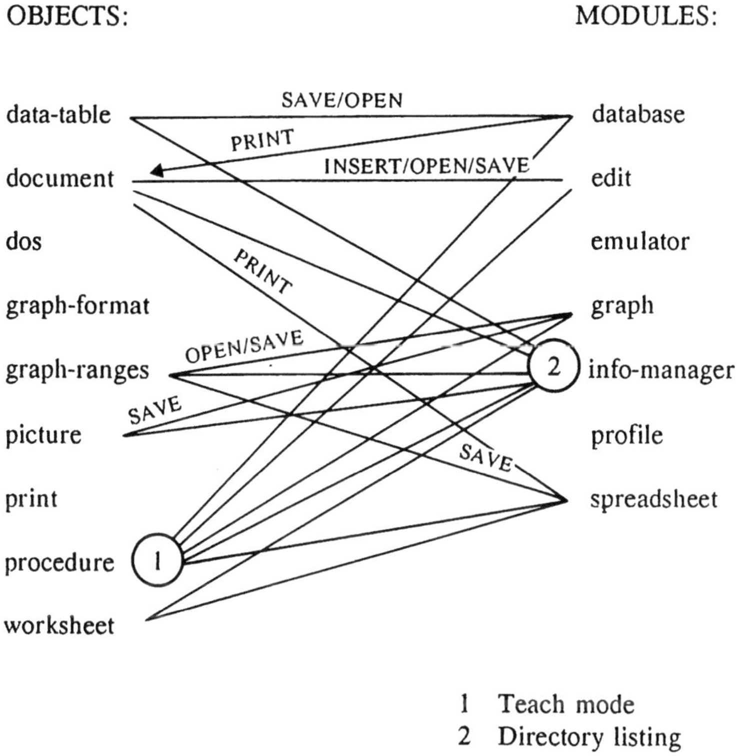

Figure 3. A subject's representation of relations between objects and tools

5.3.3. Preference for Modes

In some of the tools of the system it is the possible to choose a mode, e.g., input the coordinates of a range of cells, or point at the screen to corners of the range. All imagers preferred pointing, but only two of the nonimagers.

5.3.4. Representation of the Mental Model

A teach-back procedure was used to get an idea of the type of representation students used for their mental model of the system. The students were asked to give an overview of the transactions with the system that were needed to accomplish a certain goal, in such a way that their overview would be understandable to a colleague who had either only knowledge of the traditional office procedures for this task, or, in another question, had experience with separate systems like editors or database tools.

Table 2. Representation of subject's semantic structure of objects and tools

A	B	
data-table	database	A = individual file in B
	spreadsheet	A = input file for B
	emulator	A via emulator to/from mainframe
	info-manager	for description
document	edit	A = individual "file" in B
	emulator	A via emulator to/from mainframe
	info-manager	for description
	spreadsheet	saved as "document" or as part of one
dos	emulator	
graph-format	graph	specifications of what is under a graph
graph-ranges	graph	columns or rows of which a graph is made
picture	graph	displays the picture
	edit	references a saved picture that
		e.g. is to be included in a report
print	edit	send data to screen or printer
	graph	idem
	spreadsheet	idem
procedure	database }	collects actions. stored in a"procedure"
	spreadsheet }	so that they can be called repeatedly
		(made with assistance of "teach")

All imagers and three nonimagers presented some kind of model for at least two of the three situations. The resulting representations are illustrative of the types of model that the students used. One used images at the task-level only (Figure 4). Another explained the solution in terms of the verbal component of the metaphor of the task level:

> The calculator says which parts of the worksheet are important for the draftsman.
>
> These data are put on a separate sheet of paper (RANGES) and are sent to the draftsman.

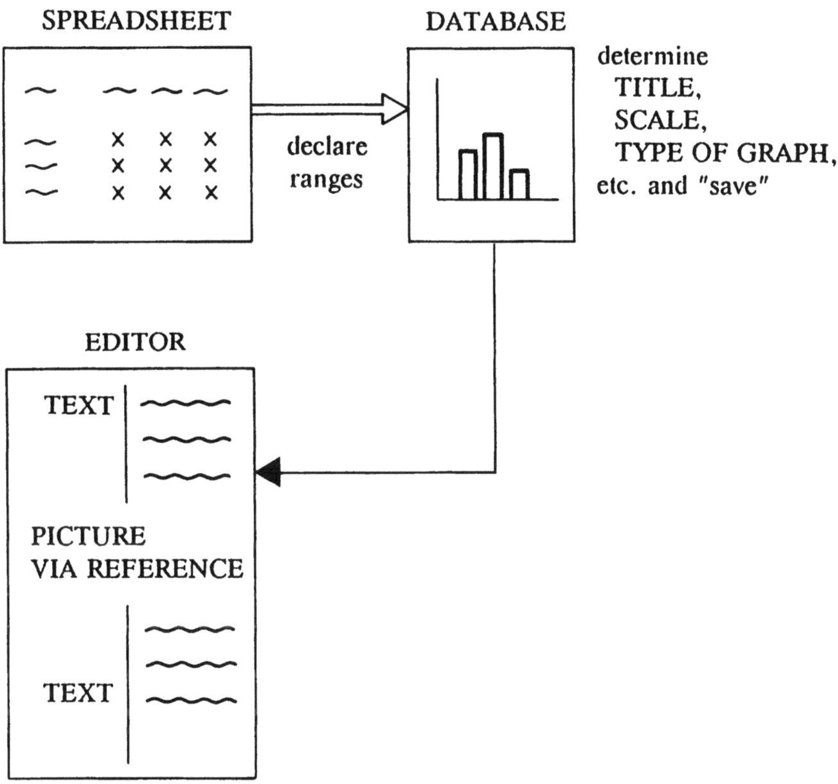

Figure 4. A subject's image representation at task level

> The draftsman makes, from that paper (RANGES), a drawing and places this drawing in the typists tray.
>
> The typist types the notes and puts the drawing in the location indicated.

Four of the students displayed a list of commands with semantic annotations, such as the following:

1 open worksheet with SPREADSHEET

2 copy → view with SPREADSHEET

3 call "view" from GRAPH with assistance from ?-statement → "range"

4 build with assistance of GRAPH/time series "PICTURE" (reference sheet)

5 build report-text with "input"

6 insert "PICTURE" (reference sheet) with EDITOR/insert

One used a flow-chart at the semantic level (Figure 5), and finaly, one student used a representation at key stroke level (semantically annotated, see Figure 6). This student explicitely stated that he was unable to represent anything that would be understandable for a colleague without experience with computerized tools (which seems reasonable with his style of representation).

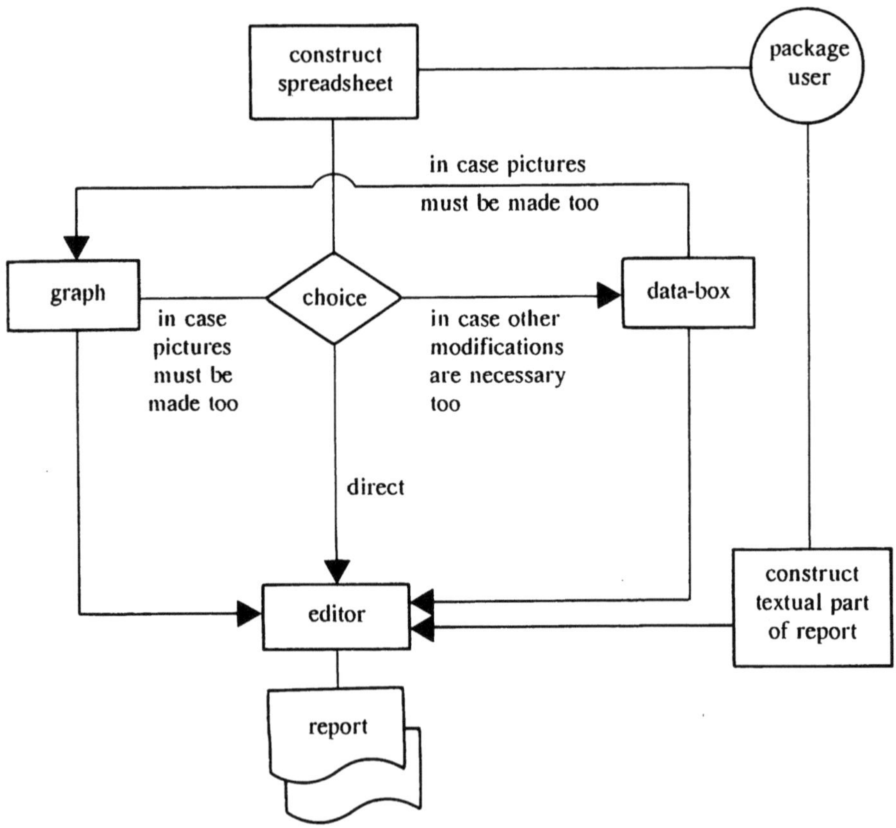

Figure 5. A subject's flow-chart representation with semantics

enter the
following: IN ↴
(go to folder of choice with arrows)

OP ↴

TO ED OP ↴ (here name of document that must be opened, and thus must be in the buffer)

F2 WO OP ↴ (here name of spreadsheet that is to be input)

F4 indicate range with arrow ↴

TO ED ↴ indicate where spreadsheet must begin

hereafter save everything and close or work further

Figure 6. A subject's key-stroke representation

6. Discussion and Conclusion

Research on teaching in real life situations has to cope with the restricted opportunities that are allowed by teachers and students. Observation is often the only way to collect data that are necessary both for the development of theory, and for evaluation. Our interest was in the acquisition of realistic notions about the usability of the conceptual analyses of Norman (1983) and Moran (1981), and in the use of metaphors in relation to the development of mental models.

For this field study we derived expectations that we, rather boldly, called "hypotheses". Our conclusions regarding these four hypothesis are as follows:

1. The virtual machine or user interface can be described with the help of the different levels described by Moran. This is a useful base for constructing a teacher's conceptual model that can also be tuned to a special user group and task domain (in our case managers who delegated tasks from the viewpoint of report production; we also developed other variants for administrators)
2. We succeeded in refering to knowledge at the task level that was generally available for the user group as a whole. In order to construct manageable educational metaphors of the semantic level of the virtual machin we had to deviate from the user interface because of its internal inconsistencies.

We constructed side remarks along with our systematic semantic metaphor, pointing to inelegant features of the user interface that the students had to view as design bugs

3. The questionaire we used turned out to help us to get an indication of both the quality and correctness of aspects of the mental model, and of the method of representation the students used. These representations reflected the different levels Moran introduced. In the products of this small group only a purely syntactic representation could not be detected
4. The group of students in this field study was too small to get more than a first impression of the relations between individual differences and the mental models. As the prior knowledge of the external task domain seemed to be rather sophisticated for all students in this study, no relation to this variable could be detected. The preferred mode of representation of information as measurable on the dimension imager/nonimager seems to be relevant for the disposition of the resulting mental model, especially regarding correctness and completeness

In this first course only one kind of metaphor was used, so we are not able to say anything regarding the interaction of teaching strategy (choice of metaphors) and individual differences. We have an indication that the metaphors our teacher applied were not too bad at communicating the kind of semantic knowledge that was intended, for students that may be called imagers. On future courses the teacher will have to apply other methods in order to take care of the learning styles of the other students (the nonimagers). After the introduction of the metaphor at task level, an example will be handed out that shows different successive phases in the processing of a real-life task performed with the system. The different semiproducts (in fact images of objects created and handled in the system during the proces) will each be printed on a separate sheet. These sheets will be stapled together in the actual order of creation by the system. No indication of the command syntax will be provided on this occasion. On behalf of the nonimagers, who showed insufficient benefit from the rather unstructured exploration of the different tools (apparently not being guided by a mental model of sufficient completeness to start with), alternative excercises will be provided, consisting of detailed problems that stress elaboration of syntactic structure and related semantics. These are intended to help students who prefer guided practice to free exploration of the semantic space. New observations will be collected to validate this method.

References

Black J. & Moran T. (1982). Learning and remembering command names. In: *Proceedings of the conference on human factors in computer systems, Gaithersburg*, ACM, New York.

Carroll J.M. (1983). Presentation and form in user-interface architecture. *Byte*, pp. 113-122.

Carroll J.M. & Thomas J.C. (1982). Metaphor and the cognitive representation of computing systems. *IEEE Transactions on Systems, Man, and Cybernetics*, 12, pp. 107-116. IEEE Computer Society, Silver Spring.

Clanton C. (1983). The future of metaphor in man-computer systems. *Byte*, pp. 263-270.

Douglas S.A. & Moran T.P. (1983). Learning text editor semantics by analogy. In: *Proceedings of the Conference on human factors in computer systems, Boston.* A. Janda (Ed.), ACM, New York.

Galambos J.A., Wikler E.S., Black J.B. & Sebrechts M.M. (1983). How you tell your computer what you mean: Ostension in interactive systems. In: *Proceedings Conference human factors in computer systems, Boston.* A. Janda (Ed.), ACM, New York.

Green T.R.G. (1984). Cognitive ergonomic research at SAPU, Sheffield. In: *Readings on cognitive ergonomics - mind and computer.* G.C. van der Veer, M.J. Tauber, T.R.G. Green & P. Gorny (Eds.) Springer, Heidelberg.

Halasz F. & Moran T. (1982). Analogy considered harmful. In: *Proceedings of the conference human factors in computer systems, Gaithersburg.* ACM, New York.

Houston T. (1983). The allegory of software. *Byte*, pp. 210-214.

Lindsey P.H. & Norman D.A. (1977). *Human information processing* Academic Press, New York.

Moran T.P. (1981). The Command Language Grammer: a representation for the user interface of interactive computer systems. *International Journal of Man-Machine Studies*, 15, pp.3-50.

Van Muylwijk B., van der Veer G.C. and Waern Y. (1983). On the implications of user variability in open systems - An overview of the little we know and of the lot we have to find out. *Behaviour and Information Technology*, 2, pp. 313-326.

Norman D.A. (1983). Some observations on mental models. In: *Mental Models.* A.L. Stevens & D. Gentner (Eds.) Erlbaum, Hillsdale, N.J.

Rohr G. & Tauber M.J. (1984). Representational frameworks and models for human-computer interfaces. In: *Readings on cognitive ergonomics - Mind and computers.* G.C. van der Veer, T.R.G. Green, M.J. Tauber & P. Gorny (Eds.) Springer, Heidelberg.

Simons P.R.J. (1980). *Vergelijkenderwijs: onderzoek naar de invloed van metaforen op het leren.* Van Spaendonck drukkerij, Tilburg.

Singley M.K. & Anderson J.R. (1985). The transfer of text-editing skill. *International Journal of Man-Machine Studies*, 22, pp. 403-423.

Van der Veer G.C., Van Muylwijk B. & Van de Wolde G.J.E. (1978). Cognitive styles and differential learning capacities in paired-associate learning. In: *Cognitive psychology and instruction.* A.M. Lesgold, J.W. Pellegrino, S.D. Fokkema and R. Glaser (eds.). Plenum Press, New York.

Van der Veer G.C., Tauber M.J., Waern Y. & Van Muylwijk B. (1985). On the interaction between system and user characteristics. *Behaviour and Information Technology*, 4, pp. 289-308.

Waern Y. (1983). Prior knowledge as obstacle and help in computer aided tasks. *Working papers from the cognitive seminar*, 17. Department of Psychology, University of Stockholm, Stockholm.

Expert Systems and Artificial Intelligence

Chapter 16. Artificial Intelligence and Cognitive Psychology: A New Look at Human Factors

David S. Brée

1. Introduction

Engineers and psychologists have traditionally cooperated in the study and design of interfaces between humans and the machines they wish to control. In the scientific literature, the results of work have been labelled Human Factors. This field has been dominated by people interested in the mechanical aspects of the interaction between man and machine; for example, the physical layout of control panels so that the hand and eye movements may be kept to a minimum. The redesign of the cockpit of fighter aircraft is a classic case of the results of such cooperation.

We are now witnessing the beginning of a new development in human factors: an interest in the computational aspects of the interaction between man and machine. One of the earlier studies in this area is a study of the hand movements required for touch typing. Unlike earlier studies which were concerned with optimizing the layout of a typewriter keyboard, Rumelhart and Norman (1982) wrote a computer program to simulate the typist. Their aim was to establish what information processing skills were required of the typist. Once this was known, then the knowledge could be applied in the design of computer assisted training programs for novice typists. Rumelhart and Norman are both members of an increasing group who call themselves cognitive psychologists, or, if they have entered the area from a different discipline, cognitive scientists. They frequently cooperate with a new type of engineer, the knowledge engineer, who is interested in artificial intelligence. Artificial intelligence, or AI for short, is concerned with the creation of computer programs that perform tasks, which up until the time these programs were created, were regarded as intelligent, i.e. the province of the human mind. It is this marriage of cognitive psychology and AI that is bringing a new look to the human factors field.

One of the recurrent themes in the human factors area is that hard science drives out soft science (Card, 1984). Engineers are for ever inventing new mechanical and, nowadays, electronic devices that quickly render obsolete older inventions. And with this obsolescence, the psychological studies built around the old machinery become less relevant. A good illustration of this is the virtual disappearance of the need for a detailed knowledge of the arm reach that a machine operator can be expected to have. The result of replacing mechanical control panels by electronic boards means that operators can sit comfortably in their chairs and operate their apparatus without stretching. For example, lighting equipment in a theatre used to be controlled by a vast bank of rheostats. These were moved by locking their control arms onto shafts which were rotated whenever a lighting change had to be made. The electricians, and there were usually at least two, spent most of their time locking and unlocking the controls onto the shafts, which occupied the whole of a wall in a major theatre. Nowadays there is only one electrician, who is faced with a panel in which each circuit or group of circuits is controlled by entering its number on the console and adjusting the level accordingly. The levels are stored for recall on cue during a performance. The electrician only has to push one button to establish the next cue change, a task which could easily be given to the stage manager, as he has to push a button to give the electrician his cue (The ideas in my original sketch for such a control board (Brée, 1965), incorporating a joystick, are at last being implemented.) The moral of the story is that we will continue to see technological developments altering our machines to such an extent that we must expect, as psychologists, always to be behind with our studies. Technological development is followed by psychological adaptation.

Most machines are designed around the task that has to be done. This is true even of the new electronically controlled variety. One of the technological developments on the horizon is that electronic machines can now be designed to be user oriented. By user oriented I do not mean that the machines should be designed to be physically comfortable or visually pleasing, which of course they should be. Rather, I mean that the software that runs the machines should be designed with the cognitive processing skills and limitations of the user in mind.

In this chapter, I will explore how this may come about, and will look at the following areas: artificial languages, text processing, spreadsheets, database interfaces, and expertsystems. I shall point to some fruitful topics for research, from possible Ph.D. theses to potential major research projects, in each of these areas.

2. Artificial Languages

The development of artificial languages has shown a steady evolution towards easier-to-use styles. In the 1950s we were still working with machine language, literally telling the machine what it had to do step by step. It was not until the 1960s that symbolically oriented languages began to be used. At that time mathematically oriented languages, such as Fortran and Algol, as well as the first qualitatively oriented languages, such as IPL-V (now extinct) and Lisp, favored in AI quarters, were implemented. That decade also saw the beginnings of special purpose languages, such as Sol and Dynamo for simulating dynamic systems.

The first half of the 1970s witnessed the introduction of easy-to-understand languages, so that people could very quickly start to write their own programs. This was the decade of such classics as Logo for children, Cobol for databases, Pascal for teaching good programming, and Basic for everybody. The second half of the 1970s was when computing started to become quite popular outside specialist fields. The advent of the microcomputer stimulated the widespread use of computation and the developers of special purpose packets responded with the first generation popular software packets, e.g., Wordstar for text processing, Lotus 1-2-3 for spread sheets, dBaseII for database management, together with software for specific tasks such as hospital registration and games for children. It also saw the beginning of graphics packets for low-resolution screens (Busigraph) and very slow plotters (Energraphics).

The first half of the 1980s has seen an attempt to provide multiple input-output facilities for software packets. The use of windows has become prominent (Loops) and the mouse has made it easy to interact with the screen to give commands, as in the software developed for the Macintosh. The advent of laser printers has made it possible to integrate text and diagrams in the output, although the software is still in its infancy. And finally the workstation in which all the different modes of input and output are flexibly integrated has recently come on the market.

The future in this area is going to develop quickly with the integration of AI techniques into the standard interfaces that are provided with artificial languages. These advances will be both of a passive and an active nature. Passive facilities provide checks on the user, to make sure that his work meets certain minimum requirements. Active facilities make suggestions to the user about what should come next (see Table 1).

Table 1. Programming aids

Passive cooperation	Active cooperation	Requirements
Syntax checkers	Syntax suppliers	
Semantics control	Program generators	Metaknowledge
Validity checking	Intention augmentation	User knowledge

At the simplest level we have had programs that check the syntax of a user's program before attempting to work with it. Most compiled artificial languages make a first pass through a potential program to ensure that the syntax of all the statements is correct. This facility can easily be provided online rather than at the time of compilation so that the user is immediately made aware of errors. On the active side we can expect to see programming environments which provide the syntax as they go along. For instance every BEGIN statement must be followed by an END, which is something that can easily be provided automatically. Together with good layout editors, this facility can be most helpful to beginning programmers, as has been seen in the Solo language for teaching AI to psychologists (Eisenstadt, 1983).

At the semantic level matters are not so simple. There is at present no way of checking that the semantics of a program is as it should be. In fact most programming languages do not provide any strong semantics component. For instance, once a variable is declared to be an integer then all arithmetic operations are permitted, by the rules of syntax. It does not, however, always make sense to perform all arithmetic operations on integers. The variable *year* would normally be an integer. It makes sense to subtract one year from another to get a time interval; it is unlikely to make sense if two years are multiplied together. It would be nice if such mistakes could be spotted for us by the machine. Better still would be a machine that could write its own programs to do what we ask of it in a higher-level language. This is, of course, the raison d'être of the so-called high-level programming languages. However, the compilers for such languages, which convert our commands into machine readable code, do so in a most slavish manner. What we would like to see are programming environments which are capable of generating high level code from instructions that are not completely specified. To do so they will require some problem solving ability. The current developments of programmers' assistants in AI are steps in this direction. What will be required is an understanding of how present-day programmers go about the business of converting the instructions that they get from system designers into working programs. One thing that is clearly required to accomplish this task is to understand more about metaknowledge. The programmer understands many things about the structure of data and control. This kind of knowledge will need to be incorporated into any semi-automatic program generator. Understanding how programmers work is a task which has come under the purview of psychologists (Kharney, 1982).

At the next level up, a program should do not only what is sensible, but also what is intended by the programmer. There is a branch of computer science that is concerned with proving that algorithms perform correctly. However, the scope of such work has been limited to well-defined problems such as one finds at the bottom of all programming languages, e.g., that a procedure for array multiplication can be proved actually to do the task it purports to do.

For programs of any extent, this approach does not seem to be a fruitful path, as anyone who has worked with a commercial software package is quickly made painfully aware. My pet example is the well known database manager dBaseII which quite easily and unintentionally can be put into a state when it will first tell you, correctly, that an unknown file is not present, but upon being asked a second time it will inform you that it *is* there. Ashton-Tate, the supporters of dBase, have even produced a thick volume (Castro, Hanson & Retig, 1985) describing the errors in their software, or rather some of them for it does not include this one, nor many, many others I suspect. Software houses spend much money on departments whose sole responsibility is to find errors in software packages. Much of this knowledge could be incorporated into AI programs for error detection. A solution is very badly needed.

The next step is to provide software that in fact does what the programmer intends, i.e., it finds proofs rather than just checking them. This is the dream of any software house. Many mistakes in software packets are due to errors in the original design rather than in the implementation of that design. What is needed is an automatic systems designer. Studying such highly paid individuals would surely lead to an interesting Ph.D. thesis.

3. Text Processing

With the advent of the personal computer, the processing of text has become one of the main occupations for computers; the development of text-processing software packages is proceeding rapidly. However, this also has a short history behind it. What I believe was one of the first text processors was developed at Carnegie-Mellon University. It (or its printer) would only produce upper case letters, with the result that the Ph.D. thesis describing it, which was of course the first document to be produced with it, was very tiring to read.

The development of text processors for users of mainframe machines took place in the 1970s. The distinguishing characteristic of these text processors is that they intertwine their textual and their control characters. The result is that the original text is unreadable. To get an output the text file must be passed to a separate layout routine which runs off the text on the printer. Typical examples of this manner of working are Waterloo script and NROFF. This, combined with the problems of getting any real-time access on university computers in the 1970s , was a sufficient deterrent to even the computer-literate users to keep them from writing directly on the machine. The major exception to this general rule was Knuth (1982), who developed his own text processor, TEX, capable of handling mathematical formulas and delivering book quality output from the general purpose computer.

The 1980s saw the development of text processors for use on microcomputers. The processors themselves were made interactive in the sense that menus were provided for various different subtasks, e.g., moving text, special printing facilities. Control characters were still present in the text but became translucent; a magic key made them vanish when they were not wanted.

Nowadays we are being offered a whole range of text processors. The modern ones are claimed to have WYSIWYG or "what you see is what you get (more or less)." They are also being linked to proportional printers. This immediately provides a difficulty for the WYSIWYG claim. For instance MS Word, one of the more friendly text processors, is not (yet?) capable of providing proportional letters on the screen. This may not seem too much of an inconvenience until one starts to make tables with fixed column layout, using a proportional printer. There are, however, systems that are really WYSIWYG, for instance the Ops system provided with the Sun workstation, which prints by sending the screen image to a laser printer. To be really effective, this method requires that the screen has as fine a grain as a laser printer, which is mostly not the case nowadays.

Another facility that is now commercially available is spelling checkers. These usually work as separate processors, checking an entire text for spelling errors after it has been completed. This is a time consuming processes. A recent innovation in this area is Turbo Lightning, from Borland, which is sufficiently fast to be able to check spelling directly when a word has been completed. However, present spelling checkers are unsuitable for languages with compounding such as Dutch (or with agglutination such as Finnish). The logical next step is to provide active rather than passive help in this area. Most of the words we use can be predicted after the first four or five letters, provided the place of the word in the syntax of the sentence is known.

The next step in text processors is likely to be a syntax checker. Present text understanding and translation systems have this facility as a necessary requirement. There is no technical reason why it cannot be incorporated into a text processor. The only limitations at present are the costs of internal memory and the lack of completely satisfactory syntactic rules. The former has been solved, and personal computers with 2-16 Megabyte memories are only a year or so away. The problem of satisfactory syntax rules is more difficult. For the simple sentences we use most of the time, the matter is relatively easy; e.g., to recognize that

Tom learned me my tables

is incorrect depends only on classifying *learned* as an intransitive verb. The major exception is ellipsis; e.g.,

John took his dog for a walk and Mary did too

is syntactically complex. Ellipsis is notoriously difficult semantically; how many dogs were taken for a walk? An active collaborative text processor would not wait for the user to make mistakes, but would provide word inflections as the words were being input. To do this requires an efficient set of syntactic rules, something that is certainly not yet available for Dutch.

That a sentence which is quite correct syntactically can be nonsense is well known, e.g., Chomsky's *Colourless green ideas sleep furiously.* What is not so well known is how to detect such sentences automatically. To spot that something that is *green* cannot be *colourless* is not too difficult; if something lacks a property dimension then it cannot have a value of that dimension as an attribute. More difficult is to decide whether *ideas* could be *green.* A rule to the effect that abstract nouns should not have visible properties would banish *blue thoughts.* At the more detailed level, the combination of verbs and nouns can pose problems not only for machines but also for nonnative speakers: one *rides a bicycle* but *drives a car* (in Dutch both are *ridden*). This whole area is beginning to be mapped. There will need to be some considerable effort before semantic checkers are part of text-processing packages. On the active side, we all experience our ability to predict what our neighbor/spouse/teacher is going to say next. Would it be possible or desirable to have a semantic predictor that some of the time filled in what we wanted to write just before we got to it, stopping to ask for a new word only one word in three, say? Word prediction would be a nice topic for a Ph.D. in itself. It would be a good area in which to test the claims for the frame based theories of sentence comprehension (Schank & Abelson, 1977; Schank, 1982). Whether a word predictor would be more depressing than stimulating is an open question.

We are constantly being asked to evaluate arguments, either explicitly as referees or implicitly every time we listen to a reasoned defence of a point of view, as in the daily newspaper editorials. (When I was at primary school I was always floored by the lack of consistency in supposedly quality newspaper editorials; I simply lacked the required presuppositions which were available to any adult. Similarly, missing presuppositions occur in geometry proofs; Brée, 1969). A program that could analyze an argument and detect its flaws would be most handy. There is even the beginnings of a commercial interest in such matters. A semiautomatic abstraction service has been proposed by more than one company. In order to do abstraction well, a program would need to be able to distill the essence of the argument in an article. The whole area of reasoning and argumentation theory (Toulmin, 1969; Körner, 1974; Keers, 1976; Lambert & Ulrich, 1980) will need to be re-explored with a much finer-toothed comb.

An active argument generator is an interesting possibility. A machine that would think up arguments in support of desired actions would be a politicians' delight. Of course, the counter tool would be developed with the same technology, so commerce would thrive at the expense of the taxpayer. A more serious, if not so important, use would be in suggesting lines of investigation for research. Based on a collection of research facts, arguments in favor of certain interpretations could be developed that depended on certain missing data, thus suggesting lines for empirical investigation.

Back in the land of the present, we see that the input mode for text is being extended. The possibility of using handwriting on a pressure pad as a means of input is being investigated (Thomassen et al., this volume). My first reaction was astonishment at this regression to the use of handwriting. However, I recently came upon an ideal application for such a device: to register the state of individual animals as they are being inspected on a farm. Farmers do not want to carry keyboards around their necks, but a pressure pad would be acceptable. The major research effort in this area is on voice input, which is also discussed in this book (see Pols, this volume).

Lastly, mundanely, but commercially and scientifically interesting, is the presentation of integrated text, tables, and figures with a good layout. The chapters for this volume were originally prepared with a text processor, but one that did not have the intelligence to avoid having a page with only one line on it. The whole area of good page layout, at present in the heads of typesetters, should be studied and captured before typesetters become a rare and then extinct breed.

I believe that we are at long last comprehending the complexities that are involved in processing written language up to the sentence level. The time of rash promises in this subdomain are over and the time for commercial applications is approaching. At more macro levels, I do not think that we are

Table 2. Text processing

Passive cooperation	Active cooperation	Requirements
Spelling check	Rest of word predict	Spelling rules
Syntax check	Correct inflections Function word prediction	Syntax rules
Semantic check	Content word prediction	Knowledge frames
Logic check	Provide argument	Argument theory Understanding theory
Voice input	Voice output	Phoneme recognition Word recognition
Integrated outputs	Automatic layouts	Theory of layout

really aware of the size of the problem. So if you are contemplating a career as an applied cognitive scientist then go for the sentence level or the layout area (see Table 2). If you want to make an academic mark then try for a Ph.D. at the level of whole texts. Semantics is an open field for both types of career.

4. Spreadsheets

What text processors are for writers, spreadsheets are becoming for managers, an everyday desktop tool. Spreadsheets are trivially simple to describe and easy to use. All they really are is a means for displaying a large matrix piece-wise on the VDU screen. Each cell of the matrix has two properties, a value and a formula for calculating this value from values found elsewhere in the matrix. Some initial values cannot be calculated, but must be supplied. For example, the profit and loss statement of a company can readily be put into the form of a spreadsheet. Intermediate results, such as operating profit, gross profit, profit after taxes, and retained earnings are calculated on the basis of the performance data of the company and its dividend decision, which must be supplied by the user. Output from spreadsheets, besides just the simple calculated results, is usually provided via automatically generated graphs. For instance, a spreadsheet containing the performance figures for a company for each month will be able to display these results over time.

Spreadsheets became available at the beginning of the 1980s. Nowadays we are seeing the development of special-purpose spreadsheets. Software houses are busy providing spreadsheets for the financial modeling of a company, to keep track of performance and to predict cashflow requirements. To avoid any misunderstanding, a financial model in this sense is not a model based on empirical observation, as an economist might build; it is simply a set of concepts linked by defining formulae. The result of their efforts has been that the software packages are no longer transparent to the user and a trained person has to be called in to help use them (e.g., the Dutch FCS/EPS financial modeling spreadsheet). There is a silver mine awaiting the first cognitive psychologist who takes the trouble to understand how managers make financial decisions, and uses this knowledge in the design specifications for a financial modeling spreadsheet. The psychologist will have to overcome much resistance from the traditional systems designers in this area (who are more keen on adding facilities to their products than on scrapping those that are not used), so that the user can easily know what he has to do to get what he wants. There is a crying need for designers of "GWYN" software packages (gives what you need software). The result will be achieved via a theory of spreadsheet design, one of the items that will be part of future human factors textbooks.

At present spreadsheets have to be designed in a rather time consuming manner. It takes about a couple of hours to design a simple spreadsheet suitable for household accounting. The result is that professionals tend to buy spreadsheets that have been specially made up for their branch. These cannot be easily adapted to the inevitable idiosyncracies of each user's situation. It is well within the possibilities of present day AI to create an intelligent interface for spreadsheet packages that actually does the major part of the spreadsheet design work on the basis of what it knows about the meaning of words such as *taxes* and *profit*. Tidying up the layout is also a task that could well be delegated to an intelligent program. Such an interface would be built using domain knowledge incorporated into a conceptual network (Table 3) - a potential Ph.D. topic with interesting commercial consequences.

Table 3. Spreadsheets

Passive cooperation	Active cooperation	Requirements
Mouse orientation	Self-designing Self-development	Spreadsheet theory Domain knowledge

5. Database Interfaces

If you have ever tried to reserve two seats side by side for yourself and your companion on a train leaving Amsterdam for anywhere, you will have been told that "the computer cannot do it" or some other such untruth. (I hesitate to call such misrepresentations a "lie" because the speaker invariably believes them!) The computer can of course do "it," but simply has not been given the appropriate program for doing so. There is much amiss in the interface between humans and their databases.

Databases, of which reservation systems are just one example, are just large filing cabinets with transparent cards. Each card has data stored on it in a particular form, the database model. Different types of data are stored on cards in different files. The files are crossindexed. This whole is managed by a program, the database management program. These creatures have been around since World War II, being highly useful for such important government activities as the census. Originally each database manager was created specially for its operation out of the raw material of some general purpose low-level programming language. In the 1960s special purpose languages were developed, e.g., Cobol which is still the most widely used language in business, for the writing of database managers.

The 1970s saw the development of languages for developing database managers. Primitives in these languages are oriented to manipulating records of data and performing data extraction. They can be used to design a database manager quickly and cheaply, provided that one does not try to do anything at all complicated, since then even the best known languages turn out to have serious flaws.

The 1980s has seen · the development of the general purpose database manager. These are rather like the general managers of any organization; they know how to manage, and it really is not supposed to matter what it is they are managing, from uranium mines to newspapers. A general database manager, such as Micro Pro's Data star, only has to be given the model of the database which it is to manage and it gets on with the job of managing it. It is even possible to get reports on the database from many aspects, using a report generator, e.g., the companion Report star. These are not programming languages at all but software packages in which the database designer's requests are interpreted to produce a database manager.

Current trends are towards using AI techniques to assist in the design of database managers. I currently have a project for the development of an intelligent interface to a database of any construction that is based on an expert system approach (which I will come to in a moment). But the whole area is open to an invasion from a cognitive point of view, in order to upgrade our present databases into knowledge bases.

For instance, one of the current topics in database circles is consistency checking (Table 4). It turns out to be quite difficult with traditional means to ensure that a database is consistent. Transactions that for some reason get broken off in the middle is one problem, as yet undetected bugs in the database manager itself is another. But the most pervasive problem is in establishing what the relationships should be between all the different variables that

Table 4. Database interfaces

Passive cooperation	Active cooperation	Requirements
Consistency check	Consistency maintenance	Deduction maps
Efficiency checking	Self-programming	Metaknowledge
Design checking	Self-designing	Database theory
Self-development		Domain knowledge

may coexist in a large database in such a way that if one value is changed, then all the other values which depend on this one value are changed simultaneously. To do this at present requires precise programming of all these relationships and the changes that must be brought about. What is needed is some general means for representing relationships between concepts in such a way that a truth maintenance system can automatically take care of the consequences of any changes. Then the designer would not have to consider how to achieve this consistency, but would only have to be concerned with specifying what the consistency relationships should be.

Another concern of the designer of database management systems is efficiency. Efficiency has traditionally been an area outside the interest of AI. If a system was getting into space or time problems, one simply bought more memory or a faster machine. However, such brute force solutions cannot be applied in the commercial world, and the checking of database managers for efficiency is a time-consuming task that could be automated to a considerable degree. This would require a formal knowledge of efficiency measurement of programs and a set of heuristics for detecting potential efficiency shortcomings. As a first cut at this problem, a cognitive psychologist might fruitfully pick the brains of an expert in database checking. More ambitious is the semiautomatic programming of database managers, a task that would require a theory of programming in this area to be sufficiently formalized so that it could be incorporated into a program. Another Ph.D thesis?

Even more ambitious, and certainly beyond the reach of a single Ph.D student but maybe a good topic for a large scale research project, is the semiautomatic design of databases. The idea is that the professional manager, for instance, who knows little about the theory of database design, can be lead to give sufficient information on his needs that an intelligent program, which incorporates the theory of databases together with heuristic rules for their design, can design a database for the manager. I think this area will provide cognitive scientists of one form or another, not only with large funds but also considerable travail for the next decade.

6. Expert Systems

A highly popular topic at the present time is expert systems. Expert systems, ESs for short, are designed to combine three strengths from the AI tradition:

- A general problem solving ability, which in the case of ES is labeled the inference engine
- A large amount of qualitative knowledge arranged in some semistructured way, here called the rule base

- A user-friendly interface for constructing the system

The present generation of expert systems stems from an idea originally introduced into computing science in the late 1960s, that of a collection of conditional rules arranged as a set. Each rule consists of a condition and an action. At any particular moment, the rules are divided into two subsets, those which are applicable and those that are not. The way this sorting is done depends on the design of the ES, but is frequently based either on selecting those rules whose condition part is fulfilled (called forward chaining), or on selecting those rules whose outcome is a current goal (called backward chaining). Some means are then required for sorting the applicable rules into an order and choosing the most appropriate to actually be executed. Eventually a path is found, either from the known facts to the goal or vice versa.

The 1970s saw the development of a few special purpose expert systems, in particular in reasonably well-structured areas such as spectrometry, the prescription of medicine for bacterial infections, and the interpretation of oil-well borings.

The 1980s have seen the introduction of expert system shells. These play a similar role here to database software packages. They enable someone who is not an experienced programmer to develop rapidly a simple ES that demonstrates some ability. As usual, more advanced work still has to be tailored to the situation, which is possible with most ES shells as they are written in interpretive languages, giving the programmer direct access to the language even while he remains inside the shell. These shells have provided various facilities to represent the rules and to control their application via the inference engine. We have seen, in particular, the development of "contexts," so that the rules can be divided up, enabling subtasks to be tackled in subcontexts. The arrangement of these contexts then becomes an interesting design issue: should they, for instance, be hierarchical or parallel. These shells are a mixed blessing. They enable small ESs to be developed quickly; but they tend to freeze the methodology. Too many ESs have been built using the simple rule-based approach where a model-based approach would have been more appropriate, simply because rule-based shells are available.

The developments that we can expect in the design of ESs and ES shells hinge on developments in our understanding of the way to represent and apply knowledge. One of the first improvements will be the development of a system for providing adequate defense for the use of rules. At present, all rules are defended in the same way. They are applied either because their condition part is true, or because their action part is a desired goal. One would like to distinguish between a defense based on local context, as presently provided, and a defense based on global knowledge of the area under investigation, for instance, when a particular rule has been found to work in similar cir-

Table 5. Expert systems

Passive cooperation	Active cooperation	Requirements
Rule defense	Rule detection	Metaknowledge
User knowledge	User goals	Domain knowledge
		Motivation theory

cumstances in the past, or when it has been recommended by a particular specialist in the area (Table 5).

On the active side, current research is concerned with developing ESs that are capable of learning from their mistakes. The automatic rewriting of rules and even their generation is the goal here. For this, a theory of knowledge acquisition and manipulation is required, a wonderful domain for the cognitive psychologist.

Another area where development is only just beginning is in the creation of a cooperative interface to an ES. The incorporation of knowledge not only about the area but also about the user is one way of achieving this. If this is combined with a theory of goals and the relationship between goals and knowledge, then an ES can provide the user with information that was not requested but is likely to be found useful (Siklossy,1981). This will require the incorporation not only of domain knowledge, but also a means for deciding what a user knows (a theory of knowledge testing) and what he is likely to want (a theory of the relationship between motives and knowledge). An area for the ambitious cognitive psychologist to win his spurs.

7. Conclusion

Looking over what is required to advance from software with passive cooperation to software with active cooperation, we see two main types of knowledge that will need to be developed for our "new look" in human factors. One concerns knowledge about the domain in which the software package is operating, e.g., about syntax, semantics, and pragmatics of natural language for the design of active text processors, or about domain knowledge for ESs. This requires a considerable amount of detailed work on the part of cognitive psychologists in order to achieve a better understanding of the information processing requirements in these tasks.

The other main item that should be on the agenda concerns theories about how knowledge is to be represented and processed. A good example of this is to be seen in the current development of ES shells, which are now turning from the original basic systems of production rules and linked systems of concepts, to providing facilities for the representation of knowledge that people have of how things work - process knowledge. Another topic that comes repeatedly on our agenda is meta-knowledge, or how to represent in a machine what a person knows.

These two points, specific domain knowledge and general metaknowledge, will form the heart of the new look in human factors.

The technological developments that have occurred in the last two decades have provided man with a new basis for arranging his affairs. The electronic chip is spawning an industry whose products will effect our daily lives to the same extent that the combustion engine has done. The technical applications of hardware and software developments will be flooding the market at an ever-increasing pace. Cognitive psychologists have the opportunity of playing a significant role in these developments. They will be able to do so if they make the effort to become familiar with the underlying technology. If they fail to do so, we shall all be inflicted with technologically advanced, but highly frustrating, artifacts. If they do rise to the challenge, we can expect to have supple tools at our disposal, to do with as we see fit - for good or ill.

References

Brée D.S. (1965). *A design for a new lighting console.* Unpublished manuscript, Carnegie Institute of Technology, Pittsburg, PA.

Brée D.S. (1969). *The understanding process; as seen in geometry theorems and the missionaries and cannibals problem.* Ph.D. thesis (University Microfilms, No. 69-18588). Carnegie-Mellon University, Pittsburg, PA

Card S.K. (1984). *Human factors and the intelligent interface.* Keynote address at the Human Factors Conference, New York.

Castro L., Hanson J. & Retig T. (1985). *Advanced programmer's guide featuring dBase III and dBase II.* Ashton-Tate, Culver City, CA.

Eisenstadt M. (1983). A user friendly software environment for the novice programmer. *Communications of the Association for Computing Machinery*, 27, pp. 1056-1064.

Keers C. (1976). *Argumentatie: redeneren-argumenteren-debatteren.* (2nd ed.). Samson, Alphen aan den Rijn.

Kharney H. (1982). *An in-depth study of the cognitive behaviour of novice programmers.* (Technical report No 5), Human Cognition Research Laboratory, Open University, Milton Keynes.

Körner S. (Ed.). (1974). *Practical reason.* Yale University Press, New Haven, CT.

Knuth D. (1982). *TEX book.* Addison-Wesley, Reading, MA.

Lambert K. & Ulrich W. (1980). *The nature of argument.* Macmillan, New York.

Pols L.C.W. (1988). The use of speech in man-machine interaction. In: *Human Computer Interaction: Psychonomic Aspects.* G.C.v.d. Veer & G. Mulder (Eds.). Springer-Verlag, Heidelberg.

Rumelhart D.E. & Norman D.A. (1982). Simulating a skilled typist: a study of skilled cognitive-motor performance. *Cognitive Science*, 6, pp. 1-36

Schank R.C. (1982). *Dynamic memory.* Cambridge University Press, Cambridge.

Schank R.C. & Abelson R.P. (1977). *Scripts, plans, goals and understanding.* Erlbaum, Hillsdale, NJ.

Siklossy L. (1981) Experiments with a query adjusting knowledge based system. In: *Proceedings of the Fifth International Congress on Cybernetics and Systems*, World Organization of General Systems and Cybernetics, Mexico City.

Maarse F.J., Schomaker L.R.B. & Teulings H.J., (1986). Automatic identification of writers. In: *Human Computer Interaction: Psychonomic Aspects.* G.C.v.d. Veer & G. Mulder (Eds.). Springer-Verlag, Heidelberg.

Toulmin S.E. (1969) *The uses of argument.* Cambridge University Press, Cambridge.

Chapter 17. Knowledge and Expertise in Expert Systems

Bob J. Wielinga and Bert Bredeweg

1. Expert Systems

An important trend in current artificial intelligence (A.I.) research concerns expert systems. Expert systems are computer programs that are able to solve complex problems at a high level of expertise (Buchanan & Shortliffe, 1984). Most are also capable of explaining why and how they came to a particular solution. They derive their capabilities from a body of knowledge about a particular domain. This knowledge comprises both declarative (factual) knowledge and procedural knowledge, i.e., knowledge describing how to solve particular problems.

Most expert systems of the first generation represent their knowledge of a domain in the form of rules. Such rules consist of a number of conditions and a conclusion. If the conditions are found to be true in a certain problem-solving context, the conclusion is added to the database of problem-specific information. An important advantage of the use of rules as a knowledge representation formalism is modularity: rules can easily be added or deleted without affecting the operation of other rules. This allows the incremental growth of a knowledge base from early prototype to final system, without major revisions of the architecture. Another advantage of rule-based systems is that human (expert) knowledge often appears to have a rulelike character. If an expert is asked to explain why a certain conclusion was made, the answer will often be of the form "Because X and Y were true I concluded that Z was likely to be the cause of the problem." Such knowledge is easily captured by an inference rule of the form: "If X and Y then conclude Y."

A large number of rule-based expert systems have now been developed. The performance of these systems varies between different domains, but in general they perform remarkably well. For example, the performance of the MYCIN system (Shortliffe, 1979) has been tested against the performance of top medical experts in the USA and was rated as belonging to the top ten. So, with respect to performance in their application domain, expert systems can behave in a way similar to a human expert. However, the similarity in performance does not necessarily mean that expert systems can be viewed as cognitive models of human expert behavior. In the following we will further investigate the differences between expert systems and human experts, and try to identify why these differences occur.

2. Shortcomings of Current Expert Systems

If we take a closer look at expert systems of the first generation and compare their behavior to that of human experts, there are, despite the similarity of the levels of performance, some striking differences between the two. When problems move away from the domain in which the problem solver is an expert, the human expert shows behavior called graceful degradation, i.e., the problem-solving performance slowly decreases as the problems get further away from the original domain. Expert systems, however, show no graceful degradation, their problem-solving suddenly becoming very poor, or even erroneous, when they have to solve problems on the edge of, or outside, the original domain. Moreover, expert systems in general have no knowledge of their own expertise, i.e., they do not know in what domain they are an expert, whereas human experts surely have a notion about their own expertise and are quite capable of deciding whether a problem falls within their body of knowledge (Table 1).

Table 1. Comparison of expert systems with human experts

	Expert systems	Human experts
Solving	good	good
Failure	sudden	graceful
Explaining	rules	background
Explaining	solving trace	task structure
Flexibility	none	present

Another difference concerns the explaining facilities. Generally, expert systems have only two ways in which they can explain how they came to a particular solution : (1) naming the rule that was applied (why), and (2) showing the solving-trace (how). Human experts, on the other hand, have a large amount of background knowledge about the rules they applied (if they did apply rules), and can also use their knowledge of the overall task structure and of how to reach a solution, as a source for explanation. While expert systems can only use their knowledge in a very specialized way, human experts are able to use their knowledge for a variety of purposes (problem solving, explanation and justification, teaching, etc.). In general, it appears that human experts are much more flexible in the ways in which they can use their knowledge than expert systems.

3. Why Are Expert Systems Limited?

There are a number of reasons why expert systems are limited in the ways described above. One major problem concerns the way in which the system decides what knowledge to apply when. The rule base in first-generation expert systems is in general unstructured and there is no direct means of controlling the reasoning process. The control in these systems is implicit rather than explicit, for any of the following reasons: (1) there is no explicit control available, (2) control is managed by some additional parameters, (3) control depends on the order of the rules in the expert system, or (4) control is imposed by adding some extra conditions in rules. The consequence of the lack of explicit control is that knowledge of a domain has to be represented in such a way that implicit control is incorporated. For example, screening rules (Clancey, 1983) contain conditions which are logically superfluous, but which are needed to prevent the system from asking silly questions of the user. However, embedding such control information in the knowledge of a domain severely limits the range of applicability of a system.

Another problem concerns the knowledge captured in a rule. First-generation expert systems often use heuristic rules which associate data about the problem with solution classes. However, the underlying model which is the justification of the rule is not available. An example is the following heuristic rule:

IF
  the patient has a fever
  and the patient has a stiff neck
  and the patient has had neuro-surgery
THEN
  the best therapy is gentamycine

A more detailed version of the same rule, but with the inference structure that was implicit in the rule above made more explicit, is as follows:

fever → infection
infection and stiff neck → meningitis
meningitis and neurological surgery → staphylococcus
staphylococcus → gentamycine

In words this can be read as follows: a fever is caused by an infection, an infection causing a stiff neck is likely to be meningitis, meningitis in combination with neurological surgery is a strong indication for staphylococcos as the underlying cause of the disease.

So, in spite of the fact that the rules are correct and are the basis for impressive problem-solving performance, they leave out much of the underlying knowledge that the human expert possesses. This causes the shallow behavior of expert systems: they are unable to explain their reasoning at a level deeper than that of simple association. Consequently, a system based on shallow rules will not be able to teach adequately or give acceptable justifications. In addition, the knowledge can only be used in one way, and no flexible behavior is possible.

4. How Can Expert Systems Be Improved?

In order to solve these problems and upgrade expert systems in such a way that the problem-solving behavior of the forthcoming generation of expert systems resembles more closely that of human experts, we need to address two major questions. First, how can we adequately analyze the knowledge of a domain in such a way that the different types of knowledge become explicit, and secondly, how can we represent knowledge in expert systems in a way that allows flexible use of that knowledge.

A solution towards the first question that we are currently pursuing (Breuker & Wielinga, 1983, 1987; Wielinga & Breuker, 1986), is based on the principle of analyzing the expert's knowledge at the epistemological level (Brachman, 1979), and representing different types of knowledge in separate layers. We distinguish between static knowledge describing concepts and relations, knowledge of different types of inferences that can be made, knowledge representing elementary tasks, and strategic knowledge. Each of these categories of knowledge is described at a separate level. The separation reflects the different ways in which the knowledge can be viewed and used. The first layer contains the static knowledge of the domain: domain concepts, relations, and complex structures such as models of processes or devices. The second layer is the inference layer. In this layer we describe what inferences can be made on the basis of the knowledge in the static layer. Two types of entity are represented at the inference layer: metaclasses and knowledge sources. Metaclasses describe the role that domain concepts can play in a reasoning process. For example, a domain concept like *infection* can play the role of a finding in a consultation process, but it may also play the role of a hypothesis. Knowledge sources describe what types of inferences can be made on the basis of the relations in the domain layer. Examples are refinement and generalization knowledge sources, which both make use of a subsumption relation in the domain layer.

The third layer is the task layer. At this level the basic objects are goals and tasks. Tasks are ways in which knowledge sources can be combined to achieve a particular goal. The fourth layer is the strategic layer in which knowledge resides which allows a system to make plans, i.e., to create a task structure, control and monitor the execution of tasks, diagnose when something goes wrong, and find ways round impasses. Each layer has its own organizational principles which reflect the constraints that apply to the ways in which the objects on a particular level can be combined. The four layers are shown schematically in Table 2.

Table 2. Layers of description of expert knowledge

Level	Relation	Objects	Organization
Domain level		concepts, relations, structures	axiomatic structure
	describes		
Inference level		metaclasses, knowledge sources	inference structure
	applies		
Task level		goals, tasks	task structure
	controls		
Strategic level		plans, metarules, prepairs, impasses	process structure

The distinction between different types of knowledge is, of course, not a novel idea. Several authors have reported ideas which pertain to the separation of domain and control knowledge, and ways of increasing the flexibility of control in expert systems. The seminal work of Davis (1980) introduced metaknowledge as a means to control inference processes in a flexible way. In the NEOMYCIN system (Clancey & Letsinger, 1984), different functions of knowledge are explicated by separating domain knowledge and control knowledge and introducing a metalevel description of the strategies that a system uses. Pople (1982) has stressed the problem of the right task formulation. He considers it a fundamental challenge for A.I. research to model the metalevel reasoning process of expert diagnosticians which determines the optimal configuration of tasks to be performed in order to solve a problem.

Besides a more elaborate metalevel reasoning, the next generation of expert systems also needs more advanced representations of knowledge of a domain.

Relations between concepts need to be explicit, for instance as in the hierarchy relation and metarule below (Clancey, in press):

Hierarchy relation

neurological surgery
    is-sub-class-of
surgery

Metarule

IF
    an attribute X is wanted
    and there exists an attribute Y
    and X is-sub-class-of Y
    and Y is not present
THEN
    X is not present

In this example the metalevel rule can use a hierarchy relation to establish a certain inference. Complex knowledge representations like KL-ONE (Brachman, 1979; Brachman & Schmolze, 1984) are needed for this purpose.

In order to represent knowledge of a domain adequately there is also a need for models at different levels of abstraction. Deep, and therefore detailed, models are needed to produce causal relations between objects and thereby facilitate support knowledge, and to perform some detailed reasoning to, for instance, distinguish between contradictory findings. Deep models use very weak solving methods and therefore cannot be used for efficient reasoning; consequently, less detailed, shallow models are also needed. Finally, there is a need for knowledge that can determine when it is necessary to jump between different models.

5. Role of Experimental Psychology

Constructing models of expertise which have the layered structure described in the previous section is difficult. Standard techniques for knowledge acquisition, such as asking an expert to formulate rules, or incrementally construct a knowledge base in cooperation with the expert, are not suitable for structuring the knowledge. What is required is a thorough analysis of expert behavior based on the analysis of thinking-aloud protocols. For the domain layer this has to be repeated for each new domain, but for the other three levels one may hope that models of similar tasks (such as diagnosis) could be based on similar knowledge at the higher levels. The strategic level in particular would appear to be rather independent of the domain at hand.

Studies in cognitive psychology of human problem solving in a variety of domains will have to show whether generic models can be formulated and validated. Such models could then form a basis for knowledge acquisition by expert systems. Expert systems based on these models would not only be easier to understand and maintain, but would also offer possibilities for more flexible behavior than the current generation of systems.

References

Brachman R.J. (1979). On the epistemological status of semantic networks. In: *Associative networks*, N.V. Findler (Ed.), Academic Press, New York. pp. 5.

Brachman R.J. & Schmolze J.G. (1984). An overview of the KL-ONE knowledge representation system. *Cognitive Science*, 9, pp. 171-216.

Breuker J.A. & Wielinga B.J. (1983). *Analysis techniques for knowledge based systems. Part 1 and Part 2.* University of Amsterdam, Amsterdam.

Breuker J.A. & Wielinga B.J. (1987). Use of models in the interpretation of verbal data. In: *Knowledge elicitation for expert systems: a practical handbook*, A. Kidd (Ed.), Plenum Press, New York.

Buchanan B.G. & Shortliffe E. H. (1984). *Rule-based expert systems.* Addison-Wesley, Reading, MA.

Clancey W.J. (1983). The epistemology of a rule-based expert system - a framework for explanation. *Artificial Intelligence*, 20, pp. 215-251.

Clancey W.J. (in press). Representing control knowledge as abstract tasks and metarules. In: *Computer expert systems.* M. Coombs & L. Bolc. (Eds.). Springer, Heidelberg.

Clancey W.J. & Letsinger R. (1984). Neomycin: Reconfiguring a rule-based expert system for application to teaching. In: *Readings in medical artificial intelligence: The first decade*, W.J. Clancey & E.H. Shortliffe. (Eds.). Addison-Wesley. Reading. MA. pp. 361-381.

Davis R. (1980). Metarules: reasoning about control. *Artificial Intelligence*, 15, pp. 179-222.

Pople H.J. (1982). Heuristic methods for imposing structure on ill-structured problems: the structure of medical diagnosis. In: *Artificial Intelligence in medicine*, P. Szolovits (Ed.), Westview, Boulder.

Shortliffe E.H. (1979). *Computer-based medical consultations: Mycin.* American-Elsevier, New York.

Wielinga B.J. & Breuker J.A. (1986). Models of Expertise. In: *Proceedings of ECAI-86*, North Holland, Amsterdam, pp. 306-322.

Chapter 18. Architectures for Production Systems: An Inside Look for Those Who Study Human-Computer Interaction

Anthony Jameson

1. Introduction

In a collection of articles such as the present one, it is appropriate to look forward, attempting to anticipate research topics which do not yet cry out for immediate attention.

At present only a small proportion of computer users interact with systems which make substantial use of techniques from the field of artificial intelligence (AI). But, as the reader is surely aware, there has been a rapid expansion in the use of expert systems, natural language interfaces, and more generally systems whose behavior is intended to exhibit some degree of human-like intelligence. It will not be possible to study the interaction of users with such systems without being aware, at least in a general way, of the various techniques used to realize them.

The chapter by De Smedt in this volume surveys and compares the major styles of knowledge representation used in AI systems. The present paper will look in greater depth at a particular knowledge-representation paradigm, namely production systems. Since this chapter presupposes familiarity with the basic ideas involved in production systems, the reader may find it useful to refer back to De Smedt's exposition on this topic. One goal is to illustrate the general point that a given AI knowledge representation technique does not have certain immutable properties; within each style many alternatives are possible. The differences by no mean concern only technical details or matters of efficiency; they often have radical consequences for the behavior of working systems and therefore for the nature of the interaction of users with the systems.

1.1. Use of PSs in Expert Systems

One more specific reasons why it is worthwhile to have an understanding of knowledge-representation alternatives within the production system (PS) paradigm, is that PSs are the core knowledge representation method for most expert systems, the first type of AI system to be widely commercialized. Perhaps even more than in other types of AI system, the nature of the interaction of users with expert systems is heavily dependent on the nature of the knowledge representation used. For example, one of the most interesting aspects of expert systems is the way in which their reasoning can be explained to the user. Explanation components take advantage of the fact that the system's knowledge is represented in the form of condition-action rules which can be understood relatively independently of one another. This fact is also exploited when experts are allowed to augment the system's knowledge base incrementally. But this accessibility of an expert system's knowledge base is only truly an advantage if the content of the individual rules, and the general reasoning strategy according to which they are applied, are congruent with the way human users or experts think about the topic in question. (In fact, the general assumption that expert knowledge can be most appropriately represented and explained in terms of a set of rules has been called into question by a number of researchers; see, for example, the chapter by Wielinga & Bredeweg, this volume.)

The problem of inappropriate knowledge representation is especially acute when a system is implemented in an expert system shell, i.e., a software development environment designed to facilitate the rapid development of rule-based systems. Since shells tend to be oriented toward ease of use, their representational possibilities are even more restricted than are those of more general-purpose PS interpreters. This pattern can produce a paradoxical situation from the point of view of human-computer interaction, as exemplified by one (highly priced) shell which is available for a popular personal computer. This shell radiates "user-friendliness" as far as the ease of entering and running a set of rules in concerned. But the expressive power of the rules is so constrained that the designer of the expert system is soon compelled to introduce artificial rules (e.g., that involve conditions which are always true or actions which have no meaning) in order to tease the desired behavior out of the system. These artificial rules, which may be more numerous than the straightforward ones, are referred to along with the latter in the explanations and traces that the shell generates, to the confusion of designer, expert, and user alike. This sort of problem will affect a larger number of computer users as more and more relatively inexperienced programmers try their hand at implementing an expert system, encouraged in part by the availability of shells for personal computers.

1.2. Use of PSs in Psychological Simulation Models

There is a second, quite different reason why knowledge representation in PSs especially merits the attention of those concerned with human-computer interaction. Unlike other AI knowledge-representation techniques, PSs have served as a knowledge-representation method in much basic psychological research relevant to human-computer interaction. The PS paradigm was developed to a large degree by psychologists seeking a suitable formalism for their simulation models of human cognitive processes. Historical sketches are given by Anderson (1983a, chap. 1) and by Neches, Langley, and Klahr (1986).

For example, Anderson and colleagues have implemented PSs which simulate the behavior of novices learning to program in the language Lisp (Anderson, 1983b; Anderson, Farrell, & Sauers, 1982; an example of a rule from one of these PSs is given by De Smedt, this volume).

A larger number of simulation efforts concern processes which are not specific to human-computer interaction but which figure prominently in it. An example in this category is Rosenbloom's (1983) work on the effects of practice on the performance of tasks in which stimulus-response compatibility is an important factor.

It might at first glance seem possible to understand and evaluate simulation models of this sort without devoting attention to the particular knowledge-representation techniques used. But it in fact proves difficult to separate the levels of psychological theory and knowledge representation completely. It is

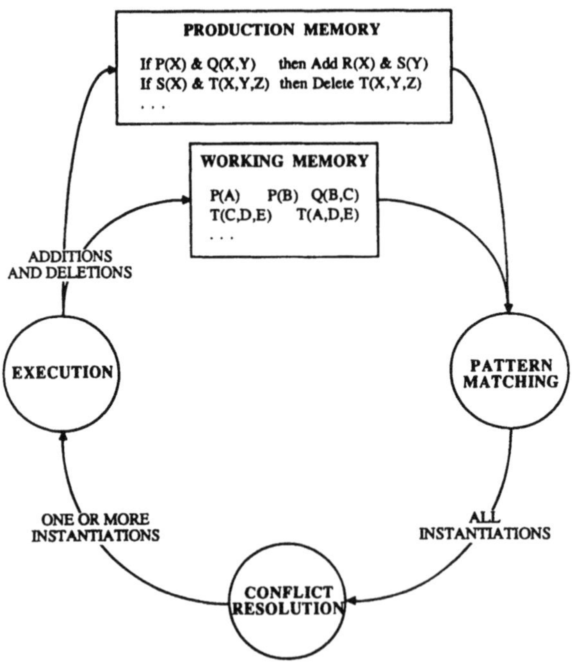

Figure 1. The basic interpretation cycle for production systems.

entirely typical that each of the two simulation models just mentioned was originally presented together with a novel PS *architecture*, i.e., a particular variant on the basic structure of a PS interpreter, which is depicted in Figure 1.

These architectures embody the researchers' hypotheses about the overall structure of the cognitive processes of interest. For example, the models of Anderson and colleagues were implemented in the architecture GRAPES (for Goal Restricted Production System language; Sauers & Farrell, 1982), which is an implementation of part of Anderson's (1983a) general ACT* theory of human cognition. The conditions and actions of PSs written for this architecture refer not only to the standard working memory but also to a special kind of data structure called a *goal tree*. (The term working memory, when used to refer to a part of a production system, bears no necessary relation to the psychological concept of working memory.) The very form of a production rule in GRAPES thus reflects the central role that the ACT* theory assigns to hierarchies of task goals as organizers of certain types of cognitive performance and acquisition.

As this research and that of Rosenbloom illustrates, much of the psychological research using PSs has been more concerned with the acquisition of cognitive skills than with performance. Given the frequency with which computer users have to adapt to new systems, researchers in this area should be especially interested in a simulation methodology which is particularly well suited to the modeling of cognitive skill acquisition. But the goal of designing a PS which can acquire new rules on its own raises many interesting knowledge-representation issues, most of which correspond to substantive psychological questions (see Neches et al., 1986, and the other papers in the same book). It is not enough for a PS interpreter to allow rules to have actions which create, modify, or delete other rules (as indicated by the upper left-hand arrow in Figure 1). For example, if existing rules are to be analyzed and modified by other rules, their condition sides must be especially simple and consistently structured. And in the conflict-resolution phase, the system must have some criteria for determining when to fire a newly created, perhaps tentative rule as opposed to an older rule which is applicable in the same circumstances. It can be seen then, that the researcher who wishes to learn from PS simulation models, like the researcher who wants to analyze the interaction between a user and an applied PS, must be aware of the most salient features of the PS architecture employed and have some understanding of their relationships to the alternatives that were not employed.

With respect to each part of the basic schema of Figure 1, it is possible to introduce meaningful alternatives when designing an interpreter. Previous writers have offered systematic discussions of these alternatives (see, for example, Davis & King, 1977; Langley, 1983). Rather than duplicating or summarizing these treatments, I will here present a complementary perspective. Since some readers of the present volume may not be accustomed to reading technical discussions of problems in AI knowledge representation, the exposition in this chapter will be quite informal; readers interested in more detailed and precise treatments can consult the papers just mentioned and the additional works referred to below.

2. Pattern Matching as a Bottleneck

I will start with the observation that most possible variations, directly or indirectly, involve the crucial process of pattern matching. Pattern matching is the most difficult problem involved in the implementation of a PS architecture. The way pattern matching works in modern PSs is very different from the mental model of the process that most readily comes to mind. Yet an inaccurate notion of how pattern matching is accomplished can severely distort one's understanding of specific PS architectural features. For example, it can make some possible techniques appear especially natural, efficient, or even inevitable even though the opposite may actually be the case. Before examining particular architectural alternatives, then, we will take an inside look at the pattern-matching problem. The most straightforward way for a production system pattern matcher to operate might be termed rule-by-rule matching: the beginning of each cycle, the matcher iterates through the production rules one by one, comparing each of the rule's conditions with each of the elements in working memory (hereafter abbreviated as WM).

This method was in fact employed in early PS interpreters, but it requires only brief reflection to see that it is extremely time-consuming if there are more than a small number of production rules and/or WM elements. For example, if 100 rules, each with three conditions, have to be compared with 100 WM elements, then on a single cycle 30,000 individual comparisons will have to be made - not to mention the large amount of additional work required to determine in which cases the three conditions of a rule were jointly satisfied, i.e., with consistent bindings of their variables. Such an explosively large amount of computation would make PSs prohibitively slow for most applications, even those for which efficiency was of minor importance.

Fortunately, various pattern-matching techniques have been worked out which are much more efficient than this rule-by-rule method. The most influential one has been the Rete algorithm developed in the 1970s by Forgy (1982). This method is employed in the widely used OPS family of PS interpreters designed by Forgy and colleagues, and it has also been incorporated into a number of more experimental architectures, including most of those mentioned in this paper.

2.1. The Rete Pattern-Matching Algorithm

I will now attempt to convey the basic strategy of this algorithm while abstracting away from the technical details. Readers who desire a more formal presentation of the Rete algorithm should refer to the 1982 paper by Forgy. For examples of recent efforts to improve the efficiency of PS pattern matching further using software and hardware techniques, respectively, see the

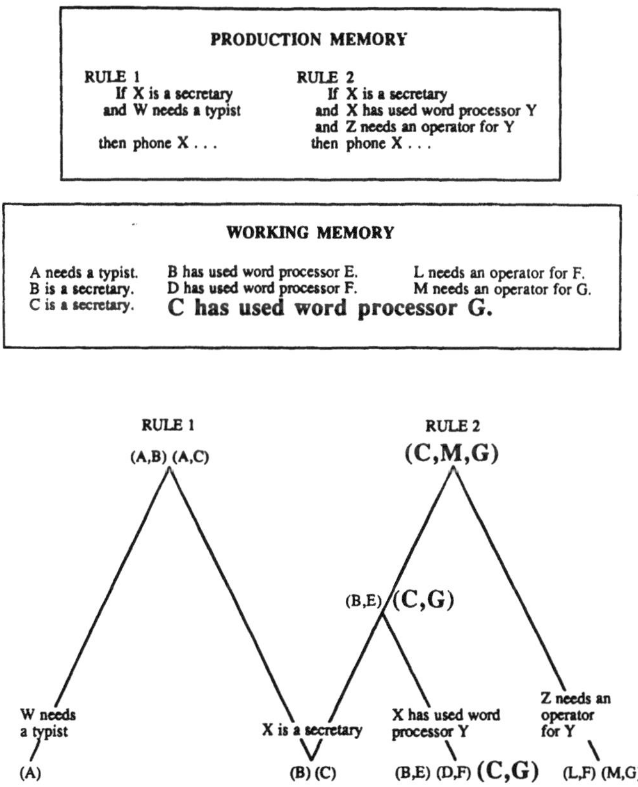

Figure 2. Illustration of the basic idea of the Rete pattern-matching algortihm. The basic situation is decribed in the text. The sets of letters within parentheses at the nodes in the network stand for sets of objects which have been found to satisfy the corresponding (combinations of) conditions. The entries in larger type represent the changes that result from the addition of the proposition "C has used word processor G" at the beginning of a given day.

papers by Schor, Daly, Lee, and Tibbits (1986), and by Forgy, Gupta, Newell, and Wedig (1984). Readers are asked to imagine themselves in the following situation, in which they would be faced with a problem similar to the pattern-matching problem for PS interpreters.

Suppose that you work as an employment agent and have a declarative database containing facts about the qualifications of particular job seekers and the characteristics of particular employers. In addition, on the basis of your experience and general knowledge, you have ideas as to what sort of employee fits well into what sort of company and what specific actions you should take when you identify an appropriate pair. These two sorts of knowledge would be represented within a PS in the WM and the production memory, respectively, as illustrated at the top of Figure 2.

Suppose further that each day's mail brings a few new changes to be made to the declarative database; your task each day is to determine what actions are to be taken on the basis of the current state of knowledge.

You might at first proceed according to the rule-by-rule pattern-matching method, considering each rule in turn and scanning the database for pairs of applicants and companies which jointly satisfied its conditions. It would soon become obvious, however, that many specific conditions were being matched against the very same data elements day after day; the only new results would involve the relatively small number of facts that had been added or deleted at the beginning of the current day. Furthermore, on a given day any specific condition which formed a part of several rules (e.g., in Figure 2 the condition "X is a secretary") would be tested several times against each data element.

A way to avoid both of these sorts of redundant testing would be to compare each fact with each rule condition only once, namely at the moment the fact first became known. You would then maintain, for each condition that occurred in some rule, a list of facts which had at some previous time been found to match it and which had not since been removed from the database.

There would remain the task, each day, of checking combinations of these facts to find sets which jointly satisfied the set of conditions for some rule. This process would also involve a great deal of redundancy, since most of the facts would remain the same from one day to the next. You might therefore begin maintaining lists of pairs of facts that had been found jointly to satisfy particular pairs of conditions, and similar lists for triads and larger combinations of facts and conditions.

A systematic way to organize all of this information would be in a network structure, as shown in the lower part of Figure 2. The various lists mentioned above are here associated with nodes in the network. They can be viewed as listing partial instantiations of rules, waiting to be compared with any new declarative facts which arrive so that the set of complete instantiations can be determined rapidly. As illustrated in the figure, when a new fact is added to the database it is a fairly straightforward operation to integrate it into this network structure and to see whether it will cause any additional instantiations of rules.

Note that this method only permits quick identification of each day's instantiations if the number of changes to the declarative database from one day to the next is in general relatively small. In the extreme case where a completely different set of facts was available each day, there would be no benefit at all in having the network of partial instantiations from the previous day.

Forgy's (1982) Rete algorithm works by maintaining a Rete network of partial instantiations which roughly resembles the network in our hypothetical example (there are many complications and additional optimizing techniques which need not be mentioned here). Figure 3, a modification of Figure 1 above, illustrates the role of this network within the basic interpretation cycle.

The execution of the production rules' actions still results in changes to WM and (in systems which learn new rules on their own) to production memory, but more importantly these changes are simultaneously used to update the Rete network. This network thus represents a sort of short cut in the interpre-

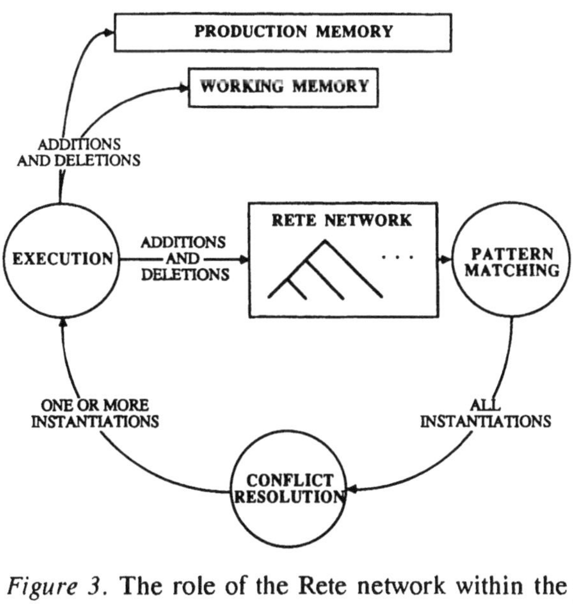

Figure 3. The role of the Rete network within the production system interpretation cycle.

tation cycle, making it unnecessary for the pattern matcher to refer to the relatively unstructured collections of declarative facts and production rules at all.

I will now examine certain architectural variants for PSs with respect to their consequences for the pattern-matching process, and will focus on two types of variants: (1) ways of storing declarative information other than in the usual WM, and (2) different conflict resolution strategies.

3. Alternative Declarative Representations

There are various reasons why it may be desirable to have some of the declarative knowledge used by a PS stored outside the system's normal WM.

3.1. Handling Frequently Changing Information

A PS may have to make use of some type of declarative information which is characterized by frequent or continual change, e.g., if this information were stored in WM, a large number of the entries of this type would have to be removed on each cycle, and a similar number of new ones would have to be added.

Information of this type is typically involved in systems designed for real-time applications (cf. Sauers & Walsh, 1983), which may have to monitor continually changing variables such as the temperatures or positions of objects. Within our illustrative example of the previous section, a rule whose actions included "phone X" might include a condition such as "the phone is not being used at the moment by someone else."

If information of this sort were stored in WM, it would of course also enter the Rete network. But this would have the consequence that the state of the Rete network would change drastically on each cycle, with many new (partial) instantiations being created and others disappearing. This would run counter to the algorithm's purpose of retaining information on partial instantiations from one cycle to the next, and it would accordingly eliminate much of the efficiency of this pattern-matching method.

A better way of handling this type of information comes to mind readily when one thinks about the illustrative example. It is natural to store highly variable information somewhere other than in WM. The conditions which refer to this information will then not be involved in the Rete network; rather, on each cycle, after the set of current instantiations has been computed by the Rete algorithm, these conditions can be applied as a sort of final check to see which ones can in fact be considered for execution on the current cycle. With reference to Figure 2, these conditions would be tested only with respect to the instantiations which reach the top of the network.

In fact, many PS interpreters do allow for the inclusion of such cyclic conditions (so called because they are checked on each cycle with respect to the instantiations which have been found to satisfy all of the normal conditions). These conditions can refer to arbitrary sources of declarative information. Although cyclic conditions make it possible to refer to frequently changing information without interfering with the optimal functioning of the pattern matcher, they by no means offer a completely general solution to the problems presented by this sort of information. For example, in the extreme case in which *all* conditions in the production rules were cyclic conditions and none referred to WM in the usual way, the Rete network would never have any content and the pattern-matching process would essentially reduce to a rule-by-rule method. More generally speaking, the larger the proportion of cyclic conditions, the more inefficient the total pattern-matching process becomes.

In sum, then, frequently changing information must be dealt with outside WM, and even then a PS will only be able to deal with it with reasonable efficiency if it is referred to by only a relatively small number of conditions.

3.2. Using Particularly Appropriate Declarative Representations

There is also a quite different sort of reason why one might prefer to use some form of declarative store other than WM: perhaps a particular alternative representation is especially well suited for the storage of a certain type of information which is needed. This might be the case, for example, for reasons of storage economy if large amounts of information were involved. Or it might be that the alternative representation made possible the use of specialized inference procedures.

As an example of this latter possibility, consider a production rule which includes the condition "Y is a microcomputer." The corresponding declarative information can be stored naturally in the inheritance hierarchy of a frame-based system. As noted in the chapter by De Smedt in this volume, such a representation makes it possible to test for relationships and attributes which may not be stored explicitly but which are readily derivable via standard inference procedures.

One way to integrate a frame-based representation into the basic PS architecture is to express conditions which refer to this representation as cyclic conditions, as mentioned in the previous section. Since such conditions can refer to arbitrary sources of information, they can, in particular, take the form of a query to an inheritance hierarchy. But as noted above, such tests must in general remain limited in number if the pattern-matching phase is not to become prohibitively time-consuming.

However, it may be quite desirable within a PS to make very heavy use of queries of this sort. In this case, there is another option available: there is in general no reason why even the normal conditions tested during pattern matching cannot refer to information stored independently of WM, provided that this other information remains constant. The reason for this restriction is that, as we saw above, the Rete algorithm only checks conditions a minimum number of times, in response to changes in WM. If, therefore, a particular condition which referred to information outside WM were to change in truth value at some time after it had first been checked, this change might never be taken into account since the condition might never be checked again. This could lead, for example, to a rule being executed even though its conditions were not all satisfied at that moment.

No such problems arise if the relevant information outside of WM is static, as would presumably be the case, for instance, with hierarchical relationships among concepts. In fact, if this provision is met it is not necessarily a bad thing for conditions referring to such outside structures to involve some quite complex processing: since the Rete algorithm minimizes the number of times that the conditions have to be evaluated, computationally expensive conditions need not slow down the pattern-matching process nearly as much as one might expect.

The general conclusions that can be drawn from the examples in this section are (1) that the nature of the conditions that it is feasible to allow in production rules depends on the consequences that their presence has for the pattern-matching process, and (2) that these consequences are seldom obvious, their recognition requiring some understanding of the way in which pattern matching is performed.

4. Alternative Conflict-Resolution Criteria

A second major way in which PS architectures can differ is in the criteria they apply in order to select for firing one or more of the instantiations produced by the pattern-matching process (see the bottom of Figure 1). Many of the issues involved here can be grasped intuitively if we consider an analogy with a familiar situation, namely a discussion within a fairly large group of participants, where a discussion leader has the responsibility for determining who is to speak next. At any given moment, the set of participants requesting a chance to speak is analogous to the set of rule instantiations which have been identified by the pattern matcher; once the discussion leader has applied some "conflict resolution" criteria to select one or more speakers, their contributions will in general bring about some changes in the set of those requesting a chance.

One general fact about PSs which this analogy helps to make plausible is that the conflict resolution criteria have a major impact on the effectiveness of the PS and the comprehensibility of its behavior to a user. If these criteria are inappropriate, for example, instantiations of critical importance may be passed over in favor of others which contribute little to the solution of the problem at hand; or the overall sequence of firings may be incoherent, appearing to switch randomly between different aspects of the topic.

4.1. Traditional Criteria

Certain conflict resolution principles have been used repeatedly in PS interpreters. Almost all of these can be understood in terms of our group-discussion analogy. For example, the *recency* criterion favors instantiations which involve WM elements that have just been added; similarly, discussants are often given the floor if they indicate that their contribution is relevant to the immediately preceding comment. The *specificity* criterion favors instantiations of rules which have relatively detailed, concrete condition sides; this is roughly analogous to the tendency of discussion leaders to prefer contributions from persons known to have specialized knowledge concerning the topic at hand, as opposed to persons who are willing to say something about virtually any topic. The *refraction* principle stipulates that an instantiation which has just been fired cannot be fired again immediately; the underlying logic is that once something has been said, there is no point in letting it be said again (unless it later becomes relevant again for some other reason). More detailed and formal analyses of conflict-resolution principles are given by McDermott and Forgy (1978), Davis and King (1977), and Neches et al. (1986).

Recall that these conflict resolution criteria are applied to the set of instantiations returned by the pattern matcher, just as the discussion leader can select a speaker from the set of participants who have indicated a desire to speak. Typically, a conflict-resolution method consists of two or more criteria to be applied in sequence, since a single criterion may not narrow the set down sufficiently.

4.2. A Priori Ordering of Rules

A further widely used conflict-resolution method makes use of a general priority ordering of the production rules, such that instantiations of higher-priority rules are chosen over others. This would be comparable to a discussion leader's policy of, for example, favoring participants with the highest academic rank. This method is used especially often in simple PS interpreters which use rule-by-rule pattern matching. The reason is that in this case the process of conflict resolution can be integrated with that of pattern matching so as to reduce the inefficiency which is inherent in the rule-by-rule method. The pattern matcher can check the rules in the order of their priority and stop as soon as it has found a single instantiation. Similarly, if a discussion leader could only find a speaker by asking the participants one by one whether they had anything to say, it would be tempting to make use of some a priori ordering of potential speakers.

But if the PS interpreter uses a pattern matcher such as the Rete algorithm which efficiently computes the set of all instantiations, then the use of an a priori rule ordering is no longer more natural or more efficient than the many other possible conflict resolution criteria. This point is worth emphasizing since it is often incorrectly assumed that an ordering of the production rules is a necessary and central property of any PS. This misunderstanding can seriously distort one's evaluation of specific PS architectures.

4.3. Rule Selection in Programmed Production Systems

Witteveen's (1984) programmed production systems represent an approach to the problem of rule selection which, like the use of an a priori ordering of rules, involves some sort of preference for certain rules at the beginning of each cycle. Each production rule *R* specifies, in addition to the usual conditions and actions

- a set of production rules which can be checked next if *R*'s conditions are *not* satisfied
- a set of production rules which can be checked next if *R*'s conditions *are* satisfied and *R*'s actions can therefore be executed

This scheme is similar to allowing discussion participants, whether or not they have anything to say themselves, to recommend one or more other participants to whom the discussion leader might turn next.

Even more than the use of a fixed ordering of production rules, this approach would greatly facilitate pattern matching if it were implemented in an interpreter which employed the rule-by-rule method. At any given moment, matching would only have to be performed for one of the rules "recommended" by the last rule examined.

But here again, if an interpreter is used which employs the Rete algorithm, there is no advantage for pattern matching if rules refer explicitly to other rules. Such a pattern matcher must in any case continually keep track of the (partial) instantiations of all rules, so the explicit references to sets of rules cannot be made use of until the conflict resolution stage, at which time they are used to select one of the current instantiations.

Programmed production systems have many interesting features which are independent of this issue (see Witteveen, 1984). The point of this brief discussion of the approach is that the assessment of a given conflict-resolution technique as being especially natural or efficient must be made with caution, since such evaluations actually depend very strongly on the pattern-matching method used.

4.4. Firing More Than One Instantiation Per Cycle

In recent years there has been considerable experimentation with conflict resolution strategies which drop the restriction that only one instantiation per cycle can be executed. The simplest and most extreme example is found in the architecture CAPS (Thibadeau, 1983; Thibadeau, Just & Carpenter, 1982). This PS interpreter executes all instantiations on each cycle.

It is notable, first, that for an interpreter which uses the Rete algorithm (as CAPS does), this exhaustive approach to rule firing is actually the simplest of all conflict-resolution strategies to implement and to apply. The conflict-resolution phase just passes the set of all instantiations on to the execution phase untouched. A conflict-resolution method such as this one can be called a *parallel* method. If several instantiations are executed on the same cycle, they are in effect executed simultaneously, in the sense that none of the executions is affected by the results of the other ones.

In fact, the main motivation for the use of such a method in CAPS was a desire to simulate human performance on tasks where a considerable amount of parallel processing is observed (e.g., reading, as in Thibadeau et al., 1982). The CAPS conflict-resolution strategy is thus an example of how the basic psychological assumptions underlying a PS simulation model can be reflected in the architecture in which the model is embedded.

CAPS also illustrates how a PS architecture can affect the general style in which the production rules must be formulated. It may already have occurred to the reader that the use of a parallel conflict-resolution method might give rise to peculiar, inconsistent behavior. For example, on a single cycle two rules might fire which drew mutually contradictory conclusions. To minimize such possibilities, the typical CAPS production system consists of rules which draw conclusions only gradually. Each proposition in WM has an associated numerical degree of activation, or confidence. A proposition is only considered true if its activation is greater than some threshold (e.g., 1.0). The typical action in a CAPS rule is to increase the activation of some proposition by a slight amount, so that it may take a number of cycles before the proposition is finally considered true (if indeed it ever reaches the threshold at all). Overall, such a PS is comparable to a discussion group in which at any moment several people may be talking, most of whom are expressing only tentative opinions which are ignored except by the few other persons who are in a position to confirm or contradict these opinions. Only when a sufficient amount of confirmation has been given is a conclusion announced as a fact so that all participants can take it into account.

In other words, CAPS production systems tend to be unusually fine grained. Since relatively little happens on a typical cycle, even though several productions may be fired, the lack of a selective conflict-resolution strategy does not result in the sort of the chaos that one might expect.

5. PS Interpreters Which Support Architectural Experimentation

It should be clear by now that researchers with an active interest in PSs and human-computer interaction will want to be in a position to experiment with different PS architectures. For the researcher studying the interaction of users with PSs, this is necessary so that the conclusions drawn will not depend in unknown ways on particular characteristics of the architecture used. For the theorist attempting to model psychological processes, it is important to be able to use an architecture which reflects or at least is compatible with his basic assumptions about these processes.

There is a potential problem here in that the implementation of a new PS architecture is in general a substantial software development effort, even if parts of existing interpreters are borrowed. In response to this problem, PS interpreters have been introduced in the past few years which are intended to allow the designer of a PS to experiment with different architectures while using a single interpreter.

5.1. The Interpreter HAPS

The architecture HAPS (for Hierarchical Augmentable Production System) introduced by Sauers and Walsh (1983) is intended to provide additional flexibility in implementing expert systems. For example, it supports various uses of goal trees (mentioned in Sect. 1.2 above). Declarative knowledge can be stored not only in WM but also in arrays, tables, or other representations which may be especially appropriate. Conflict-resolution criteria can refer, among other things, to statistics on the system's previous experience with particular production rules.

5.2. The Interpreter PRISM

The emphasis on extensibility and customizability is even stronger in the interpreter PRISM, developed by Langley and colleagues, which is primarily intended to support the implementation of psychological simulation models. The name is an acronym for Program for Research into Self-Modifying Systems, which reflects its architects' particular interest in models of human learning and development. Langley (1983) and Neches (1982) discuss the basic philosophy of PRISM and examples of its use, which illustrate the diversity of the specific systems which can be realized. The comments in the present paper refer to a more recent version of the interpreter which has been developed by Langley at the University of California at Irvine. The purpose of PRISM is to allow the designer of a PS to specify a particular architecture within the space of possible PS architectures. Where a normal PS interpreter would have a specific function or data structure, PRISM typically has a schema with several slots which can be filled in by the designer. Most of these slots are to be filled via the specification of a sequence of calls to Lisp functions (the interpreter itself is implemented in Lisp). PRISM provides a number of commonly used functions as building blocks. In addition, the designer can write new Lisp functions to fill the slots in schemas.

This method is used to add flexibility at each part of the basic architecture summarized above in Figure 1. For example, there is a general schema for a WM which allows the designer to specify, among other things, what numerical attributes (such as activation levels, as in CAPS) are to be associated with each WM entry and how these numerical attributes are to be updated when an entry which is already present in WM is added again. The designer can actually specify several WMs with different properties to be used by a single PS. Similarly, there is a general schema for a production memory with slots to specify, among other things, what conflict-resolution strategy is to be employed.

The pattern matcher uses the Rete algorithm. Arbitrary Lisp functions can be used in the conditions, and specific conditions may be specified as cyclic tests (cf. Sect. 3.1), so that they can refer to arbitrary sources of information. The use of the Rete pattern-matching algorithm allows for great freedom in specifying conflict-resolution strategies (if more than one production memory is defined, a different conflict-resolution strategy can be specified for each one).

The production rules' actions can in principle consist of calls to arbitrary Lisp functions, but most actions can be defined with the help of schemas for certain commonly used complex actions, e.g., those which provide for the simulation of spreading-activation processes.

Finally, a package is included which supports the automatic creation and modification of production rules, so that several types of procedural learning can be simulated.

6. Conclusions

Implicit in the above exposition are several recommendations for future research involving both knowledge representation in PSs and human-computer interaction. The most general recommendation is that this be recognized as a research topic which will increase in importance as AI systems based on PSs become more widely used.

Secondly, research must take into account the fact that PSs, like other AI knowledge representation methods, do not have certain fixed properties whose consequences for human-computer interaction can be determined once and for all. It is therefore necessary for researchers to be aware of the dimensions of possible variation. This in turn requires at least a general understanding of the central problems involved in implementing such variants. In the case of PSs, most variations can only be appreciated accurately if their relationship to the pattern-matching process is understood. Where actual implemented systems are used in research, preference should be given to flexible knowledge-representation packages which support the realization of variants on and combinations of established techniques.

Finally, it should be emphasized that the use of PSs to construct simulation models of the psychological processes involved in human-computer interaction need no longer be confined to the few institutions which have extensive experience in this area. The emergence of PS interpreters designed to support the realization of diverse architectures substantially reduces the amount of AI expertise and programming effort required to implement interesting simulation models.

Acknowledgement

Preparation of this chapter was supported in part by the foundation PSYCHON, which is financed by the Netherlands Foundation for Pure Research (ZWO).

References

Anderson, J.R. (1983a). *The architecture of cognition.* Harvard University Press. Cambridge, MA.

Anderson, J.R. (1983b). Learning to program. In: *Proceedings of the Eighth International Joint Conference on Artificial Intelligence*, Karlsruhe, Federal Republic of Germany, pp. 57-62.

Anderson J.R., Farrell R. & Sauers R. (1982). *Learning to plan in LISP* (interim report). Department of Psychology, Carnegie-Mellon University, Pittsburgh, PA.

Davis R. & King J. (1977). An overview of production systems. In: *Machine Intelligence*, vol. 8, E.W. Elcock & D. Michie (Eds.), pp. 300-332. Wiley, New York.

Forgy, C.L. (1982). Rete: A fast algorithm for the many pattern/many object pattern match problem. *Artificial Intelligence*, 19, 17-37.

Forgy C., Gupta A., Newell A. & Wedig R. (1984). Initial assessment of architectures for production systems. In: *AAAI-84: Proceedings of the National Conference on Artificial Intelligence*, Austin, TX (pp. 116-120).

Langley, P. (1983). Exploring the space of cognitive architectures. *Behavior Research Methods and Instrumentation*, 15, pp. 289-299.

McDermott J. & Forgy, C. (1978). Production system conflict resolution strategies. In: *Pattern-directed inference systems*, D.A. Waterman & F. Hayes-Roth (Eds.), pp. 177-199. Academic Press, New York.

Neches, R. (1982). Simulation systems for cognitive psychology. *Behavior Research Methods and Instrumentation*, 14, pp. 77-91.

Neches R., Langley P. & Klahr D. (1986). Learning, development, and production systems. In: *Production system models of learning and development.* D. Klahr, P. Langley, & R. Neches (Eds.), MIT Press, Cambridge, MA.

Rosenbloom, P.S. (1983). *The chunking of goal hierarchies: A model of practice and stimulus-response compatibility* (Report CMU-CS-83-14 8). Unpublished doctoral dissertation, Department of Computer Science, Carnegie-Mellon University, Pittsburgh, PA.

Sauers R. & Farrell, R. (1982). *GRAPES user's manual* (interim report). Department of Psychology, Carnegie-Mellon University, Pittsburgh, PA.

Sauers R.& Walsh, R. (1983). In: On the requirements of future expert systems. In: *Proceedings of the Eighth International Joint Conference on Artificial Intelligence*, Karlsruhe, Federal Republic of Germany, pp. 110-115.

Schor M.I., Daly T.P., Lee H.S., & Tibbitts, B.R. (1986). Advances in Rete pattern matching. *Proceedings of AAAI-86, the Fifth National Conference on Artificial Intelligence*, Philadelphia, PA, pp. 226-232.

Thibadeau R. (1983). CAPS: A language for modeling highly skilled knowledge-intensive behavior. *Behavior Research Methods and Instrumentation*, 15, pp. 300-304.

Thibadeau R., Just M.A. & Carpenter P.A. (1982). A model of the time course and content of reading. *Cognitive Science*, 6, pp. 157-203.

Wielinga B.J. & Bredeweg B. (1987). Knowledge and expertise in expert systems. In: *Human Computer Interaction: Psychonomic Aspects*. G.C.v.d.Veer & G.Mulder (Eds.), Springer-Verlag, Heidelberg.

Witteveen, C. (1984). *Programmed production systems*. Unpublished doctoral dissertation, University of Utrecht, The Netherlands.

Interaction with Information Systems: Input Aspects

Chapter 19. A Provisional Evaluation of a New Chord Keyboard, the Velotype

Leon P.A.S. van Noorden

1. Introduction

Recently a new keyboard for text processing, the Velotype, was introduced. The makers of the Velotype promised that it would be possible to type three times as fast on this keyboard as on the normal QWERTY keyboard, or that it could be learned in a shorter time.

As this new keyboard deviates considerably from the standard keyboard it is not plausible for it to be just plugged in instead of the old keyboard and used after a little adaptation by the typists. In order to get the greatest benefit from the innovation it is not only necessary to replace the keyboard but also to at least adapt the training and perhaps the work organization. An organization cannot take the risk of changing all this at once. To try out a large change one must have at least a good idea of the potential of the new resource. The first step, therefore, is a provisional evaluation of it use in a way that has no consequences for the work organization. In this paper we will present the results of such an evaluation of the Velotype and discuss the potential for its use.

2. Operation of the Velotype

The Velotype distinguishes itself from a normal typewriter by the fact that it enables a number of characters to be entered simultaneously. Its keyboard contains three sections of keys. The middle section contains the vowels, and the right and left sections both contain the consonants (see Figure 1). Since there are fewer keys than characters in each section, some characters have to be formed by a combination of keys. If keys are pressed in all three sections the consonants of the left-hand field go to the left-hand part, the vowels of the middle go to the middle and the consonants of the right-hand section go to the right-hand part of the output character string. This principle derives from certain types of shorthand writing machines (e.g., Palantype). If two or three characters are chosen in one of the sections, language statistics determine the succession of characters in the output string. If several successions are possi-

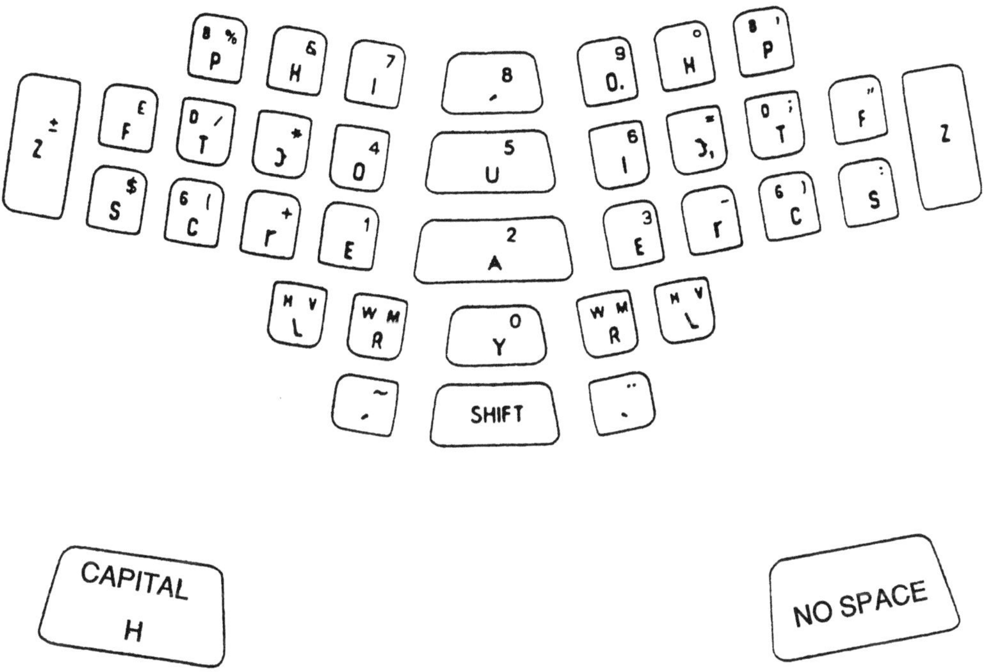

Figure 1. The Velotype keyboard.

ble in a language the less frequent ones need exceptional key combinations. Each output string is separated from the previous string by a character space unless the no-space key is pressed by the wrist. Key capitals can be formed by using the other wrist, but after a dot capitals are generated automatically.

The possibility of pressing keys simultaneously gives the impression that the promise of fast typing will be fulfilled, but the fact that sometimes more keys have to be pressed for one character and that a number of exceptional combinations have to be learned made us wonder whether this is true. Since there is no ready answer to this question, we made an empirical evaluation of this keyboard.

3. Method

3.1. Introduction

To evaluate the Velotype as an alternative to the normal keyboard we measured the performance of three different groups of subjects on texts normally used to test QWERTY typists. We measured the speed and number of errors. For comparison, the same texts were typed by a number of QWERTY typists. To get an impression of the specific problems of Velotyping we registered the chords produced by the subjects and the time interval between them.

3.2. Subjects

To approach a real-life setting the best comparison would have been that between a group of Velotypists with a number of years experience in a professional environment with an equivalent group of QWERTY typists. At the time of our investigation, however, no such subjects were available due to the newness of the Velotype. Instead, we attempted to approach the real-life situation as closely as possible by inviting the following three groups of subjects:

1. *Velotype "apprentices"*: a group of young unemployed adults (aged 17-22), who followed a Velotype instruction course. The private organization which provided this course guaranteed that all participants who could reach a speed of 500 characters per minute (c.p.m.) would get jobs. We were able to test subjects after 60, 127 and 167 h training. For admission to the Velotype course subjects had to pass an exam on their ability to take down Dutch dictation. The groups studied after training for 127 and 167 h consisted mainly of the same subjects. The 60-h group consisted of different subjects. The numbers of subjects were 3 (60 h), 10 (127 h), and 12 (167 h) respectively
2. *Velotype "demonstrators"*: three subjects, aged 14, 15 and 18. These participants were trained by their father or uncle, who was one of the inventors of the Velotype. The number of training hours were calculated by adding up the times spent doing each different exercise, instead of adding up the times taken up by the training sessions as was the case in the other groups
3. *Secretaries*: two secretaries who tried to use the Velotype in their professional environment after completing a Velotype course (total experience about 150 h). On several occassions they had to go back to using the normal keyboard to produce work quickly.

All subjects in all groups were native Dutch speakers and had received most of the Velotype training in this language.

3.3. Texts

Text I consisted of sentences from training and test material used by the typing school of the Dutch PTT. It contained normal text, numbers and a few abbreviations, like *PTT*.

Text II consisted of two parts, IIa and IIb. Text IIa was plain text but with a number of words that we judged to be potentially difficult, considering the keyboard layout. Text IIb was again a piece of PTT training material, but with a high concentration of potentially difficult words.

Text III was a section of a Dutch novel, plain text only, without difficult words. This text was added to the test after we had tested the 127-h group, the first group in the experiment, because the participants and their teacher considered texts I and II rather difficult.

All texts were in the Dutch language. The number of characters, including spaces and carriage returns, were 1253, 759, 517, and 1604, for texts I, IIa, IIb, and III, respectively. The texts can be found in Den Held and Van Noorden (1984).

3.4. Procedure

Only the secretaries were tested in their working environment. The other subjects came to our laboratory one at a time. Before they started the actual test, subjects were given two exercises containing about 1000 characters each for warming up and to adjust themselves to the sensitivity of our laboratory Velotype. (In the first production series this was not the same for all machines.) The order of presentation of the test was randomized. The subjects were instructed to type the texts as fast as possible without making too many errors. Error correction was allowed. The speed was calculated on the basis of the number of characters in the output string, including spaces and carriage returns, per minute, averaged over the whole text (c.p.m.).

4. Results

4.1. Results Achieved by Velotype Apprentices

The results obtained with the various texts by the groups of Velotype apprentices are presented in Table 1 and 2. Statistical tests are given in the Appendix. From Table 1 it can be seen that the speed increases with training time and varies considerably from one text to another. The speed was lower in text IIb especially which contained many abbreviations. Table 2 shows the error percentage (errors that remained in the output) relative to the total number of characters.

Table 1. Mean speed in characters per minute (±S.D.) as measured in the different groups of Velotype apprentices on four different texts

	Training time (h)		
	60	127	167
Text			
I	128± 5	179±37	192±31
IIa	125±10	171±24	192±36
IIb	93± 2	126±19	137±29
III		167±13	245±47
	(n = 3)	(n = 10)	(n = 12)

Table 2. Percentage of errors

	Training time (h)		
	60	127	167
Text			
I	0.53	0.69	0.55
IIa	0.57	0.77	0.50
IIb	0.67	0.75	0.77
III	0.19	-	0.29

It can be seen that the fastest text, III, has a smaller percentage of errors. The other error rates do not differ significantly. There is no evidence that fewer errors are made as the typist receives more training. The percentage, however, is well below the 1% standard used in typewriting exams.

4.2. Results Achieved by Velotype Demonstrators

The Velotype demonstrators were tested in our laboratory before a demonstration for personnel of the text-processing department. The total number of hours of practice has been estimated by adding the times these subjects needed to do the exercises. They timed all their exercises and recorded these times in their books. This is quite different from the estimation by adding up hours of training as was the case with the other groups of subjects. Table 3 shows the speed and error rates of these subjects.

Table 3. Speed and accuracy of demonstration subjects

Text	Training time (h) 80	160	240
	Speed (c.p.m.)		
I	281	299	402
IIa	274	274	350
IIb	214	188	256
III	427	410	607
	Percentage errors		
I	0.80	1.28	1.60
IIa	0.39	1.32	1.32
IIb	1.16	1.73	3.85
III	0.56	0.87	1.12

It can been seen from Table 3 that these subjects were much faster than those who attended the Velotype course. However, their error rate was also much higher, i.e., well above the 1% standard for typewriting exams. There is a similar large variation from one text to another.

4.3. Results Achieved by Secretaries

In a large business firm two secretaries were given the opportunity to take a 50-h course in Velotyping. The problem in their situation was that at the end of the course they were not fast enough to do all their work on the Velotype. Especially in rush situations they went back to their QWERTY keyboard. At the time of our test both secretaries had had about 150 h experience of working with the new keyboard, hours of training and work taken together.

We tested them in their own work environment on their own Velotype. Therefore we could not make registrations of their chords and interchord times. The speed was determined with a stopwatch by timing the beginning and end of the various texts. Speeds and error rates are shown in Table 4, which shows that the speed was similar to that achieved by the 167-h group of Velotype apprentices, but that the error rate was much higher.

Table 4. Speed and error rate of two secretaries

Text	speed c.p.m.		Percentage error	
	1	2	1	2
I	217	212	2.5	0.7
IIa	208	210	2.1	1.9
IIb	190	176	4.1	2.1
III	232	244	2.1	0.7

4.4. Results Achieved by the QWERTY-keyboard Control Group

Twelve typists of a text-processing department of the PTT were willing to type the same texts. Since we asked inexperienced and contest typists not to take part, our subjects could be considered reasonably good typists with 2-5 years experience. To register the interkey times the tests were taken with a computer terminal keyboard (Digital VT 100). The positions of some punctuation marks were different from those on their own keyboards (Wang). Therefore, a few training texts were presented before the actual tests. The results are given in Table 5, and show that the speed reached on the QWERTY keyboard depends less on the type of texts than that reached with the Velotype. The error rate is within the 1% norm. The speed can be considered normal for this group of typists, especially if we take into account that the tests were not taken on the keyboard layout the typists were used to. Table 6 gives some results from the literature by way of comparison.

Figure 2 shows a compilation of the results we have obtained so far. When the error rate was over 1% the speed was adjusted. For each error 2.35 was added, this being the mean time taken for error correction by the Velotype apprentices with 167 h training. It is clear that only the demonstration sub-

Table 5. Speed and error rate of QWERTY typists

Text	Speed c.p.m.	Percentage error
I	273	0.3
IIa	236	0.5
IIb	245	0.4
III	264	0.2

Table 6. Some data on typing speeds

reference	*N*	Range	Mean	*SD*
PTT test, text III	12	199-317	265	40
Long, Nimmo-Smith, and Whitefield (1983)	16	189-377	265	49
Droege and Hill (1961)	575	215-435	325	56
Philips (1957)	15	240-380	317	49
Salthouse (1984)				
Experiment I	34	161-585	307	-
		(85-520)[a]	(274)[a]	
Experiment II	40	120-549	322	-
		(115-490)[a]	(300)[a]	-

[a] These speeds have been corrected with respect to errors.

jects could produce texts on Velotype much faster than normal typists, and moreover, this only applies to plain text.

5. A Closer Look at Velotyping

5.1. Influence of the Number of Characters per Chord

We found that speed varied considerably from one text to another. Since the most difficult text contained a large number of abbreviations, e.g., "hdr TNZ," it seemed probable that in this text a large number of single-character "chords" were produced. We therefore analysed the chord length distribution from one text to another. Figure 3 illustrates this distribution as found in the group with 167 h practice, and confirms that the slowest text also contains the most one-character chords and that the fastest text contains the largest mean number of characters per chord.

5.2. Time to Produce a Chord as a Function of its Length

One-character chords slow down velotyping speed only if these chords take more time proportionally. To investigate this effect we calculated the mean interchord time as a function of the number of characters in the chords. The results are presented in Figure 4 separately for chords which do and do not use the "no space" key. Only correct chords were used in the calculation.

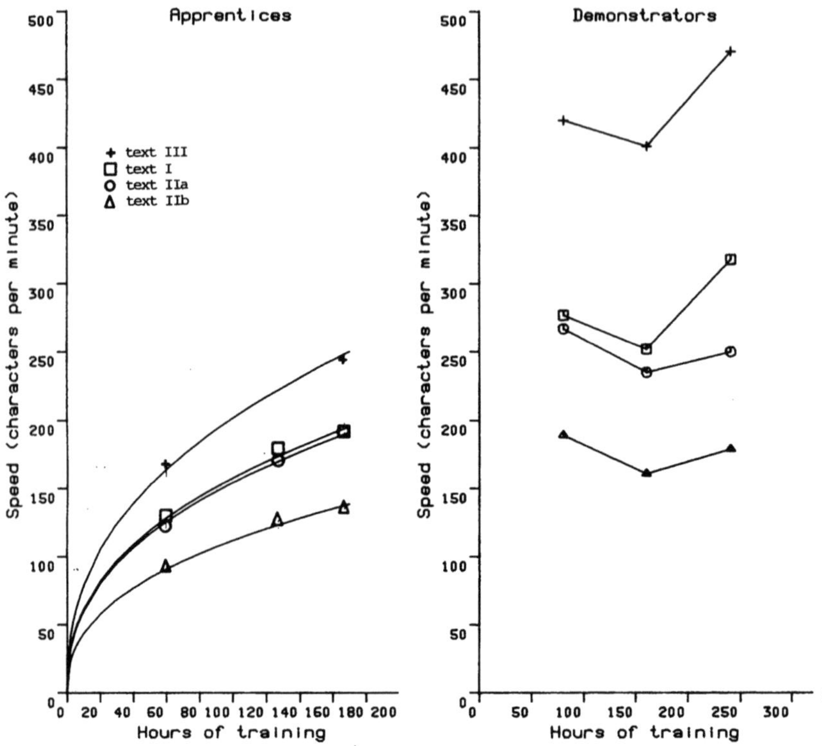

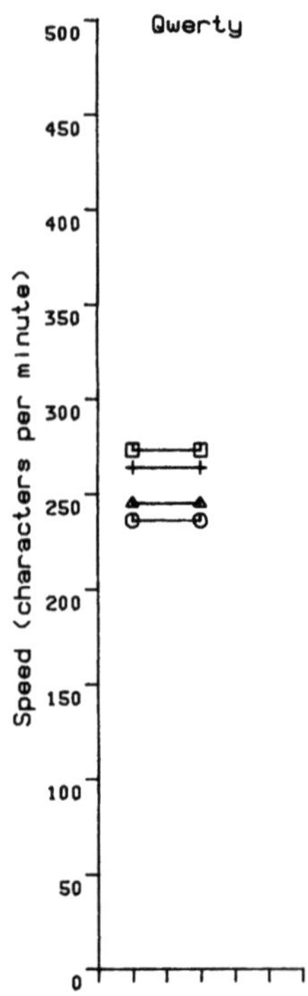

Figure 2. Speed of Velotype apprentices, Velotype demonstrators, and QWERTY typists.

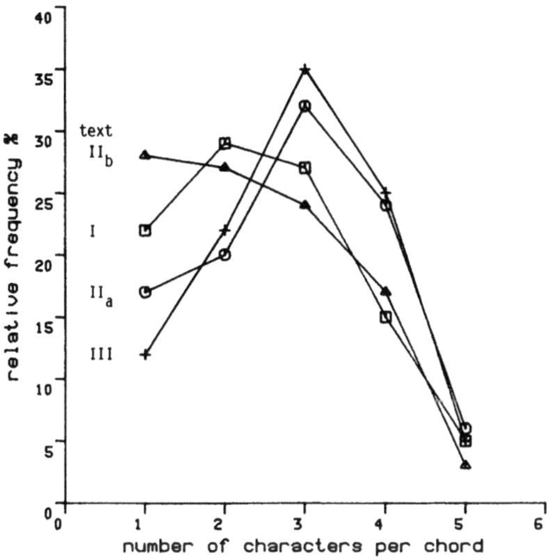

Figure 3. Relative frequency of occurence of chords as a function of the number of characters per chord.

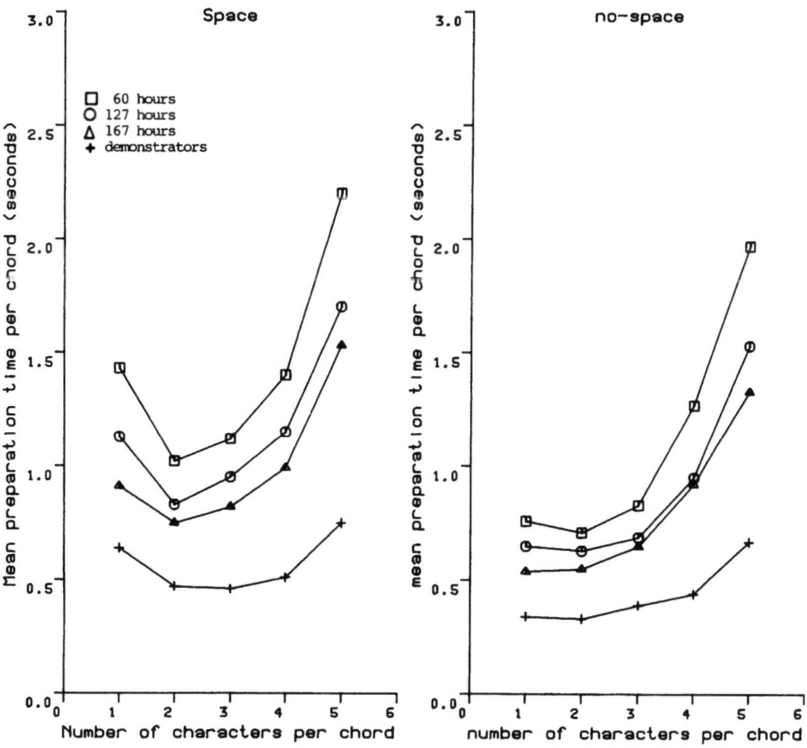

Figure 4. Mean preparation time per chord as a function of the number of characters per chord.

The following conclusions can be drawn from these results. Interchord times clearly depend on the number of characters in the chord. The average time to produce chords of 2 or 3 characters is relatively small, while chords of 1, 4 and 5 characters take longer. Inspection of the distribution of the interchord times of single-character chords reveals that this distribution is clearly multimodal. There are a number of very short interchord times, but also a large number of relatively long ones. It can be shown that the latter are related to the short forms.

Although pressing the "no space" key is an extra action in a chord, the mean times for these chords are smaller. Two tentative explanations can be given for this result: (1) the chord complexity of the second and third syllables is, on average, less than that of the first syllable; (2) the decision times, reading pauses, etc., tend to occur between, not within, words.

5.3. Particularly Difficult Chords

The Velotype keyboard is constructed on the basis of the observation that the most common syllable is of the form consonant-vowel-consonant. If we study the mean time to produce each particular chord we indeed find that these chords are the fastest to produce. For example, *men*, *tal*, *hun* take less then 500 ms (the values pertain to the 167-h group), but syllables with two vowels in the middle, like *keer* and *voor* take from 800 to 1200 ms. Most difficult are syllables with several consonants both at the beginning and at the end, like *Frank* and *strekt* which take about 2000 ms. The word *dwaas* turned out to be extremely difficult (3500 ms). This five-character word requires eight keys to be pressed. Only one subject showed the insight that it is much faster to divide the word in two chords, *d* and *-waas*. Perhaps this touches upon one of the basic difficulties of the Velotype; that of making the decision how to divide up less frequently occurring words if there are no natural syllable boundaries.

5.4. Error Recovery

Inspection of the chord registration showed that the Velotype apprentices and demonstrators made about 10% error chords. This figure was nearly independent on training time. Of these errors chords, about 14% were not corrected by the apprentice groups. The demonstrators, however, left 38% of the error chords uncorrected.

The number of error chords is high compared with the number of error key strokes in QWERTY typing (1.5%), even if one takes into account that the mean chord length is about three characters. The percentage of uncorrected error key strokes in QWERTY typing is about 12%. This corresponds with the value found by Neal and Emmons (1984), 11%, and is not far from the 14% of the Velotype apprentice group.

Error recovery takes time by erasing the error chord and often a few additional chords which were typed in between making the wrong chord and halting to go back. The mean time to correct an error dropped from 3.7 s in the 60-h group to 2.3 s in the 167-h group. The percentage of total typing time spent in error recovery varied from 15% for text III to 26% for text IIb.

5.5. Types of Errors

The relative frequencies of the different types of error are as follows (cf Gentner et al., 1983):

Substitution	40%
Insertion	22%
Omission	15%
Upper-lowercase	9%
Other	23%

6. Discussion

At the end of this first evaluation we must return to the question of whether the Velotype is a useful keyboard. In this evaluation we started with the assumption that the Velotype could replace the QWERTY keyboard for the regular typist in the office. We tested the Velotypist with tests similar to admission tests for normal typists. However, this evaluation cannot be considered as a final empirical test because there was no fully experienced Velotypist available. In view of the steady increase in speed with training time in the Velotype apprentice, we can try to make a prediction of the speed obtainable after 1000 h practice. As Yamada (1983a,b) has indicated, this period is often mentioned as the period after which no more perceptible increase in speed occurs.

To make the prediction we fitted a general learning curve $y = a \exp(b \ln(x))$ (Thurstone, 1919) to the data, in which y stands for the number of letters per minute, and x for the total time elapsed from the beginning of practice (power law of practice, see for instance Card, Moran & Newell, 1983). The fitted values of a were 17.3, 23.9, 24.5, 31.3, for texts IIb, IIa, I and III respectively, and b was 0.405 in all cases. These produce the curves shown in Figure 2. With these values the correlation coefficient r equals .998, and the predicted values after 1000 h are 285, 375, 400 and 515 c.p.m., respectively.

This is an optimistic estimate, since it supposes that after the end of the Velotype training course speed continues to increase at the same rate. From normal typing, however, it is known that this is not always the case. It depends, among other things, on the emphasis on accuracy in the task. On the other hand the results of the three demonstration subjects showed that, for plain text at least, a speed of 500 c.p.m. is obtainable. However, it should be kept in mind that these subjects were trained in special circumstances, and that their error rate was not low enough.

From the large variation in speed across texts it must be concluded that the Velotype is not well-suited for all types of work. In some cases it is convenient to be able to type letter by letter, e.g., in abbreviations and when making corrections with a text processor. Although we did not verify the latter by means of experiments, we suppose that this would be a very complicated job when using Velotype. The principle of the QWERTY keyboard is much more generally applicable. It is so much like the way people write that even schoolchildren can use the keyboard with a one- or two-finger "hunt-and-peck" method without special training. It can be used by people of all standards, up to a 400-c.p.m. audiotypist.

The Velotype, therefore, is a keyboard for the specialist. Or is it? We should consider the situations in which it could be useful, i.e., for the bulk input of text from written material and from spoken material. An important task of keyboard specialists is to transform handwriting into printed text. More often than not the deciphering and grammatical improvement of the manuscript will be the limiting factor. Jaarsveld (1983) found that difficult manuscripts cannot be read at a speed of more than 500 c.p.m. Copying clean print will become less important as more and more of these texts are stored in an electronic from or can be read by an optical scanning device. Clean print that includes composing instructions which must be copied may be an exception, and in fact, a number of Velotypists are employed for this application.

There are two main sources of spoken text that are transformed into print, tape-recorded speech and speech in meetings. In the former case, we believe the Velotype can be used to its full potential as the only limiting factor is typing speed. However, as regards speech in meetings we wonder whether the Velotype is suitable for making a literal report. Downton, Newell, and Arnott (1980) found that stenographers using Palantype reached their limit at 180 words/min (i.e., about 900 c.p.m.). Palantype has fewer keys, there is no error correction, no capitals and commas are produced, and a kind of phonetic shorthand is obtained. At this speed, one in every three to five chords is faulty. We wonder whether the same speed can be reached with the Velotype, which is adapted in such a way as to produce faultlessly spelled text. It should be investigated more closely whether, after revision of the crude input, the overall production time and quality are better for the Velotype or for a device like the Palantype, which is designed for a high speed of real-time speech copying.

It must be concluded that the Velotype is a very ingenious keyboard which may eventually be used for some specialized applications. In the meantime, it must be admitted that the currently available knowledge of typing processes does not enable us to decide which is theoretically the best keyboard design and what the best training methods are.

Acknowledgements

The author is indebted to Martin den Held, for conducting the experiments, and to Rob van Leeuwen, for methodological advice and statistical analyses.

Appendix: Statistical Tests of the Data used in Tables 1 and 2.

Table A1. Fischer's *t* test (one tailed) applied to the data underlying Table 1: Velotyping speed in the various groups of apprentices.

	Training times (h)								
	60:127			60:167			127:167		
Text	*t*	*df*	*p*	*t*	*df*	*p*	*t*	*df*	*p*
I	1.54	9	.079	2.22	13	.02	0.38	18	.35
IIa	2.11	10	.031	1.98	13	.03	0.66	19	.26
IIb	1.94	10	.04	1.64	13	.06	0.43	19	.34
III	-	-	-	1.79	13	.05	-	-	-

Table A2. Fischer's *t* test (one-tailed) applied to the data underlying Table 2: Velotyping error rate as function of training time.

	Training times (h)								
	60:127			60:167			127:167		
Text	*t*	*df*	*p*	*t*	*df*	*p*	*t*	*df*	*p*
I	-0.64	9	.73	-0.06	13	.53	0.85	18	.20
IIa	0.45	11	.32	0.30	13	.38	-0.21	20	.58
IIb	-0.20	10	.57	-0.22	13	.59	-0.03	19	.51
III	-	-	-	-0.99	13	.83	-	-	-

Table A3. Fischer's *t* test (two tailed) applied to the data underlying Table 2, Velotyping error rate compared with respect to the four texts used.

	Texts								
	I:IIa			I:IIb			I:III		
Training time (h)	*t*	*df*	*p*	*t*	*df*	*p*	*t*	*df*	*p*
60	-0.25	2	.83	-0.6	2	.61	3.6	2	.07
127	0.44	6	.68	-1.29	6	.25	-	-	-
167	0.58	11	.57	-1.46	11	.17	3.1	11	.01
	IIa:IIba			IIa:III			IIb:III		
	t	*df*	*p*	*t*	*df*	*p*	*t*	*df*	*p*
	-0.27	2	.81	3.0	2	.1	1.7	2	.23
	-1.17	8	.28	-	-	-	-	-	-
	-1.45	11	.17	2.3	11	.04	2.6	11	.03

References

Card S.K., Moran T.P. & Newell A. (1983). *The psychology of human computer interaction.* Lawrence Erlbauw Assosciates, Hillsdale, New Jersey.

Downton A.C., Newell A.F. & Arnott J.L. (1980). Operator error performance and keyboard evaluation in Palantype machine shorthand. *Applied Ergonomics*, 11, pp. 73-80.

Droege R.F., & Hill B.M. (1961). Comparison of performance on manual and electric typewriters. *Journal of Applied Psychology*, 45 (4), pp. 268-270.

Gentner D.R., Grudin J.T., Larochelle S., Norman P.A. & Rumelhart D.E. (1983). A glossary of terms including a classification of typing errors. In: *Cognitive aspects of skilled typewriting*, W.E. Cooper, (Ed.), Springer, New York.

Den Held M. & Van Noorden L. (1984). *Een eerste evaluatie van de Velotype t.b.v. het gebruik binnen de PTT.* SWO-1 report 769/4, CD-PTT, The Hague.

Van Jaarsveld H.J. (1983). *On reading handwriting.* Thesis, Katholieke Universiteit Nijmegen.

Long J., Nimmo-Smith I. & Whitefield, A. (1983). Skilled typing: a characterization based on the distribution of times between responses. In: *Cognitive Aspects of Skilled Typewriting*, W.E. Cooper, (Ed.), Springer, New York.

Neal A.S. & Emmons W.H. (1984). Error correction during text entry with word-processing systems. *Human Factors*, 26, pp. 443-448.

Philips N.V. (1957). *Onderzoek typemachines.* Internal report.

Salthouse T.A. (1984). Effects of age and skill in typing. *Journal of Experimental Psychology: General*, 113 (3), pp. 345-371.

Thurstone L.L. (1919). The learning curve equation. *Psychological Monographs*, 26.

Yamada H. (1983a). Certain problems associated with the design of input keyboards for Japanese writing. In: *Cognitive aspects of skilled typewriting*. W.E. Cooper (Ed.), Springer, New York.

Yamada H. (1983b). The dvorak simplified keyboard: Practice belies theory. *Computer*, 16 (3), pp. 80-81.

Chapter 20. Real-time Processing of Cursive Writing and Sketched Graphics

Arnold J.W.M. Thomassen, Hans-Leo Teulings, Lambert R.B. Schomaker

1. Introduction

The advances that have recently been made with respect to intelligent workstations and software also involve highly sophisticated recognition algorithms. The latter open up attractive possibilities for accessing the computer by means of the "natural" linguistic communication modes of speech and writing. Yet the large-scale introduction of keyboard-and-screen text editors with the many human-machine interaction problems associated with that revolution, and the spectacular potential of speech processing soliciting huge and lasting research investments in that area, seem to be responsible for the relative oblivion of the study of handwriting and drawing as efficient modes of human-computer interaction. The present contribution intends to point out the attractiveness and feasibility of using pen and paper as a natural communication device in an office work environment.

Admittedly, as compared with the keyboard, handwriting does have some serious drawbacks due to its relative slowness, attention demands, and fatigue. These disadvantages are more prohibiting the longer the text involved and the more routine the writing task. However, for shorter notes, for editing comments, and for the composition of nonroutine texts, where writing speed is secondary to careful formulation and accurate positioning, handwriting may be the most efficient mode. This is also the case, of course, for filling out forms, addressing mail, writing out cheques, and other writing tasks which are difficult to achieve with typewriters and text editors. Moreover, the natural use of the pen can be most effective in situations where various marks and symbols are used in combination with text, with editing comments in existing documents, both handwritten and from line printers, and with graphics, as we shall see in the present paper. Neglecting in our research and development the use of the pen as a processing mode in the modern office would therefore be a denial of the possibility of a "universal" communication facility that is in fact within reach. It would, moreover, overlook the enormous economic interests involved in satisfactory solutions for the automatic processing of the large variety of handwritten documents in our society. Finally, it would be a denial of the contributions made by several promising research projects during the past 25 years. In the paragraphs to follow, we shall refer to some of this earlier work as well as to some recent research including that at our laboratory.

Working with paper and pencil in an office environment not only involves the production and revision of handwritten words and alphanumeric characters. Symbols of various kinds are often produced, such as those in mathematical expressions, and the characters of different writing systems such as Greek, Cyrillic or Chinese. Moreover, sketches of all sorts, such as tables, tree structures, flow charts, and logic circuits, are drawn roughly. And, finally, formulae of different degrees of complexity may belong to one's handwritten output. It would be of an advantage if a single system could be designed that is capable of dealing with all these forms of graphemic, symbolic, and graphic output: i.e., a system that would not only be able to read handwritten letters, digits, words, and text-editing comments, but that would also read hundreds of nonalphanumeric characters and symbols, that would interpret formulae and roughly sketched graphics, and that would render these in a neat, orderly fashion, properly grouped and aligned.

The present paper, although not devoted to all of these aspects, intends to draw the attention of human-computer interaction specialists to the feasibility of such a universal graphics system. Many problems still have to be solved, but the attempts thus far have been very stimulating. The next section of this paper is devoted to a discussion of the different access modalities that have been introduced in addition to the keyboard; it appears that the mouse is a handy instrument, but that the pen connected to a graphic tablet has many specific advantages.

2. Editing Text Files

2.1. Some Cursor Control Modalities

A variety of workstation facilities have been developed in order to achieve easy, quick, and flexible access to (usually text) information on the screen for editing or manipulating purposes. These devices, most of which have been reviewed by Embley and Nagy (1981), require the user to move a pointer (cursor) towards a position on the screen that needs to be changed. Apart from the keyboard, where usually four keys are responsible for the step-by-step movement of the cursor, we distinguish five types of analog control. A first category is formed by the knee control and the joystick, the latter allowing fine precision and being applicable over a wide range of functions. Second, there are the pair of thumb wheels and the track ball, which, unlike the first category, respond to manipulation but remain in place themselves.

The mouse, which is actually an encased and inverted track ball, constitutes an interesting third class of its own. Its unique property is that the excursions it makes on the desk evoke corresponding movements on the screen. The mouse is judged to be quick as a device and to lead to relatively few errors, but also has some disadvantages. The light pen, or its slight modification, the light pistol, and the touch panel which require the arm and hand to be moved towards and across the screen, all belong to a fourth category having the advantage of being simple and direct. A drawback is, however, that arm movements are tiring and that additional control by keys is required to mark the intended movements.

The electronic pen used on a graphic tablet, which forms our fifth class, also has the advantage of simplicity and directness. Moreover, it can be used in the normal horizontal writing plane with a normal, relaxed, and supported hand position. The graphic tablet is usually covered by a paper sheet for graphic output by a ballpoint stylus; accurate feedback is obtained from the paper where drawing or writing is produced, as well as from the screen. The advantages of using the latter system will be considered later. A new development where the electronic pen leaves an electronic light trace in the tablet, which itself also serves as a display screen (so-called flatscreen) will only be touched upon in the present context. We now turn to some human-factors aspects of using the pen in editing work. Some of its features will be compared with those of the mouse.

2.2. Ergonomic Features of Pen and Paper

To the extent that an instrument's shape and function approach these of an ordinary writing instrument such as a pencil, fibre-tip or ball-point pen, an adult user may be expected to be capable of manipulating it easily and flexibly without further practice. This is obviously the case with most of the pens that are supplied with the modern graphic tablets. We noted above that prolonged writing is relatively slow and cumbersome if it is to result in an unambiguous trace. As a principal support, however, and for shorter comments and various unusual characters and formulae, as well as for designing, sketching and for error correcting and making jumps across the page for any other reason, the pen seems to be by far the most favored instrument.

As compared with the mouse, the pen is light and small so adequate visual control of the trajectory is available. It can be very accurately manipulated for these reasons, and also, of course, because it is highly compatible with well-practiced pointing and writing movements. The direction of a trajectory of the pen on the graphic tablet, moreover, is not dependent on the orientation of the device, as is the case with the mouse whose response varies, for example, with wrist angle. Similarly, a "natural" jumping movement made with the pen above the tablet is processed as such; this in contrast to jumps of the mouse above the desk which are merely neglected. Furthermore, in editing texts, etc., the pen itself can be used both for finding the place in the text and for making the actual symbolic, graphic, or textual entry; this results in a highly efficient, unitary system. Moreover, there is perfect correspondence (compatibility) between the place where, and the plane in which a mark is to be made when pen-and-paper are used. This again compares favorably with the mouse, which is operated in a working plane (desk) that deviates in position, orientation and dimension from the plane (screen) where the effect is intended and effected. Finally, a pen is not so much of an additional object on the office desk as a mouse is; although supplied with a wire, the pen is merely a writing stylus, which is needed on any office desk.

2.3. Screen Versus Hard Copy Text Processing

Apart from the above ergonomic considerations of using pen and paper, there is also ample evidence in the literature that reading from a hard copy is generally preferred to reading from the screen (for reviews see Dainoff, 1982; Embley & Nagy, 1981; Helander, Billingsley & Schurick, 1984; National Research Council, 1983; Padmos, Pot, Vos & De Vries-Mol, 1985). Specific empirical evidence concerning speed is provided by Gould and Grichowsky (1984). They observed a 20%-30% time gain when comparing hard-copy proof reading with screen proof reading. A similar difference of 24.1% in favour of reading printed text was found by Kruk and Muter (1984). No doubt, having a full-size overview of a printed page and the ease of searching for the correct page as well as changing paper pages are additional advantages when dealing with multi-page manuscripts.

An interesting simulation experiment involving both reading and writing was carried out by Gould and Alfaro (1984). They compared the revision of documents with a familiar full-screen text editing system to that with the pen on hardcopy pages. The authors observed a 50%-90% time gain under the latter condition. It appeared that in keyboard editing substantial amounts of time where involved in searching between places in the document and the corresponding places on the screen, in deciding what action to take, and in rereading the revised passage. Results of this kind suggest that it would be extremely attractive to have a system that allows the operator (the principal or the secretary) merely to write or trace the editorial comments and marks directly onto (an overlay on) the printed or handwritten page. This is truly an example of direct manipulation (Shneiderman, 1983) in editing.

Let us now look into the feasibility of recognition of handwriting by the computer. In the following section, after having distinguished different styles of writing, we shall present a brief review of earlier research.

3. Automatic Recognition of Handwriting

3.1. Types of Script

As regards the automatic recognition of handwriting, it is desirable first to make some distinctions. The numeric character ensemble is generally assumed to comprise only the 10 different digits, written without connections and roughly in a single style. The alphabetic characters occur in many different styles, all of which are commonly subdivided into capitals (or upper case) and lower case letters. Block letter characters are produced to look like printed letters, also to the extent that they are separated by spaces. Cursive script, in contrast, is a running style of writing, involving the flowing production of upper and lower case letters virtually without pen lifts, and in principle connecting all the letters in a word. Presumably, the easiest script for automatic recognition is capital block letters; cursive script, the characters of which are both difficult to segment and highly variable in shape, and the many mixed styles that are typical of natural, unconstrained writing are more difficult to recognize.

Processing handwritten documents by computers has a history of about 25 years. Not only the Latin alphabet in its various forms but also many other writing systems, including Chinese and Japanese kanji and kana, have received attention in pattern recognition research. The recognition procedures attempted thus far are highly diverse, and the number of problems encountered in most of them is considerable. With respect to performance, the two extremes are that neatly and discretely written words in "standard" capitals can be read almost perfectly, whereas there is as yet no system available that produces correct interpretations of cursive sequences written without constraint by arbitrary writers.

3.2. Early Work

The oldest attempts at handwriting recognition followed the procedure of calculating the best fit to templates of the ensemble. Naturally, only block letters written according to very precise specifications are amenable to such matching. From the early sixties onwards, more sophisticated procedures subsequently employed "syntactic" methods of detecting the characters' structural features, i.e., their constituent basic elements (primitives) and their relationships. The output of such a detection procedure is a compact, coded representation of the characters. Their identification subsequently takes the form of class assignment on the basis of stored feature sets. The latter procedure is capable of handling a much larger variety of letter shapes and therefore in principle is suitable for reading cursive script. Whenever possible, contextual constraints (e.g., language statistics, word knowledge) are employed to attain the most likely interpretation.

A survey of several early approaches to the recognition of (cursive) handwriting is provided by Lindgren (1965). He reviews work between 1960 and 1965, undertaken within the realm of speech research, where it was hoped to gain a better insight from handwriting because of its similar but less complex problems associated with segmentation, variability, and context. These forms of cursive script recognition did not attempt to tackle unconstrained writing. They were commonly based on extraction of features from accurately produced script. This occurred either at the word level, avoiding segmentation problems (Earnest, 1963), or it followed a letter-to-letter approach complemented by a whole-word approach (Frishkopf & Harmon, 1961). Even in these early attempts, the sequential or graphic constraints of the handwriting movement were somehow taken into account. The latter authors, moreover, actually studied the writing trace as a function of time.

The third line of research reviewed by Lindgren is that of Eden, which by its attempt to generate handwriting first, can be characterized as analysis by synthesis (Eden & Halle, 1961). Eden's work was mainly concerned with the generation of handwriting "by rule." The rules generated letters and words from 18 different strokes, which in turn were made up of only four different "primitives." Recognition concerned the analysis of the dynamic writing signal into its component strokes (Mermelstein & Eden, 1964). All these recognition systems, moreover, used linguistic constraints for error detection and correction. Nevertheless, their achievements did not reach the critera of acceptability, or in the words of Harmon quoted by Lindgren (1965), they had "not advanced much beyond the stage of being laboratory toys."

3.3. More Recent Work

The literature of the more recent years has been reviewed by Harmon (1972) and Suen, Berthold, and Mori (1980) for example. Much of the work is concerned with the effectiveness of bulk input of handwritten alphanumeric data into data-processing systems (e.g., Spanjersberg, 1978). The procedure is usually a purely "optical" character recognition (OCR) which, following scanning and various preprocessing procedures to detect, normalize, clean, and thin up the characters' contours, determines specific features in their global and local trajectories; the latter invariant primitives are then represented by codes in a syntactic pattern recognition mode (e.g., Ali & Pavlidis, 1977).

The recognition of unconstrained handwriting has been attempted for the last 20 years. However, in order to achieve an acceptable level of correct identification, standard digits and capital letters, often written in boxes, are usually required. Reduction in the size and variability of the character set (e.g., following the ANSI norm X3.45 by the American National Standard Institute, drawn up in 1974), results in an adequate recognition rate. If writers follow the specifications, and especially if they receive feedback during a brief training period, correct recognition can be of the order of 99.0%-99.5%. However, if writers are untrained and unconstrained, correct identification is only 90%-95%; if a document is estimated to contain about 10 crucial characters to be recognized, there is an unacceptably low probability of a correctly read document (see, e.g., Himmel, 1978).

It is of interest to note here that the vast majority of the errors and rejections in automatic recognition concern the products of only about 15% of writers, so selection, where possible, certainly does pay. Another point to be noted is that it appears to be counterproductive to put too many constraints upon letter shapes: this reduces speed and the writer's willingness to cooperate (see, e.g., Apsey, 1978) as well as the application range of the system.

4. Handwriting Movement Recognition

4.1. Graphic and Dynamic Constraints

As stated above, many, though not all (e.g., Sayre, 1973), of the handwriting recognition procedures mentioned, somehow take the temporal sequence of the writing movement into account. That is to say, they are partly based upon the graphic constraints in the production of the written material. Obviously, stroke order and stroke direction can disambiguate in a large number of cases, especially where adjoining and crossing contours are to be segmented. Examples involving discrimination based on stroke order and stroke direction are shown in Figure 1. It can also be deduced from these examples, however, that certain idiosyncratic character formations, although written clearly, could be misread because of their unusual temporal stroke sequence. Moreover, certain stroke sequences will never contribute to the characters' identification; we are familiar with this problem in cases such as *200* and *ZOO*, where higher-order context is required to solve ambiguities. It should be noted, moreover that in many cursive script sequences, like *cl* or *d*, the segmentation of letters can only be achieved in an interactive process switching between letter segmentation and word recognition. For examples of the ambiguities of segmentation, see Figures 2 and 3.

Basing handwriting recognition upon the dynamic constraints of the actual handwriting movements is going a step further than employing graphic constraints. Making full use of these constraints in an analysis-by-synthesis

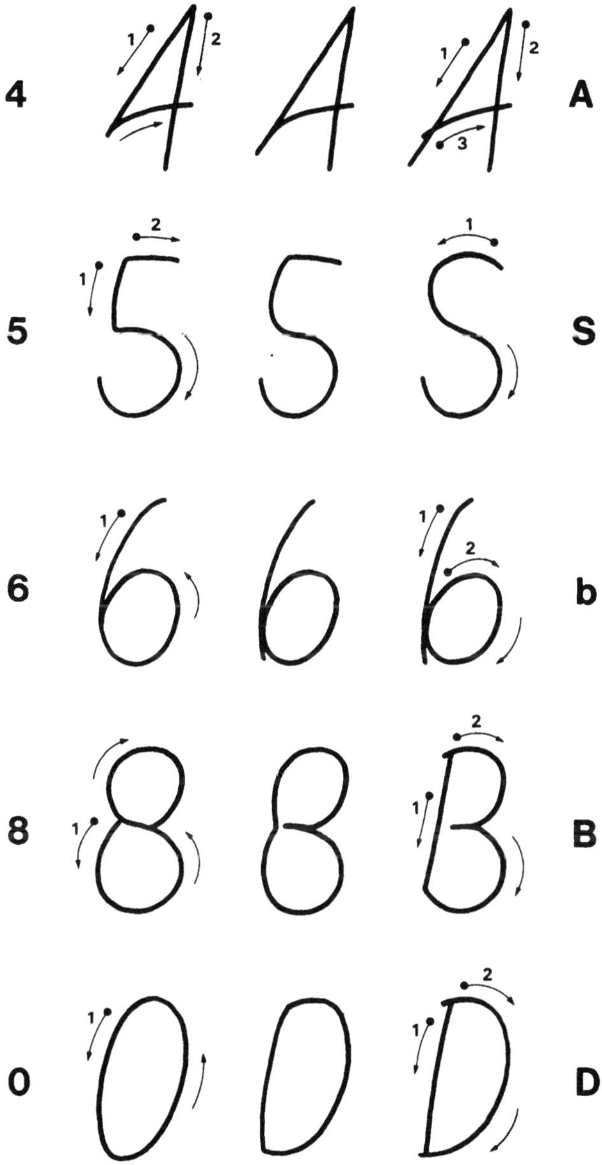

Figure 1. Some examples of disambiguation of alphanumeric characters by considering number, order, and direction of strokes. The central column contains ambiguous character shapes. Dotted arrows indicate starting points and directions.

(a) (b) (c) (d) (e) (f) (g) (h)

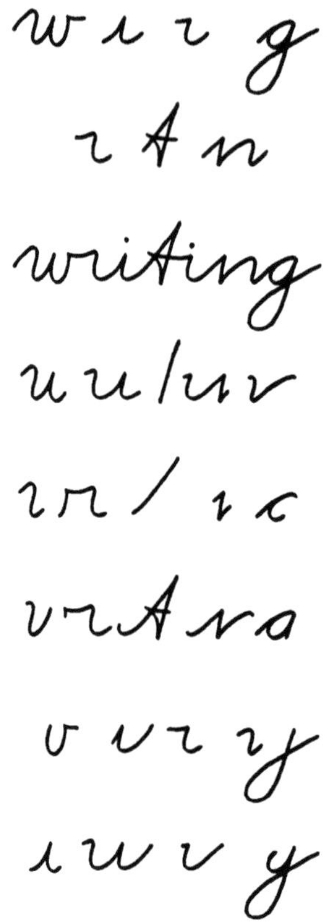

Figure 2. The cursively written word *writing* (c) and its build-up from correctly (a, b) and incorrectly identified (d-h) segments (the later segments have been chosen arbitrarily).

approach requires a model describing the psychomotor process and the prevailing mechanics, dynamics, and context effects in natural handwriting. Such a model is not available, although a number of very useful attempts have been made with respect to certain essential details (Denier van der Gon, Thuring, & Strackee, 1962; Dooijes, 1984; Eden & Halle, 1961; Morasso & Mussa Ivaldi, 1982; Vredenbregt & Koster, 1971). Whatever their merit may be, recognition procedures based on these attempts are wholly lacking.

4.2. Modelling of Handwriting

A model of handwriting suitable to support a recognition system is being developed by the present authors and Maarse and Van Galen, also at Nijmegen. It intends to take account of the following factors. A written word

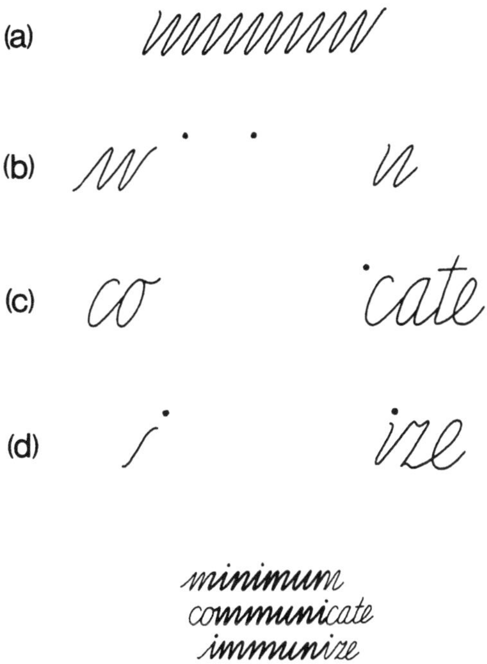

Figure 3. The 22 strokes of (a) constitute an ambiguous sequence, which in the context of (b) forms the central part of *minimum* in that of (c) the letters 3 - 7 of *communicate*, and in (d) the five initial letters of *immunize*; no down stroke in (a) serves the same function in (b), (c), or (d).

in someone's handwriting reflects the person-specific stored and retrieved representation of the word's characters and his or her individual psychomotor, mechanical, and muscular performance capabilities and preferences. The actual production of the word involves many joints and antagonistic muscle pairs. These, however, are incorporated in three principal, directional subsystems. The first, mainly represented by the fingers, corresponds to the letters' near-vertical movements, especially their down strokes; the second, which is primarily performed by the wrist, produces the small horizontal excursions of the letter strokes and their connections which occur mainly in up strokes; the third directional subsystem is in principle taken care of by the upper arm which produces the large rightward displacement when writing successive letters within and between words. Although these general directional systems thus each have primary executing effector systems with their own biomechanical features, the performance of a word can in principle be achieved in very many different ways, according to the large number of degrees of freedom in the arm-wrist-finger system with its 32 joints. Indeed, it must be assumed that the stable representation of handwriting characters in a person's motor memory is abstract, that is, independent of the exact orientation, size and muscles with which they are executed, and even independent of the arm-wrist-finger system itself.

The model of handwriting, furthermore, assigns a central position to vertical strokes (especially down strokes) because they appear to be the most elementary performance units both in motor and in graphic terms. In its attempt to describe well-practiced cursive writing, the model requires a high degree of temporal constancy across different performances, but an even higher degree of relative spatial constancy, since the attainment of spatial goal positions in near-vertical strokes has been shown to take priority. These strokes, moreover, appear to have a stable representation, to be relatively insensitive to disturbances, and to be triggered by simple commands which result in ballistic movements.

In the dynamic cursive-handwriting recognition system described briefly below, an attempt is made to make full use of the characteristics of the writing model under construction. The principal step in this respect is the selection of the stroke, defined by minima in the absolute velocity signal, as the most elementary production and recognition unit capable of being represented by a relatively simple code and suited to act as a meaningful constituent element ("primitive") in the letters and words to be identified.

4.3. A Model-Based Handwriting Recognizer

The present section will review the basic features of the recognition system as it has thus far been developed in Nijmegen as part of the Esprit project on image and movement understanding. A more complete account is provided by Teulings, Schomaker, and Thomassen (1986). The recognizer has been used only for the identification of cursive words of a few writers, avoiding digits. The first stage is that of recording the movements of the pen tip on the digitizing tablet, which is covered by a sheet of ordinary writing paper. The pen's position is sampled at a rate of 105 Hz in terms of x and y coordinate values. With the present hardware (Calcomp 9240) and software, this yields an accuracy of 0.02 mm per sampling point. Also, the pen-up movements above the tablet, as well as axial pressure are recorded; the pressure data, however, are thus far only used to separate pen-up and pen-down movements. The digitized data are subjected to certain preprocessing procedures which place the coordinate values on a time scale, calculate velocity in x and y directions, and execute low-pass filtering.

Segmentation constitutes the next stage in the recognition process. A word written without any constraints as to size, space, or orientation, is scanned in temporal order to detect the segmentation points, i.e., the instances where the pen speed reaches a minimum. Using a selection procedure involving these minima, the word's baseline is estimated, this being needed for the normalization of its orientation. The selection discards, for example, segmentation points belonging to loops in downward extenders and other outliers. The segments separated by zero crossings of the vertical velocity, given the baseline as reference, are denoted strokes. Subsequently, the height of the characters can be determined, as is illustrated in Figure 4.

The recognition process proper starts by coding the successive strokes in a sequence in order to obtain the coded representation of a segment of writing that could possibly be a letter. The code for each stroke refers to its elementary shape, direction, and length. A sequence of stroke codes is subsequently matched against the stored code sequences for the (presently only lower case

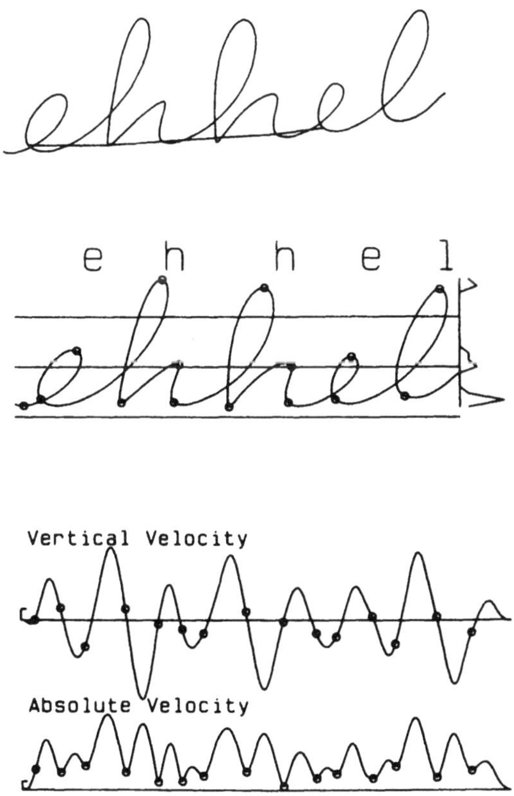

Figure 4. Recognized letter sequence *ehhel*, following normalization of its orientation. Horizontal lines correspond to the obtained baseline. The small circles in the sequence correspond to velocity minima found near y-velocity minima and their distributions are indicated to the right of the normalized word.

cursive) letters of the alphabet. A match results in a recognized character, and a sequence of recognized characters make up a recognized word. In a considerable number of cases a longer code sequence can be subdivided into various different 'recognizable' subsequences, such as *de* and *clc* sequences. In these cases consultation of a writer's individual features (see Maarse, Schomaker & Teulings, 1986) and of a word dictionary (and lower-order language statistics such as trigram frequencies as well as higher-order linguistic constraints such as syntax) is essential in order to exclude impossible and unlikely interpretations. Obviously, segmentation into characters requires an interaction with word recognition of the kind discussed above (see also Figures 2 and 3). It is of interest to note that, although in this procedure words constitute the units upon which recognition is based, the units classified and coded are not words, but strokes as letter segments in words.

Although the system, which was described in very general terms, is in principle writer-independent, it may actually need some interaction with most writers during an acquisition phase, where rejected and incorrectly recognized characters are given the proper label by the user. It is to be expected that a system of this kind, which is explicitly based on a model of the production of handwriting, will be capable of recognizing bottom-up the vast majority of the handwritten output of the writers with whom it is familiar. Applying top-down error correction as indicated should lead to the near-perfect interpretation of a person's alphanumeric output. Other systems that are currently being developed (e.g., Tappert, 1986), even though they only take graphic stroke order and pen lifts into account, are reported to have a very high potential recognition rate. In any case, the use of the pen and graphic tablet for alphanumeric data entry and editing would seem to be a feasible and a very attractive facility in the office of the future.

4.4. Future Developments

Looking ahead, the above-mentioned universal system for entering numbers as well as words, symbols and strange characters, proof-correction marks and other editing comments, hand-sketched drawings, graphs, and flow charts, as well as complex mathematical formulae, seems to be within reach. It is of course a matter of further research investment, but in principle all these applications can be developed. In fact, considerable work along the above lines has been devoted, for instance, to Chinese characters. Moreover, some interesting work in the area of error correcting using handwriting as input has been done by Suenaga and Nagura (1980).

An interactive system for the interpretation of hand-sketched line figures such as flow charts and logic circuit diagrams and for their "professional" plotting by a graphics subsystem been proposed by Lin and Pun (1978). More

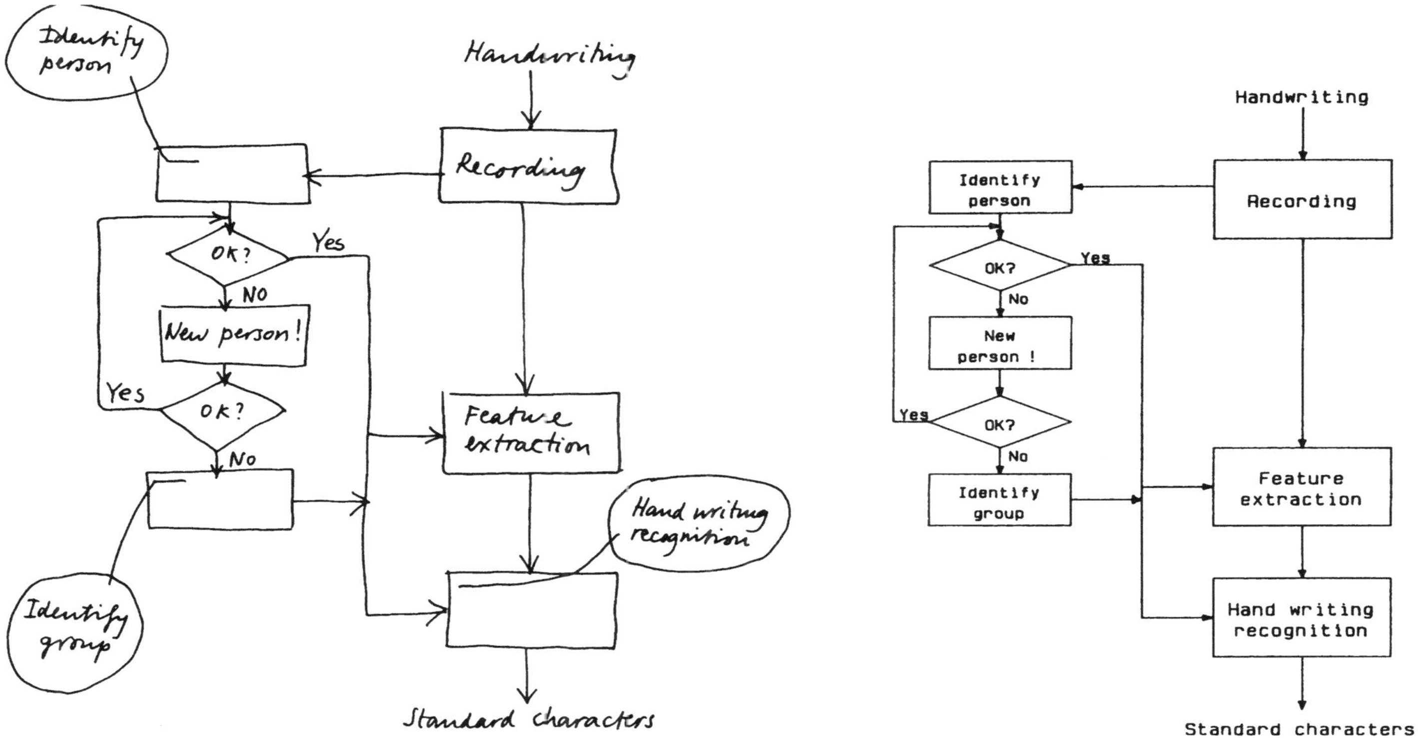

Figure 5. A hypothetical example of the automatic processing of combined graphic and cursively written material entered on a graphic tablet (from Maarse et al., 1986).

recently, a system for the syntactic interpretation of complex mathematical formulae written on a graphic tablet has been designed by Belaid and Haton (1984). The formula reader, of course, works in conjunction with a character-recognition system. An illustration of a system to be used for combined graphics and text is given in Figure 5. Furthermore, Plamondon and Baron (1986) recently described a prototype of an on-line character recognition system interfaced with a software tool which is dedicated to the detailed design and coding of computer programs. The user interacts with the software tool by means of handwritten alphanumeric and simple graphic symbols without any command entry. Another recent development that could be linked to the kind of graphic-tablet use we have in mind is the "tree doctor" program by Desain (this volume). It is an interactive program, making use of direct manipulation with a mouse, for handling, drawing, and changing graphic tree structures. Manipulations of this kind seem to be feasible for all kinds of graphic representations and formulae, again using the pen on a graphic tablet. In other words, in many respects the future of the pen-and-tablet as a universal device in the office does not seem too far ahead.

It seems very likely that with properly developed hardware (built-in graphic tablets, transparent flatscreens, flexible, portable tablets, wireless pens) and highly advanced intelligent software, the electronic pen and tablet could be used for a large variety of textual and graphic purposes. Such a workstation could interpret hundreds of different symbols both as data and as instructions; it could read a writer's various styles of handwriting and their mixtures; it could easily be adapted to different writers who would need only minimal instruction and feedback; it would interpret sketched lines and curves as parts of regular diagrams, graphs and drawings; it would localize words in an earlier produced printed or handwritten page and it would perform editing instructions and correct errors according to proof-reading conventions. Moreover, it would be able to serve many other functions after selection from a menu.

In brief, the pen and tablet could develop into the desired universal editing workstation without a keyboard. Of course, this would have specific advantages in environments where conventional keyboards are not available or wanted. However, it is unlikely that one single interaction modality, however ingenious, will be the most efficient for dealing with all the tasks where one might wish to exchange information with the computer. Instead, it is to be expected that highly intelligent, multimodal, "symbiotic" human-computer interfaces will be designed which allow the operator to make full use of his or her robust, natural (perceptual, motor, and linguistic) skills. Beside speech, handwriting and drawing will no doubt be amongst these skills.

5. Some Suggestions for Research

We wil conclude by making a few comments concerning ergonomic and psychonomic research that will be required in the near future if handwriting is to take the place it deserves as an input modality in human-computer interaction. The prospect of using handwriting as an input modality opens up a whole area of ergonomic research in the field of text processing. Before specifying a limited set of narrow research topics, we shall first indicate two general topics, one more fundamental, one more applied. Taking handwriting seriously as a means of communication with computers not only involves a reappraisal of the skill of handwriting but also demands fundamental insight into its psychomotor and mechanical aspects. The field is as yet much less developed than those of speech and typewriting, but basic psychonomic and biomechanical research of handwriting and other graphic skills has attracted an increasing amount of attention during the past few years, as witnessed by the organization of international conferences (Thomassen, Keuss, & Van Galen, 1984; Kao, Van Galen & Hoosain, 1986) and by the recent foundation of the International Graphonomics Society (IGS). It is hoped that the near future will see a rapid increase in basic knowledge and formal modeling of handwriting. As has been indicated here, this is instrumental to the development of recognition algorithms.

A special research goal is the optimization of coding, storage, and retrieval of handwritten material in documents. Presently, the International Standards Organization (ISO) is concerned with norms for the design of office document architecture (ODA). It is of essential importance that not only are text, image, and voice documentation normalized, but that special norms for handwriting (its compression, classification, and identification) and for other hand-produced graphic output are developed. The ergonomic research to support such norms has not been conducted thus far. The applications range far beyond the mere recognition of handwriting. Such norms could have consequences for normalizing the printed and cursive styles of handwriting to be taught in schools, as well as of proof-reading marks, and for prescriptions as regards handwritten editing and formatting of comments in printed and handwritten documents.

Narrower research topics with some degree of urgence include (1) ergonomic work with a pen on flatscreen displays simulating the writing trace ("electronic ink"); (2) psychonomic work on feedback procedures during the acquisition phase and during the operational phase of a handwriting recognition system; (3) determining the learnability of specific character shapes by children and adults; (4) determining the natural stroke order and directional tendencies in spontaneous drawing and writing; (5) designing optimal handwriting alphabets for automatic processing; (6) finding the ergonomic and psychonomic features of using microcomputers in the teaching of writing that involves normalized alphabets; (7) studying relationships between the dynamics of handwriting movements and their static trace in order to improve the off-line reading of finished handwriting; and (8) designing nonalphabetical handwritten symbols and markers for editing and various graphic purposes.

References

Ali F. & Pavlidis Th. (1977). Syntactic recognition of handwritten numerals. *IEEE Transactions on Systems, Man and Cybernetics.* SMC-7, pp. 537-541.

Apsey R.S. (1978). Human factors of constrained handprint for OCR. *IEEE Transactions on Systems, Man and Cybernetics.* SMC-8, pp. 292-296.

Belaid A. & Haton J.-P. (1984). A syntactic approach for handwritten mathematical formula recognition. *IEEE Transactions on Pattern Analysis and Machine Intelligence.* PAMI-6, pp. 105-111.

Dainoff M.J. (1982). Occupational stress factors in visual display terminal (VDT) operation: A review of empirical research. *Behavior and Information Technology,* 1, pp. 141-176.

Denier van der Gon J.J., Thuring J.Ph. & Strackee J. (1962). A handwriting simulator. *Physics in Medicine and Biology,* 6, pp. 407-413.

Desain P. (1988). Treedoctor: A package for animation and manipulation of tree structures. In: *Human-Computer Interaction: Psychonomic Aspects.* G.C. van der Veer & G. Mulder (Eds.). Springer, Heidelberg.

Dooijes E.H. (1984). *Analysis of handwriting movements.* Ph.D. Thesis, University of Amsterdam. Krips Repro, Meppel.

Earnest L.D. (1963). Machine recognition of cursive writing. In: *Information processing 1962.* C.M. Popplewell (Ed.)., North-Holland, Amsterdam, pp. 462-466.

Eden M. & Halle M. (1961). The characterization of cursive writing. In: *Information Theory.* C. Cherry (Ed.), Butterworths, London. pp. 287-299.

Embley D.W. & Nagy G. (1981). Behavioral aspects of text editors. *Computing Surveys,* 13, pp. 33-70.

Frishkopf L.S. & Harmon L.D. (1961). Machine reading of cursive script. In: *Information Theory.* C. Cherry (Ed.). Butterworths, London. pp. 300-316.

Gould J.D. & Alfaro L. (1984). Revising documents with text editors, handwriting-recognition systems and speech-recognition systems. *Human Factors,* 26, pp. 391-406.

Gould J.D. & Grichkowsky N. (1984). Doing the same work with hard copy and with cathode-ray tube (CRT) computer terminals. *Human Factors*, 26, pp. 323-337.

Harmon L.D. (1972). Automatic recognition of print and script. *Proceedings of the IEEE*, 60, pp. 1165-1176.

Helander M.G., Billingsley P.A. & Schurick J.M. (1984). An evaluation of human factors research on visual display terminals in the workplace. *Human Factors Review*, 3, pp. 55-129.

Himmel D.P. (1978). Some real-world experiences with handprinted optical character recognition. *IEEE Transactions on Systems, Man, and Cybernetics*. SMC-8, pp. 288-292.

Kao H.S.R., Van Galen G.P. & Hoosain R. (Eds.). (1986). *Graphonomics: Contemporary Research in handwriting*. North-Holland, Amsterdam.

Kruk R.S. & Muter P. (1984). Reading of continuous text on video screens. *Human Factors*, 26, pp. 339-345.

Lin W.C. & Pun J.H. (1978). Machine recognition and plotting of hand-sketched line figures. *IEEE Transactions on Systems, Man and Cybernetics*. SMC-8, pp. 52-57.

Lindgren N. (1965). Machine recognition of human language. Part III: Cursive script recognition. *IEEE Spectrum*, 2, pp. 104-116.

Maarse J.F., Schomaker L.R.B. & Teulings H.-L. (1988). Automatic identification of writers. In: *Human-Computer Interaction: Psychonomic Aspects*, G.C. van der Veer & G. Mulder (Eds.), Springer, Heidelberg.

Mermelstein P. & Eden M. (1964). Experiments or computer recognition of connected handwritten words. *Information and Control*, 7, pp. 225-270.

Morasso P. & Mussa Ivaldi F.A. (1982). Trajectory formation and handwriting: A computational model. *Biological Cybernetics*, 45, pp. 131-142.

National Research Council (1983). *Video displays, work and vision*. National Academy Press, Washington.

Padmos P., Pot F.D., Vos J.J. & De Vries-Mol, E.C. (1985). *Gezondheid en welbevinden bij het werken met beeldschermen 1: Report of a preliminary study*. Report 8412139. Ministerie van Sociale Zaken en Werkgelegenheid, The Hague.

Planmondon R. & Baron R. (1986). Handwritten interaction between a dedicated microcomputer and a software tool: System prototyping. *Journal of Microcomputer Applications*, 9. pp. 51-60.

Sayre K.M. (1973) Machine recognition of handwritten words: A project report. *Pattern Recognition*, 5, pp. 213-228.

Shneiderman B. (1983). Direct manipulation: A STEP beyond programming languages. *IEEE Transactions on computers*, 16, pp. 57-69.

Spanjersberg A.A. (1978). Experiments with automatic input of handwritten numeric data into a large administrative system. *IEEE Transactions on Systems, Man and Cybernetics.* SMC-8, pp. 286-288.

Suen C.Y., Berthold M. and Mori S. (1980). Automatic recognition of hand-printed characters - the state of the art. *IEEE Proceedings*, 68, pp. 468-487.

Suenaga Y. & Nagura M. (1980). A facsimile based manuscript layout and editing system by auxiliary mark recognition. *Proceedings of the 5th International Conference on Pattern Recognition, IEEE Computer Society*, pp. 856-858.

Tappert C.G. (1986). An adaptive system for handwriting recognition. In: *Graphonomics: Contemporary research in handwriting.* H.S.R. Kao, G.P. van Galen & R. Hoosain (Eds.), North-Holland, Amsterdam.

Teulings H.-L., Schomaker L.R.B. & Thomassen A.J.W.M. (1986). *Compatible software library for low-level processing of cursive script.* Esprit Report TK3-WP1-DI1.

Thomassen A.J.W.M., Keuss P.J.G. & Van Galen G.P. (Eds.). (1984). *Motor aspects of handwriting: Approaches to movement in graphic behavior.* North-Holland, Amsterdam.

Vredenbregt J. & Koster W.G. (1971). Analysis and synthesis of handwriting. In: *Philips Technical Review*, 32, pp. 73-78.

Chapter 21. Automatic Identification of Writers

Frans J. Maarse, Lambert R.B. Schomaker and Hans-Leo Teulings

1. Introduction

Using handwriting as a means of input to a computer has several advantages, currently not appreciated sufficiently. The use of pen (and paper) gives the user the opportunity of providing the computer with textual and graphic information in a "natural" fashion and it is expected that the keyboard will continue to be an obstacle for large-scale human-computer interaction. Equivalent arguments have been used by Zue (1985) for speech recognition, and speaker verification or recognition, but in spite of years of effort the performance of the available (commercial) speech recognition systems is still inferior to that of humans. Since the early 1960s efforts have been made towards computer recognition of handwriting. The disappointing results made it necessary to restrict the set of patterns to be recognized. Methods used in attempts to improve recognition results include limitation of the set of characters to be recognized (e.g., to digits; Impedovo, Marangelli, & Plantamura, 1976; Shridhar, & Badreldin, 1985), use of standard character types (Apsey, 1978), and imposition of spatial restrictions (Spanjersberg, 1978; Suen, 1979).

These methods may provide some results from the purely technical point of view, but the restrictions (e.g. writing within boxes or lines) proved to be unsatisfactory to users. Therefore, studies are being undertaken to develop methods that give the computer user the opportunity to use his personal cursive handwriting as a means of input without being disturbed by many restrictions on orientation, shape or vocabulary (Thomassen, Teulings, & Schomaker, 1987). Under these conditions, reduction of the recognition problem can only be achieved if the recognition system itself can reduce the set of patterns to be recognized. For instance, by estimation of an individual's handwriting parameter values the system can tune the recognition to a specific writer. Once the personal handwriting characteristics are known, they can be stored to enable the system to detect the identity of the user on later occasions. For each new user a description of his personal handwriting characteristics has to be added to the system, or the handwriting has to be classified as belonging to some general type of handwriting. Figure 1 shows the global flow chart of a handwriting recognition system with a writer-identification stage. In fact, the process of recognition is extended with an extra, less complicated recognition phase, the identification of the current writer, which facilitates the more complex phase of handwriting recognition itself.

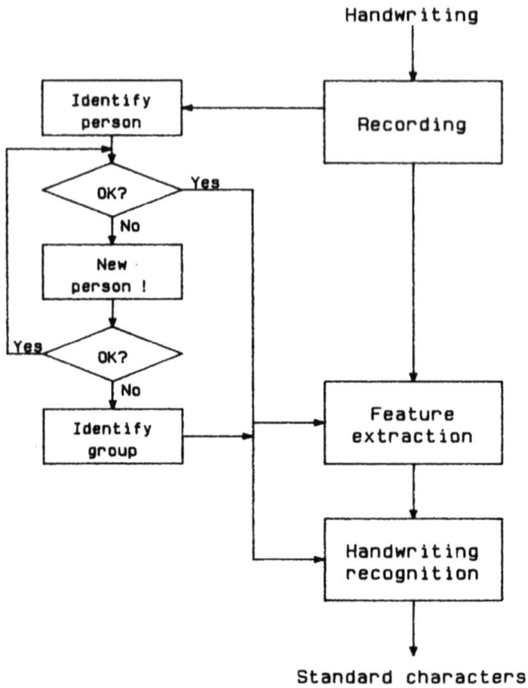

Figure 1. Flow diagram of a pattern recognition system for handwriting extended with a system for identification of the individual (left).

The left part of the figure shows the possible steps in identification of the individual. On the basis of the result of the identification, parameters are selected that apply to the given (type of) handwriting. Important individual characteristics of handwriting are cursive vs block print, handwriting slant, individual choice of letter and symbol shapes and their variants, relative size of handwriting constituents, time-dependent changes in stroke size within words, and pen speed. Figure 2 shows two examples of ambiguity in handwriting that could be solved if writer-dependent knowledge were available in the recognition system. In the first example, the first three letters are the same in both patterns, but the interpretation is determined by the fourth letter. If the recognition system knew that the user writes smaller at the end of a word than at the beginning it would recognize the word correctly. In the second example it is clear that in "normal" handwriting the word *clip* has to be read. If the recognition system uses the knowledge that the sample is produced by a writer who uses a large X progression, the pattern will be correctly recognized as *dip*. These examples indicate in what ways identification of individuals may be useful in handwriting recognition. Here we will concentrate on this identification stage. Central issues are the choice of handwriting material and methods of determining the values of relevant parameters.

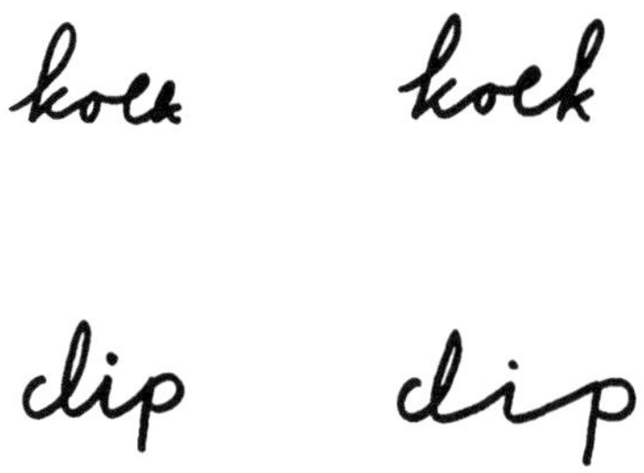

Figure 2. Some handwriting samples that are especially prone to cause errors in automatic handwriting recognition.

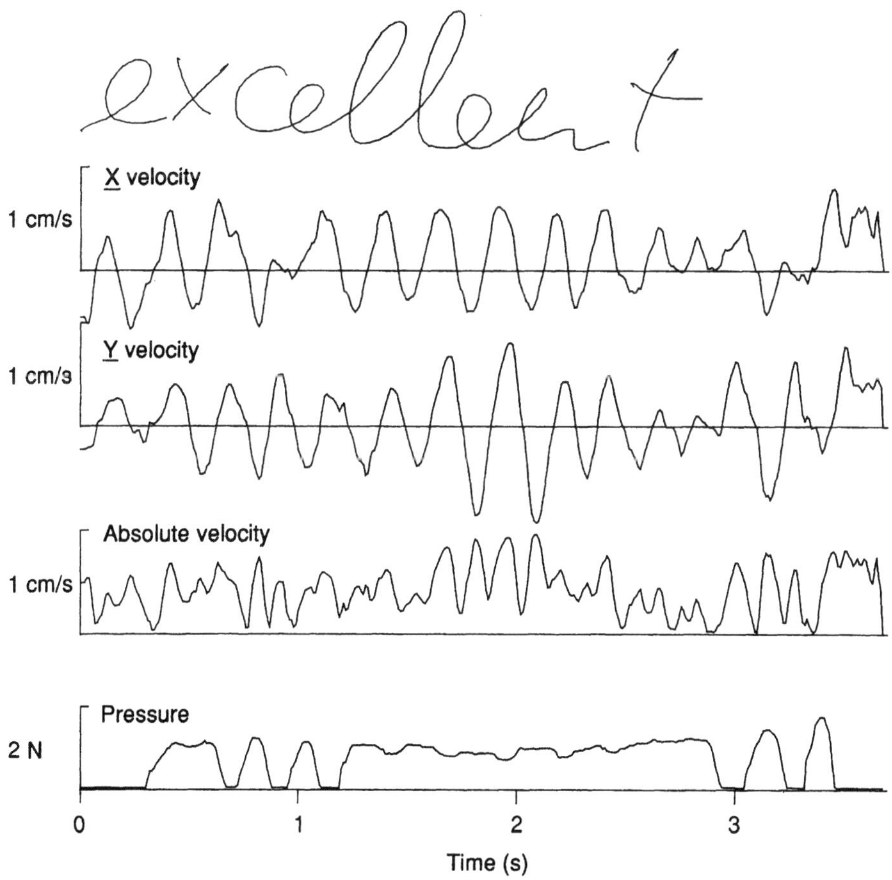

Figure 3. A handwriting sample with x and y velocities and pen pressure vs time, which are used in the determination of the personal handwriting characteristics.

In the literature on this subject, essentially three methods have been described. In the first method, a recording of a handwritten signature is used. Crane and Ostrem (1983) achieved 95%-99% correct classification in a group of 58 individuals, using 14 spatial and temporal parameters of the handwriting trace. Parameters used were stroke size, total writing time, etc. However, this method only works for users known to the system, and a disavantage is that the writer has first to identify himself. However, we are searching for a procedure whereby the system itself can recognize the user.

A second method, described by Azari (1977, 1983) and Duvernoy (1976), is based on pages of handwritten text. The parameters used here concern the layout, word length, and vertical spacing on a page. Recording is done by spatially digitizing a page of text within a field of about 1000 × 1000 pixels. This density is unfortunately not enough to obtain relevant information about the shapes and sizes of individual letters. Temporal information cannot be evaluated either. On the other hand, parameters that can be determined easily from spatially digitized pages are "ink" density and handwriting slant.

The third method uses findings from psychomotor research concerning movement grammars and trajectory formation (Thomassen et al., 1988; Dooijes, 1983). Typical findings are that some writers tend to reduce the size towards the end of a word, that there are specific relations between height, width, and slant (Maarse & Thomassen, 1983), and that handwriting is executed at a specific pace (Teulings & Maarse, 1984; Maarse, Schomaker & Thomassen, 1986). Figure 3 shows a typical sample of handwriting, recorded with a digitizer, together with the corresponding velocity and pen pressure time functions. As can be seen, spatial as well as temporal characteristics can be derived from such a recording. Findings from psychomotor research have indicated in what way the signals can be segmented. The psychomotor approach can be compared with the technical approach used in speaker identification and recognition (Doddington, 1985), where "low-level" dynamic acoustic features are used. These features include characteristics of the speech signals such as pitch frequency, spectral amplitudes, bandwidth, and characteristic voicing aperiodicities.

2. Experiment

In an experiment described in Maarse, Schomaker & Teulings (1986), we searched for specific parameters that could be used to identify subjects. We defined 13 parameters. From earlier handwriting studies, the most of these parameters were known to be relevant with respect to this type of psychomotor behavior:

T_r Relative writing duration: this is total pen-down duration divided by total writing duration

v Mean absolute pen velocity in pen-down segments

P Mean axial pen pressure

ϕ Handwriting slant, determined from the mean direction of long, downgoing strokes (Maarse & Thomassen, 1983)

Rnd A roundness measure: this is the mean length of the long up- and downstrokes divided by the mean length of the short strokes going from left to right and from left to right

Z_c Z transform of the Pearson coefficient of correlation between velocities in x and y directions

H_d Length of the descender loops, as in *j, g, y*

H_c Corpus height: this is the vertical size of letters such as *m, n, a*

H_a Length of the ascenders, as in *b, h, k, l*

W_x Width of letters, derived from the horizontal stroke size

dP Increase of pressure during words

dH Decrease of vertical stroke size during words

Twenty subjects produced eight lines of text each (a total of 160 lines). One-half of this material was used to calculate discriminant functions by means of the SPSS DISCRIMINANT program. The remaining 80 lines were entered in a test in which an attempt was made to identify the writer of a line on the basis of the discriminant functions obtained. Of the 80 lines, 77 were attributed to the correct writer. When the number of parameters was reduced to five, this figure increased to 79 out of 80. These five parameters were P, ϕ, v, W_x, and T_r. The reason for this increase is that estimation of some of the parameter values from a single line is unreliable.

3. Discussion

The automatic recognition of handwriting is still in its infancy. The method of writer identification and classification described in this paper may be a valuable tool in future recognition systems. On the basis of a limited amount of handwriting, the writer could be identified by the system, which could in turn select from a database the set of statistically reliable global parameter values for that person to tune the recognition system. If identification succeeded, a set of writer-specific letter descriptions could also be selected. The determination of the identity of the writer could be based on a minimum certainty of 95%. The results described here indicate that this probability can be reached fairly easily, although replication of the study is necessary.

It can be argued that successful automatic recognition of handwriting depends to a large extent on knowledge concerning the production mechanisms. Availability of the temporal information helps to disambiguate many segments of handwriting that are virtually impossible to recognize on the basis of spatial information only. In future handwriting recognition systems, however, it should be possible to infer some temporal characteristics from the spatial handwriting trace. Until then, more success is to be expected from handwriting recognition systems that make use of temporal or at least sequential information to be interpreted in terms of production mechanisms, and spatial information.

What is needed here is knowledge of handwriting production mechanisms (handwriting being a type of human motor behavior) and of handwriting grammar. Individual handwriting is chararacterized by idiosyncratic letter shapes, motor dynamics and degree of variability. Similarly, in speech recognition, knowledge of speech mechanisms is being used to improve speech recognition and speaker identification (see Leung, 1985).

Another potential application of the procedure is person identification by cursive script rather than by signature. The person could be asked to write some words or sentences randomly selected by the system, thus making forgery even more difficult than in identification systems based on signature. In this application, however, much higher reliability figures than 95% would be necessary. Improvement of the reliability of the identification procedure requires a search of parameters that are independent of rotation, size, and content. In speech recognition the "fixed-text" approach has been more successful then the "free-text" approach (Doddington, 1985). Which is more useful for handwriting recognition is a question that should be the subject of further studies.

It should be noted that several methods and techniques used in speech recognition are also suitable for handwriting recognition. In some respects, however, handwriting recognition is less complicated. For example, the lower storage requirements make the use of time-costly data compression techniques virtually unnecessary. In other respects, solving the problems of the handwriting recognition requires the development of specific methods from both signal-processing theory and artificial intelligence.

Successful use of handwriting recognition depends largely upon the ergonomics of the devices used for recording the handwriting. Before the digitizer can become a standard peripheral for computers, the shortcomings of the existing pens for them must be dealt with. Many of the commercially available pens are too large and thick, and often the pen tip cannot be seen by the user at all. Moreover, the cord connecting the tablet and pen is a nuisance, although this could be overcome by building a transmitter into the pen. A final problem to be solved is the spatial dissociation between the action on the tablet and the result on the CRT screen. The solution to this problem would be an integrated liquid-crystal flat panel with digitizer. Such a system would combine all the advantages of the writing pen and the mouse, and avoid the disadvantages of the mouse and the light pen (Thomassen et al., 1988).

References

Apsey R.S. (1978). Human factors of constraint handprint for OCR. *IEEE Transactions on Systems, Man and Cybernetics*, 8, pp. 292-296.

Azari B. (1977). Handwriting identification by means of run-lenght measurements. *IEEE Transactions on Systems, Man and Cybernetics*, 12, pp. 878-881.

Azari B. (1983). Automatic handwriting identification based on the external properties of the samples. *IEEE Transactions on Systems, Man and Cybernetics*, 12, pp. 878-881.

Crane H.D. & Ostrem J.S. (1983). Automatic signature verification using a three-axis force-sensitive pen. *IEEE Transactions on Systems, Man and Cybernetics*, 13, pp. 329-337.

Doddington G.R. (1985). Speaker recognition - Identifying people by their voices. *Proceedings of the IEEE*, 73, pp. 1651-1664.

Dooijes E.H. (1983). Analysis of handwriting movements. *Acta Psychologica*, 54, pp. 99 114.

Duvernoy J. (1976). Optical pattern recognition and clustering: Karhunen-Loeve analysis. *Applied Optics*, 15 pp. 1584-1590.

Impedovo S., Marangelli B. & Plantamura V.L. (1976). Real-time recognition of handwritten numerals. *IEEE Transactions on Sytsems, Man and Cybernetics*, 6, pp. 145-148.

Leung H.C. (1985). *A procedure for automatic alignment of phonetic transcriptions with continuous speech*. Thesis, MIT, Cambridge, MA.

Maarse F.J. & Thomassen A.J.W.M. (1983). Produced and perceived writing slant: Differences between up and down strokes. *Acta Psychologica*, 54, pp. 131-147.

Maarse F.J., Schomaker L.R.B. & Teulings H.-L. (1986). Kenmerkende verschillen in individueel schrijfgedrag: Automatische identificatie van schrijvers. *Nederlands tijdschrift voor de psychologie*, 41, pp. 41-47.

Maarse F.J., Schomaker L.R.B. & Thomassen A.J.W.M. (1986). The influence of changes in the effector coordinate systems on handwriting movements. In: *Graphonomics: Contemporary research in handwriting.* H.S.R. Kao, G.P. van Galen, & R. Hoosain (Eds.). North-Holland, Amsterdam. pp. 33-46.

Shridhar M., & Badreldin A. (1985). A high-accuracy syntactic recognition algorithm for handwriting numerals. *IEEE Transactions on Systems, Man and Cybernetics,* 15, pp. 152-158.

Spanjersberg A.A. (1978). Experiments with automatic input of handwritten numerical data into a large administrative system. *IEEE Transactions on Systems, Man and Cybernetics,* 8, pp. 286-288.

Suen C.Y. (1979). A study on man-machine interaction problems in character recognition. *IEEE Transactions on Systems, Man and Cybernetics,* 9, pp. 732-736.

Teulings H.-L. & Maarse, F.J. (1984). Digital recording and processing of handwriting movements. *Human Movement Science,* 3, pp. 193-217.

Thomassen A.J.W.M., Teulings H.-L, & Schomaker L.R.B. (1988). Real-time processing of cursive writing and sketched graphics. In: *Human-Computer Interactions: Psychonomic Aspects.* G.C.v.d.Veer & G.Mulder (Eds.). Springer-Verlag, Heidelberg.

Zue V.W. (1985). The use of speech knowledge in automatic speech recognition. *Proceedings of the IEEE,* 73, pp. 1602-1615.

Chapter 22. The Use of Speech in Man-Machine Interaction

Louis C.W. Pols

1. Introduction

Speech plays an important role in communication between people. This natural and direct way of communication would also be a desirable form of interaction between man and machine. However, at present the technical possibilities are limited, especially with respect to speech input, and it is doubtful whether it is useful to introduce the present systems with their limited vocabulary and poor performance. With present-day knowledge it is possible to realize subsystems for specific applications. Speech input/output (I/O) computer facilities should be compared with other interfaces like the alphanumeric keyboard, function keys, monitor, mouse, light pen, graphic tablet, touchscreen, joystick, and trackball. Speech should not just replace another interface which itself already functions quite well, but should add something. A great advantage of speech is that almost everybody knows spoken language, and therefore no training is required, although most man-machine conversations do require strict protocols. Most speech I/O applications somehow belong to a category in which the hands and/or eyes are already busy with other jobs (Nye, 1980). Market prognoses with respect to speech technology so far have been too optimistic regarding speech synthesis and speech recognition, although speech coding for speech storage and forwarding applications currently getting much attention. Several speech technology companies did not survive the early period of development, initial applications, and limited success, although in each case other companies have taken over their position (Lea, 1980b). Furthermore, several large organizations like IBM, CMU, and AT&T Bell have long-term speech research programs. The use of speech technology in science-fiction stories has created the belief that most problems are already solved, despite the fact that many scientific, technical, and ergonomic problems still exist. Because of the general theme of this book, with its special emphasis on psychonomic aspects, I will mainly discuss ergonomic, evaluative, and technical aspects. Relevant references will be given at appropriate places for those interested in more details.

2. Areas of Application for Speech I/O

Before describing in the following sections aspects of speech input, storage, and output in greater detail, in this section I will give a short survey of the main areas of application for speech I/O (Sciences & Techniques, 1984):

1. *Industry (and defense)* (*Beek & Vonusa*, 1983). Most industrial applications are in the field of "command, control, and communication." Specific examples include computer-aided design and manufacture (CAD/CAM), spoken messages like alarms, and spoken input for quality control at production lines.
2. *Office systems.* In the office of the future there will probably be advanced workstations in which speech interfaces will have a prominent position (SPIN, 1984).
3. *Aids for the handicapped.* In my opinion, there are two major fields of applications in this area, one being communication aids, and the other being voice-controlled equipment like wheelchairs, home and hospital appliances, control functions in cars, and professional aids like voice-controlled text editors and speaking desk calculators (Soede, 1985).
4. *Education.* In this area applications include interactive dialogue systems for programmed learning, although dialogue systems themselves have a much wider range of uses, such as expert systems for medical diagnoses. Much simpler speech facilities for educational purposes include devices such as "Speak & Spell", the very first commercial product with the Texas Instruments speech chip (Frantz & Wiggins, 1982).
5. *Consumer products.* This is a potentially very large area of applications. Various examples of "speaking products" already exist, such as in car dashboards, ovens, clocks, elevators, and cameras, but this is not the place to discuss the usefulness of such applications. With the availability of a telephone in almost any home, virtually unlimited application areas become available, such as banking, ordering products from mail-order companies, or getting information about airplane or train departures over the telephone.

3. Aspects of Speech Communication

The problems of speech I/O in man-machine interactions can only be understood if one realizes that this type of interaction is part of the much larger area of speech communication. Below I will give a short overview of the technical aspects of speech communication, excluding fields like psychoacoustics, speech and hearing disorders, or linguistics.

a. *Telecommunication.* This usually implies a natural speaker, a channel like radio, telephone, telegraph, or television, and a listener. Distortions can be introduced at the transmitting or receiving ends (background noise, reverberation, competing sounds) or in the channel. In the digital telephone a waveform coder and decoder (codecs) are used. This allows digital transmission, which is less error sensitive. It also permits scrambling and introduces possibilities like digital mobile telephones.

b. *Speech Coding and Speech Storage.* Speech coding (Flanagan et al., 1979) for efficient transmission implies analysis and resynthesis of a spoken text by applying more or less sophisticated techniques of waveform coding at specific bit rates. The bit stream can be transmitted and/or temporarily stored, as in voice mail. Some of the many waveform coding techniques are pulse code modulation (PCM), delta modulation (DM), and adaptive differential pulse code modulation (ADPCM). Hardware realizations of various types of coders are presently available or under development.

c. *Speech Synthesis.* If the waveform is not coded, but some form of parametric coding is used, we talk about speech synthesis. Such types of coding make use of the fact that the acoustic signal is a speech signal, for instance by performing voiced or unvoiced silence detection and pitch extraction. Some of the many possibilities are linear predictive coding (LPC), formant coding, and the use of bandfilters (channel vocoder, Gold, Blankenship, & McAulay, 1981). A bit rate of 2.4 kb/s is an achievable goal in this area. Medium band coders like subband coding (SBC), time domain harmonic scaling (TDHS), or multipulse LPC take an intermediate position, both in terms of bit rate and in terms of using speech knowledge. Parametric speech synthesis is also the basis of text-to-speech synthesis by rule. Here, the parameters are not derived by analyzing the spoken text, but are generated using rules on the basis of a graphemic input. The parametric representation can partly be achieved by concatenating phonemelike units like allophones, or syllable-sized units like diphones or demisyllables. Various speech chips are available which can be controlled by LPC-based or formant-based parameters. Complete text-to-speech synthesis systems have been developed for various languages. A well-known one for American English with a very high speech quality was MITalk (Allen, Hunnicutt, Carlson, & Granström, 1979), now commercially available as DECtalk (Klatt, 1982; Gutcho, 1985). This is also the only system that can generate speech with several different voices. The most highly developed system for Dutch is a diphone-based system (Elsendoorn, 1984). For the time being this system works with a quasiphonemic input, but the duration rules need further development. In December 1985 a national research program was started in the Netherlands to improve this and another (allophone-based) system at the various levels involved, like grapheme-to-phoneme conversion, stress assignment, intonation rules, context dependency and temporal organization, lexicon, syntactic and semantic rules, basic units, parametric analysis and coding, speaker dependency, intelligibility and quality evaluation, and hardware realization. This ambitious research program is sponsored by SPIN, a government program stimulating research in information technology. For a natural dialogue it is not sufficient to be able to generate speech from text;

text generation from a "concept" is also required, as well as speech understanding (Kempen, Konst, & De Smedt, 1984).

d. *Speech Recognition.* In this area one can differentiate various levels of complexity, from recognizing a few known words from one known speaker to understanding unrestricted conversation. For many years it has been possible to recognize a small set of words from a known speaker by using a training procedure and some form of template matching, generally preceded by nonlinear time normalization (Dixon & Martin, 1979). Every new speaker requires training in order to achieve a reference set of words. This approach is not feasible for vocabularies of, say, more than 100 words, where segmentation and labeling are required. These segments can have the form of acoustic segments, or phonemelike or diphonelike units. Nowadays a popular approach is the use of hidden Markov chains (Bridle, 1984). For a limited vocabulary of connected words, like telephone numbers, storehouse codes, or ZIP codes, dynamic time warping (nonlinear time normalization) and template matching still appears to be a successful approach (Bridle, Brown & Chamberlain, 1982). IBM recently demonstrated a system for the recognition of 5000 words using the hidden Markov model on centisecond segments with phonemelike labels (Jelinek et al., 1985). The firm Kurzweil has promised a similar 15,000-word system relatively soon. MIT aims at recognizing vocabularies of up to 20,000 words by first assigning global features to word segments, which allows for a substantial reduction in word candidates (Huttenlocher & Zue, 1984). Several speech recognition systems with vocabularies of about 1000 words have been developed in an ARPA-sponsored research program (ARPA is a well known network of computer-systems in the USA). In 1976, at the end of that five-year program, only HARPY met the requirements (Klatt, 1977; Lea and Shoup, 1980; Lowerre & Reddy, 1980). Meanwhile, several other approaches, like LAFS (lexical access from spectra: Klatt, 1986), and SERAC, a system using a "society of experts" all generating and verifying phonetic hypotheses (De Mori, Laface, & Mong 1985), have been described. Up to now no commercially available speech recognition system exists.

e. *Speaker Recognition and Verification.* The verification of a person's identity by his voice (Dupeyrat, Tual, & Vanuexem, 1984; Strube, Helling, Krause, & Schroeder 1985) is a potentially very useful application, especially if for instance conducting banking transactions by telephone should become common. Speaker verification is already used incidentally for admission to secure access premises. Voice characteristics are also sometimes used in court, although the so-called voiceprints must be considered scientifically doubtful.

f. *Miscellaneous* Aspects of speech recognition are also used in somewhat less common applications like speech monitoring (scanning various communication channels for incidental speech messages), language recognition, keyword spotting (the keyword can for instance be the name of a station or an important politician), in a phonemic vocoder (very low bit rate speech coding implying phonemelike recognition), and emotion detection, including stress detectors and the very unreliable lie detectors.

4. Evaluation of Speech I/O in Man-Machine Interaction

4.1. Speech Coders

High quality speech can be achieved using various coding techniques at 64 kb/s, the norm set by CCITT, the standardization committee of PTTs. However, for speech storage applications, like in advanced workstations, this bit rate is rather high. In the digital telephone the aim is a bit rate of 16 kb/s, whereas for temporary storage 9.6 kb/s seems to be an achievable goal. This will not be possible without some loss of quality, and certain voices will probably turn out to be "difficult voices" for such systems. Therefore, intelligibility and quality evaluation under various conditions and for several voices is indispensable. A mean opinion score (MOS) on a five-point scale from bad to excellent is frequently used (Goodman & Nash, 1982). This is a quick, but not very accurate, procedure. Paired-comparison tests are generally considered more sensitive, but take substantially more time. For intelligibility testing, lists of phonetically balanced (PB) CVC (consonant-vowel-consonant) words (logatoms) can be used, or for instance the diagnostic rhyme test (Voiers, 1982). Steeneken (1982) has developed a Dutch version of the latter test. Although the intelligibility is generally fairly high for speech coders, it can drop appreciably in a noisy environment. Within the framework of an Esprit-sponsored project called SPIN (Speech Interface at Office Workstation), in which I also participate, a quality and intelligibility evaluation will be performed for several types of speech coders (Pols & Boxelaar, 1986; Boxelaar & Pols, 1985). In this evaluation we will also study speaker identifiability on the basis of smaller or larger amounts of coded speech. Another partner in this project will evaluate the ergonomic aspects of speech I/O, including storage, in an advanced office workstation developed by Nixdorf.

4.2. Speech Output

The speech quality of systems for text-to-speech synthesis by rules is not yet very good and so far always has a machinelike sound. However, the intelligibility itself can be rather high, as is apparent from several tests at the segment or phoneme level. The initial- and final-consonant intelligibility of a rule synthesis system using dyads (somewhat similar to diphones), developed by Olive (1980), was 83% correct in CVC test words with an open response set (Pols & Olive, 1983). Recently Logan, Pisono, & Greene (1985) measured the initial- and final-consonant intelligibility for eight different text-to-speech systems, including one male and one female voice of DECtalk, the English version of the Swedish multilingual Infovox, and some rather simple systems like Votrax Type'n'Talk and Street Electronics Echo. They used the modified rhyme test (MRT) with six alternatives (House, Williams, Hecker, & Krijter, 1965), but also ran an experiment with an open response version. The average consonant error in the closed set was 0.53% for natural speech, 3.25% for the male voice (Paul) of DECtalk, 5.72% for the female voice (Betty), 27.4% for Votrax, and 35.6% for Echo. Five systems were also tested with the open format; the word error rate was then at least three times higher than for the closed format. The closed response MRT is an efficient test procedure and requires hardly any training from the subjects, however, not all consonants are tested with equal frequency of occurrence and, more seriously, the six alternatives restrict the responses to a subset which is not always representative of the peculiarities of a specific synthesis system. For instance, for the dyad system the most frequent error for an initial *b* was a *v* response (Pols & Olive, 1983), however, out of the 14 (out of 50) times that *b* occurred in the initial position in a block of six words, *v* is present only once as a possible response in the six alternatives (Nye & Gaitenby, 1973). We believe that CVC word lists with open responses give a better indication of the intelligibility at a phoneme level. However, it is clear that it is not sufficient to test a rule-synthesis system at this level only. One should at least evaluate the system at word and sentence level as well, in order to test multisyllabic words, stress assignment, prosodic rules, and so on. Beyond that, one would like to know, among other things, if there is an extra memory load with synthetic speech, whether comprehension is reduced, what the effect is of training, and whether one can listen to synthetic speech for long periods of time. D.B. Pisoni's research group at Indiana University has also gained much experience in these types of testing (Manous, Pisoni, Dideni, & Nusbaum, 1985; Pisoni, 1982; Schwab, Nusbaum, & Pisoni, 1983; Luce, Feustel, & Pisoni, 1983; for a literature survey, see Boxelaar & Pols, 1985). As part of the earlier mentioned Esprit project SPIN, we will evaluate the quality and intelligibility of a French, an Italian, and possibly a German rule-synthesis system, all three of them presently being under development (Pols & Boxelaar, 1986). Also, in the SPIN research program on analysis and synthesis of speech, special attention will be devoted to the evaluation of the two Dutch rule-synthesis systems which are to be improved and extended over the next few years. In a seminar on speech synthesis and speech recognition, recently organized by World Trade Center Electronics in Eindhoven, Buiting (1985) discussed the ergonomic aspects of speech synthesis systems. He emphasized the unique properties of speech for information exchange between user and system, but warned against misuse of speech when equivalent, or better, alternatives are available.

4.3. Speech Input

There is a great need for standardization in evaluating speech recognition systems. As far as commercial systems are concerned this means in practice a limitation to isolated- and connected-word recognition systems. The problem is that one frequently tries to compare almost incomparable scores. What should be done, for instance, with a 0.5% error score for tape-recorded isolated digits from one French speaker if one would like to know whether that system would be useful for 10 to 50 English words from a number of different speakers spoken directly into the microphone in a noisy environment? A field test could give the answer, but every new vocabulary or environment would require a new test. There are some possibilities for solving these problems. One practical solution would be to agree upon a limited set of tape-recorded test vocabularies from a number of speakers in a number of languages of various vocabulary sizes and complexities. Any new system then could be tested with these vocabularies by an independent organization. For actual applications it could then be possible to extrapolate the test results to the specific application intended. Various organizations like the American National Bureau of Standards (Pallett, 1982), the British Speech Technology Assessment Group, the French coordinated research group GRECO, the NATO research study group RSG-10 on Speech Processing, the European organization COST, and the IEEE Standards Working Group on Speech I/O (Baker, 1982) are all involved in some way in compiling speech databases for evaluating speech recognition systems (Baker, Pallett, & Bridel, 1983). On top of that, several laboratories have their own database for testing word recognizers (Doddington & Schalk, 1981). Pols (1982) studied the human performance on a connected-digits database which was also used to evaluate various hardware systems (Bridle et al., 1983). Chollet and Gagnoulet (1982) suggested comparing the performance of a specific system with a reference recognition system. Another way to evaluate speech recognition systems is to apply a more basic approach, like the human equivalent noise reference (HENR) method (Moore, 1977). With this method the difficulty of any specified vocabulary is estimated, based on the confusions made by human listeners at various signal-to-noise ratios. Curves for standard vocabularies, like digits, spelled alphabet, and military alphabet, can then be used to calibrate the performance of an automatic speech recognition system by finding that signal-to-noise ratio at which human performance is equal to system performance. Makino and Wakita (1984) described a method to calculate the similarity between word pairs in a vocabulary on the basis of their phonemic representation. Taylor (1981) has described two methods to derive a particular figure of merit, called effective vocabulary capability (EVC), which is based on the internal confusions between the words in the vocabulary. Woodard and Nelson (1982) suggested an information theoretic approach using the relative information loss (RIL). In the English Alvey program on information technology (Holmes, 1985) there is a strong speech component, mainly in the area of man-machine interfaces. In that area, suggestions have been made to develop evaluation methods for automatic speech recognition systems. A third form of evaluation is to set the requirements beforehand and to test which system meets those requirements at the end of the project. This was the approach taken by the ARPA Speech Understanding Project. The goal was "to accept continuous speech, from many cooperative speakers, in a quiet room, with a good quality microphone, with slight adjustment for each speaker, accepting 1000 words, using an artificial syntax, yielding less than 10% semantic error, in a few times real time." As said before, only HARPY met that goal (Lea, 1980b).

5. Conclusions

Hopefully it has become clear from the preceding sections that speech and language technology (ZWO, 1984) can play an important role in man-machine interaction. A spoken dialogue is a very natural way of interacting. Signal processing, phonetic and linguistic sciences, and information technology have contributed towards achieving such a spoken interaction. There have been substantial improvements in the last 20 years, but the process of a spoken dialogue remains a very complex matter in itself, and much more fundamental and applied research is required before a natural spoken conversation between man and machine is possible. With the present emphasis on speech technology the psychonomic and ergonomic aspects should not be neglected since the human user is always on one end of the communication chain.

References

Allen J., Hunnicutt S., Carlson R. & Granström, B. (1979). MITalk- 79: The 1979 MIT text-to-speech system. In: *ASA-50 Speech Communication Papers*, J.J. Wolf and D.H. Klatt (Eds.), Acoustical Society of America, New York, NY. pp. 507-510.

Baker J. (Chairman) (1982). *Guidelines for performance assessment of speech recognizers.* IEEE Standards Working Group on Speech I/O.

Baker J.M., Pallett D.S. & Bridle J.S. (1983). Speech recognition performance assessments and available data bases. *Proceedings of the IEEE*, ICASSP83, pp. 527-530.

Beek B. & Vonusa R.S. (1983). General review of military applications of voice processing. *Speech Processing*, AGARD Lecture Series No. 129, NATO (North Atlantic Treaty Organization), pp. 1.1-1.20.

Boxelaar G.W. & Pols L.C.W. (1985). *State-of-the-art report about intelligibility evaluation of speech coding and text-to-speech synthesis systems.* IFA Report 79.

Bridle J.S. (1984). Stochastic models and template matching: Some important relationships between two apparently different techniques for automatic speech recognition. *Proceedings of the Institute of Acoustics*, 6 (4).

Bridle J.S., Brown M.D. & Chamberlain R.M. (1982). An algorithm for connected word recognition. *Proceedings of the IEEE* ICASSP82, pp. 899-902.

Bridle J.S. et al. (1983). *Connected word recognition for use in military systems.* AC/243 (Panel III/RSG10) Project One Report.

Buiting H. (1985). *Ergonomie van spraaksynthese systemen.* (Written version of paper given at Seminar Spraaksynthese en Spraakherkenning, Eindhoven).

Chollet G. & Gagnoulet B.P. (1982). On the evaluation of speech recognizers using a reference system. *Proceedings of the IEEE*, ICASSP82, pp. 2026-2029.

De Mori R., Laface P. & Mong Y. (1985). Parallel algorithms for syllable recognition in continuous speech. *IEEE Transactions on PAMI 17*, pp. 56-69.

Dixon N.R. & Martin T.B. (Eds.) (1979). *Automatic speech and speaker recognition*, IEEE Press.

Doddington G.R. & Schalk T.B. (1981). Speech recognition: turning theory to practice. *IEEE Spectrum*, 18, pp. 26-32.

Dupeyrat B., Tual D. & Vanuxem P. (1984). *Automatic speaker verification: A state of the art*, (Interim Report 1 of Esprit Project 64).

Elsendoorn B. (1984). Heading for a diphone speech synthesis system for Dutch, *IPO Annual Progress Report*, 19, pp. 32-35.

Flanagan J.L., Schroeder M.R., Atal B.S., Crochiere R.E., Jayant N.S. & Tribolet J.M. (1979). Speech coding, *IEEE Transactions or COM*, 27, pp. 710-737.

Frantz G.A. & Wiggins R.H. (1982). Design case history: Speak & Spell learns to talk. *IEEE Spectrum* 19, pp. 45-49.

Gold B., Blankenship P.E. & McAulay R.J. (1981). New applications of channel vocoders. *IEEE Transactions on ASSP*, 29, pp. 13-23.

Goodman D.J. & Nash R.D. (1982). Subjective quality of the same speech transmission conditions in seven different countries. *IEEE Transactions on COM*, 30, pp. 642-654.

Gutcho L. (1985). DECtalk - A year later. *Speech Technologie*, 3, pp. 98-102.

Holmes J.N. (1985). Speech technology in the U.K. Alvey Program. *Speech Technology*, 3, pp. 44-47.

House A.S., Williams C.E., Hecker M.H.L. & Kryter K.D. (1965). Articulation-testing methods: Consonantal differentiation with a closed-response set. *Journal of the Acoustical Society of America*. 37, pp. 158-166.

Huttenlocher D.P. & Zue V.W. (1984). A model of lexical access from partial phonetic information. *Proceedings of the IEEE*, ICASSP84, pp. 26.4.1-26.4.4.

Jelinek F. & IBM Speech Recognition Group (1985). A real-time, isolated-word, speech recognition system for dictation transcription. *Proceedings of the IEEE* ICASSP85, pp. 23.5.1-23.5.4.

Kempen G., Konst L. & DeSmedt K. (1984). Taaltechnologie voor het Nederlands. Vorderingen bij de bouw van een Nederlandstalig dialoog- en auteursysteem. *Informatie*, 26, pp. 878-881.

Klatt D.H. (1977). Review of the ARPA speech understanding project. *Journal of the Acoustical Society of America*, 62, pp. 1345-1366.

Klatt D.H. (1982). The Klattalk text-to-speech conversion system. *Proceedings of the IEEE*, ICASSP82, pp. 1589-1592.

Klatt D.H. (1986). The problem of variability in speech recognition and in models of speech perception. In: *Invariance andvariebility of speech processes*, J.S. Perkell & D.H. Klatt, (Eds.), Lawrence Erlbaum, Hillsdale, pp. 300-319.

Lea W.A. (Ed.) (1980a). *Trends in speech recognition.* Prentice Hall, Englewood Cliffs, NJ.

Lea W.A. (1980b). Speech recognition: Past, present, and future. In: *Trend in speech recognition*, W.A. Lea (Ed.), Prentice Hall, Englewood Cliffs, NJ., pp. 39-98.

Lea W.A. & Shoup J.E. (1980). Specific contributions of the ARPA SUR project. In: *Trends in speech recognition*, W.A. Lea (Ed.), Prentice Hall, Englewood Cliffs, NJ., pp. 382-421.

Logan J.S., Pisoni D.B. & Greene B.G. (1985). Measuring the segmental intelligibility of synthetic speech: Results from eight text-to-speech systems. *Research on Speech Perception Progress Report* 11, pp. 3-31.

Lowerre B. & Reddy R. (1980). The Harpy speech understanding system. In: *Trends in speech recognition*, W.A Lea (Ed.), Prentice Hall, Englewood Cliffs, NJ, pp. 340-360.

Luce P.A., Feustel T.C. & Pisoni D.B. (1983). Capacity demands in short-term memory for synthetic and natural speech. *Human Factors*, 25, pp. 17-32.

Makino S. & Wakita H. (1984). Lexical analysis for word recognition based on phoneme-pair differences. *Journal of Acoustical Society of America*, 76, Suppl. 1, S89 (A).

Manous L.M., Pisoni D.B., Dedina M.J. & Nusbaum H.C. (1985). Comprehension of natural and synthetic speech using a sentence verification task. *Research on Speech Perception Progress Report* 11, pp. 33-57.

Moore R.K. (1977). Evaluating speech recognizers. *IEEE Transaction on ASSP*, 2, pp. 178-183.

Nye J.M. (1980). The expanding market for commercial speech recognizers. In: *Trends in speech recognition*, W.A. Lea (Ed.), Prentice Hall, Englewood Cliff, NJ. pp. 461-468.

Nye P.W. & Gaitenby J.H. (1973). Consonant intelligibility in synthetic speech and in a natural speech control (Modified rhyme test results). *Haskins SR* 33, pp. 77-91.

Olive J. (1980). A scheme for concatenating units for speech synthesis. *Proceedings of the IEEE* ICASSP80, pp. 568-571.

Pallett D.S. (Ed.) (1982). *Proceedings of the National Bureau of Standards Speech I/O Workshop*. D.S. Pallett (Ed.).

Pisoni D.B. (1982). Perception of speech: The human listener as a cognitive interface. *Speech Technology*, 1, p. 10-23.

Pols L.C.W. (1982). How humans perform on a connected-digits data base. *Proceedings of the IEEE* ICASSP82, pp. 867-870.

Pols L.C.W. & Boxelaar G.W. (1986). Comparative evaluation of the speech quality of speech coders and text-to-speech synthesizers. *Proceedings of the IEEE* ICASSP86, pp. 901-904.

Pols L.C.W. & Olive J.P. (1983). Intelligibility of consonants in CVC utterances produced by dyadic rule synthesis. *Speech Communication*, 2, pp. 3-13.

Schwab E.C., Nusbaum H.C. & Pisoni D.B. (1983). Some effects of training on the perception of synthetic speech. *Research on Speech Perception Progress Report* 9, pp. 39-77.

Sciences & Techniques (1984). *L'ordinateur prend la parole. Reconnaissance et synthese vocales.* Numero 2, Hors serie.

Soede M. (1985). *Ergonomische aspecten van spraak in- en uitvoer bij hulpmiddelen voor gehandicapten.* (Written version of paper given at Seminar Spraaksynthese en Spraakherkenning, Eindhoven.

SPIN (1984). *Speech interface at office workstation*, Technical appendix to Esprit project 64.

Steeneken H.J.M. (1982). *Ontwikkeling en toetsing van een Nederlandstalige diagnostische rijmtest voor het testen van spraakkommunikatiekanalen. IZF-report 1982-13.*

Strube H.W., Helling D., Krause A. & Schroeder M.R. (1985). Word and speaker recognition based on entire words without framewise analysis. In: *Speech and speaker recognition*, M.R. Schroeder (ed), Bibliotheca Phonetica 12, Karger, Basel. pp. 80-114.

Taylor M.M. (1981). *Issues in the evaluation of speech recognitionsystems.* DC IEM draft paper.

Voiers W.D. (1982). Measurement of intrinsic deficiency in transmitted speech. The diagnostic discrimination test. *Proceedings of the IEEE*, ICASSP82, pp. 1004-1007.

Woodard J.P. & Nelson J.T. (1982). An information theoretic measure of speech recognition performance. *Proceedings of the National Bureau of Standards Speech I/O Standardization Workshop.* D.S. Pallett (Ed.).

ZWO (1984). *Taal- en Spraaktechnologie in Nederland*, ZWO-report.

Searching for Information in Information Systems

Chapter 23. Search Strategies in Internal and External Memories

Jos Beishuizen

1. Introduction

Should the structure of external databases correspond to the structure of long term memory? This question is relevant to human factor specialists engaged in the design of user friendly information retrieval systems. The question presupposes agreement on the assumption that external cognitive acts are performed in the same way as analogous internal mental acts. This assumption is not new and might be considered as the opposite of the internalization hypothesis set forth by, for example, Vygotsky (1978) and Piaget (1953). The internalization hypothesis holds that intelligence as such is the product of perceptual-motor activities of the young child. Manipulations of concrete objects are internalized and integrated into the individual's mental equipment to deal with the environment.

However, two a priori objections can be raised against the hypothesis that a retrieval system paralleling human long term memory enables efficient information retrieval. First, human memory search is not necessarily the most efficient way of retrieving information. Loftus and Fathi (1985) showed that personal events are usually remembered in forward order (i.e., in chronological order), although a backward reconstruction (i.e., starting with the most recent event) produces a higher recall score. Here the natural order of reproduction does not seem to be the most efficient approach. Secondly, human memory is equipped with a visual mode of representing data. Visual information plays an important role in remembering and is even used in several mnemonic techniques for improving recall. Up until now, however, visual data and search facilities have not been available in common information retrieval systems. Based on these two objections the conclusion that external databases should reflect the organization of long-term memory does not seen warranted.

Rejection of the correspondence assumption does not imply that designers of information retrieval systems should ignore research on long-term memory. In this paper we will try to deduce guidelines for the design of external databases, based on memory research, the study of human problem problem solving, and on our own data.

2. Research on (Very) Long Term Memory

Recent attempts to reveal the structure of (very) long term memory have been realized with the help of two different research methods: (1) the study of the "natural" use of long-term memory, and (2) testing models of human memory by computer simulation. Norman and Bobrow's (1979) model of long-term memory search resulted from experiments based on the former research line. However, the model was also adopted in simulation studies following the latter research strategy (e.g., Kolodner, 1983). Although Norman and Bobrow's (1979) model of the kernel retrieval cycle was not very precise or even original, it served as a source of inspiration for research on (very) long-term memory. Even in our own work on search strategies in external memories the model proved to be a useful starting point. For this reason Norman and Bobrow's model will be explained, together with a short description of some aspects of Kolodner's CYRUS system as far as they seem relevant to the issue of this paper.

2.1. Norman and Bobrow's Kernel Retrieval Cycle

Norman and Bobrow (1979) studied the way people remember events stored in their personal memory, such as the names of classmates or teachers from high school. This type of remembering always involves a process of reconstruction of the original event (Bartlett, 1932). During searching a vague description of the event to be retrieved becomes clearer and more complete until finally the information is recaptured in memory. In this process three stages can be distinguished:

1. *Construction of a retrieval specification.* A retrieval specification has to be built which serves as a basis for the selection of memory elements and as a criterion for the evaluation of the relevance of the selected memory elements. The chances of finding the facts sought, partly depend on the discriminability of the retrieval specification, i.e., the degree to which relevant and irrelevant information can adequately be discriminated using the retrieval specification
2. *Selection of memory elements.* Memory elements differ with regard to the ease with which they can be recognized during information retrieval. The "deeper" a memory element has been processed (Craik and Lockhart, 1972), the more cues for the element are available and the easier it will be recognized
3. *Evaluation of memory elements.* Selected elements are checked for the presence of the information to be retrieved using the verification criteria of the retrieval specification. If the desired information is not available the retrieval specification must be updated and extended, thereby increasing its discriminability.

The three stages can be identified within one cycle of the kernel retrieval process. Usually several cycles will be needed for a complete reconstruction of an event. Norman and Bobrow assume that a retrieval process comprises an iteration of several kernel retrieval cycles.

2.2. Kolodner's CYRUS Model

Together with the somewhat older EPAM models (Feigenbaum & Simon, 1984), the development of CYRUS means a major step forward in our understanding of human information retrieval. CYRUS has been developed to test a theory on the organization of long-term memory. The theory has been implemented in an intelligent fact retrieval system. This system uses data describing the political careers of two former U.S. Secretaries of State, Cyrus Vance and Edmund Muskie. CYRUS has been based on the notion of scripts as the basic units of long term memory (Schank & Abelson, 1977). Scripts guide the generation of hypotheses during the interpretation of incoming information. The elements in CYRUS are called E-MOPs, episodic memory organization packets. An E-MOP is a description of individual events and may contain other E-MOPs. Each E-MOP contains general information pertaining to all events or E-MOPs within itself. For instance, within the E-MOP *diplomatic meetings* this content frame of general information explains who the regular chairman of these meetings is (in the case of the CYRUS retrieval system, the former Secretary of State Cyrus Vance), who the participants in diplomatic meetings are, and which topics are negotiated. All events and E-MOPs within an E-MOP share the general information. However, the characteristics by which they can be differentiated are also available in the form of indices leading to an individual event or to an E-MOP. These indices need to be specified in order to address an individual event or E-MOP. For instance, the E-MOP *diplomatic meetings* contains an index *Begin* giving access to a particular event and an index *Camp David Accords* leading to the same event: a diplomatic meeting between Vance and Begin about the Camp David Accords. This example shows that any event may be accessible via more than one index. In CYRUS an E-MOP can be addressed via 10 indices on average. CYRUS is called a locked conceptual framework because an event can be "unlocked" if and only if an index to that event has been specified. If an index leads to a set of events organized in an E-MOP, then within that E-MOP a new index must be specified in order to continue the search process. Generation of indices and accessing new E-MOPs proceeds until a single event is found. This model forbids the retrieval of events by the mere fact that they are part of an accessed E-MOP. No summing up of events is allowed or, to put it in Kolodner's (1983, p.288) own words: "In a reconstructive memory, memories are not directly enumerable. Instead, the features that describe individual memories must be reconstructed."

CYRUS represents not only a memory model but also a retrieval system. Two components can be distinguished: the kernel retrieval cycle, and the so-called retrieval strategies which are called into action whenever the kernel retrieval cycle fails to come up with the information required. The kernel retrieval cycle starts whenever a retrieval specification contains indices with which information can be sought. After selection of indices, the events referred by each index are addressed simultaneously. If an event turns out out to be an E-MOP then again an index must be specified in order to continue the search process within that E-MOP. For each individual event the content is mapped against the retrieval specification. In case of a match the event is returned as the information to be retrieved. In case of a mismatch, the retrieval process has failed and special retrieval strategies are activated to extend the retrieval specification and to find new indices.

Comparing Kolodner's CYRUS system with Norman and Bobrow's kernel retrieval cycle one important difference is relevant to our study. Norman and Bobrow consider memory search as an iteration of retrieval cycles. After each cycle either the memory element is delivered or the retrieval specification is updated and a new retrieval cycle is initiated. On the other hand, Kolodner assumes a recursion of cycles. After an index has been selected and an event has been chosen, a hierarchically subordinated new retrieval cycle must be started if this event turns out to be an E-MOP (i.e., a collection of events) instead of a single event. In this way a hierarchy of retrieval cycles is set up until an individual event has been found which can be evaluated on its relevance with respect to the retrieval specification. The difference between Norman and Bobrow and Kolodner is rooted in Kolodner's non-enumerability assumption which precludes the set theory approach which has been adopted by Norman and Bobrow.

3. Searching Information: Solving an Ill-Defined Problem

Williams and Hollan (1981) characterized information retrieval as an example of problem solving: based on incomplete evidence an event must be reconstructed. To this characterization can be added that the problem to be solved is an ill-defined problem. Ill-defined problems are to be distinguished from well-defined problems in three respects. First, the criteria to evaluate retrieved information are usually vaguely specified. At the outset the retrieval specification is vague and incomplete (see above). During the search process the criteria become clearer and more sharply outlined. Secondly, the search instruments to carry out the task have a "broad" and "weak" character (Newell, 1973). In contrast to this, the instruments in a well-defined problem, for instance chess rules in a chess problem, are clearly defined and offer useful points of departure to the problem solver. Thirdly, databases are usually large and possess an opaque structure, at least in the eyes of an inexperienced user. In this matter chess problems again differ: the number of pieces and the number of locations on the chess board are restricted. However, the difference between well- and ill-defined problems should not be considered absolute, as both problem types are extremes on a continuum.

The ill-defined character makes the consultation of external databases an arduous task. An important heuristic method is the decomposition of the problem goal into several subgoals, a strategy which brings the problem solver closer to attaining the final goal (Reitman, 1965). In this process of decomposition the internal representation of the problem plays an important role. The way problem solvers create an internal representation of the problem or "problem space" (Newell & Simon, 1972) has received attention in studies dealing with differences in problem solving between experts and novices. Hayes and Simon (1974) studied the way in which novices interpret written problem instructions. Novices tend to start generating and trying out hypothetical solutions before they have completely encoded the problem instructions. Subsequent solution attempts lead to failure because the problem has not been fully understood. Therefore, the problem solver has to return to the instructions to interpret new problem details and continue the solution process. Experts behave in a different manner. Their original problem representation is usually adequate. The encoding process has been guided by their knowledge of problem types (Simon & Simon, 1978) or recurrent "patterns" (Greeno, 1976) in problem statements. Experts actively seek these types or patterns whilst reading the problem instructions. Their domain knowledge contains a lot of patterns which facilitate the encoding process. Simon (1980) figured out that experienced chess players possess about 50000 patterns with which they quickly encode chess configurations.

Novices and experts differ in problem-solving strategies. Novices are bound to general heuristics, like means-ends analysis. Experts can take patterns in the problem space as points of departure in the solution process. Larkin, McDermott, Simon, and Simon (1980) designed two computer models which could solve problems in the semantically rich domain of physics: a novice model working with a means-ends strategy and an expert model recognizing patterns in the problem presentation. The performance of the models appeared to parallel the behavior of a human novice and a human expert.

Apart from this distinction between novices and experts, other individual differences in problem solving strategies are worth mentioning in the context of this study. Newell and Simon (1972) payed attention to the difference between a breadth-first approach and a depth-first approach. Subjects following a breadth-first approach consider, at any decision point, as many alternatives as are available. According to the depth-first approach a line of reasoning about a possible solution is followed until a decision has been reached either to accept or to reject the alternative. In actual problem-solving protocols a mixture between both tendencies can be expected. De Groot (1965) described the method of progressive deepening. A chess player, using two solution plans to solve a chess problem, often works intermittently on both plans. Plan A is elaborated, then plan B, then plan A, etc., until one plan can be accepted as the better solution or rejected as the worse alternative.

4. Extension of the Norman and Bobrow Model

Kolodner's claim that memory elements are not enumerable is based on the observation that search latencies do not increase as the number of memory elements to be checked grows. Sequential checking of lists of items growing in length would result in increasing latencies. In fact, Kolodner makes two assumptions at the same time: checking items is a sequential process, and memory items are not enumerable. Her line of argument is difficult to follow because she does not apply the sequentiality assumption in the CYRUS system. On the contrary, she assumes parallel searching along all available tracks until elementary episodes are encountered or the search process fails. Under these circumstances the difference between a breadth-first approach and a depth-first approach vanishes. The hypothesis that the same conditions hold for human information retrieval seems unrealistic. Here at least some degree of sequentiality is supposed. Therefore, the pros and cons of the nonenumerability assumption have to be reconsidered because some potential drawbacks may be masked by the fact that CYRUS searches in parallel.

The direct consequences of the nonenumerability assumption are the hierarchical structure in which memory elements are organized and the recursive succession of retrieval cycles. Both features are undesirable in an external database. A database with a hierarchical structure is useful for those experienced users who know and understand the hierarchy. Since the sequence in which indices can be entered into the system is fixed, a user overlooking a certain keyword inevitably gets stuck in an impasse. Choosing an alternative route via backtracking is difficult if one has not kept track of the search path which led to the dead end. Our conclusion is that it is easier to retrieve information in an unknown domain if the user can consult the list of keywords recognized by the system. With this list the user can enter keywords in any preferred order. This way of structuring the database does not require extensive experience with the hierarchy of indices and, apart from that, allows for individual differences in search strategies. Problem-solving research has shown that stable individual differences do occur both between experts and novices and between users with the same level of experience.

The above mentioned considerations have led to the design of a new model of the search process which comes close to Norman and Bobrow's original idea (see Figure 1). It should be kept in mind that this model is a representation of a search strategy in an external database, whereas Norman and Bobrow's model depicted an internal memory search process. The first stage in our

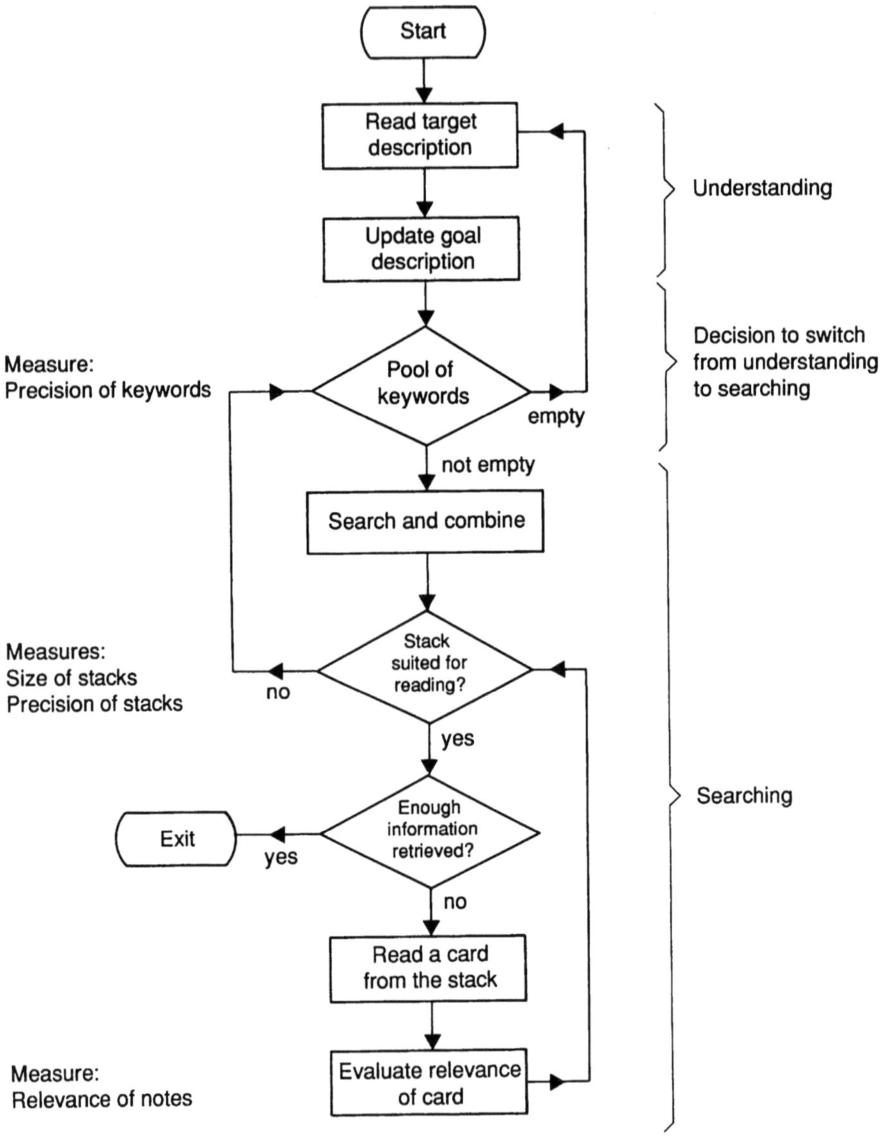

Figure 1. Model of a search process in an external database; see text for explanation.

model is the stage of understanding the target description, i.e., the description of the search task at hand. Reading the target description leads to the construction of an (internal) goal description. A goal description results in the selection of one or more keywords as relevant points of entry into the database. These selected keywords form the pool of keywords with which the user starts searching and combining: the searching phase (see Figure 1). In the context of our experiments, searching means entering keywords and thereby creating subsets of elements of the database. Combining means the merging of two sets either by interaction or by union. Using this operation the searcher not only combines sets of elements but, at the same time, keywords referring to particular aspects of the target description. The search and combine operations eventually lead to a subset or stack of memory elements which is considered suitable for reading and evaluation. If the created stack is not suitable for reading (e.g., contains too many items or misses certain relevant aspects of the target description) then the pool of keywords must deliver a new keyword with which new search and combine operations can be carried out. The decision point "Is the stack suited for reading?" with two possible outcomes has not been included in Norman and Bobrow's model. In their model a retrieval cycle has to be run through before a new selection of elements can be made. By adding a decision point at which the readability of a newly created stack is judged, a compromise has been reached between the recursive flow of control in Kolodner's model and the iterative nature of Norman and Bobrow's succesion of retrieval cycles. After a readable stack has been created the elements of this stack (denoted by the term cards in Figure 1) are read and evaluated on their relevance to the target description. If this pool is the stack runs out of cards before the relevant information has been spotted the pool of keywords is reconsidered. If this pool is empty then the target description has to be reread in order to extend the (internal) goal description and the pool of keywords. In this way the model lends room to expert and novice strategies and also to breadth-first and depth-first approaches.

In experiment I the validity of the model was empirically tested. In experiment II attention was focused on individual differences in the search and combine phase of the model.

5. Experiment I: Evidence for the Extended Search Model

5.1. Introduction

In Experiment I the main question was whether the model (see Figure 1) adequately described the way in which users carry out the experimental task. A common method to test the validity of a model is to write it down in a computer program and to run the program and human subjects on the same task. Comparison of the subject's behavior and the protocols of the simulation program sheds light on the adequacy of the model. However, experiment I followed a less rigorous method because adequate artificial intelligence techniques were not available. Instead, we deduced some behavior characteristics which, according to the model, should determine the outcome of the search process. These parameters reflected major decision aspects of the model: the quality of the keywords used by the subject, the quality of the subsets of memory elements which the subject considered suitable for reading, and the quality of the evaluation by the subject of selected memory elements. If the model is valid, then each of these aspects should uniquely describe part of the variance in the search results. If the model is not valid, then no relation should appear between the parameters and the search outcome. If one of the parameters, e.g., the quality of the keywords, accounts for all variance in the search result, then the distinction of several stages in the model is not valid. We used a multiple-regression analysis to estimate the contribution of each of the parameters to the variance in the search performance. This analysis quantifies the amount of joint and separate influence of the selected parameters on the dependent variable. Of course it does not explain the detected relations. If the same parameters could be analysed in another model, then this new model would also be corroborated by the data. Therefore, the regression analysis technique must be considered as a first test of the power of some parameters reflecting main aspects of the model of a search process in an external database.

5.2. Method

Subjects. Eighteen pupils from the sixth grade of two elementary schools and 36 pupils from the third grade of two secondary schools in Amsterdam participated. All subjects were selected from within the same range of intelligence: the upper 25% of the Raven Standard Progressive Matrices.

Materials. In the experiment a database containing 180 "cards" was used, describing (1) the organization and the social-economic functions of the Tailors Guild in the Golden Age in Amsterdam, and (2) the clothing that was worn at that time. The database was stored in a PDP 11/55 computer, for which a visual display unit was set up in the school connected via a telephone line. There were two search tasks, each of which was presented to half of the subjects, each with a different target description: (1) the training needed to become a master in the tailor trade (task A), and (2) the social provisions in the Tailors Guild (task B). The relevance or irrelevance of the cards with relation to each of the target descriptions was derived by the experimenter on an a priori basis.

The database was accessible with a program providing six operations for information retrieval. The database consisted of numbered cards. Each card contained a short text, the contents of which normally fitted on a 24×80 screen. The cards could be independently requested by number. In addition, a list of keywords enabled the subject to select cards dealing with a specific topic. On the basis of an entered keyword the program made a subset or "stack" of cards. The program could supply the unity and intersection of two stacks. A separate dictionary provided the meaning of difficult words included in the text of the cards. At the start of the first session the children learnt to use this program. The experimenter read an instruction out loud and the subjects practiced with a database consisting of 33 cards on which different birds were described.

In defining the parameters used to represent the descriptive value of the model, the concept of precision value played an important role (borrowed from research on the working of an automated documentation system (Salton, 1975). The precision value of a selection from the the database was defined as the proportion of relevant information in the selection. If, in a stack of 12 cards, three contain information on the subject of the search task, then the precision value of the stack is equal to 3/12 or 0.25. In this way a precision value can be calculated for each keyword. The average precision value of the keywords given by the subject was the first measure that we entered in the regression analysis. This measure gave an indication of the quality of the internal goal description the subject used while carrying out the search task. The second and third parameters represented the decision to read in a stack that had been made (see Figure 1). As explained, making a stack does not imply that all its cards have to be read. The decision to read, also depends on the size of the stack. To evaluate the contribution of this characteristic to the decision to read we calculated the size of the stack from which each requested card originated. The average of these stack sizes was entered in the regression analysis as a relevant parameter. The keyword (or keywords) with which the subject made a stack and the relevance of the cards previously read also played a role in the decision to (continue to) read. This aspect was discounted in the third parameter, the average precision value of the stacks from which the displayed cards originated. The notes made by the subject during the execution of the task were used for the fourth and last parameter, which was the proportion of relevant cards from which the subject made notes.

As dependent variable for the quality of the result of the search, the precision value of the set of cards the subject read and judged was used as the search score, i.e., the percentage of relevant cards read and judged by the subject. Thus, the amount of relevant information retrieved was related to the number of cards selected by the subject (usually 20), within the time limit of the experimental session (1 h). The dependent measure (precision value of cards read) was thus based on the a priori categorization by the experimenter.

Procedure. The subjects received instruction on the operations by which information could be traced. This was followed by the experimental search task. The execution was stopped as soon as the subject had read and judged 20 cards, or the time limit of 1 h was passed. The subject had no insight into the keyword list but had to extract suitable keywords from the target description.

5.3. Results

The explanatory power of the model parameters was tested by a regression analysis in which the influence of the experimental factors was controlled statistically. The level of significance for rejection of the null hypothesis was set at 5%. In order to describe the variations in the dependent variables five predictor terms were introduced into the regression equation. The factors task, sex, and school level were controlled statistically. The first variable in the regression equation was the IQ score, recorded in order to control for differences in intelligence. After this, the model parameters were included in the regression equation. The order of inclusion was determined by the supposed importance of each of the parameters. The precision value of the keywords was assumed to be the key factor in the search process. If our extension of Norman and Bobrow's model was superfluous then the size and precision value of the selected stacks should not explain an independent part of the variance in the search results. However, if our contribution made sense then part of the variance in the dependent variable should be described by the second and third model parameters. The fourth parameter, the relevance of the notes taken by the subject, was the last variable in the regression equation. We had no precise idea of whether and how the relevance judgements influenced the search results. The results of the regression analysis are shown in Table 1.

Table 1. Results of the regression analysis

Variables	df	*F*	*P*	Percentage of variation explained
IQ	1, 41	3.60	0.06	8.07
Precision of keywords	1, 40	18.97	0.00	29.57
Size of stacks	1, 39	24.23	0.00	23.90
Precision of stacks	1, 38	108.11	0.00	28.46
Relevance of notes	1, 37	3.77	0.06	0.93
Total	5, 37	74.13	0.00	90.92

The IQ score did not provide a significant contribution to the variance in the search score. The parameters precision of keywords, size of stacks, and precision of stacks independently of each other accounted for 30%, 24%, and 28% of the variance, respectively. The percentage of relevant notes did not provide a significant contribution.

5.4. Discussion

The behavior of the subjects as measured with the search score seemed to be well described in terms of the search model. The derived parameters explained 82% of the variance in the search score. Inspection of the contribution of the individual parameters showed that the average precision value of the keywords used accounted for 30% of the variance in the search score. In other words, the choice of the keywords is a factor that exercises great influence on the ultimate results. Keywords are directly deduced from the target description. Careful reading of the description, both in the beginning and in the course of the search task, appears to be of great importance in finding relevant information.

There is, however, more to be said. After partitioning out the variance of the first parameter, the average size and the average precision value of the stacks from which the subject received information explained more than 50% of the variance in the search score. This implies the importance of not only the choice of relevant keywords, but also of the correct combination of stacks and the choice of those stacks (of all created stacks) that offer the greatest chance of relevant information. These are, in general, small stacks. The findings support the extension that we made to Norman and Bobrow's model of internal memory search. They had sketched the retrieval process as a formulation of a goal description, the selection of memory elements, and the evaluation of these elements. Our results suggest that, when external memories are searched, cards are not only selected on the basis of keywords (as in Norman and Bobrow's model), but also on the basis of size and precision value of the created stacks. In this respect the successful subjects distinguished themselves from the less successful ones.

6. Experiment II: Individual Differences in Search Strategies

6.1. Introduction

To identify task-associated search characteristics and to distinguish them from systematic search behavior, we constructed a new database in which information had to be traced on the basis of a vague target description. The new domain was better structured than the Tailors Guild domain, because an extensive list of keywords was made available to the subjects, and the form and content of the domain better matched existing foreknowledge which could be used by the subjects during the search task.

This second experiment was also of a descriptive nature: it was directed at revealing patterns or strategies present in the search behavior.

6.2. Method

Subjects. A group of 30 subjects from the third grade of a secondary school in Amsterdam took part in this experiment. The average level of the subjects on the Raven Standard Progressive Matrices was 52.6 (maximum score 60) and 30.0 on the Verbal Analogies subtest of the Differential Aptitude Test (maximum score 50).

Materials. The database consisted of 210 job descriptions. The number of keywords was limited to 49, of which 31 described functional requirements, five a level of education, and 13 referred to a job sector. The subjects were asked to find five suitable jobs for a client whose profile, in terms of weak and strong qualities, educational level, and job sector preference, was given. The list of keywords recognizable by the system was then placed at the disposal of the subjects. The subjects were asked to search for suitable jobs for three profiles (I, II, and III). The first profile served as a practice run. The sequence of the remaining profiles (II and III) was varied randomly across subjects.

Procedure. Each subject first received an explanation of the use of search operations and then began the experimental tasks. The experimenter provided the profile and asked the subject to study the text and then to mark the possible relevant keywords on the list of keywords. Subjects were allowed to read as many cards as they wished (the maximum was no longer limited to 20 cards). When the subject thought he had found five suitable jobs or when 75 minutes had passed, the search task was ended.

6.3. Results

A global inspection of the protocols gave the impression that two different strategies existed. In strategy A the subject first selects jobs using two keywords. Then the intersection of the two sets is found. If the intersection con-

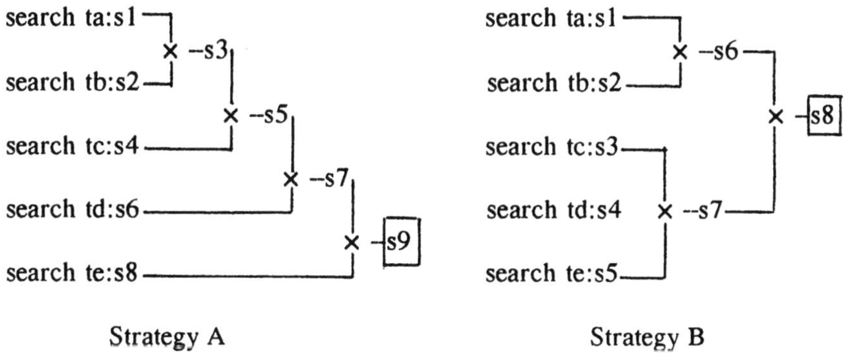

Figure 2. Examples of both strategies. Jobs are sought using five keywords: ta, tb, tc, td, and te. For each strategy the keywords are given on the left-hand side of the figure. An intersection is indicated by a square bracket and an ×. The sequence of the steps is indicated by s1 - s9. The enclosed digit shows the intersection for which jobs are finally evaluated on relevance.

tains too many jobs, the subject then makes a selection with a new keyword and intersects this selection with the previous intersection. Following this approach the subject eventually ends up with an intersection containing a limited number of jobs (usually about five). Given the profile, the subject then evaluates the relevance of the jobs. If all the keywords in the profile have not yet been utilized, and if five suitable jobs have not yet been found, the subject then sets up a new "search tree." If all the keywords have been used the subject stops.

In strategy B the subject first makes a subset of jobs for each keyword in the profile. Then intersections of subsets (and of intersections) are made until an intersection with a limited number of jobs is reached. The subject evaluates the relevance of these jobs, given the profile, and then stops. An example of both strategies is shown in Figure 2.

To discover the extent to which a strategy was consistently followed by a subject we analyzed the protocols using a computer program. The program contained a production system in which both search strategies were represented (see Figure 2). This production system specifies, for each search state, the next move according to the search strategies. For each move the protocol analysis program predicted the following step for both strategies and compared the prediction with the actual search operation carried out by the subject. The program determined if, and to what extent, the subject followed one of the two strategies (for details of the protocol analysis, see Beishuizen, 1986).

Two protocols were analysed in this manner for each subject. Table 2 gives the results of this analysis. From the proportion of correctly predicted moves, it appears that for 27 of the 30 subjects, both protocols were best predicted by following one of the two strategies.

Table 2. Results of the protocol analysis according to strategies A and B.

	Number of subjects	Proportion of correctly predicted moves
Both protocols according to strategy A	10	0.8146
Both protocols according to strategy B	17	0.7884
One protocol according to A, One protocol according to B	2	
Undecided	1	

6.4. Discussion

The new database with job descriptions brought forward two different strategies for information retrieval (see Figure 2). Strategy A corresponds to the depth-first approach: starting from two keywords as a point of departure the user immediately creates an intersection to see what the result is. If the created stack does not meet the two criteria for readability (i.e., the stack is reasonably small, and has been constructed with a representative sample of relevant keywords) then a new keyword is entered and added to the target stack. This process continues until a suitable stack has been made, the user runs out of keywords, or the target stack becomes empty. In strategy B a breadth-first approach is preferred. First, all keywords which can be deduced from the target description are entered. In this way the subject aims at a complete representation of the target description in terms of keywords. After that the subject starts combining stacks until a suitable stack has been created. Both strategies are equally effective. The information retrieval system allows for different approaches to be applied and successfully brought to an end.

7. Guidelines for the Design of External Databases

Internal and external memories differ in two respects: (1) the user is experienced with his or her own memory but is not necessarily familiar with the structure of an external database; and (2) external search proceeds in sequential order, whereas internal memory search is probably at least partially a parallel process. Close examination of Kolodner's CYRUS system makes the differences clear. A hierarchical organization of memory elements and a strictly recursive concatenation of retrieval cycles are both not to be considered as friendly for the inexperienced, sequentially working user. Based on these considerations and on the experiences in the two reported experiments some guidelines for designing external databases are proposed.

7.1. Structure of the Database

Experiment I showed that users differ in the way they approach an unknown database in order to find vaguely specified information. These differences were observable since our database is equipped with a rich structure of keywords. Each item in the database is accessible by, on average, seven keywords. Moreover, each keyword is directly available since the keywords are not arranged in a hierarchical order which the user must work through before arriving at the desired keyword. Every user can choose his own entry point and search in any direction he prefers. In this way the database structure offers a maximum amount of freedom in which every search style can be used. However, a word of caution seems appropriate. The list of keywords may be too long to be manageable by novice or even experienced users. Under these circumstances communication should be made easier by providing a natural language interface or by providing some hierarchical structuring in the list of keywords. A menu-driven presentation of keywords may, however, be turned into a user-friendly interface by supplying the user with a facility to preview upcoming selections before a choice on the current menu level has been made. Snowberry, Parkinson, and Sisson (1985) showed that this help facility significantly increases the accuracy of search. In this and other ways the cumbersome handling of hierarchical menus may become easier.

7.2. Search Strategies

Experiment II showed that individual users differ in the strategies with which they carry out a search task. A database should offer the opportunity for users to employ their preferred working style. This again implies that a hierarchical organization of keywords precluding any approach but the depth-first strategy should be avoided if possible. Both depth-first and breadth-first strategies should be admitted. A second implication of this argument is that recursive searching may be less user friendly than iterative searching. Systems that automatically create intersections after the entering of a new keyword are in fact restricting the searcher's freedom of action. Every intersection should purposefully be made by the user.

7.3. Interface

The user should be kept well informed about the search process. Graphics seem to be suitable for this purpose. In particular, if a recursive approach has been chosen the user needs extensive process information. Facilities for backtracking to an earlier level in the hierarchy and for undoing the last choice of keywords seem necessary. The designer should be aware of the fact that most users are unfamiliar with the network of keywords covering the database and have only limited knowledge of the way the search commands should be operated. A facility for advice or coaching may contribute to the development of an adequate search skill, and may, after a period of getting acquainted with the organization of the domain to be searched, turn the novice into an expert.

References

Bartlett F. (1932). *Remembering: A study of experimental and social psychology.* Cambridge University Press, London.

Beishuizen J.J. (1986). *Leren opzoeken van informatie.* Thesis, Vrije Universiteit. Stichting voor Onderzoek van het Onderwijs, 's Gravenhage

Craik F.I.M. & Lockhart R.S. (1972). Levels of processing: A framework for memory research. *Journal of Verbal Learning and Verbal Behavior,* 11, pp. 671-684.

Feigenbaum E.A. & Simon H.A. (1984). EPAM-like models of recognition and learning. *Cognitive Science,* 8, pp. 305-336.

Greeno J. (1976). Indefinite goals in well structured problems. *Psychological Review,* 83 (6), pp. 479-491.

Groot A.D. de (1965). *Thought and choice in chess.* Mouton, Den Haag.

Hayes J.R. & Simon H.A. (1974). Understanding written problem instructions. In: *Knowledge and cognition.* L.W. Gregg (Ed), Erlbaum, Hillsdale, N.J.

Kolodner J. (1983). Reconstructive memory: A computer model. *Cognitive Science,* 7, pp. 281-328.

Larkin J.H., McDermott J., Simon D.P. & Simon H.A. (1980). Models of competence in solving physics problems. *Cognitive Science*, 4, pp. 317-345.

Loftus E.F. & Fathi D.C. (1985). Retrieving multiple autobiographical memories. *Social Cognition*, 3 (3), pp. 280-295.

Newell A. (1973). Artificial intelligence and the concept of mind. In: *Computer models of thought and language*, R.C. Schank & K.M. Kolby (Eds.), Freeman, San Francisco.

Newell A. & Simon H.A. (1972). *Human problem solving*. Prentice-Hall, Englewood Cliffs, N.J.

Norman D.A. & Bobrow D.G. (1979). Descriptions: An intermediate stage in memory retrieval. *Cognitive Psychology*, 11, pp. 107-123.

Piaget J. (1953). *The origins of intelligence in the child.* Routledge and Paul Kegan, London

Reitman W.R. (1965). *Cognition and thought.* Wiley & Sons, New York.

Salton G. (1975). *Dynamic information and library processing.* Prentice-Hall, Englewood Cliffs, N.J.

Schank R.C. & Abelson R.P. (1977). *Scripts, plans, goals, and understanding.* Erlbaum, Hillsdale, N.J.

Simon H.A. (1980). Problem solving and education. In: *Problem solving and education: Issues in teaching and research.* D.T. Tuma & F. Reif (Eds.), Erlbaum, Hillsdale, N.J.

Simon D.P. & Simon H.A. (1978). Individual differences in solving physics problems. In: *Children's thinking: what develops?* R. Siegler, (Ed.), Erlbaum, Hillsdale, N.J.

Snowberry K., Parkinson S. & Sisson N. (1985). Effects of help fields on navigating through hierarchical menu structures. *International Journal of Man-Machine Studies*, 22, pp. 479-491.

Vygotsky L.S. (1978). *Mind in society: The development of higher psychological processes.* Harvard University Press, Cambridge, MA.

Williams M.D. & Hollan J.D. (1981). The process of retrieval from very Long-Term memory. *Cognitive Science*, 5, pp. 87-119.

Chapter 24. Keywords Instead of Hierarchical Menus

Bernard A. Weerdmeester

1. Introduction

Videotex systems, providing a great variety of information, were developed around 1970 to serve experienced as well as inexperienced users. Therefore simple access methods are needed. Information retrieval from videotex systems is usually performed by means of numerical choices from hierachical menus, detailing the subject more and more. Early in the search process, when only general keywords have been entered, the users have to select an information provider, the owner of the information in a videotex database. After selecting the information provider and getting to the related general page the users can reach detailed information by means of the information providers' own search method. This is often another menu structure. At this stage it is very difficult to change to another information provider or to return to the main dialogue, other than by starting over again. During the search process the users are not informed whether there is an answer to their question, online help is not provided and the only assistence can be obtained from the printed directory.

Menu systems are easy to learn for inexperienced users. They can, however, be tedious for experienced users and not all kinds of information or tasks are equally suitable for hierarchical presentation (Dumais & Landauer, 1984). The search and access routes depend on a rigid, partly arbitrary organization imposed by system designers. Young and Hull (1982) call the confusion resulting from this organization a "cognitive mismatch" between the designer of the frame and the user.

Past studies on access to Videotex systems have revealed low percentages of correctly answered questions (e.g. Vrins, Velthoven & Frankhuizen, 1982). Researchers in different countries have mentioned the lack of adequate (detailed) subject indexing as one of the reasons for this (Goillau & Stewart, 1978; Kromrey, 1984). Alphanumeric keyword searching was suggested as one of the solutions.

In view of the worldwide lack of alphanumeric search systems for videotex services, the Netherlands PTT developed an experimental keyword search method for Viditel, their national videotex system. A research group, consisting of software and human factors engineers defined and implemented the new system in Viditest, the test system of Viditel.

2. Requirements

Many researchers have formulated requirements for human-machine dialogues applicable to interactive retrieval systems (Wasserman, 1973; Kennedy, 1974; Vigil, 1983):

Communication should take place in a terse "natural" language

The dialogue should allow the same message to be expressed in more than one way

The basic operations of searching should be "and," "or," and "not"

The computer behavior should be logically consistent under all circumstances

The computer system should give help when requested or whenever it perceives that the user is in difficulty

Abbrevations should be allowed wherever possible

Error messages should be polite, meaningful, and informative

Short-cuts should be provided for knowledgeable users

Some additional requirements for videotex systems were specified by Vrins et al. (1982). They proposed that users of a videotex system should always be informed about the size (number of pages) of the selected information, and, if the selected information was of an acceptable size, additional information about the contents of the selected set should be given.

Current search methods all require users to select an information provider before they actually get to the information required. Experiments by Vrins et al. showed that 50% of the user decisions concerning the selection of an information provider did not lead to correct answers to their questions. Therefore the possibility of shortcutting information providers' databases is required.

If the kind of information is of a great variety, as in videotex systems, a dialogue is desirable which gives the users relatively great freedom of choice of keywords, and also provides the opportunity for quick access to the mass of available information.

3. Characteristics

On the Viditest system a search method based on keyword search was implemented, with the following characteristics:

A keyword list of about 8000 keywords. The content of this list is considered more or less stationary. This means that only small fluctuations in the composition are allowed. In this way system reactions after entering keywords will be most consistent. For specific or very topical keywords information providers may create their own "sub-keyword lists". Sub-keywords are only relevant after the name of the related information provider has been entered

Intersection of the information related to the keywords. Negations and unions are possible by preceding the entered keywords respectively by the terms "NOT:" and "ALSO:". Because of the differences in meaning between Boolean expressions and normal language only intersections are recommended for casual users and used in the experiments

Qualitative and quantitative feedback on the progress of the search process. Quantitative feedback is given by means of the number of pages selected, qualitative feedback is given by means of a short description of the contents of a page by means of a describer, a related but not entered keyword

Keywords, names of information providers, and geographical names are all treated in the same way. This is in contrast to existing methods where specific searching of one of these categories requires the selection of a specific search method

Easy control possibilities. One of the possible problems of keyword methods for videotex systems is that information providers try to attract customers by indexing nonrelated, but popular, keywords to their pages. This has an impact on the perceived reliability of the system. Therefore control possibilities are planned to avoid favoring specific information providers

4. User Dialogue

Dialogues were determined for all parties involved, e.g. the users, the information provider and the system manager. Only the user dialogue, which consists of two phases, will be described here.

4.1. Phase 1

In phase 1 a user is asked to enter one keyword at a time. After entering a keyword its existence is checked. If it does not exist the user is informed and asked to enter another keyword. If it exists, the system replies with the number of pages associated with this keyword, after which the user is invited to enter another keyword.

If this exists the system performs the intersection of the sets of pages which are associated with the keywords. The result of this intersection is reported to the user by showing the number of selected pages. If the number of selected pages is not low enough in the user's opinion, the procedure can be repeated by entering more keywords.

4.2. Phase 2

Phase 2 of the dialogue starts when the user is satisfied with the number of selected pages and asks for a listing of these pages by means of the function key PAGE LIST. In this phase the user is supplied with a menu of the

Table 1. Phase 2 of the user dialogue

Viditest DNL	960a	0c
hotels japan 3 pages found another keyword or PAGE LIST		
1. KLM tokyo		0c
2. KLM osaka		0c
3. JAL tokyo		0c
enter your choice		

selected pages. Each possible choice is numbered and gives the name of the information provider of a selected page, the maximum price of a frame in that page, and, if applicable, another not yet entered keyword associated with that page (Table 1).

If the set of selected pages does not fit within the window on the screen the user can go forwards and backwards through this list as well as return to the first phase. A return is possible by entering more keywords or by deleting already entered keywords. In phase 2 the user can make a choice from the page menu. The system then retrieves the first frame of the page via the normal videotex processes (this could be regarded as a "phase 3"). The user then can use the ordinary videotex commands to see more information. The user can also return to the keyword dialogue, and the system shows the same menu as before leaving the dialogue. This facility can be regarded as the system's memory function.

4.3. Help Facilities

Several features have been developed to assist users to find their way to the desired information. Some help facilities are explicit (at the users' request) and some implicit (always offered by the system when available). The help functions are summarized in Table 2.

Table 2. Help facilities

	Implicit	Explicit
Morphological	Spelling	Completion
Semantic	Synonyms	Hierarchical
Procedural	Messages	On-line help

A short description of the various help functions is as follows:

1. *Implicit morphological help.* Alternative spellings can be used. The keyword system recognizes alternative spellings of keywords as well as the preferred spelling

2. *Explicit morphological help.* At the user's request a list of keywords is presented, which reflects the alphabetical environment of a given keyword. This feature is still provided, though the length of the list is now limited to one
3. *Implicit semantic help.* If the user enters a keyword to which no page numbers are assigned, a search is made for another keyword with a similar meaning. If this "synonym keyword" exists, the keyword entered is replaced by the synonym
4. *Explicit semantic help.* At the user's request the system may offer a list of keywords, the meanings of which are closely related to the meaning of the keyword entered. There are two different types of semantic relations which may exist between keywords. The system recognizes:
   a. Associative relations, where keywords share in some respect a certain field of interest
   b. Hierarchical relations, where one keyword possesses a more restricted meaning than the other

   The different types are handled by the system in the same way. The only way for the user to recognize one type from the other is by means of the number of related pages. For hierarchical (lower) relations this number is always the same or lower, but for associative relations the number of related pages may be higher
5. *Implicit procedural help.* Various messages may help the users during their dialogue session. These messages are often called "error messages." The question, however, is whether these are users' errors. In fact, it was the system designer who made the error by not understanding users' behavior
6. *Explicit procedural help* At any time during the dialogue session the user can ask the system for procedural help. The system then shows the possible commands or other information useful in the current phase of the dialogue

5. Method

Experiments were performed to determine whether the newly developed method is better than the best comparable existing search method. The chosen existing method is a numerically operated subject list. By this method users choose from an alphabet menu by keying numbers (A=11, B=12, C=13). After the user has repeated this until the first part of the chosen subject is defined precisely enough, a list of subjects and related information providers is offered. The users can choose from this list and enter the information of the information provider, usually at a general level.

The main differences between the new and the existing search methods are summarized in Table 3.

Table 3. Differences between the search methods

	New keyword search method	Existing keyword list
Number of keywords	More than one (intersections)	One at the time
Feedback about choice	Immediately	After a few steps
Relations between keywords	Semantic	None
Feedback about selected information	Yes	No
Help	Available	Not available

For example, when a user wants to know where to buy a Philips CD player in Amsterdam, only "CD player" can be selected from the existing subject list. The keyword search method allows users to intersect the information related to Philips, Amsterdam, and CD player(s) in a random order.

5.1. Subjects

The 32 subjects for the experiment were selected from a total of 800 inhabitants of Leidschendam who had expressed their willingness to cooperate. They were matched for age, education, sex, and experience with keyboards. People who had taken part in Viditel experiments before were not invited.

5.2. Questions

There were 50 questions in the experiment, 25 of which were used for each subject. The questions had been partly derived from questions used in earlier experiments (Vrins et al, 1982). Use was made of this large number of questions in order to minimize the influence of particular questions on the total result. The answers to all questions were available in Viditest. The subjects were not aware of this. Examples of questions are: "How many years of study does it take to become a dental technician?" and "What is on the program at the "Concertgebouw" in Amsterdam this week?". In pilot experiments we tried to embed the questions in short stories to avoid the use of keywords in the questions. However, this resulted a high number of falsely interpreted questions, and so direct questioning was used in the experiments.

5.3. Design

Each subject was asked to come to the laboratory twice. On the first occasion subjects were asked to carry out 10 searches using a particular search method, and on the second occasion to carry out 15 more searches using the same method. All questions occurred the same number of times. The factors in the analysis of variance were the two search methods and the two questions. Dependent variables were the number of correctly answered questions and the search time. The following definitions of these variables were used:

A question is answered correctly if the page containing the information answering the question is reached, provided the search time does not exceed 10 minutes

The search time starts when the subject presses the first key after reading the question. It ends when the last key is pressed in a successful search for an answer or when the subject states that he is unable to find the answer

5.4. Procedure

After a date had been agreed with the subjects for their visit to the laboratory, they were sent a description of the search method and of the layout of the keyboard. On their arrival at the laboratory the layout of a Viditel page was explained to them, as was the use of some function keys. These keys, such as SEND, HELP and PAGE LIST were added to evaluate their use in case of futur multifunction terminals. Keys like HELP and PAGE LIST are only meaningful for the new search method, since in the existing method online help is not provided and lists of pages are always offered in an implicit manner. Before the actual experiment, three trials were carried out in which the instructor explained why certain keywords were right or wrong and which search strategy was best.

6. Results

Table 4 shows the main results obtained with the two search methods. Analysis of variance showed that the new method produced more correctly answered questions ($F(1,777)=26.475, p<0.001$) and that less time was taken to answer the questions correctly ($F(1,582)=8.214, p<0.005$).

Table 4. Performance measures

	Percentage correctly answered	Search time (s)
New search method	83	127
Existing keyword list	67	155

6.1. Subjectiveness

After each session, the subjects were asked to give their opinion on the search method and the keyboard. The new search method was not found significantly more difficult than the existing method. The keyboard however, was thought to be difficult ($t(30)=3.92, p<0.001$). This is probably due to the function keys needed for the new method.

6.2. Failure

The experiments revealed the same causes for failure in both search methods, as can be seen in Table 5. The numbers in Table 5 are percentages of the incorrect answers. Before the experiments the correct answers were defined, as were the correct related keywords and information providers. Within the information of the correct information provider it was possible to select incorrect information. If subjects did everything correct, but stopped halfway, their answer was classified in Table 5 under "other".

Finding the right keyword is the most difficult step. This can be due to the previously mentioned cognitive mismatch between the person who indexed the keywords to the pages and the user. Finding the first keyword is particularly

Table 5. Origins of incorrect answers (%)

	Choice of keyword	Choice of information provider	Choice with information providers' data	Other
Keyword search	73	22	5	0
Existing subject list	70	21	6	3

important. Of all the failures, 59% resulted from an incorrect first keyword. Because only intersections could be used this could never lead to a correct answer. Choosing the wrong information provider was often due to incorrect indication of unused related keywords in the second phase of the dialogue.

7. Recommendations

Based on the results of these experiments, the following recommendations are made:

1. *Implementation.* As a tool for answering specific questions, the new search method was found to be a major improvement on existing search methods. Based on the results of the experiment, implementation of the new method in Viditel and other Prestel-oriented systems is recommended. This will probably have taken place in the Netherlands, as well as in Australia, at the time of publication of this study
2. *Morphological help.* Presentation of one morphologically similar keyword (as implemented) is often insufficient. Therefore more keywords should be offered with the same initial letters, from which the user can then make a choice. However, selection from a long list of synonyms should be avoided
3. *Making explicit functions implicit.* When a nonexistent keyword is entered, the user should immediately be offered a list of similar existing keywords. The same applies to the page list. If such a list exists and is offered immediately, the user may at least get some ideas from it. In many cases, the list will even enable the user to make a choice, provided it contains the right describers

4. *Improvement of describers.* The describing keyword in the page list (describer) must be more specific and more destinctive.

8. Future Developments

One of the problems with testing videotex systems is that the information does not answer the users' own questions. This makes it very hard to motivate subjects in experiments. In the future, when videotex systems might be used for telephone directories, home shopping, or home banking, motivation of subjects in experiments will be easier. After many years of laboratory experiments, field experiments with specific user groups will be useful. Within the Netherlands Viditel system such a group of specific users might be composed of frequent users, such as transport bureaus, travel agencies, or bankers.

To reach the general public the dialogue of videotex should be intelligent and should probably make use of speech recognition and speech synthesis. The structure of the information should be improved to make easy access possible. It should be made clear to the users whether there is no answer to their question at all, or whether it is just that the particular system does not provide the answer.

To facilitate the process of indexing the keywords to the pages a system should be developed which compares the contents of a frame with the keyword list. All similarities should be presented to the indexer as possible keywords. However, composing a frame is nearly as subjective a process as indexing, and so this will probably not resolve the problem of cognitive mismatches.

9. Summary

One of the biggest problems with computerarized databases is the retrieval of information from them. A user-friendly search system is of the greatest importance, especially when these databases contain a great variety of information and are used by a great number of people with different background.

At the Dr. Neher Laboratories of the Netherlands PTT. a group of researchers from different disciplines developed and tested an alphanumerically based search system for their national videotex service Viditel. Though the results showed that the new method was significantly better than the best existing method, a 100% score was not achieved. This is partly due to the fact that retrieval of information is more difficult when the search terms are assigned by others than if it is done by the searchers themselves. The results of the experiments led to suggestions for (simple) improvements of the method.

The results were so hopeful that implementation of the new search method is recommended in videotex systems.

References

Dumais S.T. & Landauer T.K. (1984). Describing categories of objects for menu retrieval systems. *Behavior Research Methods, Instruments & Computers*, 16 (2), pp. 242-248.

Goillau P.J. & Stewart T.F.M. (1978). *An evaluation of different information access methods for the post office 'viewdata' service.* Loughborough University, HUSAT memo n. 168.

Kennedy T.C.S. (1974). The design of interactive procedures for man-machine communication. *International Journal of Man-Machine Studies*, 6, pp. 309-334.

Kromrey H. (1984). Bildschirmtext: ein neues Kommunikations- und Informationssysteem. *Massacommunicatie*, 1, pp. 12-24.

Vigil P.J. (1983). The psychology of online searching. *Journal of the American Society for Information Science*, 34(4), pp. 281-287.

Vrins A.G.M., Velthoven R.H. van & Frankhuizen J.L. (1982). Search method evaluation in the Dutch videotex system. *Displays, April*, pp. 101-105.

Wasserman T. (1973). The design of idiot-proof interactive systems. *Proceedings of the National Computer Conference*, 45, AFIPS Press, Montvale, New Jersey, pp. 357-364.

Young R.M. & Hull A. (1982). Cognitive aspects of the selection of viewdata options by casual users. In: *Proceedings of the 6th International Conference on Computer Communication.* M.B. Williams (Ed.), pp. 571-576.

The Use of Natural Language in Interaction with Information Systems

Chapter 25. Natural Language Communication with Computers: Some Problems, Perspectives, and New Directions

Harry C. Bunt

1. Introduction

This paper presents a view on where we stand in the realization of natural-language dialogue systems and where we should direct research efforts in order to make further progress in this area.

These topics will be addressed in the following way. First, I will briefly discuss the kind of dialogue between man and machine most likely to be of serious interest: a dialogue with the purpose of exchanging certain factual information. Such a dialogue is called an "informative dialogue." In the next section a selective overview will be presented of the most significant work in building dialogue systems where natural language plays a certain role: question-answering systems and interactive systems which make use of messages in "canned" natural language. The section will close with a discussion of the inherent difficulties in the interpretation of natural language by computer. This will be followed in the next section by considering natural informative dialogues between people, both in spoken form and via computer terminals. Observations on these dialogues reveal a variety of problems that should be addressed in order to make automatic dialogue systems sophisticated enough to be of real value. One of the conclusions will be that man-machine dialogues should not be restricted to question-answer pairs. The fifth section will outline a theoretical framework for the study of those problems involved in designing systems that allow more complex dialogues than question-answer pairs. The next section will sum up the various kinds of problems in the design of dialogue systems that have emerged in the preceding sections, dividing these into three categories (linguistics, psycholinguistics, and computer science), and indicates some new developments and directions in research relevant for dealing with these problems. General conclusions on the prospects of realizing intelligent dialogue systems will be drawn in the final section. There is also an Appendix, containing the Dutch originals of the English dialogue samples used in the main text.

2. Informative Dialogues

The term informative dialogues has been coined in analogy with the term informative questions. Informative questions are utterances that not only look like questions, but are also intended to function as questions in the proper sense of the word, i.e., as requests for information. Other kinds of questions, which we might call noninformative, are, for example, rhetorical questions, examination questions, politeness questions ("How do you do?"), "involving" questions ("And what do you think of this, Peter?"), and exclamatory questions ("Isn't she cute?").

Like a question, a dialogue usually has the goal of accomplishing a certain transfer of information, but it can have many other purposes as well. Noninformative dialogues are, for instance, politeness dialogues like "How do you do?" "Very well, thank you," television interviews, where one partner has the primary aim of getting the other partner to speak out on something, and conversations intended to convert someone, to convince him of something, or to gain his support or vote. By analogy with the notion of an informative question as a pure request for information, an informative dialogue is defined as a verbal interaction in which two partners participate with the sole purpose of accomplishing the transfer of the information they request or offer. In its simplest form, such a dialogue consists of an informative question followed by an answer. In real-life situations, an informative dialogue never consists of a question and an answer only. There is usually some introductory material before the actual question and, after a question-answer pair, some form of acknowledgement and often a response to that. In a later section we will see what natural informative dialogues look like.

There are two reasons, why informative dialogues should be of particular interest; a scientific and a practical one. The scientific one is that virtually any kind of dialogue, whether "informative" or not, depends on the transfer of information. That is, a dialogue with more complex purposes can be viewed as an informative dialogue where the participants try to realize intentions additional to straightforward information transfer. The study of informative dialogues is therefore basic to the study of dialogues in general. The practical reason is that dialogues purely motivated by the goal of transferring factual information are the most obvious form of communication that makes sense with a computer. Other motivations, such as convincing someone of something, creating a nice atmosphere, or making a good impression, simply do not arise in connection with a machine.

3. Informative Dialogues with Computers

There are two kinds of computer programs which are sometimes called dialogue systems, namely question-answering systems, where a dialogue consists of a question-answer pair, and interactive systems which allow more complex dialogues but where the dialogue has to follow a rigid scheme, allowing the user only a very limited choice of natural language expressions at each point in the schema.

3.1. Natural-Language Question-Answering Systems

After some preliminaries during the 1960s (see Simmons, 1965, 1969), the first question-answering systems of serious interest were developed during the early 1970s. Three systems fairly sharply stand out in this period: the REQUEST system, designed by Petrick and collaborators; the LSNLIS system developed by Woods and colleagues, and Winograd's SHRDLU system. These systems stand out for two reasons: on the one hand because they demonstrated for the first time the possibility, at least in principle, of using natural language in a nontrivial way for obtaining information from a computer, and on the other hand because they incorporated theoretically interesting new ideas about language processing. Since the mid-1970s, several other question-answering systems have been built which either explored new ideas, such as PHLIQA or TENDUM, or tried to develop existing techniques to a point where they might be useful in practical applications, such as ROBOT and LIFER. In addition, a new generation of spoken-language processing systems were developed, such as SPEECHLIS and SPICOS. Other novelties, explored in systems of the 1980s, are the combination of linguistic input with visual data in the HAMRPM system and the development of facilities for the

Table 1. Question-answering systems mentioned in this section, with approximate year of completion and main references.

REQUEST/TQA (1973; 1978)	(Petrick, 1973; Damerau, 1978)
LSNLIS (1972)	(Woods, Kaplan & Nash-Weber, 1972)
SHRDLU (1972)	(Winograd, 1972)
PHLIQA (1975; 1979)	(Medema et al., 1975; Bronnenberg et al., 1980)
GUS (1977)	(Bobrow et al., 1977)
ROBOT/INTELLECT (1977)	(Harris, 1977)
LIFER (1977)	(Hendrix, 1977)
SPEECHLIS (1978)	(Bates, 1978)
HAM-RPM (1980)	(von Hahn et al., 1980)
KLAUS (1980)	(Haas & Hendrix, 1980)
TENDUM (1984)	(Bunt et al., 1985)
TELI (1986)	(Ballard, 1986)
SPICOS (1986)	(Niedermair, 1986; van Deemter et al.,1986)

user to extend the system's vocabulary and grammar interactively in the KLAUS and TELI systems. Attempts to design a system which allows a more complex dialogue than (essentially) a question-answer pair resulted in the GUS program and the TENDUM system. Table 1 lists the systems mentioned here in chronological order, according to their year of construction (which cannot always be specified unequivocally, as the construction process has often stretched over a number of years) along with an indication of the main bibliographical references. A more extensive survey of "language-processing systems" can be found in Winograd (1983).

In order to identify the most crucial issues to be addressed if useful natural-language dialogue systems are to become a reality, I shall consider in the rest of this section some of the limitations of those systems which are the richest in ideas: SHRDLU, LSNLIS, REQUEST, PHLIQA, and TENDUM.

The REQUEST system, nowadays called TQA (Transformational Question Aswerer), derives its strength and its weakness from one and the same characteristic. The work on this system started in the second half of the 1960s, and it was intended as an application of the theory of transformational generative grammar (TGG) put forward by Chomsky (1965). From a linguistic point of view, this was a very interesting enterprise at the time. However, during the 1970s generative grammarians abandoned many of the TGG ideas of the 1960s, with the result that, as the development of the system went on, REQUEST found itself resting on a theoretically more and more obsolete basis. Moreover, from the point of view of automatic language interpretation the TGG approach suffered from at least two major problems. One is that TGG was explicitly formulated as a model for language generation, which caused a great deal of technical problems for parsing (e.g., deletion transformations). The other is that the TGG model has always been underdeveloped from a semantic point of view. Due to a great deal of ingenuity on the part of the system designers, computational solutions have been found for many of the problems which the grammar formalisms cause for parsing; in addition, a semantic component has been added. Altogether, the strength of the system does not so much lie in the specific choice of its theoretical basis, but in the fact that *some* theoretical basis was chosen and kept fixed for quite a number of years. The reality of building natural-language processing systems is that, whatever theoretical basis is chosen, it takes a large number of man-years to produce anything substantial; moreover, much of the investment goes into working out "details" which have not been given sufficient attention by theoretical linguists. However, in view of the developments in linguistics that have taken place in the last 15 years, both in syntax and semantics, it seems clear that continuing to work on the basis of the 1965 theoretical linguistic insights is not the best strategy.

The LSNLIS system has been particularly influential in computational linguistics because it developed the concept of augmented transition networks

(ATNs), and demonstrated that ATNs are a computationally attractive technique for representing the grammar of natural-language fragments. The SPEECHLIS system, mentioned above, was essentially a reincarnation of LSNLIS with spoken input; a peculiarity of SPEECHLIS is that it incorporated an ATN with application-specific phrase categories. The use of a grammar with such special-purpose categories has become known as the semantic grammar approach, which is in fact rather a euphemism for grammars with application-dependent, linguistically ad hoc syntactic rules. The ROBOT system, also mentioned above, is an ATN-based question-anwering program that is marketed commercially under the name INTELLECT. Many other ATN-based language processing systems have also been developed in the area of machine translation (e.g., Witkam, 1985).

The appearance of SHRDLU, the third of the systems from the early 1970s caused a shock and a great deal of excitement in the scientific community. This is partly due to the spectacular demonstration dialogue that Winograd used in his publications and presentations of the system. The central idea explored in SHRDLU is that effective language interpretation should take the form of integrated linguistic and nonlinguistic information processing: Winograd regarded the separation of linguistic from nonlinguistic information processing as artificial, and due to linguistic tradition and prejudice. Consequently, the distinction between morphological, syntactic, semantic, and pragmatic processing would be even more artificial. Moreover, Winograd propagated a procedural view of the incorporation of linguistic knowledge, thereby breaking away from the traditional view of linguistic knowledge in terms of descriptive rule systems. Altogether, Winograd's approach to language interpretation can be said to be a truly computational view. Rather than bothering about formal constraints on the form of rules in a grammar, as linguists since Chomsky had typically been doing, Winograd propagated the exploitation of the computational powers of an information-processing machine with a high-level programming language.

SHRDLU has been very succesful in two respects. In the first place it made clear to a large audience that there may be exciting prospects in computer interpretation of natural language. Secondly, it demonstrated that, if one does not bother too much about linguistic generalization, the exploitation of the information processing capacities of a computer can result in an impressive performance on a limited class of natural-language inputs.

On the other hand, the impact of SHRDLU on subsequent work has been much smaller than that of LSNLIS for instance. The reason is that the design decisions that allowed SHRDLU to make a spectacular first appearance have also prevented it from being a fruitful basis for subsequent work. A critical look at SHRDLU's abilities has revealed an extreme lack of robustness and a rather shocking lack of linguistic generalization. As part of a critical examination of several question-answering systems, Petrick (1976, p.318) reports:

> The syntactic and semantic coverage provided by SHRDLU appears to be spotty. Although a large number of syntactic constructions occur at least once in sample sentences appearing in published dialogue, our attempts to combine them into different sentences (involving no new words or concepts) produced few sentences that [Winograd felt] the system could succesfully process. ... The gaps that were encountered were attributed primarily to syntactic limitations. The actual users of the system with whom the author has spoken reported similar syntactic gaps and also mentioned encountering sentences that, although syntactically acceptable, produced anomalous computer responses.

The sources of this disappointment are precisely the central claims underlying the system design. First, there is the rejection of the use of a formalism for describing linguistic structures in a way adequate for capturing syntactic and semantic generalizations. Secondly, the reliance on computation rather than formal structure leads to an interpretation process where the intermediate results take the form of expressions in a programming language, which are suited for execution but not for inspection of their formal properties. For example, if SHRDLU is asked one of the following questions

> Is a red block red?
> What is the color of a red block?

the system is in trouble if there is no red block present in the current state of its toy world, in the sense that it fails to understand the question. This is because the recognition of a noun phrase like "a red block" leads to a semantic representation in the form of a LISP procedure that looks for such a block. Since this procedure is executed as part of the interpretation of the input, the language processing is blocked if it fails. Therefore, the system reports that it is unable to analyse the sentence. This points to two fundamental problems concerning SHRDLU's design. First, the procedure representing a phrase should not be executed until it can be decided that the execution makes sense; in the examples this is not the case, and this can only be decided after the entire sentence has been analyzed. However, it is extremely difficult to discover this if the representation that is built for the sentence as a whole is only a piece of LISP code. Secondly, it is very doubtful whether the semantic representation of a noun phrase in cases like those above should be procedural in character at all. From a semantic point of view, what is essential is that "a red block" refers to an object with a red color, and that the colour attribute plays a particular role elsewhere in the sentence. But these are static, structural facts which one would typically prefer to express in a descriptive, predicate-logic type of language rather than in a programming language.

The first question-answering system that appeared on the scene after SHRDLU and incorporated significant new ideas was PHLIQA, developed at Philips' Research Labs since between 1972 and 1978. A first implementation was completed in 1975, and a second in 1978. The design of PHLIQA was based on two important ideas concerning the semantic interpretation of natural language, which are best explained with reference to an approach to meaning which has become popular in semantic theory during the last decade in the form of Montague grammar. In this approach, the interpretation of natural-language expressions goes via a translation into a formal, logical language, of which the semantics are defined separately. This definition consists of two components, a *model* and a set of recursive *interpretation rules.* Using M to designate a model and R to designate a set of interpretation rules, the semantic definition is thus a pair, I = (M, R).

The first idea underlying PHLIQA is a computational elaboration of the concept of a model. A model, in this context, is a combination of two things: a specification of the objects in the domain of discourse, called a *model structure*, and an assignment of interpretations to the terms of the language, called a *model assignment.* (These interpretations are individual objects in the model structure, or sets of such objects, or relations between objects, etc.). Formally, a model is a pair, M = (D, F), with model structure D and model assignment function F. The recursive interpretation rules R describe for each complex expression of the language how its interpretation is constructed from the interpretations of its constituents. In PHLIQA, the database describing the state of affairs in the discourse domain is treated as representing a model of the logical language into which natural-language queries are translated. For example, the collection of database records that describe cities is treated as the interpretation assigned to the constant CITIES. Looking up the value of a constant in the database then corresponds to the application of a model assignment function to that constant.

I would like to draw attention to three interesting aspects of this approach. First, there is the advantage that the database, an essential part of any question-answering system, but usually treated as something that just happens to be "in the machine," is given a precise and satisfactory formal status. Secondly, the entire interpretation process is an exact implementation of an articulate linguistic semantic theory. And thirdly, PHLIQA does not need a separate module for performing deductions. This is a consequence of following a semantic (model-theoretic) rather than a syntactic (axiomatic) approach to meaning; the PHLIQA database is not viewed as a collection of axioms from which the truth of other statements must be deduced, as in SHRDLU and other systems.

The second important idea underlying the PHLIQA design is that the translation of natural-language expressions into the formal language for which the database serves as a model, may be performed in a number of steps, each resulting in an expression in a language belonging to the same family as the target language. This approach, where each step in the process deals with specific aspects of the semantic analysis, has been called "multilevel semantics" (Medema et al., 1975). A special feature is that the interpretation of content words is postponed to a late stage, and is preceded by the analysis of logical form. The delay of lexical disambiguation is achieved by translating each content word into a term of a formal language which still has the full potential ambiguity of the natural-language term. This leads to a stage of semantic representation in a formal language with the unusual property of having ambiguous constants. The mathematical consequences of this approach have been discussed by Landsbergen & Scha (1979); from a practical point of view it has the advantage that the first part of the interpretation process is independent of the domain of discourse. A change of application area would only imply changes in the interpretation of lexical items at a later stage. Also, a change of input language, say from English to Dutch, would only require a change in the first part of the process; the modules that take care of later stages can remain the same. More generally, the modularity of the interpretation process is of course a positive feature from the point of view of system development and maintenance.

Compared to SHRDLU, LSNLIS and REQUEST, PHLIQA clearly fares better from a semantic point of view, as it has a solid basis in semantic theory. For example, PHLIQA is capable of a considerably more sophisticated treatment of quantification than the other systems. However, paradoxically this also introduces new problems: as the system is able to make finer distinctions in interpreting its inputs, corresponding requirements have to be put on its outputs. As in other question-answering systems, the emphasis in the design of PHLIQA has been on the processing of natural-language inputs and not on the generation of natural-language outputs. This has the result that the following dialogue with PHLIQA may occur:

(S, system; U, user)

U: Did the German firms buy more than 5 computers in 1975?
S: No.
S: Do you want a search for another interpretation of your question?
U: Yes.
S: Yes.

The problem here is that the answer to the collective interpretation of the question is positive and that to the distributive interpretation is negative, but the system is unable to distinguish these interpretations in its output. For most systems, this problem simply does not arise because the distinction is not made at all. More generally, as the input interpretation component is able to make more subtle distinctions, a useful system should be able to express the different readings in a way comprehensible to the user. The semantic representations that the system builds up internally are quite unsuitable for this purpose. To express the differences in natural language, on the other hand, requires a highly sophisticated natural-language generation capacity, as it implies the generation of natural-language sentences of an unusual semantic precision.

Unfortunately, PHLIQA was implemented on experimental hardware in a Philips-internal system programming language, which was abandoned some time after the project was discontinued. As a result, the program was lost when the hardware was taken out of service.

In the early 1980s the design started of the TENDUM dialogue system, which inherits several of the basic ideas of the PHLIQA system. The TENDUM project is a cooperative enterprise of the Computational Linguistics Unit at Tilburg University and the Institute for Perception Research in Eindhoven, a joint institute of Philips and the Eindhoven University of Technology. In essence, the TENDUM design is based on a combination of the PHLIQA approach to semantics with a theory about the mechanisms underlying informative dialogues. The crucial assumption of this theory, which will be outlined later, is that a dialogue is conceived in terms of communicative actions that change both partners' state of knowledge, hence the name to the system: "Tilburg-Eindhoven system for Natural-language Dialogue based on User Modelling." Another feature of TENDUM is that semantic interpretation is coupled to a new grammar formalism, called *augmented phrase-construction grammar* (Bunt, 1985b, 1986a). So far, TENDUM has only been developed to a point where it is little more than a question-answering system; further work on various components is needed to turn it into a real dialogue system. For instance, the output of the system consists at the moment of a set of communicative actions, organized in a "plan" describing constraints on the performance of the actions in relation to other actions and their outcome. Both the individual actions and the plan structure are represented in a formal language; the task of transforming this output into natural language has been explored only marginally so far (but see Bunt, 1986a). Still, TENDUM seems to be one of the few systems under development, if not the only one, where the interpretation and generation of discourse is undertaken as governed by a system of rules, based on a formal pragmatic theory. Earlier systems that allowed dialogues of a certain complexity, such as GUS (Bobrow et al., 1977) relied on the use of application-specific dialogue schemes. Apart from the inherent difficulties in language interpretation that all question-answering systems run into, as discussed later, TENDUM has to deal with problems concerning dialogue pragmatics and user modeling that have not been faced in other systems, simply because it has higher ambitions than other systems when it comes to supporting a form of communication based on general principles for conducting natural-language dialogue. These problems will also be discussed later, in connection with a theoretical perspective on informative dialogues.

3.2. Quasi Natural-Language Dialogue Systems

Question-answering research has generally been concerned with building systems that allow miniature dialogues with user initiative, consisting of a question-answer pair where the question is in natural language and the answer is not. Another form of interaction is one where the system has the initiative in a dialogue that may consist of several turns, but where the user inputs allowed at each turn are very severely restricted. A simple example of this approach is provided by a program allowing the user to obtain information about incoming and outgoing airplanes. The system begins by trying to identify the relevant flight:

S: Flight number?
U: Unknown.
S: Place of departure?
U: Montreal.
S: Scheduled time of arrival?
U: Sorry, Toronto.
S: Incorrect time.
Again: Scheduled time of arrival?
U: 12:15
S: Unknown flight.

The last message from the system refers to the fact that there is no flight from Montreal scheduled at 12:15; there is one from Toronto at that time, but the correction of the place of departure has not been recognized as such. The heart of the problem here is that this dialogue is based on the idea that the reaction to a question should be an answer. That people in practice may do many other things has not been taken into account. In fact, one may ask whether this kind of communication can be called natural-language communication at all. The individual utterances are in natural language, of course, but the sentences produced by the systems are simply preprogrammed and do not reflect any language-generation ability; similarly, the user inputs allowed at each point in the dialogue are restricted to a fixed finite set which is simply listed in the program, and their processing does not reflect any language-understanding ability. I therefore think it is actually misleading to call the capability of performing such a dialogue a natural language capability.

Even more misleadingly, software products which allow the use of natural-language words instead of mathematical symbols are sometimes advertized as allowing natural-language inputs. For instance, the sophisticated spreadsheet program JAVELIN is promoted by saying that "input to JAVELIN takes place in natural language" (Software Newsletter 9, in Software Magazine, 5, 1985, p.1). What is meant is that the user may write formulas like "profit = turnover − expenses" instead of "L = X − Y", using ordinary words rather than mathematical variables. This is really nothing more than the use of mnemonic variable names.

There is one area of man-machine communication where an extremely restricted use of natural language is of interest for man-machine communication, and that is the case of spoken input. A fairly extreme example of such a system is provided by an experimental speech input-output dialogue system built at the Institute for Perception Research in Eindhoven in the late 1970s (Muller, Nooteboom, & Willems, 1977), which has been a valuable tool in the study of informative dialogues. An example of a dialogue which a naive subject conducted over the telephone with the system, is the following. (The English text given here is a translation from the Dutch original, which can be found in the Appendix).

S: Computer information system Eindhoven. You may obtain information concerning departure times of intercity trains. From Eindhoven, intercity trains run in four directions: Den Bosch, Venlo, Weert, Tilburg. Your direction is ...
U: Eh,.. Tilburg, eh, around ten o'clock.
S: Direction Tilburg. Today?
U: Yes, around ele-
S: The next few departures?
U: Round ele-.. eh, Tilburg, eleven in the morning ...
S: Please answer clearly yes or no.
U: Ah!
S: The next few departures?
U: Eh, Tilburg, eleven in the morning...
S: Please answer clearly yes or no.
The next few departures?
U: Yes.
S: Direction Tilburg.
U: Eleven in the morning.
S: The next few departures are: 9.38, 10.08, and 10.38.
Do you want more information?
U: Yes, direc-
S: Same direction?
U: Direction Tilburg, eleven in the morning.
S: Please answer clearly yes or no.

U: Yes!
S: Same direction?
U: Yes.
S: Same day?
U: No, Friday.
S: Which other day?
U: Friday, round ele-
S: Friday.
U: Yes. Friday.
S: In the morning, the afternoon or the evening?
U: In the morning.
S: Round which hour between 5 and 13?
U: Eleven.
S: Tilburg, Friday. Departure times are: 10.38, 11.08 and 11.38.

Experimentation with this kind of dialogue may, for instance, provide valuable insights into the relation between the formulation of a question and the formulation of the responses that are elicited (see Bunt, 1984, 1985a; Van Katwijk et al., 1979).

3.3. Inherent Difficulties in Computer Interpretation of Natural Language

The quasi natural-language systems discussed in the previous section do not attempt to *understand* the user's utterances, but only to *recognize* them. That is, all the system does is try to match the input with a finite list of items. In the case of speech input this is of course not a trivial task, but here the difficulty of the task is not caused by the natural language, but by the use of speech. The use of spoken input gives system designers an excuse, one might say, for not taking the input language seriously with regard to understanding. For systems with keyboard input the situation is different. In that case the reason for not attempting to make natural language inputs understood is simply that it is extremely hard to make a computer understand natural language in the first place.

What is it that makes this task so difficult? One of the well-known characteristics of natural languages is that they are *infinite* systems; no natural language is adequately described as a finite set of expressions, and it is sometimes thought that this is why natural language is so difficult for computers to deal with. But a moment's reflection will make it clear that this is not the case. Any high-level programming language allows an infinite variety of correct program texts, which can nonetheless be interpreted succesfully by a computer. Is the source of the problem, then, that programming languages have precise definitions, while natural languages do not? When we look at definitions of a programming language, what we see is specifications of correct expressions, that is, definitions of the *syntax* of the languages. It is true that we do not have complete and precise descriptions of the syntax of any natural language, but that is a problem that we can get around in any practical computer application by restricting the full range of syntactic variation that is allowed, thereby effectively defining a sublanguage of a natural language (what linguists since Montague have called a fragment of a natural language). We do have very good instruments like augmented transition networks and (augmented) phrase-structure grammars for describing the syntax of natural-language fragments in computationally tractable ways. If the restrictions of the fragment are chosen in a reasonably natural way, given the application, the user may hardly ever notice them. In that case we have a "habitable" fragment of the language (Watt, 1968), which for the user is virtually indistinguishable from real natural language. All the question-answering systems considered above are based on this approach, though not always with explicit attention to the habitability of the language fragment they cover.

However, there is yet another part of the definition of a language, and that is its semantics. For a programming language, the semantics are hardly ever defined with the same explicitness and formal rigour as the syntax; it is not uncommon that a programming language is in fact defined semantically by its compiler or interpreter, which relates expressions in the language to more complex expressions in a lower-level language, and ultimately to sequences of the primitive operations that the hardware can perform. In a sense, this is also how Winograd approaches the semantics of natural language in the SHRDLU system; there is no explicit formal definition of meaning, but a translation of sentence constituents to expressions in a programming language. This, we have seen, constitutes one of the fundamental weaknesses of the SHRDLU system. Here we touch upon a fundamental problem for designing natural-language dialogue machines: they have to capture and process the meanings of natural-language expressions, and we still only have a limited knowledge of how this can be done.

The study of meaning in natural language has traditionally not been the focus of linguistic investigation (which has instead been the study of syntax), and to the extent that linguists and philosophers have been occupied with semantic theory, it has mostly not been systematic and formal enough to be useful for computational purposes. And, although this has changed somewhat with the advent of Montague grammar, it is quite unlikely that linguistic and philosophical studies in semantics will solve the problems that the computational meaning hunter faces. The reason is that to understand the meaning of an expression is essentially to relate the concepts occurring in the expression and their combination to a body of already present knowledge of what the expression is about. Theoretical semanticists typically take this body of knowledge for granted, feeling that it is not *their* job to say anything about it. For example, Thomason (1974, pp.48-49) argues that:

> It is the business of semantics to account for meanings. A central goal of this account is to explain how different kinds of meaning attach to different syntactic categories; another is to explain how the meanings of phrases depend on those of their components .... But we should not expect a semantic theory to furnish an account of how two expressions belonging to the same syntactic category differ in meaning. The task of explaining the particular meanings of various basic expressions will obviously presuppose, if not factual information, at least a minutely detailed terminology for classifying things of all kinds. Perhaps even pictures or a museum ... At any rate, lexicography will have to borrow from all areas of human knowledge.

In other words, semantics is not supposed to deal with the meanings of individual lexical items, and especially stays away from relating language to bodies of knowledge. And yet this is precisely what is needed for a language understanding system.

The world knowledge in the question-answering systems mentioned above is generally restricted to the expert knowledge of facts in a limited domain, that are needed to provide the answers to the users' questions. However, equally important for language understanding is general, "common-sense" knowledge. This may readily be appreciated by reflecting on why it is that a sentence like "John and Mary have three children" has one clearly preferred reading. The study of "common-sense" knowledge and its representation is receiving some attention in artificial intelligence circles (see for example Hobbs & Moore, 1985), but is still far from providing techniques that are ready for use in machine understanding systems.

So far, we have only considered understanding in terms of relating language to knowledge about the world. However, that is only one aspect of language understanding. Another crucial aspect of understanding language in communication is the determination of the *intention* of the speaker. In the above dialogues with (quasi-)natural-language systems we find several instances where the computer fails to understand the user's intention. In the first dialogue of the preceding subsection, for example, the computer failed to understand the intention to correct a previous answer. Also, the cumbersome character of the second dialogue in the same section is caused by the persistent partial mismatch between the intentions underlying the user's and the computer's utterances; for instance, the computer fails all the time to understand those parts of the user's perfectly cooperative, "overinformative" answers which supply information that was not explicitly asked for. Where understanding the factual semantic content of a sentence means that the content is related to a body of factual knowledge, understanding the user's intentions means that the semantic content of an utterance is related to the user's goals, plans, beliefs, expectations, etc. Modeling the user's beliefs, goals, etc., is therefore a prerequisite for the ability to represent a user's intentions. Another prerequisite for dealing effectively with intentions is to know what linguistic devices people use to convey their beliefs and intentions. The study of such devices takes place in linguistics in the subdiscipline called pragmatics (and also in psycholinguistics, especially in connection with spoken language). At a small scale, it has also been undertaken in artificial intelligence (Allen & Perrault, 1978) although, altogether, it is still an underdeveloped area of investigation.

4. Natural Informative Dialogues

In this section I shall consider some of the characteristics of natural informative dialogues between people. This will give some idea of some further issues to be addressed in order to develop acceptable natural-language computer dialogue facilities. I shall consider two kinds of dialogue, those where the communication takes place via computer terminals and those where telephones are used. Communication via terminals is technically comparable to the man-machine situation with keyboard input; the telephone situation is comparable to that of spoken man-computer interaction and has the further advantage that the linguistic behaviour in spoken dialogues, by virtue of its greater spontaneity, reveals people's preferences for natural dialogue structures more clearly.

4.1. Dialogues via Computer Terminals

Of course, people don't normally communicate through computer terminals, so perhaps we should not call this kind of dialogue natural. The dialogues we consider here are natural in the sense that there are no restrictions on the use of the language and that each participant assumes the other to be a fully competent and cooperative speaker, and behaves accordingly. These dialogues are therefore as natural as possible in the given circumstances. By studying them we can obtain an idea of what a man-computer dialogue might ideally look like, if the computer were a perfectly competent dialogue partner. (Which is not to say, of course, that an ideal person-computer dialogue should be like a person-to-person dialogue in all respects.)

The detailed comparative study of dialogues via terminals in contrast with spoken dialogues is of interest both from a linguistic and psycholinguistic point of view. For studies of this kind the reader is referred to Cohen (1984); here, I will restrict myselves to briefly considering an example of a terminal dialogue for the purpose of identifying some characteristic properties which it seems obvious would be desirable in man-machine dialogues, and which present serious problems.

The following terminal dialogue was recorded at the Institute for Perception Research in Eindhoven in the context of a joint research project with the Computational Linguistics Unit in Tilburg. Of the two participants, one had been trained to behave in spoken dialogues like the employees at the telephone information service at Schiphol, Amsterdam Airport. The other participant was a subject who had no experience in the use of computer terminals, and who had been told that she participated in a psychological experiment concerning the influence of modern media on communication. The subject was told a short story about a person who has planned a holiday trip to Spain and wants to know some details about the travel; the subject was asked to act as being in the position of that person. The story was based on the recording of a natural dialogue over the telephone with the information service at Schiphol. (The English text given here is a translation from the Dutch original; the original can be found in the Appendix.)

(S, subject; I, information service)

1. I: Schiphol information.
2. S: I have booked for flight IB 885, next Saturday, to Alicante.
   What time should I report at Schiphol?
3. I: You should check in half an hour before departure at the latest.
4. S: So between what time and what time?
5. I: Between twelve and one-thirty.
6. S: Do you also have information about departure and arrival times
   of trains?
7. I: In Holland?
8. S: Yes.
9. I: I do.
10. S: What is the last train from Breda I can take to be
    there in time for that flight, IB 885?
11. I: The train of 12.06
12. S: What is the arrival time in Alicante?
13. I: 17 hours.
14. S: What is the duration of the bus travel Alicante Benidorm?
15. I: We don't have information about that.
16. S: Thank you.
17. I: You're welcome.

This example illustrates several points that have been found more generally in natural terminal dialogues. First of all, the idea that informative dialogues consist roughly of question-answer pairs that accomplish the desired information transfer is not realistic. In this example, only five of the subject's nine utterances were factual questions; the others were a "prelude" to a question (2), a meta-question (6), an answer to a meta-question (8) and an acknowledgement (16). On the part of the information source, four of the nine utterances were factual answers; the others were a general introduction (1), a request for clarification (7), an answer to a meta-question (9), a notification of lacking information (15), and an acknowledgement (17). This illustrates the rather surprising observation we made, in a variety of circumstances where people conducted a natural informative dialogue without visual contact, that only sóme 50% of the utterances are factual questions and answers. The other half consists mainly of communicative actions that serve to ensure that the dialogue proceeds smoothly and stays on (or returns to) the right track; these are called *dialogue control* acts. The occurrence of this high percentage of dialogue control acts is partly due to matters of politeness, but it is also a consequence of the fact that, except in cases of trivial simplicity, it is difficult and certainly unnatural for people to express in a single sentence what information they want. The normal situation is, rather, that some interaction is needed to arrive at a desire for information which is articulate enough to be expressed in a single sentence.

Secondly, and related to the previous point, most of the individual utterances are impossible to interpret correctly or even to interpret at all when considered in isolation. Of the subject's utterances only the first one, the question on the bus travel in line 14, and the final "Thank you" are semantically selfcontained. Of the other participant's utterances, only the opening sentence "Schiphol information" and the closing sentence "You're welcome" can be interpreted in isolation. In fact, these two don't call for any genuine semantic analysis at all; they are purely conventional dialogue openers and closers, that have only to be recognized as such. All other utterances in the dialogue contain explicit or implicit references to previous utterances, which must be taken into account in the interpretation. Two rather dramatic instances of utterances that cannot be interpreted succesfully in isolation, though for very different reasons, are "Yes" (8) and "What is the arrival time in Alicante?" (12). Answers like yes and no can of course never be interpreted without reference to a preceding question; however, it is important to note that answers *in general*, not just answers to yes-no questions, can only be intepreted correctly in connection with a certain question. Groenendijk and Stokhof (1984) have argued this from a theoretical point of view, and we see it illustrated here in I's answer "You should check in half an hour before departure at the latest" (3). This answer should be interpreted as saying something only in relation to the kind of flight being discussed; in response to a question about another kind of flight, such as an intercontinental one, the answer would not be correct. A more instructive, though made-up example, from Groenendijk and Stokhof (1985), is that the sentence "John and Mary are in the garden" as an answer to the question "Who is in the garden?" means something different as an answer to the question "Which children are in the garden?" Another kind of difficulty arises in the case of "What is the arrival time in Alicante?" (12); here, the addressee must understand that the question does not refer to the train mentioned in the immediately preceding context, but rather to the flight mentioned in the beginning. One can easily imagine a computer program going wrong here.

Two particular linguistic devices for indicating that an utterance should be interpreted relative to an element in the dialogue context can be seen at work: anaphoric words like "that" (15) and "there" (10) (referring back to "Schiphol" in line 2!), and elliptic constructions such as "In Holland?" and "What is the arrival time in Alicante?" Both phenomena are notorious stumbling blocks for computer interpretation of natural language.

4.2. Spoken Dialogues

The following dialogue was recorded in the context of the same experiment as the one in the previous section. The subject used a telephone with a simulated connection to Schiphol (the original Dutch text is again in the appendix).

(S, subject; I, information service)

1. I: Schiphol information.
2. S: Yes, good morning, eh, this is Mrs. De Bruin in Arnhem, eh,
   I wanted to ask something, eh, I have to meet someone
   today at Schiphol who comes from Munich....
3. I: Yes,
4. S: Could you, eh, tell me then what time exactly that,
   eh, I would have to be there?
5. I: Do you know the flight number?
6. S: Yes, eh, I forgot what it was exactly, but she comes by Lufthansa.
7. I: O.K., then it's LH 906 or LH 988.
8. S: Oh, eh, I don't think it was 988.
9. I: Then it will be LH 906. That one is expected at 4.15.
10. S: 4.15.
11. I: That's right. The other one comes at 19.45.
12. S: Great thank you.
13. I: Oh, no thanks.
14. S: Good morning.
15. I: Good morning.

In comparison with the terminal dialogue, it seems clear that the speech situation calls for more "social talk" then the rather "impersonal" situation of keyboard and display. Also, in the speech situation people express their thoughts more overtly: such little elements as the "Yes" (6), the "O.K." (7), the "Oh"

(8), the repeated "4.15" (10), and the "That's right" (11) are typically absent in the more considerate terminal dialogues. One may suspect that this difference relates to the fact that talking is easier and faster than typing and also, again, to the fact that the terminal situation is "impersonal" compared to the telephone situation. Also in line with these considerations is the fact that in spoken dialogues people tend to introduce their questions more elaborately, and often close the topic of a question explicitly. Utterance 10 and the first one in line 11 illustrate the latter point. We found that in spoken dialogues the most frequently occurring pattern is not the question-answer pair, but the quadruple question-answer-(partial) repetition-confirmation, sometimes preceded by a separate introduction of the question topic. In terminal dialogues, (partial) answer repetitions and confirmations have not been found.

The (partial) answer repetitions which are typical of spoken dialogues are in fact quite intriguing. Their function does not always seem to be the same; sometimes they are clearly meant as verifications, on other occasions they mainly seem to serve the purpose of filling one's turn and gaining time to plan a continuation of the dialogue, and there are still other functions that repetitions may have. For an investigation into these matters the reader is referred to Beun (1986a).

Of particular importance is that spoken dialogues usually contain a substantial amount of verification, although the above dialogue does not illustrate this clearly. Terminal dialogues contain verifications too, but considerably fewer. The importance of this point is that people in informative dialogues apparently often have uncertain knowledge about something, and a desire to get rid of their uncertainties. This means that, if a computer dialogue system is to work with a model of the user, this model will have to incorporate uncertain knowledge and should allow uncertain knowledge to be turned into certain knowledge. Uncertain knowledge plays an interesting role in the above dialogue at the point where the two partners together figure out what the relevant flight number is (8 and 9). The little piece of reasoning which is carried out by partner I can be spresented schematically as follows:

(p = flight number is LH 906, q = flight number is LH 988)

I knows that either p or q
I knows that S suspects that not q
I suspect that p

This is an example of the apparently simple reasoning that people seem to do effortlessly in conversation; yet, when we think of a machine that should have the same kind of ability, we realize that it is not easy at all. In fact, logicians have not yet been able to present any mathematically correct and empirically reasonable logical calculus which involves two agents and the attitudes "knowing" and "suspecting", which could serve as a basis for a machine to make such deductions.

I would like to also note a point on the positive side, namely that one problem which does *not* present itself as a particularly pressing one is that of ill-formed input. It is sometimes suggested that spoken language is a big mess, full of ungrammatical sentences. Our dialogue material does not confirm that. What is found, and may give a somewhat messy impression, are the many hesitations, especially in the beginnings of dialogues, and unfinished sentences followed by hesitations or signals of selfcorrection. By and large, however, the sentence fragments separated by hesitations either form correct sentences when they are joined, or they constitute pairs where the first element is an unfinished sentence and the second is a correct, complete sentence meant to replace the first one. Genuine ungrammaticalities occur only rarely; it therefore seems that the occurrence of "ill-formed" inputs, often thought to be a plague for language-processing computers, is not one of the most pressing problems, at least in the context of informative dialogues.

5. A Theoretical Perspective on Informative Dialogues

5.1. Questions, Answers, and Other Communicative Actions

The question-answering systems discussed earlier are almost invariably based on the idea that a user asks selfcontained questions, to which the computer reacts in one of two ways. Either an answer to the question can be computed, in which case that is the reaction, or for some reason it cannot, in which case a failure message is generated. Most question-answering systems, like computer programs in general, are notoriously defective when it comes to producing informative failure messages; we have seen an example of this in the case of SHRDLU, where the failure of a procedure to find a physical referent for a noun phrase caused the parsing program to fail, and gave rise to message that suggested a linguistic problem. The PHLIQA system is able to produce quite articulate messages, owing to the modular organization where each module has a well-defined task at which it can fail. As a consequence, PHLIQA can report whether there is a parsing problem, an interpretation problem given the system's world model, a problem with an unfulfilled presupposition, or a lack of information in the database. Similarly, the TENDUM system is designed to be able to issue special messages when a conflict is detected with the current user model, or between the user's beliefs about the subject domain and the system's knowledge. However, with the partial exception of TENDUM, none of these systems can deal in a principled way with inputs other than questions, or generate communicative actions other than answers and failure reports.

Yet, if we take the idea of informative natural-language dialogues with a computer seriously, it is obvious from what we have seen about natural informative dialogues that a dialogue system should be able to process and generate things other than questions and answers.

If we want a system to deal with a variety of communicative actions, such as questions, corrections, verifications, answers, and confirmations, then we first need to determine which types of communicative action should be distinguished in this context. Subsequently, we must give an explicit formal characterization of these concepts which can be made operational in a machine. Unfortunately, the existing theories of communicative action, which have been developed mainly on the borderline of linguistics and philosophy in the framework of speech act theory (Searle, 1969; Allwood, 1976), do not have the explicitness and formality required for this purpose. Levinson (1983) argues that the most promising approach for arriving at such a theory would appear to be one where speech acts are characterized in terms of their context-changing effects, as has for instance been proposed by Gazdar (1979) and Bunt (1977). However, as the notion of context in general is an extremely broad and vague one, which is intuitively not any clearer than that of a speech act, for a general theory of communicative action this hardly seems to be a feasible approach. I believe, however, that by limiting ourselves to purely informative dialogues we can obtain a notion of context which is sufficiently clear and manageable to provide the basis for an explicit formal characterization of communicative actions.

5.2. An Analysis of the Notion of Context in Informative Dialogues

On the basis of our observations about natural informative dialogues we can identify the key dimensions of the notion of context, relevant to this kind of communication.

We may begin by noting that the very notion of an informative dialogue means that we have two partners A and B and the sole purpose of obtaining or sending factual information. Obviously, the communicative actions that A and B perform have the effect of changing their information in certain ways. So, basic to the notion of context we are looking for, must be what A and B know and in what respects they want to expand their respective knowledge. However, we must be careful using the term knowledge, for two reasons.

First, we should perhaps speak of belief rather than knowledge, in order to avoid the suggestion that the relevant concept of knowledge is that where something can be known only if it is true. The course of an informative dialogue between A and B is not determined by what is actually true in the world, but by what A and B *believe* to be true. What is meant here by saying that A knows that x, is just that A has the information x available, without implying any commitment to the actual truth of x.

Secondly, we have already noticed that a substantial part of what the partners in a natural informative dialogue do is verify information which they have available, but which they do not fully trust. In accordance with the terminology used in the schematic representation in the previous section, I shall indicate this situation as A *suspects* that x. Surely, in natural informative dialogue situations some "suspicions" are stronger than others, so we should perhaps have a continuum of suspicion attitudes with knowledge as the upper limit and ignorance as the lower limit. However, in our empirical dialogue material we have not found compelling reasons to introduce stronger and weaker suspicion attitudes. The minimal distinction that must be made in order to account for the occurrence of verifications is that between knowing and suspecting; that is, between having information which is fully trusted and having information which is not fully trusted. So, in describing the context of an informative dialogue, two important types of elements we must take into account are

A knows that p
A suspects that p

with the interpretation of knows and suspects as discussed above. The same applies, of course, for partner B. What p may stand for will be discussed below.

It is important to realize that not only the information available to the partners is crucial in an informative dialogue, but also the information which is not available and which they want to become available. There are two ways in which one may want information to become available: one may want it to become available to oneself or one may want it to become available to the partner. In other words, one may want to know something or one may want to make something known to the other. These are the only kinds of goals that may underly an informative dialogue. It is thus crucial to take into account, as part of the context that gives rise to an informative dialogue, elements of the form

A wants to know whether p
A wants to make known that p

I shall now refine this by considering what p may be. The pieces p of information that A and B may want to know or to become known, are in the first place specific facts about the state of affairs in the dicourse domain; that is what the dialogue is all about. However, sometimes the partners in an informative dialogue want to make known or to know certain information about themselves or the other partner. Examples of this can been seen in the dialogue about trains in the preeceding section, where participant S wants to know what information the other participant has available in line 6, where participant I wants to know for certain in line 7 that the partner is referring to trains in Holland, and where participant I wants to make known in line 15 that she does not have information about buses in Spain. Similarly, in the spoken dialogue about flights, participant S wants to make known in line 2 that she wants to know something, and participant I wants to know in line 5 whether the other participant knows a flight number. Apparently, we should allow the pieces of information *p* to be information about what the speaker knows or what the other knows. Moreover, when we look more closely at an example such as line 5 in the latter dialogue, we see that participant I wants to know something where this cannot be expressed in the format "A wants to know whether *p*", which only allows for the case where one wants to know whether a certain proposition is true. We therefore need a more general form, namely

A wants to know the value of *x*,

where *x* may be a proposition, in which case the value is either TRUE or FALSE, but may also be something else, such as the flight number of a certain airplane, or the time. This generalization is also required for the know attitude and the suspect attitude: one may know (or suspect) that a plane has flight number KL 402, but one may for example also suspect that the partner knows what the flight number is. Apparently, we must distinguish between the following two cases:

A knows the value of *x*
A knows that the value of *x* is *y*

A similar distinction must be made for suspecting. In combination with the observation that the objects of the various attitudes, indicated by *p* and *x* in these formulae, may be aspects of the discourse domain as well as aspects of the dialogue partner, this means that we should allow context elements with nested speaker/attitude references, such as

A knows that B does not know the arrival time of flight KL 402
A knows that B wants to know the arrival time of flight KL 402
A knows that B suspects that the arrival time of flight KL 402 is 12:45
A knows that B suspects that A knows the arrival time of flight KL 402

and so on. In sum, what we find as the most crucial elements of the context can be described by the following rules:

1. [A, B] [knows, suspects, wants to know, wants to make known] the value of *x*, where *x* is information about the discourse domain, propositional or otherwise
2. [A, B] [knows, suspects, wants to make known] that *p*, where *p* is a proposition expressing information about the discourse domain
3. [A, B] [knows, suspects, wants to know, wants to make known] the value of *p*, where *p* is a proposition of the form of 1, 2, 3, or 4

4. [A, B] [knows, suspects, wants to make known] that *p*, where *p* is a proposition of the form of 1, 2, 3 or 4

With the assumption that know, suspect, want to know, and want to make known are the basic attitudes of the participants in an informative dialogue, these rules describe the ingredients that may be hypothesized to make up the essence of the context that gives rise to and is changed during an informative dialogue.

5.3. Context and Communicative Action

We have explored the notion of context for informative dialogues as a potential basis for defining communicative actions, the idea being that different types of communicative action can be defined in terms of their effects on the context. The effects on a context as outlined above consist primarily of additions to the addressee's information. For instance, if speaker A asks speaker B whether flight KL 402 comes from Montreal, this provides addressee B with at least the following pieces of information:

1. A wants to know whether flight KL 402 comes from Montreal
2. A suspects that B knows whether flight KL 402 comes from Montreal

If B answers A that this is indeed the case, then this provides A at least with the following piece of information:

3. B knows that flight KL 402 comes from Montreal

However, this is not all, since the performance of a communicative act by a speaker does not only influence the information of the partner, but also his own. When one performs a communicative action, one normally assumes that, unless there is evidence to the contrary, the action does transmit the information which it conveys when it is correctly understood. For instance, asking the question whether flight KL 402 comes from Montreal not only has the effects 1 and 2 on B, but also the following effects on A:

4. A suspects that B knows that A wants to know whether flight KL 402 comes from Montreal
5. A suspects that B knows that A suspects that B knows whether flight KL 402 comes from Montreal

As 1-2 and 4-5 illustrate, there is a simple relationship between the effects on the addressee and those on the speaker. The relationship is that for every effect E*j* on the addressee that a communicative action has when correctly understood, there is a corresponding effect on the speaker of the form: A suspects that E*j*. This form expresses simply that the speaker suspects his action to have its usual "direct" effect. It should be emphasized that the only effects considered here, called direct, are those which are indissolubly connected to the understanding of the communicative action (in speech act theory these are often called illocutionary effects). Of course, an action like answering that flight KL 402 leaves at 10.30 may have a great many other effects besides the addressee knowing that the speaker believes that, such as the effect that the addressee starts running to the ticket office. Such indirect effects obviously play no part in the characterization of communicative actions, and are therefore not considered here.

Note that the direct effects E*j* on an addressee B in the case of correct understanding of a communicative action are always of the form E*j* = B knows that C*j*, where C*j* is a *condition on the speaker.* The above examples illustrate this. The conditions C*j* are the conditions that the speaker must satisfy in order to perform the communicative action according to the (implicitly known) rules of the informative dialogue game, which stipulate cooperativeness, rationality, honesty, etc. (see Allwood, 1976, for a discussion of dimensions of cooperative linguistic behaviour). Let us call these conditions the *appropriateness conditions* of the communicative action in question. (In the pragmatic literature one finds the terms felicity conditions and correctness conditions, but these usually have a broader meaning than what is intended here.) For a communicative action with appropriateness conditions {C*1*, ..., C*k*}, performed by speaker A and addressed to B, the following direct effects are tied to the correct understanding of the action (the direct effects in the case of incorrect understanding are of course unpredictable):

1. B knows that C*j*
2. A suspects that B knows that C*j*

   (where *j* = 1, ..., *k*)

This is not the end. For the participants A and B surely both know, at least upon reflection, that these effects occur. Therefore,

3. B knows that A suspects that B knows that C*j*

By the same token, A knows, at least in principle, that the situation described by 3 obtains:

4. A knows that B knows that A suspects that B knows that C*j*

It seems that, in principle, there is no end to this iteration of speaker/attitude combinations, though for practical purposes it may be reaonable to impose a limit somewhere.

It may be observed that the direct effects of a communicative act follow from the appropriateness conditions through a simple general principle. This means that the simplest way of characterizing communicative actions is not in terms of their effects, but in terms of their appropriateness conditions! So for instance, we can characterize the distinction between an "open" yes/no question and a check with the same semantic content *p* by postulating that they both have the appropriateness conditions (1) that the speaker wants to know whether p is true, and (2) that the speaker suspects that the partner knows whether p is true, while the check has the additional appropriateness condition (3) that the speaker suspects p to be true. In a similar way we can characterize confirmations, corrections, negative checks, and so on.

This brief exposition was intended to indicate a possible direction for providing an explicit characterization of the notion of communicative action, which might be the basis of a computer dialogue system able to participate in a more natural kind of dialogue than a pure question-answering system. The TENDUM dialogue system (Bunt et al., 1985) incorporates a simple and crude first implementation of this approach. This entails a whole range of new research questions that have hardly been addressed before, such as:

1. What constitutes an empirically valid set of communicative action types for man-machine informative dialogues?
2. How do people recognize communicative action types?
3. How can we incorporate the recognition of communicative action types in a model for linguistic interpretation?
4. Is the notion of context, outlined in the previous section, a reasonable one?
5. If the answer to the previous question is affirmative, can we give a mathematically correct formalization of this notion, in order to get a sound basis for performing the logical calculations that are needed in informative dialogues? (Compare the problem described in the section on spoken dialogues.)
6. If the answer to the first question is positive, and a mathematically acceptable formalization can be given, then can we design a computationally acceptable implementation?

These are all fundamental questions, to which at least partial answers will have to be given before we can hope to build linguistically "intelligent" dialogue systems.

6. Research Problems and Perspectives

In the previous sections we have come across a wide variety of research problems, to which at least partial solutions will have to be developed if we want to construct machines with which we can have reasonably intelligent informative dialogues in natural language. These problems differ very much in character. Some are of a linguistic nature, such as the resolution of anaphora and ellipsis in dialogue. Others are of a psycholinguistic nature, such as the linguistic encoding of intentions in communicative actions. Still others belong to computer science, either to theoretical branches like the design of knowledge-representation systems for user modeling, or to more practical branches when it comes to efficient implementation of parsers and language interpretation models. Some of the problems may be called technical in the sense that there are well-established techniques that can be used to develop solutions; in other cases the problems are of such a new, often interdisciplinary, and fundamental nature that we still need to work on the development of appropriate research methods and suitable theoretical frameworks. This is particularly true of the problems relating to the encoding and recognition of communicative intentions, including the modeling of these phenomena in formal grammars and algorithms for language generation and interpretation. The theoretical perspective on these matters, outlined above, is only the beginning of a framework in which issues of this kind can be studied.

The general emphasis in this paper on *problems* in the development of natural-language dialogue systems should not be taken as an expression of the opinion that hardly anything has been accomplished so far. I consider each of the question-answering systems listed in Table 1 a substantial achievement. It is nonetheless fair to say that a genuine facility for natural-language informative dialogues between a computer and a "casual" user has not yet been created and not even been approximated. The specific aim of this paper was to investigate where we currently stand in this respect, why we have not come any further than we have, and what we should do in order to make substantial further progress. The identification of largely unsolved problems is of double interest in this respect, as it explains on the one hand why we haven't come further than we have, and it tells us on the other where we should direct continued research efforts. I shall therefore try to sum up the main problems, as they emerge from the above discussion of existing question-answering systems and quasi-natural-language systems, of natural informative dialogues between people, and of a theoretical perspective on informative dialogues. I shall divide the problems in three areas, namely (1) formal and computational linguistics, (2) psycholinguistics and pragmatics, and (3) computer science, in particular knowledge representation. Occasionally, I shall also indicate some recent developments which seem relevant for dealing with the problem under consideration.

6.1. Formal and Computational Linguistics

The following problems, some of a fundamental and some of a technical character, emerge from the preceding sections.

1. *The use of the (interpretation of) the preceding dialogue in the semantic interpretation of utterances.* There have been several instances of this problem in the section on dialogues via computer terminals, for example,

someone says "I have booked for flight IB 885 next Saturday to Alicante. What time should I report at Schiphol?" The difficulty is that the second sentence looks like an ordinary, complete sentence without reference to previous sentences, to which one would like to apply the sentence interpretation rules; yet it is obviously impossible to obtain a correct interpretation without taking the first sentence into account. Maybe we should consider this as a case of semantic ellipsis, assuming that there should be some specific purpose for reporting at the airport. However, purposes are typically often implied and not expressed explicitly; this doesn't mean that almost everything we say is semantically elliptic. This is a fundamental problem, largely underestimated or even overlooked in the scientific community.

Two recent developments in semantics may be mentioned here, that offer some perspective for tackling this problem. One is a proposal from Groenendijk and Stokhof (1985) for the interpretation of answers, which are in a sense always semantically elliptic; the proposal being to assign interpretations to question-answer pairs, rather than to answers in isolation. The other is Kamp's (1981) discourse representation theory (DRT), which represents an attempt to construct semantic representations of sequences of sentences in an incremental fashion. Work in the framework of DRT has so far focused on other semantic problems, however, and has only dealt with sequences of sentences rather than sequences of utterances, related to different speakers and attitudes.

2. *The resolution of anaphora and ellipsis in dialogue.* These may be considered to be technical problems, on which a good deal of work has already been done. This applies especially to anaphora, which have been a source of inspiration for the development of DRT; conversely, DRT has stimulated interesting new studies in anaphora and quantification (e.g., Van Eijck, 1985; see also the next point). Both ellipsis and anaphora constitute special cases where previous utterances must be taken into account in semantic interpretation, but they are not so hard as the first problem, since here we have explicitly marked points where the context must be consulted, marked either by anaphoric words or by the absence of certain syntactic elements. Our empirical dialogue material shows that both anaphora and ellipsis occur very frequently.

3. *The recognition of presuppositions and interpretation of quantifiers in informative dialogue utterances.* Again, these are two technical problems. Together with anaphora, the problems in interpreting quantifiers have been the primary motivation for developing DRT. The classical example of DRT is the sentence "Every farmer who owns a donkey, beats it." This sentence contains two semantic problems, which become apparent when one tries to formulate a set of rules systematically assigning semantic representations to sentences. The first problem is that the indefinite arti-

cle, which is usually interpreted as an existential quantifier, acts as a universal quantifier here. The second is that, when we try to translate the sentence into predicate logic in the usual way, we end up with the formula:

$$\forall x\ [[\mathrm{FARMER}(x)\ \&\ \exists y[\mathrm{DONKEY}(y)\ \&\ \mathrm{OWN}(x,y)]] \rightarrow \mathrm{BEAT}(x,y)],$$

which not only has the wrong quantifier. but also has the variable y in BEATS(x,y), corresponding to "it". outside the scope of the (wrong) quantifier $\exists y$.

What makes DRT particularly interesting for our present concerns is that not only problems like this can be tackled. but it also vecomes possible to give a correct treatment of definite descriptions used as intersentential anaphoric links. as in:

> I have booked for flight IB 885 from Eindhoven Airport
> next Saturday. What time should I be at the airport?

Here, the phrase "the airport" should obviously *not* be treated as quantified, carrying the presupposition that there is exactly one airport.

In spite of the amount of theoretical work already done, a great deal remains to be done; moreover, a separate effort is needed to bring the available knowledge to bear effectively in language understanding programs.

4. *The incorporation of a treatment of linguistic devices for expressing communicative intentions in formal grammars.* These devices vary in nature. Some are syntactic, such as sentence type (mood), some are lexical, reflected in the choice of particular words, and others consist in the use of punctuation marks in written language and of prosodic features in spoken language.
5. *The design of special-purpose grammars for the automatic generation of natural-language expressions with appropriate precision.* See the section on natural-language question-answering systems for an explanation of the problem.
6. *The use of both specific, domain-dependent and general, common-sense world knowledge in semantic interpretation.* When discussing SHRDLU and other systems we came across the problem of using world knowledge in an effective and controlled manner. See also the section on the inherent difficulties in computer interpretation of natural language, and point 1 in the section on computer science problems.

6.2. Psycholinguistics and Pragmatics

1. *The identification of the communicative functions that utterances in informative dialogues may have.* This is a fundamental problem, for which both theoretical frameworks have to be developed, such as the one outlined earlier (and described more fully in Bunt, 1986b), and empirical methods of investigation have to be designed. See also the next point.
2. *The identification of the linguistic devices for expressing communicative functions, and which are relevant for their recognition.* See Beun (1986a, 1986b) for explorations concerning syntactic, prosodic and other features in spoken dialogues, and Allen and Perrault (1980) for a plan-based approach to the recognition of intentions.
3. *The identification of the dimensions of user modeling which are relevant in informative dialogues.*
4. *The empirical investigation and validation of the logical properties of the dimensions of user modeling.* (cf. the section on the inherent difficulties in computer interpretation of natural language).
5. *The determination of practically useful and "habitable" fragments of natural language for informative dialogues.* (cf. Watt, 1968).
6. *The identification of a practically useful repertoire of dialogue control acts* (see the section on dialogues via computer terminals) and the establishment of their relation to aspects of language and knowledge processing in informative dialogues (cf. Bunt, 1986b).

6.3. Computer Science, in Particular Knowledge Representation

1. *The representation of general, common-sense world knowledge in an effectively useful way* (cf. formal and computational linguistic problems, point 6). This concerns the representation of such "trivial" facts as that married couples usually consist of two partners of opposite sex, that water flows from high to low, or that it's warmer in summer than in winter. Such general background knowledge heavily influences the choice of the most likely interpretation of a sentence. No generally accepted methods for representing such knowledge have yet been developed. Two recent collection of studies in this area are Hobbs and Moore (1985), and Hobbs et al.(1986).
2. *The representation of user models with the dimensions relevant in informative dialogues* (cf. psycholinguistic and pragmatic problems, point 3). This involves, among other things, the representation of ignorance and uncertain knowledge, but also the representation of knowledge in a way that does not suffer from "logical omniscience." Recent advances with respect to the latter problem have been made by Fagin and Halpern (1985).

3. *The systematic construction and updating of user models on the basis of the interpretation of his utterances.* See earlier. A separate problem is how to keep the user model consistent. Relevant work on this point has been done by Doyle (1978) and Perrault (1986).
4. *The development of a planning system for generating appropriate schemes of communicative actions on the basis of a dynamic user model.* Recent work on planning in artificial intelligence, such as that by Appelt (1981) can probably serve as a basis for such a system, once we have well-established repertoires of communicative actions and effective user models.

6.4. Other Developments

There are two positive developments in recent years that have not yet been mentioned, and that I consider as quite important. One is that logicians and mathematically oriented computer scientists are turning to the design of knowledge representation formalisms, partly inspired by the need to represent "knowledge states" in distributed processing systems as in the work by Fagin and Halpern (1985), and partly inspired by the study of the logical properties of databases (cf. Levesque, 1984). This is currently bringing the design of such formalisms to a much higher level of sophistication.

The second is the tendency among groups of theoretical linguists and computer scientists to work together in developing grammar formalisms. This concerns especially the design of new enriched forms of phrase-structure grammar, such as generalized phrase-structure grammar (Gazdar et al.,1985), head grammar (Pollard, 1984), APC Grammar (Bunt, 1985b) and others, but it also concerns lexical-functional grammar and government-binding grammar. The linguists involved are interested in the computational aspects of their grammars, and the computer scientists involved are interested in the linguistic generalizations achievable in their parsers. This is certainly a healthy development, which offers far better prospects for constructing systems with a substantial coverage of natural language than before.

7. Conclusions

In conclusion I would like to say that, since the appearance of the most valuable question-answering systems during the 1970s, no real breakthroughs have been achieved in terms of working dialogue systems. However, our awareness and understanding of the problems involved has grown in very significant ways. This, combined with the recent joining of forces by linguists, logicians, and computer scientists, gives us good reason to believe that the prospects for building intelligent dialogue systems are by no means poor, provided that we are not afraid to expend substantial effort on the challenging, often fundamental problems that are involved.

Appendix: Original Dialogue Texts in Dutch.

The dialogues in the main text (3.2, 4.1, and 4.2) are translations into English of texts that were originally in Dutch. The original texts are listed here.

S: Inlichtingenautomaat Eindhoven. U kunt informatie krijgen
over vertrektijden van intercitytreinen. Intercitytreinen
rijden vanuit Eindhoven in vier richtingen: Den Bosch,
Venlo, Weert, Tilburg. Van toepassing voor u is...
U: Eh,.. Tilburg, eh, rond tien uur.
S: Richting Tilburg. Vandaag?
U: Ja, rond el-
S: Eerstvolgende vertrektijden?
U: Rond el-, eh... Tilburg, elf uur 's ochtends...
S: Antwoordt u alstublieft duidelijk met ja of nee,
U: Ja!
S: Eerstvolgende vertrektijden?
U: Eh, Tilburg, elf uur 's ochtends,..
S: Antwoordt u alstublieft duidelijk met ja of nee,
eerstvolgende vertrektijden?
U: Ja,
S: Richting Tilburg,
U: Elf uur 's ochtends
S: De eerstvolgende vertrektijden zijn: negen uur achtendertig,
tien uur acht, en tien uur achtendertig. Wilt u meer inlichtingen?
U: Ja, rich-
S: Zelfde richting?
U: Richting Tilburg, elf uur 's ochtends.
S: Antwoordt u alstublieft duidelijk met ja of nee,
U: Oh.
S: Zelfde richting?
U: Ja.
S: Zelfde dag?
U: Nee, vrijdag.
S: Welke andere dag?
U: Vrijdag, rond elf
S: Vrijdag,

U: Ja, vrijdag.
S: 's Ochtends, 's middags, of 's avonds?
U: 's Ochtends.
S: Rond welk uur tussen vijf en een?
U: Elf uur.
S: Tilburg, vrijdag. Vertrektijden zijn: tien uur achtendertig, elf uur acht, en elf uur achtendertig.
I: Schiphol inlichtingen.
S: Ik heb geboekt voor vlucht IB885, a.s. zaterdag naar Alicante. Hoe laat moet ik mij melden op Schiphol?
I: U moet uiterlijk een half uur voor vertrek inchecken.
S: Dus tussen hoe laat en hoe laat?
I: Tussen twaalf en half een.
S: Hebt u ook informatie over aankomst- en vertrektijden van treinen?
I: In Nederland?
S: Ja.
I: Dat heb ik
S: Wat is de laatste trein uit Breda die ik kan nemen om er op tijd te zijn voor die vlucht a.s. IB 885?
I: De trein van 12.06
S: Wat is de aankomsttijd in Alicante?
I: 17 uur.
S: Wat is de duur van de busreis Alicante Benidorm?
I: Daarover hebben wij geen inlichtingen.
S: Dank u.
I: Tot uw dienst.

I: Schiphol inlichtingen.
S: Ja, goedemorgen, eh, u spreekt met mevrouw de Bruin in Arnhem, eh, ik wilde iets vragen, eh, ik moet iemand ophalen op Schiphol die uit Munchen komt vandaag...
I: Ja,
S: Kunt u eh, mij vertellen hoe laat precies dat, eh, ik daar zou moeten zijn?
I: Weet u het vluchtnummer?
S: Ja, eh, ik weet niet meer precies wat het was, maar ze komt met de Lufthansa...
I: O.K., dan is het LH 906 of LH 988.
S: Oh, eh, ik geloof niet dat het 988 was.
I: Dan zal het LH 906 zijn. Die wordt verwacht om vier uur vijftien.
S: Vier uur vijftien.
I: Dat klopt. De andere komt om negentien uur vijfenveertig.
S: Mooi, dank u wel.

I: Geen dank hoor.
S: Goedemorgen.
I: Goedemorgen.

References

Allen J.F. & Perrault C.R. (1978). Analyzing intention in dialogues. *Artificial Intelligence*, 15 (3).

Allwood J. (1976). Linguistic communication as action and cooperation. *Gothenburg Monographs in Linguistics*, 1.

Appelt D. (1981). *Planning natural language utterances to satisfy multiple goals.* Dissertation, Stanford University.

Ballard B.W. (1986). User specification of syntactic case frames in TELI. In: *Proceedings COLING' 86.* Association for Computational Linguistics, Bonn, pp. 454-460.

Bates M. (1978). The theory and practice of augmented transition networks. In: *Natural language communication with computers*, L. Bolc (ed). Springer, New York. pp. 191-260.

Beun R.J. (1986a). The function of repetitions in spoken information dialogues. In: *IPO Annual Progress Report 20.* pp. 91-98.

Beun R.J. (1986b). Declarative question acts. In: *Preacts of conference structure of multimodal dialogues*, Venaco, Corsica.

Bobrow D.G. & the PARC Understander Group (1977). GUS-1, a frame driven dialog system. *Aritificial Intelligence*, 8 (2), pp. 155-173.

Bronnenberg W.J., Bunt H.C., Landsbergen S.P.J., Scha R.J.H., Schoenmakers W.J., & Utteren E.P.C. van (1980). The question answering system PHLIQA1. In: *Natural language question answering systems.* MacMillan, London; Hanser, Munich, pp. 217-305.

Bunt H.C. (1977). Towards an analysis of dialogue organization principles. In: *IPO Annual Progress Report 12.*

Bunt H.C. (1984). Taal, kennis en computer. *Tilburg Studies in Language and Literature*, 5.

Bunt H.C. (1985a). Artificial Intelligence and the information processing behind simple dialogues. In: *Teaching Thinking.* W.A. van de Grind & J.P. van Wouwe (Eds.), Forum Humanum the Netherlands, Leiden. pp. 27-37.

Bunt H.C. (1985b). *Mass terms and model-theoretic semantics.* Cambridge University Press, Cambridge.

Bunt H.C. (1986a). Information dialogues as communicative action in relation to partner modelling and information processing. In: *Preacts of conference structure of multimodal dialogues*, Venaco, Corsica.

Bunt H.C. (1986b). Utterance generation from semantic representations augmented with pragmatic information. In: *Natural language generation*. G.Kempen (Ed.), Kluwer/Nijhoff, The Hague.

Bunt H.C., Beun R.J., Dols F.J.H., Linden J.A. van der & Schwartzenberg G.O. thoe (1985). The TENDUM dialogue system and its theoretical basis. *IPO Annual Progress Report*, 19, pp. 105-113.

Chomsky N. (1965). *Aspects of the theory of syntax*. MIT Press, Cambridge, MA.

Cohen P.R. (1984). The Pragmatics of referring and the modality of communication. *Computational Linguistics*, 6, (3/4), 135-149.

Damerau F.J. (1978). The derivation of answers from logical forms in a question answering system. *American Journal of Computational Linguistics*, Microfiche 75.

Deemter C.J. van, Brockhoff G., Bunt H.C., Meya M. & De Vet J.M. (1986). From TENDUM to SPICOS, or how flexible is the TENDUM approach to question answering? In: *IPO Annual Progress Report*, 21, pp. 83-90.

Doyle J. (1978). *Truth maintenance systems for problem solving*. MIT Artificial Intelligence Laboratory Memo AI-TR-419.

Eijck J. van (1985). *Aspects of quantification in natural language*. Thesis, University of Groningen.

Fagin R. & Halpern J.Y. (1985). Belief, awareness and limited reasoning. In: *Proceedings of the 9th International Joint Conference on Artificial Intelligence*. Kaufmann, Los Altos, CA.

Gazdar G. (1979). *Pragmatics*. Academic Press, New York.

Gazdar G., Klein E., Pullum G.K. & Sag I. (1985). *Generalized phrase structure grammar*. Harvard University Press, Cambridge, MA.

Groenendijk J.A.G. & Stokhof M.B.J. (1985). *Studies on the semantics of questions and the pragmatics of answers*. Thesis, University of Amsterdam.

Haas N. & Hendrix G.G. (1980). An approach to acquiring and applying knowledge. *American Journal Computational Linguistics*, Microfiche 47.

Hahn W. von, Jameson A., Hoeppner W. & Wahlster W. (1980). The anatomy of the natural language dialogue system HAM-RPM. In: *Natural language based computer systems*, L. Bolc (Ed.), Hanser, Munich, pp. 119-254.

Harris L.R. (1977). User-oriented data base query with the Robot natural language query system. *International Journal of Man-Machine Studies*, 9, pp. 697-713.

Hendrix G.G. (1977). LIFER: A natural language interface facility. *SIGART Newsletter*, 61, pp. 25-26.

Hobbs J.R., Blenko T., Croft W., Hager G., Kautz H.A., Kube P. & Shoham Y. (1986). *Commonsense summer: final report*. CSLI Report 85-35, Stanford, CA.

Hobbs J.R. & Moore R.C. (1985). *Formal theories of the commonsense world*. Ablex, Norwood, NJ.

Kamp H. (1981). A theory of truth and semantic representation. In: *Formal methods in the study of language*. J.A.G. Groenendijk, T.M.V. Janssen & M.B.J. Stokhof (Eds.), Mathematisch Centrum, Amsterdam, pp. 277-322.

Katwijk A.F.V. van, Nes F.L. van, Bunt H.C., Muller H.F. & Leopold F.F. (1979). Naive subjects interacting with a conversing information system. In: *IPO Annual Progress Report*, 14, pp. 105-112.

Landsbergen S.P.J. & Scha R.J.H. (1979). Formal languages for semantic representation. In: *Aspects of automatized text processing*. S. Allen & J.S. Petofi (Eds). Buske, Hamburg, pp. 59-111.

Levesque H. (1984). The logic of incomplete knowledge bases. In: *On conceptual modelling*. Brodie (Ed.), Springer, New York.

Levinson S. (1983). *Pragmatics*. Cambridge University Press, Cambridge.

Medema P., Bronnenberg W.J., Bunt H.C., Landsbergen S.P.J., Scha R.J.H., Schoenmakers W.J. & Utteren E.P.C. van (1975) PHLIQA1: Multilevel semantics in question-answering. *American Journal of Computational Linguistics, Microfiche* 32.

Muller H.F., Nooteboom S.G. & Willems, L.F. (1977). An experimental system for man-machine communication by means of speech. *IPO Annual Progress Report*, 12.

Niedermair, G. (1986). Divided and valency-oriented parsing in relation to partner modeling and information processing. In: *Preacts of conference structrue of multimodal dialogues*. Venaco, Corsica.

Perrault C.R. (1986). An application of default logic to speech act theory. In: *Preacts of conference structure of multimodal dialogues*, Venaco, Corsica.

Petrick S.R. (1973). Transformational analysis. In: *Natural language processing*. R. Rustin (Ed.), Algorithmic Press, pp. 27-41.

Petrick S.R. (1976). On natural language based computer systems. *IBM Journal of Research and Development*, 20 (4), pp. 314-325.

Pollard, C.R. (1984). Generalized phrase structure grammars, head grammars, and natural language. *Doctoral Dissertation*, Stanford University.

Searle J.R. (1969). *Speech acts*. Cambridge University Press, Cambridge

Simmons R.F. (1965). Answering English questions by computer: A survey. *Communications of the ACM*, 8, 53-30.

Simmons R.F. (1969). Natural Language Question-Answering Systems, *Communications of the ACM*, 13, 15-30.

Thomason R.H. (1974). Introduction to R. Montague, In: *Formal Philosophy*. Yale University Press, New Haven.

Watt W.C. (1968). "Habitability". *Journal of the Amercan Society of Information Sciences*, 19.

Winograd T. (1972). *Understanding natural language*. Academic Press, New York.

Winograd T. (1983). *Language as a cognitive process*. Addison-Wesley, Reading, MA.

Witkam A.P.M. (1985). *DLT, distributed language translator - A multilingual facility for videotex networks*. BSO Company, Utrecht.

Woods W.A., Kaplan R.M. & Nash-Webber B. (1972). *The lunar sciences natural language information system*. BBN Report 2265, Bolt Beranek and Newman, Cambridge, MA.

Appendix: Color Plates

Chapter 1. The Legibility of Visual Display Texts

Floris L. van Nes

Figure 3. The Teletekst general index page at the end of 1981. The way in which the available space has been used, the tabulation, and the use of color are not optimal. The letters and numbers are formed from a 6 × 10 dot matrix.

Figure 4. A Teletekst subject index page from March 1982. This index is clearer than the one in Figure 3, but it is open to question whether a subject index page should be used to refer to all other subject indexes. The fact that the words "*VAN DE*" at the top of the page differ in both color and shape from the rest of the heading makes it look as though they are not part of it. The letters and numbers are formed from a 12 × 10 dot matrix; O has been used wrongly instead of the numeral null.

teletekst
Hoofdinhoud 16de proefperiode,100
PAGINA's met RUBRIEKSOVERZICHTEN zijn:
105 Nieuws 205 Consument
225 Vrije tijd 255 Beurs
305 Weerberichten 355 Verkeer
405 Sportrubriek 505 Omroep
De rubrieksoverzichten bevatten de
nummers van alle pagina's die,al of
niet in uitzending,onder deze rubrieken
voorkomen Alfabetisch zoeken kunt u met
de pagina's 200 tot en met 204.
Veelgevraagde pagina's:
101 Laatste nieuws 102 Weerkaart
523 Ondertitel-info 208 Voor doven
212 Vacatures 233 Natuur

OVERZICHT VAN DE
OMROEPRUBRIEK
AVRO 506 RTV-actueel 517
VARA 507 School-TV 520
KRO 508 Zendschema radio 521
NCRV 509 Zendschema TV 522
TROS 510 Over ondertitels 523
VPRO 511
Veronica 513 Omroep Brabant 527
IKON 514 Radio Oost 529
Teleac 515 ROZ Limburg 530
NOS 516 Radio Noord 531
Overzichten:
Beurs 255 Sport op 405
Nieuws op 105 Verkeer op 355
Consument op 205 Vrije Tijd op 325
Weer op 305 Overzicht op 500
Alfabetisch zoeken: pagina 200 t/m 204

Figure 5. This motto of the IPO letter designers is, from top to bottom, alternately hard and easy to read. This was achieved by selecting colors such that the luminance contrast between text and background was alternately low and high. A 6 × 10 dot matrix was used for letters and numbers.

Figure 6. In this figure the motorway numbers are amongst the most conspicuous elements because they are a different color, an aid to searching which enables the reader to find them quickly. The other text items shown in yellow: "*geen middenbermbeveiliging*" (no central crash barrier), "*70 km/u*" (70 km/h) and "*VERVOLG PAG. 118!*" (continued on page 118!) are a different color for another reason, to indicate their importance. A 6 × 10 dot matrix was used for letters and numbers.

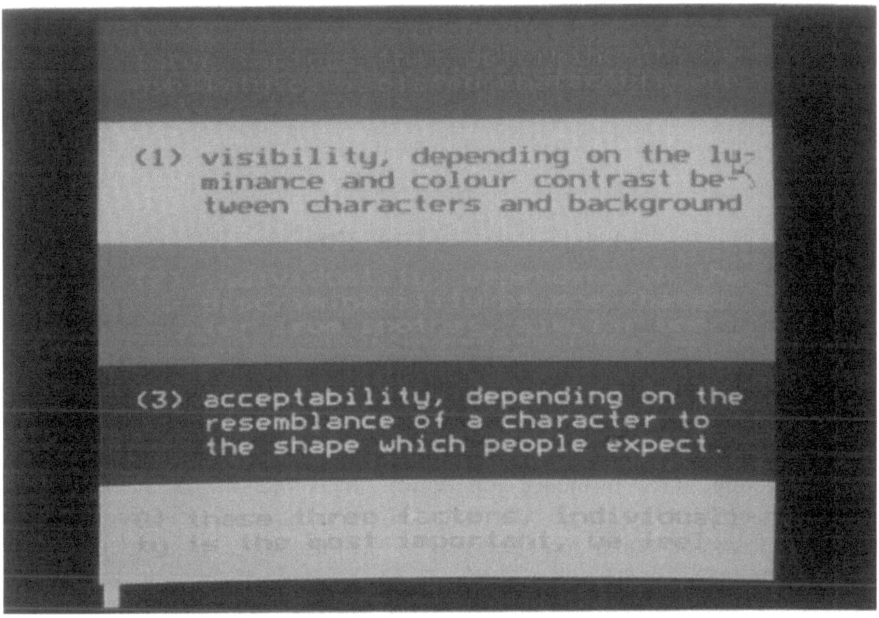
(1) visibility, depending on the lu-
minance and colour contrast be-
tween characters and background
(3) acceptability, depending on the
resemblance of a character to
the shape which people expect.

P117 Proef tt P117 9 mei 10.28/34
VERKEERSBEELD
Op de volgende wegen kunnen door werk-
zaamheden aan de weg vertragingen ont-
staan:
-autosnelweg Eindhoven-Weert (A 2): de
afrit Leende is voor verkeer uit de
richting Weert afgesloten.Verder
rijbaanversmallingen en snelheids-
beperkingen;
-autosnelweg Rijswijk-A'dam (A 4): bij
Leidschendam twee rijstroken in beide
richtingen, geen middenbermbeveiliging
en max.snelheid 70 km/u.;
-autosnelweg Den Oever-Sneek (A 7) ter
hoogte van de brug op de Afsluitdijk
in beide richtingen een rijbaan;
-autosnelweg A'foort-Zwolle (A 28) bij
Hoevelaken ri.Zwolle een rijstrook af-
gesloten. VERVOLG PAG.118 !

Chapter 2. The Use of Color in Visual Displays

Charles M.M. de Weert

Figure 3. Designed by Vicario (1978) to demonstrate chromatic changes due to figural properties (A and B). Here it is used to demonstrate how changes in color and luminance influence the figural interpretation. In A luminance differences are present, in B only color differences occur. The organization in depth planes is much more evident in the luminance picture. C and D present examples of monocular depth. In D the depth impression is strongly reduced due to the absence of luminance contrasts.

Figure 4. Examples of the pseudocoloring. A is the original luminance based picture. In B color differences have been added. In C the luminance relations have been removed and the different luminance levels have been substituted by colors.

A B C D

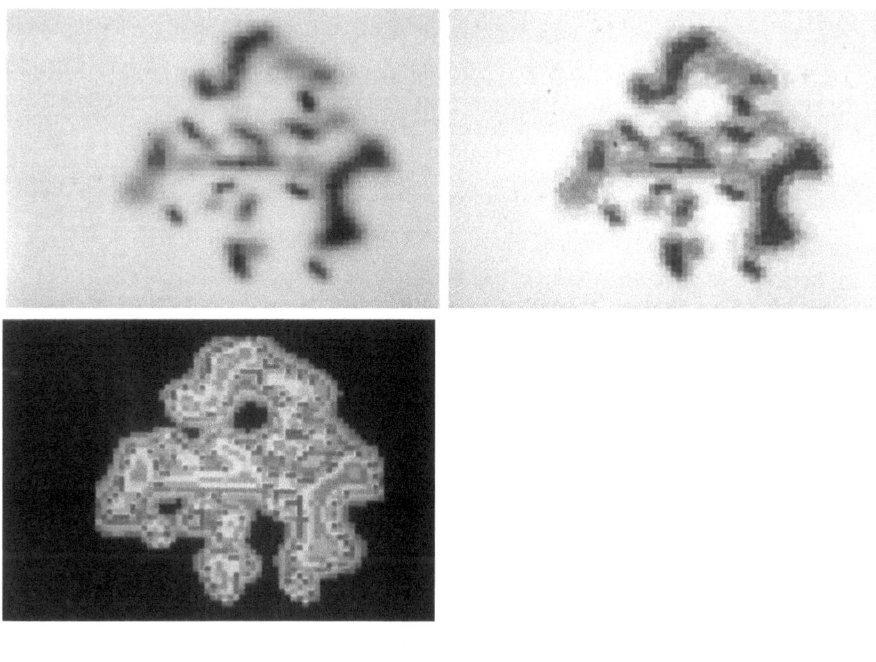

A B C

Figure 6. Examples of combinations of form, brightness, and color.

Figure 7. Star stimulus used in the color similarity measurements. Subjects were asked to report whether they saw a triangle pointing to the right or one pointing to the left.

Figure 10. The choice of relative luminance can strongly influence the possible perception of parts of the figure as separate objects (A and B); C and D show examples of direction signs.

Figure 11. Examples of stimuli used to measure the effect of the choice of the overlap colors.

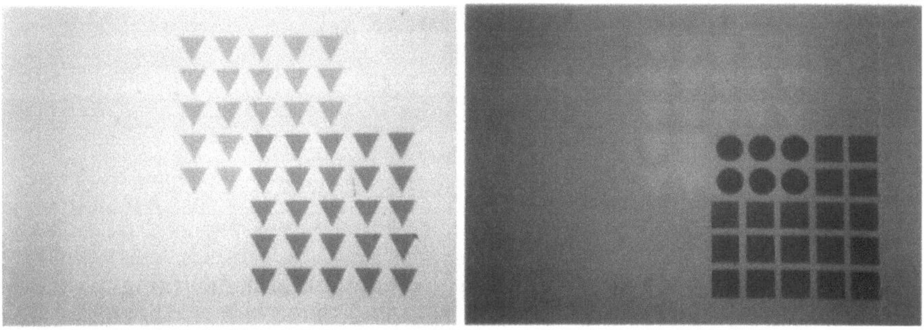

A B

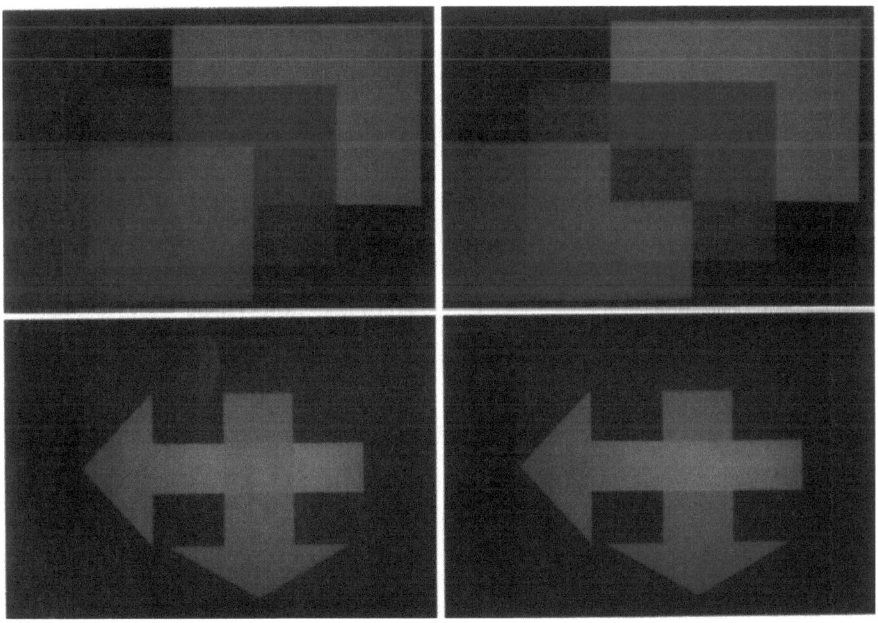

A B C D

Subject Index

MIX
Papier aus verantwortungsvollen Quellen
Paper from responsible sources
FSC® C105338
FSC
www.fsc.org

If you have any concerns about our products,
you can contact us on
ProductSafety@springernature.com

In case Publisher is established outside the EU,
the EU authorized representative is:
Springer Nature Customer Service Center GmbH
Europaplatz 3, 69115 Heidelberg, Germany

Printed by Libri Plureos GmbH
in Hamburg, Germany